A USER'S GUIDE TO TRADE MARKS:
The New Law

Julian Gyngell

LLB, Dip IPL, AITMA
Solicitor, Bird & Bird

Allan Poulter

LLB (Hons), RTMA
Solicitor, Marks & Clerk

Butterworths
London, Dublin & Edinburgh
1994

United Kingdom	Butterworth & Co (Publishers) Ltd, Halsbury House, 35 Chancery Lane, LONDON WC2A 1EL and 4 Hill Street, EDINBURGH EH2 3JZ
Australia	Butterworths, SYDNEY, MELBOURNE, BRISBANE, ADELAIDE, PERTH, CANBERRA and HOBART
Canada	Butterworths Canada Ltd, TORONTO and VANCOUVER
Ireland	Butterworth (Ireland) Ltd, DUBLIN
Malaysia	Malayan Law Journal Sdn Bhd, KUALA LUMPUR
New Zealand	Butterworths of New Zealand Ltd, WELLINGTON and AUCKLAND
Puerto Rico	Butterworth of Puerto Rico, Inc, SAN JUAN
Singapore	Butterworths Asia, SINGAPORE
South Africa	Butterworths Publishers (Pty) Ltd, DURBAN
USA	Butterworth Legal Publishers, CARLSBAD, California and SALEM, New Hampshire

A CIP Catalogue record for this book is available from the British Library.

ISBN 0 406 00577 X

Typeset by B & J Whitcombe, Nr Diss, Norfolk, IP22 2LP
Printed in England by Clays Ltd, St Ives plc

A User's Guide to Trade Marks:
The New Law

Preface

Introduction For all concerned, our patience has been
rewarded: the Trade Marks Act 1994 ('the 1994 Act') came into
force on 31 October 1994.[1] It has been over four years since the
Department of Trade and Industry published the Government's
White Paper 'Reform of Trade Marks Law'[2] ('the White Paper') and
many will need to be reminded that the European Commission's
first proposal for a directive to harmonise the laws of the Member
States relating to trade marks was submitted to the Council as long
ago as 25 November 1980.[3] That said, those numerous individuals
and organisations who have been responsible for debating, drafting
and ultimately delivering the new legislation should be commended
for their respective and collective efforts.

The 1994 Act gives effect to and implements the EC's trade mark
harmonisation directive of December 1989 ('the Directive').[4] It
repeals the Trade Marks Act 1938 ('the 1938 Act') in its entirety;[5] it
makes provision in connection with the Community Trade Mark

---

1 Pursuant to an order made by SI No 1994/2550 in accordance with section
   109(1); different days have been appointed for different provisions and different
   purposes and these dates are noted in the text of the Act which is set out in the
   Appendix.
2 September 1990, Cm 1203.
3 OJ No C351, 31.12.1980.
4 Council Directive to Approximate the Laws of the Member States relating to
   Trade Marks OJ No L40, 11.2.89; 89/104/EEC.
5 Section 106(2), schedule 5; for a complete list of enactments which have been
   amended see schedule 4; for a complete list of enactments which have been
   repealed or revoked see schedule 5.

Regulation ('the Regulation');[6] it enables the United Kingdom to ratify and give effect to the Madrid Protocol[7] concerning the international registration of marks, as well as complying with certain of the United Kingdom's other international obligations in relation to trade marks under the Paris Convention.[8]

It is thus an understatement to say that the 1994 Act does not merely restate trade mark law. The 1994 Act embodies new jurisprudence and introduces new legal principles in relation to the law governing registered trade marks in the United Kingdom[9] which are intended to reflect the significant changes in domestic and international trade and commercial practices which have occurred since the 1938 Act came into force.

The original deadline imposed by the Directive for each Member State to amend its trade mark laws was 28 December 1991. That deadline was extended until 31 December 1992. Accordingly, since 1 January 1993, arguably the United Kingdom has been in breach of the mandatory provisions of the Directive to the extent that those provisions were not already reflected in the 1938 Act.[10]

Scope and intent of this book This is a guide to and commentary on the 1994 Act and the Rules made under it. It is not intended to be a treatise on trade mark law. The first objective has been to gather together the sections of the 1994 Act under familiar headings. Secondly, we have tried to describe how those sections are intended to apply, based on what we understand to be their object and effect in legal and commercial terms. In essence, the intention has been to put into practice the words of John Mortimer:

'The law seems like a sort of maze through which a client must be led to safety, a collection of reefs, rocks, and underwater hazards through which he or she must be piloted.'[11]

6 Council Regulation on the Community Trade Mark (EC) No 40/94 of 20 December 1993; see chapter 13.
7 The Protocol Relating to the Madrid Agreement Concerning the International Registration of Marks, adopted at Madrid on 27 June 1989, not yet ratified by the UK (Cm 1601); see chapter 14.
8 The Paris Convention for the Protection of Industrial Property (Cmnd 4431).
9 See sections 107 and 108 in relation to the precise territorial extent of the 1994 Act.
10 This topic is outside the scope of this book. For a discussion of this issue see for example: 'The Trade Mark Directive – Could it have Direct Effect?' D Guy and J Gyngell, Trademark World February 1993.
11 *Clinging to the Wreckage* (1982).

This has not proved to be easy and, to continue the nautical theme, we have not always found the charts easy to decipher.

Although we will consider the 1994 Act and the Rules in detail, looking at the procedural and substantive issues including identifying changes to the old law under the 1938 Act, it is not the intention of this book to debate at length the issues arising under the 1938 Act and the cases decided under that Act. Instead, more time is spent putting forward suggestions as to how the courts may interpret and apply the new law under the 1994 Act. Some help in this task can be derived from the decisions of courts in other jurisdictions such as France, Benelux and Denmark where legislation in compliance with the Directive has already been implemented.

Finally, it should be noted that the 1994 Act continues the tradition of previous United Kingdom trade mark legislation by providing that nothing in the Act affects the law relating to passing off[12] and therefore this subject is not considered.

Scope and intent of the Directive   There is no secret in the fact that the 1994 Act, quite correctly, embodies not merely the principles of the Directive but, in many cases, the actual words of the Directive. Therefore, it is necessary first to consider briefly the scope and the objectives of the Directive when it was adopted in December 1988. In that context, it should be remembered that when interpreting and applying the 1994 Act it is necessary to adopt a European approach which is more 'purposive' than the approach which has traditionally been adopted by English courts of construing legislation according to its literal meaning.

The Directive does not attempt to achieve full-scale harmonisation of the trade mark laws of each Member State. It is directed towards minimising those differences which can affect the free movement of goods and thus hinder the development of the single European market. It does not, therefore, address procedural matters but instead concentrates on key areas of substantive law. For instance, it sets out the grounds on which the registration of a trade mark may be refused or invalidated, but leaves Member States a free hand as to whether these grounds may be raised during ex parte examination (as is the case in the United Kingdom) or only in opposition proceedings or before the courts. It also defines the

12 Section 2(2).

rights which are conferred by the registration of a trade mark in order that those rights are less likely to be used to distort or restrict the free movement of goods and services in the EC.

The rationale behind the Directive is that differences between the trade mark systems of the Member States can produce barriers to trade. Of course, while the Directive will have the effect of harmonising certain substantive provisions of national trade mark laws, this process will not exclude the application to trade marks of other branches of the law, such as passing off, unfair competition or consumer protection. Similarly, the right of action acquired through the use of an unregistered trade mark is not affected: this is a matter of some importance in the United Kingdom.

Although some of the provisions of the Directive are merely optional, the Directive is nonetheless a useful benchmark since it sets limits on the extent to which national laws may differ. Member States may not, for example, retain or introduce grounds for refusing or invalidating a registration which are not provided for in the Directive, nor confer rights on registered trade marks extending beyond what is contained in the Directive.

It is in this context that the 1994 Act was drafted and, in many cases, it may be the only way that one can sensibly interpret the language used in certain sections which is alien to trade mark practitioners in the United Kingdom. We trust that readers will find our book helpful and we await with interest the decisions of the courts in relation to the numerous issues raised by the new legislation.

Acknowledgements To conclude, we would like to acknowledge the true support and encouragement which the partners at Bird & Bird and Marks & Clerk have extended to us in relation to the writing of this book. Our thanks also go to all our colleagues at work who have 'covered' for us time and again over the last four or five months. But the real accolades go to Teresa, Susan, Lucie, Lynda and Jacquelyn who performed heroics at the keyboard.

To Kate and Una, to Alasdair and James.

JMG   AMP
Bird & Bird   Marks & Clerk
London   London

Contents

Contents

Table of statutes

EC legislation

Treaties, convention and agreements

Table of cases

Table of cases

Glossary of terms

Abbreviation	Full title/description
The Counterfeit Goods Regulation	Council Regulation (EEC) No 3842/86
The Directive	Council Directive No 89/104/EEC of 21 December 1988 to Approximate the Laws of the Member States relating to Trade Marks
The EEC Treaty	The Treaty establishing the European Economic Community: The Treaty of Rome
The Journal	The Trade Marks Journal published by the Registrar in accordance with section 81 and rule 65
The Mathys Report	British Trade Marks Law and Practice of May 1974, Cmnd 5601

Abbreviation – *contd*	**Full title/description** – *contd*
The Nice Agreement	The Nice Agreement concerning the International Classification of Goods and Services for the purpose of the Registration of Marks of 15 June 1957 (current version: 6th edition, Cmnd 6898)
The Official Journal	The Official Journal of the European Communities
The Paris Convention	The Paris Convention for the Protection of Industrial Property, of 20 March 1883 (as revised and amended)
The Protocol	The Madrid Protocol Relating to the International Registration of Marks of 27 June 1989
The Regulation	Council Regulation (EC) No 40/94 of 20 December 1993 on the Community Trade Mark
The Rules	The Trade Marks Rules 1994, SI No 2583
The White Paper	Reform of Trade Marks Law, September 1990, Department of Trade and Industry, Cm 1203
The 1938 Act	Trade Marks Act 1938, c22
The 1994 Act	Trade Marks Act 1994, c26

1 Trade marks

1.01 Introduction The 1994 Act, although primarily directed at the subject of registered trade marks, contains provisions relating to:
(a) unregistered trade marks;
(b) well known trade marks;
(c) certification marks;
(d) collective marks;
(e) Community trade marks;
(f) international trade marks; as well as
(g) registered trade marks.
The marks referred to in (a) and (b) above are considered at the end of this chapter (paragraphs 1.10 et seq); the marks referred to in (c)–(f) are dealt with individually in chapters 11–14 respectively; while registered trade marks are the subject of chapters 2 through to 10. But, before all this, it is necessary first to examine the new definition of 'trade mark' in section 1(1) of the 1994 Act.

1.02 Trade mark: the statutory definition, s1(1) The key definition in the 1994 Act as to what constitutes a 'trade mark' is found in section 1(1) which provides that a trade mark is any 'sign'[1] which is both:
(a) capable of being represented graphically; and
(b) capable of distinguishing goods or services of one undertaking from those of other undertakings.
By way of example, the section goes on to state that a trade mark

may consist of:

> ' . . . words (including personal names), designs, letters,
> numerals or the shape of goods or their packaging.'

This is not an exhaustive list. Any sign which satisfies the two
limbs of the definition in section 1(1) is a trade mark for the
purposes of the 1994 Act. It is a feature of the 1994 Act that, apart
from the two requirements set out in the definition, there is no
limit to the categories of signs which can be considered capable
of being trade marks. Of course, the fact that a sign is a trade
mark for the purposes of section 1(1) does not necessarily mean
that it is registrable; the question of registrability is considered in
chapter 2.

It should also be noted that the term 'trade mark' is used in the
1994 Act to embrace marks which are used in relation to both goods
and services.[2]

This chapter first looks as what constitutes a 'sign' and then
considers individually the two limbs of the definition of 'trade
mark'.

1 As to the meaning of which, see paragraph 1.03.
2 As to which, see paragraph 1.06.

1.03 A 'sign' For the first time in United Kingdom trade mark
legislation the definition of a 'trade mark' refers to a 'sign'. The word
'sign' is not itself defined in the 1994 Act. It has been taken directly
from Article 2 of the Directive. Dictionary definitions are somewhat
unhelpful except in so far as they confirm that the word 'sign' has a
wide meaning that will embrace at least all those things which
would have been a 'mark' for the purposes of section 68(1) of the
1938 Act.[1] The Chambers Concise Dictionary includes within its
definition of the word 'sign':

> ' . . . a signal; a mark with a meaning; a symbol; an emblem; a
> device; an indication . . .'

It is clear, also, that a 'sign' will include certain things which may
not have been a 'mark' under the old law. In the Explanatory
Memorandum to the Regulation, the Commission states (in relation
to the corresponding definition of a Community trade mark):

> 'No type of sign is automatically excluded from registration . . .'

This approach is confirmed in the White Paper[2] which states that:

> ' . . . the word "sign" is intended to be interpreted broadly. It
> does not exclude the possibility of a combination of colours

or even a single colour, or sounds being considered to be a trade mark.'

Colours, sounds and smells   The 1994 Act neither excludes nor makes specific provision for colours, sounds or smells. Therefore, any application for the registration of a trade mark which contains or consists of a colour, sound or a smell will be examined on its own merits. The problem will be that it may be difficult to represent sounds and smells graphically.[3]

Of course, the 1938 Act did not exclude a colour or colours from being regarded as a trade mark. For example, the distinctive appearance of a pharmaceutical capsule which was half coloured and half transparent containing multi-coloured pellets was held to be capable of registration by the House of Lords in *Smith Kline and French Laboratories Ltd v Sterling-Winthrop Group Ltd*.[4] This has more recently been confirmed in another *Smith Kline and French* case where the colour pale green was adopted for pharmaceutical preparations (albeit that the application was rejected on other grounds).[5]

Phrases and slogans   Phrases and slogans were registrable in principle under the 1938 Act.[6] Problems sometimes arose under the 1938 Act where the phrase or slogan was either a descriptive statement or was not being used as a trade mark in the sense required by section 68(1), that is, it was not being used for the purpose of indicating the necessary connection in the course of trade. The elements of section 68(1) do not appear in section 1(1) of the 1994 Act and thus the only issue is whether the phrase or slogan is capable of distinguishing the applicant's goods or services.[7]

Surnames   It will be a question of fact in each case as to whether a surname is capable of distinguishing the applicant's goods or services. Very common surnames may not be so capable. However, section 1(1) itself specifically includes 'personal names' within the list of examples of trade marks.[8]

The goods themselves   In the *Coca-Cola* case,[9] Lord Templeman stated that the word 'mark', both in its normal meaning and in its statutory definition, was apt only to describe something which distinguished the applicant's goods rather than the goods themselves. Accordingly, it was held that the Coca-Cola bottle could not be a 'mark' for the purposes of section 68(1) of the 1938

Act. Section 1(1) of the 1994 Act makes it clear that a trade mark can consist of the shape of goods and therefore there is no requirement that a 'sign' must consist of something which is separate from the goods themselves. The new wording of section 1(1) should ensure that the *Coca-Cola* case would now be decided differently and thus the Coca-Cola bottle, all other requirements being met, will now be eligible for registration.

Get-up The wording of section 1(1) makes it clear that trade marks can consist of packaging and hence the get-up of goods will prima facie be registrable. The issue will be whether get-up or trade dress which is not packaging can be a trade mark. Examples of such matter will include the decor of a restaurant or retail outlet, in particular franchising operations. Strictly, any get-up or trade dress which satisfies the requirements of the two limbs of section 1(1) will be a trade mark.

The key difference between the 1938 Act and the 1994 Act, however, lies not so much in the introduction of the new concept of a 'sign' per se but in the new definition of 'trade mark' which involves satisfying the criteria set out in the two limbs of section 1(1). These criteria are discussed in paragraphs 1.04 and 1.05.

1 ie: a device, brand, heading, label, ticket, name, signature, word, letter, numeral, or any combination thereof.
2 Paragraph 2.08.
3 As to which, see paragraph 1.04.
4 [1976] RPC 511.
5 *Smith Kline and French Laboratories Ltd's Cimetidine Trade Mark* [1991] RPC 17.
6 See for example: 'I Can't Believe It's Yoghurt' [1992] RPC 533.
7 As to which, see paragraph 1.05.
8 As to the registrability of surnames see chapter 2.
9 *Coca-Cola Trade Marks* [1986] FSR 472; [1986] RPC 421; see also *In re James's Trade Mark* (1886) LR 33 ChD 392.

1.04 Capable of being represented graphically, s1(1) The first limb of the definition of 'trade mark' requires the sign to be capable of graphic representation. Essentially, this is a practical requirement which arises from the need to be able to record and publish the mark as well as to search the Register.

In the case of applications for two-dimensional word and device marks this requirement will necessarily be satisfied. However, applicants seeking to register sounds, smells or three-dimensional signs (and any intangible/non-visual signs) will have to find a way to represent their signs graphically to the satisfaction of the Registrar. For example, certain sounds may be capable of being represented in musical notation, some shapes can be represented by one or more photographs or series of drawings. Alternatively, each could be described in words; in the United States of America there have been such cases.[1] While these options may be valid in certain circumstances, it needs to be remembered that the sufficiency of the representation for the purposes of the first limb of section 1(1) will be tested, inter alia, by reference to whether a third party searching the Register will be able to ascertain the scope of the registration so that he can avoid infringing the proprietor's exclusive rights.

The requirement of graphic representation would suggest that the Registry will not be obliged to accept, nor will it be sufficient for an applicant to deposit, either three-dimensional objects, recordings of sounds or specimens embodying smells.

1 Hilman Brown's registration number 556780: for the mark consisting of 'the sound of a creaking door' in respect of certain entertainment services; National Broadcasting Company Inc's registration number 916522: for the mark consisting of 'the musical notes GEC played on chimes' in respect of broadcasting services; Celia Clarke's registration number 1639128: for the mark consisting of 'a high impact, fresh, floral fragrance reminiscent of plumeria blossoms' in respect of sewing thread and embroidery yarn; Fotomat Corporation's registration number 942454: for the three-dimensional design, depicted in numerous photographs, of a retail outlet for drive-in photographic supplies.

1.05 Capable of distinguishing goods or services of one undertaking from those of other undertakings, s1(1)

The second limb of the definition of 'trade mark' is of fundamental importance and embodies the principle that a trade mark must serve to distinguish the goods or services to which it is applied.

The Explanatory Memorandum to the Regulation states that the purpose of these words is to focus attention on the question whether:

'... the relevant sign is capable of performing the basic function of a trade mark. That function, in economic and legal terms, is to indicate the origin of goods or services and to distinguish them from those of other undertakings.'

The wording of the second limb will be recognised as being not dissimilar to that used in section 10(1) of the 1938 Act (the old Part B test for registrability) in so far as the phrase 'capable of distinguishing' appears in each. The phrase in the 1994 Act will not, however, be interpreted in the same way as it was under the 1938

Act where it was interpreted to mean that the mark had to be capable in fact and in law of distinguishing the applicant's goods or services. This is because section 10(1) was interpreted in the light of:

(a) the definition of 'trade mark' in section 68(1) of the 1938 Act; and

(b) the provisions of section 10(2) of the 1938 Act, which required the court to have regard to the extent to which the trade mark was 'inherently capable of distinguishing' the applicant's goods or services.

These two provisions of the 1938 Act were read together in such a way as to result in the conclusion that a trade mark was not 'capable of distinguishing' unless it was inherently capable of distinguishing the applicant's goods or services both in fact and *in law*. The reasoning was as follows:

(a) section 68(1) required that a trade mark must indicate a connection in the course of trade between the goods or services and the applicant (or a registered user);

(b) public policy required that certain descriptive words should be available for all traders to use;

(c) by virtue of their prima facie descriptiveness and by virtue of the public policy consideration referred to in (b), certain words could therefore never indicate the necessary connection in the course of trade (and therefore could never be trade marks for the purposes of the 1938 Act); and

(d) thus, the requirement in section 10(2) that the court should have regard to the extent to which the mark was 'inherently capable of distinguishing', was not fulfilled merely by showing distinctiveness in fact because distinctiveness in fact, of itself, did not necessarily overcome the public policy considerations.

Accordingly, the phrase 'inherently capable of distinguishing' was interpreted as requiring the trade mark to be inherently capable of distinguishing *in law* the applicant's goods; the reference to 'in law' meaning that a mark could not be a trade mark if it was of such a nature that the law required the mark to be available for use by all traders.

The justification for reading in the requirement that the mark be 'inherently capable in fact and in law of distinguishing' was therefore based on two sections of the 1938 Act which do not appear in any form in the 1994 Act. It would therefore be inconsistent with the remainder of the 1994 Act for the requirement in section 1(1) to be read as requiring anything other than distinctiveness in fact, that is, that the sign must be capable of distinguishing in fact the applicant's goods or services from those of other undertakings.

1.06 Goods or services, s1(1) Although amendments in 1986[1] brought service marks within the scope of the 1938 Act, the 1994 Act takes the opportunity to simplify the position and to have, as far as possible, the same provisions governing marks for services as those for goods. The term 'trade mark' is thus used in relation to goods or services.

Retail services Under the 1938 Act it was difficult (if not impossible) to register a service mark for retail services. This was the practical effect of the Court of Appeal's decision in *Dee Corporation.*[2] In that case it was held that a service has to be charged for separately and that retail services are merely ancillary to the function of trading in goods. This decision was based on the definition of 'service mark' in section 68(1) of the 1938 Act which required that the provision of a service had to be for money or money's worth. There is no such requirement in section 1(1) of the 1994 Act, indeed the word 'service' is not defined at all. Accordingly, a sign which is used in relation to retail services (or any other service which does not involve a charge) should qualify as a trade mark provided that the two limbs of section 1(1) are otherwise satisfied. However, the remaining concern is that the Court of Appeal also held that the specification of 'retail services' was too indefinite to provide an identifiable description of the applicants' services for the purposes of registration. This must still be the case and hence an application drafted in this way may still be refused.[3]

1   Trade Marks (Amendment) Act 1984.
2   [1990] RPC 159.
3   As to which, see chapter 2.

1.07 Undertakings, s1(1) The word 'undertakings' is not defined in the 1994 Act. It is taken from the Directive and, assuming that it is therefore to be interpreted so as not to be inconsistent with Community law, it will embrace any legal or natural person including companies, partnerships, trade associations, co-operatives, individuals, state-owned corporations, regional and local authorities and statutory bodies[1] engaged in an economic activity, regardless of its legal status or the way in which it is financed and whether or not it is profit making.[2]

The EEA Treaty[3] defines an undertaking as 'any entity carrying out activities of a commercial or economic nature'.

It has been further held that undertakings engaged in the supply of services are 'undertakings' for the purposes of Article 85(1) of the EEC Treaty, as are undertakings engaged in the supply of goods.[4]

1 See the cases cited in *Common Market Law of Competition*, Bellamy and Child, Fourth edition, chapter 2.
2 Case C-41/90 *Höfner & Elser v Macroton* [1991] I ECR 1979, [1993] 4 CMLR 306; Case T-61/89 *Dansk Pelsdyravlerforening v Commission* [1992] II ECR 1931.
3 The Treaty on a European Economic Area signed on 2 May 1992.
4 eg: Case 155/73 *Sacchi* [1974] ECR 409, [1974] 2 CMLR 177.

1.08 Comparison with section 68(1) of the 1938 Act The definition of 'trade mark' in section 68(1) of the 1938 Act required the mark to be:

'...used or proposed to be used...for the purpose of indicating, or so as to indicate, a connection in the course of trade...'

The definition in section 1(1) makes no reference to the purpose for which the sign is used in order for it to be a trade mark. This is relevant when one considers, in particular, the licensing of trade marks[1] because it was this requirement in section 68(1) that led to the House of Lords deciding (reluctantly in the case of Lord Bridge) in the *Holly Hobbie* case[2] that the applicant was 'trafficking' in his trade mark, ie, because he was not using his trade mark for the purpose specified in section 68(1), he was therefore 'trafficking' and hence the registration of the applicant's licensees as registered users was refused under section 28(6) of the 1938 Act. Although attention will be focused, quite rightly, on the fact that section 28(6) has been repealed and not replaced in the 1994 Act, it is submitted that an even more important factor is the omission from the definition of 'trade mark' in section 1(1) of any reference to the requirement that a sign must be used so as to indicate a trade connection with the proprietor. The omission of this requirement means that the commercial exploitation of signs through character merchandising, franchising and other licensing operations which may amount to treating the sign as a commodity will not, of itself, mean that the sign cannot be considered to be a trade mark.

Used or proposed to be used – use in a trade mark sense Cases on
a number of different issues decided under the 1938 Act referred to
the concept of a trade mark being used 'in a trade mark sense'. This
was a reference to the trade mark being used in accordance with
and for the purposes described in section 68(1). For example, in the
Nerit case,[3] the token use of the mark was held not to be use in a
trade mark sense and hence not only was the mark struck off for
non-use under section 26 of the 1938 Act, it was also held that the
mark was not a trade mark for the purposes of section 68(1).

It will remain to be seen whether any remnants of the concept of
'use in a trade mark sense' remain under the 1994 Act. While it is
quite clear that the concept no longer forms any part of the
definition of 'trade mark', it is questionable whether the concept
may not re-surface in the context of infringement cases under
section 10, non-use cases under section 46(1)(a) or (b) and
revocation cases under section 46(1)(d).

1 As to which, see chapter 10.
2 [1984] FSR 199.
3 *Imperial Group Ltd v Philip Morris & Co Ltd* [1982] FSR 72.

1.09 Comment The Mathys Report[1] recommended that trade
mark legislation should clearly exclude the registration of the colour
or the shape of goods or the shape of containers, or smells or
sounds. Mathys submitted that to permit the registration of such
things was contrary to public policy in that no one trader should be
granted a perpetual monopoly of an arbitrarily selected
characteristic or feature, whether inherent or applied. It followed
from this recommendation that there was no amendment to the
definition of 'mark' in the 1938 Act[2] and thus the *Coca-Cola* case[3]
was decided as it was.

The statement of principle expressed in the Mathys Report has
not been rejected as such. But the overriding objective of the 1994
Act is to recognise the fact that:
(a) certain signs (which may not have qualified for registration
     under earlier trade mark legislation) are nonetheless recognised
     by consumers as distinctive of the goods or services of a
     particular trader; and
(b) the registration of such signs merely recognises the de facto
     monopoly in respect of the use of such signs which is
     enforceable by way of an action for passing off.

There is also an argument that signs which could be protected under other intellectual property legislation should expressly be excluded from trade mark registration. Once again, the 1994 Act, consistent with the objective stated above, seeks only to test whether the sign in fact functions in the market place as a trade mark and, if so, it is prima facie a trade mark and registrable unless there are express grounds for refusal.[4]

The 1994 statutory definition of 'trade mark' is therefore intended to serve the needs of commerce and to be open-ended so as to be capable of adapting to changes in trading practices. This pragmatic approach is in marked contrast to the 1938 Act (and its predecessors) and to the attitude of the courts in interpreting and applying the old law. In the past, marks have been denied registration on technical, formalistic grounds when the fact of the matter was that the mark in question was distinctive of the applicant's goods or services and would only have been used by a third party who wanted to trade-off or appropriate the benefit of that distinctiveness.

1 Paragraph 64.
2 ie: section 68(1).
3 Supra 1.03, note 9.
4 As to which, see chapter 2.

1.10 Unregistered trade marks Although section 2(2) asserts that no proceedings lie either to prevent or recover damages for the infringement of an unregistered trade mark, the 1994 Act does in fact indirectly recognise unregistered trade marks for certain purposes. It is not the intention to review in detail in this chapter the relevant sections relating to unregistered trade marks. However, it is worth noting briefly the circumstances in which an unregistered trade mark is relevant for the purposes of the 1994 Act.

Passing off, s2(2) In the first place, section 2(2) itself goes on to confirm that nothing in the 1994 Act affects the law relating to passing off.

Impediment to registration, s5(4)(a) Secondly, in the context of registrability, a trade mark cannot be registered if its use is liable to be prevented in the United Kingdom by virtue of any rule of law protecting unregistered trade marks or signs used in the course of trade.[1] A mark registered contrary to this provision is liable to be declared invalid.[2]

Defence to infringement, s11(3) Thirdly, in the context of defences to infringement, the use of an 'earlier right' in a particular locality, which applies only in that locality, does not infringe a later registered trade mark.[4] For the purpose of this defence 'an earlier right' means an unregistered trade mark or other sign which has been continuously used since before both the use and registration of the registered trade mark. Accordingly, provided that the proprietor of the unregistered trade mark can show that his trade mark is an 'earlier right' for the purpose of section 11(3), he can continue to use his trade mark notwithstanding that such use would otherwise infringe a registered trade mark.

Acts of agents and representatives, s60 Although not strictly relevant to unregistered trade marks in the United Kingdom, the 1994 Act introduces new rights and remedies for the benefit of proprietors of marks (whether registered or unregistered) in a Convention country.[4]

Specifically, the proprietor of the mark has the following options open to him in the event that his agent or representative applies for the registration of the mark in the United Kingdom:[5]

(a) to oppose the application, in which case the registration will be refused;[6]

(b) to apply for a declaration that any subsequent registration of the mark is invalid;[7]

(c) to apply for the rectification of the Register so as to substitute his name as the proprietor of the registered trade mark;[8] and

(d) to obtain an injunction to restrain the unauthorised use of the mark by the agent or representative.[9]

Well known trade marks Finally, an unregistered trade mark may also be so well known that it is entitled to the special protection which the 1994 Act confers on such marks in accordance with Article 6*bis* of the Paris Convention. These marks are the subject of the next two paragraphs.

1 Section 5(4)(a), As to which, see chapter 2.
2 Section 47(2), As to which, see chapter 5.
3 Section 11(3), As to which, see chapter 7.
4 Section 60; a Convention country means a country, other than the United Kingdom, which is a member of the Paris Convention: section 55(1).
5 Subject to the provisions set out in section 60(5) and (6).
6 Section 60(2), As to which, see paragraph 4.05.
7 Section 60(3)(a), As to which, see paragraph 5.18.
8 Section 60(3)(b), As to which, see paragraph 5.18.
9 Section 60(4), As to which, see paragraph 8.18.

1.11   Well known trade marks, s56   The 1994 Act, in accordance with Article 6*bis* of the Paris Convention, confers certain rights and remedies on the proprietor of a well known trade mark.

Section 56 provides that, for the purposes of the 1994 Act, a reference to a trade mark which is entitled to protection under the Paris Convention as a well known trade mark is to be construed as a reference to a mark which is:

'... well known in the United Kingdom as being the mark of a person who:

(a) is a national of a Convention country; or

(b) is domiciled in, or has a real and effective industrial or commercial establishment in a Convention country,

whether or not that person carries on business, or has any goodwill, in the United Kingdom.'

Meaning of 'well known'   The first issue which must be considered is what is required in order for a mark to be considered to be 'well known' for the purpose of section 56. Indeed, there has been considerable speculation as to what the answer to this question might be.[1]

Of course, the question as to whether a mark is well known is essentially one of fact. The problem is the extent to which a mark must be known before it can be said to be 'well known'. Perhaps light can be thrown on this issue by looking at those sections of the 1994 Act where well known trade marks will or may be relevant.

To start with, section 56(2) provides that the proprietor of a well known trade mark can obtain an injunction to restrain the use of his well known mark by third parties in the United Kingdom. However, an injunction will only be available if his well known trade mark is used:

(a) in relation to goods or services which are identical with or similar to the goods or services for which the mark is well known; and

(b) where such use by the third party is likely to deceive or cause confusion.

Accordingly, the injunction available to the proprietor of a well known mark under section 56(2) is certainly no broader and arguably narrower than the injunction which would be available to the proprietor of a registered trade mark pursuant to section 10(2).[2]

In any event, the injunction under section 56(2) will never be available in the circumstances described in section 10(3) (that is, where a third party uses his trade mark in relation to goods or services which are not similar to those for which the mark is protected). What can one deduce from this? It could be argued that, because the injunction is only available in limited circumstances (limited as compared with section 10(2) and (3)), the level of notoriety required should not be set too high.

However, it may be wrong to conclude that the moderate level of protection afforded by section 56(2) is necessarily indicative of the level of notoriety that will be required in order to establish that a mark is well known. Instead, one could argue that, because the 1994 Act is conferring certain protection on foreign proprietors' trade marks, which may be unregistered in the United Kingdom, it is right that such protection should be limited only to those marks with a very high level of notoriety.

Evidence In certain countries, arbitrary levels of notoriety have been adopted for the purposes of determining whether a mark is well known. This often takes the form of a stipulation as to a certain percentage market recognition of the mark in question. In practice, arbitrary levels are unsatisfactory. If such an approach is adopted then issues will arise as to what evidence will need to be submitted to the court, for example:

(a) will it only be necessary to establish a certain level of notoriety in the particular trade or service sector in which the trade mark is used and, if so, what level of market awareness will be required?

(b) will it also be necessary to establish a certain level of notoriety outside the relevant trade or service sector and, if so, what level of market awareness will be required?

(c) will it also be necessary to establish a general public awareness of the mark in question and, if so, what level of awareness?

(d) what will constitute a sufficiently representative sample? Presumably this can be answered by statisticians, although it may be difficult to define in advance given the numerous variables such as: how many people will need to be surveyed/give evidence, the extent to which those persons must be representative of the various geographical regions of the United Kingdom, as well as the various cultures, age groups, and even standards of education, not to mention gender.

Furthermore, will it be necessary to establish that the notoriety has subsisted for any particular length of time or will it be sufficient that the mark is well known as at any given date? All these matters suggest that proving that a trade mark is well known may be a logistical nightmare. Having said this, of course, in the majority of cases the notoriety of the mark may almost be a matter for judicial notice.

Conclusion   The question of whether a trade mark is well known is very much at large. Ultimately, the courts will have the pleasure of determining the meaning of 'well known' in the context of a trade mark as well as the nature and extent of the evidence that will be required to establish that a mark is well known.

Assuming, however, that it can be established that a mark is well known, the 1994 Act confers certain rights and remedies on its proprietor and these are mentioned briefly below.

Impediment to registration, ss5 and 6   In the first place, a well known trade mark is deemed to be an 'earlier trade mark' for the purposes of section 5[3] and thus can be the basis on which the registration of a later conflicting identical or similar trade mark can be refused,[4] provided that the well known mark was well known as at the date of the application for the registration of the later trade mark. A mark registered contrary to this provision can be declared invalid.[5]

Defence to infringement   Section 11 does not provide expressly that a registered trade mark will not be infringed by the use of an earlier well known mark. However, it may be the case that a mark which is well known for the purposes of the 1994 Act (see section 56(1)) will also come within the meaning of the phrase 'earlier right' for the purposes of the defence set out in section 11(3). The difficulty with section 11(3) is that it is only available where the use of the earlier right is in a 'particular locality' and where the earlier right 'applies only in that locality'. It must be assumed that the whole of the United Kingdom can be a 'locality' for the purposes of section 11(3) as, although such a conclusion strains the ordinary meaning of 'locality', the alternative conclusion would be perverse and would almost necessarily exclude well known marks from the ambit of section 11(3) because, of their nature, they are likely to 'apply' throughout the United Kingdom.

There is also a second difficulty in so far as section 11(3) is only available where the use of the earlier right is 'protected by virtue of any rule of law (in particular the law of passing off)'. A well known mark need not necessarily be protected by virtue of any rule of law (whether passing off or otherwise) because the definition in section 56(1) is wide enough to include well known marks of proprietors who do not carry on business and/or who do not have any goodwill in the United Kingdom: it is questionable whether the well known mark of such a person is indeed entitled to any protection by virtue of any rule of law. Certainly, there must be a very real question as to whether the law of passing off will provide such protection. The counter argument which may be available to the proprietor of the well known mark is that section 56(2), which confers the right on the proprietor to obtain an injunction, provides the necessary protection for the purposes of section 11(3) and, in that case, the proprietor of the well known mark will have the same defence available to him as is available to the proprietor of any other 'earlier right'.[6]

Remedies, ss56(2) and 60   The proprietor of a well known mark is entitled to restrain by injunction the use in the United Kingdom of a trade mark which is identical with or similar to his well known mark provided that the mark is being used in relation to identical or similar goods or services and where such use is likely to cause confusion.[7]

The proprietor of the well known mark may also be entitled to the benefit of the special rights and remedies set out in section 60 vis-à-vis the acts of his agents and representatives provided that he is the proprietor of the well known mark in a Convention country.[8] That is, there is no necessary inconsistency for the proprietor of a well known mark to be entitled to the benefits of both sections 56 and 60.

1 See for example: 'Trade Mark Filing Strategies and Pitfalls', MacDonald, Cook and Barr, *Managing Intellectual Property*, October 1991.
2 As to infringement under section 10(2), see chapter 2.
3 Section 6(1)(c).
4 As to which, see chapter 2.
5 Section 47(2), As to which, see chapter 5.
6 As to which, see chapter 7.
7 Section 56(2), As to which, see chapter 8.
8 As to which, see the summary in paragraph 1.10.

2 Registrable trade marks

2.01 Approach taken by the 1994 Act In contrast to the 1938 Act, the 1994 Act stipulates only that which cannot be registered rather than setting down mandatory criteria for registrability. Accordingly, all trade marks[1] are prima facie registrable unless there are express grounds for refusal. It is these grounds which are the subject of this chapter.

The grounds for refusal may be classed under four headings:
(a) absolute grounds for refusal: section 3;
(b) relative grounds for refusal: sections 5 and 6 (subject to honest concurrent user: section 7);
(c) specially protected emblems: sections 4 and 57 to 59;[2] and
(d) the failure to comply with the formalities of section 32 and the Rules.[3]

1 As defined in section 1(1): see chapter 1.
2 See chapter 15.
3 In particular, rule 11 and see chapter 3.

Absolute grounds for refusal

2.02 Signs which do not satisfy the requirements of section 1(1), s3(1)(a) Logically, if a sign does not fall within the definition of a 'trade mark' then it cannot be registered.[1]

Section 3(1)(a) is the only ground for refusal of registration under section 3 to which the proviso at the end of section 3(1) does not apply.[2] This would, at first, appear to mean that, in certain circumstances, a sign can be refused registration even if it has in fact acquired a distinctive character as a result of the use made of it. However, this misses the point that where any sign can be shown in fact to have acquired the requisite distinctive character then, by virtue thereof, it will necessarily satisfy the requirement in section 1(1) that it be capable of distinguishing the applicant's goods or services. It would then only remain to be determined whether the sign is capable of being represented graphically. This conclusion depends upon the validity of the argument advanced in chapter 1 that distinctiveness in fact will always satisfy the second limb of the definition of 'trade mark' set out in section 1(1).

1 Section 3(1)(a); as to which, see chapter 1.
2 As to the proviso, see paragraph 2.06.

2.03 Trade marks devoid of distinctive character, s3(1)(b)

Although certain signs will fall within the definition of a trade mark if they are capable of distinguishing the applicant's goods or services that, of itself, does not necessarily mean that the trade mark is registrable.

The requirement in section 1(1) may be satisfied by proving that the sign has in fact become distinctive through use because a sign which is in fact distinctive must logically be capable of distinguishing the applicant's goods or services. However, section 3(1)(b) provides that a trade mark (ie: a sign capable of distinguishing) shall not be registered if it is 'devoid of any distinctive character', subject to the proviso discussed in paragraph 2.06. This would seem to require that the trade mark must be more than merely capable of distinguishing, that is, that it must also possess some 'distinctive character'. This is reminiscent of the inherent distinctiveness requirement under the 1938 Act.

By way of example, a prima facie descriptive sign (eg a lemon-shaped container for lemon juice) could satisfy the threshold requirement in section 1(1) of being capable of distinguishing the applicant's goods and it will be the acquired distinctiveness in fact which establishes that the sign is so capable. However, one could argue that such a trade mark is nonetheless devoid of any 'distinctive character' and thus should be refused registration under section 3(1)(b). Of course, it would then be open to the applicant to seek to rely upon the proviso by submitting evidence that the trade

mark has in fact acquired a distinctive character as a result of the use
made of it prior to the date of application.

'Devoid'   There is a further issue arising out of the use of the word
'devoid' which can be defined as meaning 'destitute, free, empty'.[1]
Applying this definition to the phrase 'distinctive character' one
could argue that a trade mark will only be excluded from
registration on this ground if there is a complete absence of any
element which may serve to distinguish. The corollary to this
proposition is that a trade mark will be prima facie registrable if it
incorporates any distinctive element, notwithstanding that the
remainder of the mark may lack any distinctive quality.

Alternatively, a narrower interpretation could be taken, viz that
a trade mark will be refused registration on this ground if, when
considered as a whole, it lacks any distinctive character. The mere
incorporation of a distinctive element may or may not give it that
character. However, it is difficult to conceive of a trade mark which
incorporates a distinctive element and yet (subject to the de
minimus rule) can be said to be devoid of any distinctive character.
The narrow interpretation sits uneasily with the policy of the 1994
Act to allow the registration of trade marks which are recognised by
consumers as being distinctive of the applicant's goods or services
and it should not matter that such recognition derives from a mere
element of the mark.

'Distinctive character'   Finally, section 3(1)(b) requires some
analysis of what constitutes a 'distinctive character' when that phrase
is applied to trade marks. The adjective 'distinctive' can only mean
that the 'character' of the trade mark must distinguish the applicant's
goods or services. What then constitutes 'character' in the context of
a trade mark? It is assumed that the requisite character must derive
from an element or elements which enable the trade mark to be
recognised in the marketplace. A trade mark will, therefore, only be
refused registration under section 3(1)(b) if it is devoid of any
element which will enable it to be recognised in the marketplace.

Surnames   Unlike the 1938 Act,[2] the 1994 Act does not expressly
make reference to the registration of surnames. However, it could
be argued that surnames should be denied registration either on the
ground that a surname:
(a) is incapable of distinguishing the applicant's goods or services

and hence is not a trade mark; or

(b) is devoid of any distinctive character.

The question as to whether a surname can be a trade mark is dealt with in chapter 1. As stated in chapter 1, it will be a question of fact as to whether any particular surname fulfils the requirements of section 1(1) and the same case by case analysis will need to be carried out in order to decide whether the surname can be said to be 'devoid of any distinctive character'. Under section 9(1)(d) of the 1938 Act, the Registrar adopted the practice of refusing registration if the surname applied for occurred more than a given number of times in the telephone directory. It is suggested that such a practice is no longer valid as the issue is not whether the mark applied for is a surname but rather whether the mark applied for is 'devoid of any distinctive character'. The fact that a surname occurs any given number of times in a telephone directory must be insufficient evidence in itself that the mark applied for is necessarily devoid of any distinctive character. Of course, this proposition works both ways and the mere fact that a surname occurs rarely in a telephone directory should not necessarily preclude the Registrar from refusing the application if the surname, for whatever reason, is devoid of distinctive character.

1 The Chambers Concise Dictionary (1991).
2 Section 9(1)(d) of the 1938 Act.

2.04 Descriptive trade marks, s3(1)(c) Section 3(1)(c) provides that the following shall not be registered:

'trade marks which consist exclusively of signs or indications which may serve, in trade, to designate the kind, quality, quantity, intended purpose, value, geographical origin, the time of production of goods or of rendering of services, or other characteristics of goods or services'.

There are several elements of this sub-section which require comment.

'Exclusively' The use of the word 'exclusively' may limit the application of this ground for refusal because, arguably, any trade mark which is otherwise registrable will not be refused registration under this section provided that it merely incorporates at least a single element (subject to the de minimus rule) which does not fall within the wording of the sub-section.

'Indications' The reference to 'indications' would appear to be superfluous in the context of this section.[1] The word 'indications' is not defined in the 1994 Act and surely adds nothing to the reference to 'signs'.

'May serve to designate' The use of the word 'may' in the phrase 'may serve . . . to designate' is ambiguous as it could suggest that the Registrar is to exercise some degree of discretion enabling him to speculate as to what a trade mark may serve to designate in the future. Alternatively, and more likely, the phrase 'may serve' should be construed simply as a reference to the principle which has always been at the heart of trade mark jurisprudence (and which has been affirmed in the Directive and the 1994 Act), namely, that all traders should be entitled freely to describe or 'designate' relevant characteristics of their goods or services. It has previously been held that no one trader should be able to 'fence off' any section of the English language which another trader legitimately may wish to use so as to describe his goods or services. This remains the case under the 1994 Act.

'In trade' The phrase 'in trade' is not limited expressly to the trade in the goods or services in respect of which the registration of the applicant's trade mark is sought. However, one would expect this section to be construed so that trade marks will not be refused registration unless they are apt descriptions or designations of characteristics of the goods or services covered by the application. It must be right that a trade mark, which is descriptive of certain goods or services, may legitimately be used and registered in respect of other goods or services without impinging upon another trader's ability to describe the characteristics of his goods or services.

'Geographical origin' Although trade marks which consist of indications of geographical origin may be refused registration under this section, it may be possible to register such marks as collective marks and/or certification marks pursuant to section 49 and/or 50 of the 1994 Act.[2]

1 The wording has been adopted from Article 3(1)(c) of the Directive.
2 See Schedule 1, paragraph 3(1) in relation to collective marks which is dealt with in chapter 12, and see Schedule 2, paragraph 3(1) in relation to certification marks which is dealt with in chapter 11. Note also Council Regulation on the Protection of Geographical Indications and Designation of Origin for Agricultural Products and Foodstuffs No 2081/92 of 14 July 1992.

2.05 Generic marks, s3(1)(d) Section 3(1)(d) provides that the following shall not be registered:

'trade marks which consist exclusively of signs or indications which have become customary in the current language or in the bona fide and established practices of the trade.'

The comments in paragraph 2.04 above in respect of the words 'exclusively' and 'indications' apply equally to their use within this sub-section. The remaining wording of this sub-section, however, raises a further issue of interpretation and application.

The phrase 'customary in the current language' raises an initial problem as to whether it is qualified by the words 'of the trade' which appear at the end of the section. One would hope that this phrase is so qualified so that this ground for refusal will not catch trade marks which have simply become customary in the English language rather than customary in the language of the relevant trade.

The clear intention of this sub-section is to prevent the registration of signs which are used descriptively or generically. This must be right because a generic sign cannot function in the relevant market as a trade mark. The language used, however, raises questions as to what enquiries will be made and what evidence will be admissible to establish that a sign or indication has become either:

(a) customary in the current language [of the trade]; or
(b) customary in the bona fide and established practices of the trade.

It will be a question of fact in each case whether either of these grounds for refusal is made out.

2.06 The proviso, s3(1) Sub-sections 3(1)(b),(c) & (d) are qualified by the proviso that:

' . . . a trade mark shall not be refused registration by virtue of paragraph (b) (c) or (d) above if, before the date of application for registration, it has in fact acquired a distinctive character as a result of the use made of it'.

This represents a fundamental departure from the pre-1994 Act law relating to the registration of trade marks. Although it was possible to register a distinctive mark under section 9(1) of the 1938 Act, that entitlement was subject to the definition in section 9(2) which provided that 'distinctive' meant 'adapted . . . to distinguish . . .'

Accordingly, distinctiveness in fact was not necessarily sufficient.[1] However, under the 1994 Act, if an applicant can establish that the mark applied for has, before the date of application, acquired a distinctive character as a result of the use made of the mark, then the mark will proceed to registration as long as it is not caught by any of the other grounds for refusal which are not subject to the proviso.[2]

The proviso effectively overturns earlier decisions of the courts which had refused registration of marks in certain circumstances even where it had been shown, in fact, that the mark in question was 100% distinctive of the applicant's goods.[3]

The proviso embodies the now accepted proposition that a trade mark which is in fact recognised as designating the origin of goods or services should not be denied registration. Note, however, that the proviso only comes to the assistance of an applicant seeking registration of a trade mark which has acquired a 'distinctive character' as opposed simply to having become distinctive. Perhaps this is a distinction without a difference? It is difficult to imagine that a trade mark could have acquired distinctiveness and yet be without a 'distinctive character' but the possibility must exist. The meaning of the phrase 'distinctive character' is considered in paragraph 2.03 above.

1   See the discussion of this issue in chapter 1, paragraph 1.05.
2   ie: sections 3(1)(a), 3(2)–(6), 4 & 5.
3   See *'York'* TM [1984] RPC 231.

2.07   Signs consisting exclusively of shapes, s3(2)   The 1994 Act specifically provides that a trade mark may consist of 'the shape of goods or their packaging', but signs which consist exclusively of certain shapes are excluded from registration. These excluded shapes fall into three categories and are discussed in paragraphs 2.08 to 2.10.

Shapes   It is to be assumed that the reference to 'shape' will embrace any aspect of the three-dimensional structure or configuration of the goods in question.

'Exclusively'   The same comment needs to be made as has already been made in relation to section 3(1)(c) and (d), namely that this ground for refusal of registration only applies where the sign consists 'exclusively' of an excluded shape. Thus, one should be able to avoid an objection being successfully raised pursuant to

section 3(2) simply by ensuring that the trade mark applied for incorporates elements or features in addition to an excluded shape.

2.08 Shapes which result from the nature of the goods themselves, s3(2)(a) Section 3(2)(a) provides that a sign shall not be registered as a trade mark if it consists exclusively of:

'the shape which results from the nature of the goods themselves'.

This provision recognises the legitimate concern that the potentially perpetual monopoly afforded by a trade mark registration should not extend to a shape which results from the nature of the goods themselves. This raises two issues relevant to the application of this ground for refusal:

(a) must the shape be dictated by the nature of the goods in the sense that, by virtue of the nature of the goods, the shape is the only shape which can obtain?

(b) what elements or features of the goods will be considered to be part of their 'nature'?

Having regard to the purpose of this section, one would expect it to apply only to those shapes which are dictated necessarily by the nature of the goods and that 'nature' in this context would include those elements or features which affect the shape of the goods. Rarely, if ever, would an aesthetic feature of a product be such that it would necessarily result in any particular shape, whereas the function or intended purpose or composition of a product may dictate the shape of that product. Thus, although the definition of a trade mark includes ' . . . the shape of goods or their packaging',[1] a trade mark will not be registrable to the extent that the trade mark applied for, being the shape of the goods themselves, results from a function, intended purpose or composition of the goods for which registration is sought. Applying this principle to the *Coca-Cola* decision,[2] the Coca-Cola bottle will not be refused registration under this sub-section as its shape has no relationship to the function, intended purpose, composition or other nature of the soft drink which it contains.

1 Section 1(1).
2 *Coca-Cola* TM [1986] FSR 472 HL.

2.09 Shape of goods which is necessary to obtain a technical result, s3(2)(b) Section 3(2)(b) provides that a sign shall not be registered as a trade mark if it consists exclusively of:

'the shape of goods which is necessary to obtain a technical result'.

This is a further specific example of the general proposition stated in paragraph 2.08 above. If a shape serves a functional or utilitarian purpose, then other traders should not be prevented (at least under trade mark law) from achieving the same technical result.[1] An important practical example would be, in the computer industry, the shape of porting devices which must be of a certain configuration in order to enable computer equipment manufactured by various companies to communicate with each other.

1 This may be subject to patent or other intellectual property right protection.

2.10 The shape which gives substantial value to the goods, s3(2)(c) Section 3(2)(c) provides that a sign shall not be registered as a trade mark if it consists exclusively of:

'the shape which gives substantial value to the goods'.

The scope of this section is arguably too broad. After all, many trade marks add value to the goods or services in relation to which they are used. If a trade mark is otherwise registrable, why should it be denied registration simply because it consists of a shape which adds substantial value to the goods? To deny registration to a sign merely because it adds substantial value to the goods is not consistent with the principle which underlies sections 3(2)(a) and (b). It is always open to other traders to add value to their products provided they do so by adopting a different sign, in this case, a different shape. It would appear that the only justification for this section is that shapes which add value are to be protected under other branches of intellectual property law and that once these rights (if any) have lapsed, other traders should be free to use the shape in question.

'Substantial value' What comes within the concept of a shape giving substantial value? One needs to consider the circumstances in which the shape of the product gives substantial value to that product. The White Paper suggests that a shape will be of substantial value if it serves a utilitarian purpose, whether by making the product itself superior in performance or more attractive to the eye or by facilitating its manufacture, distribution or storage. No doubt there are other categories but, as always, the onus will be on the Registrar to establish that the shape does give

substantial value to the product. The following questions can be posed but it is difficult to provide definitive answers:
(a) will a shape which makes a product more marketable be held to 'give substantial value' to that product?
(b) will a trade mark only 'give substantial value' if the goods themselves are worth more as a result of the shape?
(c) can it be the case that products, for which shape is irrelevant or of minor importance to the purchaser, can ever be given substantial value by the adoption of a particular shape?

2.11   Comment on section 3(2)   It should be noted that there is no proviso in relation to the grounds for refusal in respect of signs which consist of shapes which is equivalent to the proviso to section 3(1). Thus, it is irrelevant that an applicant can show that a shape, which is caught by section 3(2), has in fact acquired a distinctive character as a result of the use made of the shape. This is a derogation from the general principle adopted in the Directive and embodied in the 1994 Act that a sign which in fact functions as a trade mark should not be denied registration. It could be argued that the question of registrability should be determined by asking whether the shape serves to distinguish the applicant's goods from rival products and, if it does, then the mark should be registered, except only where such registration would effectively confer a monopoly in the product itself.

2.12   Contrary to public policy or to accepted principles of morality, s3(3)(a)   Section 3(3)(a) of the 1994 Act provides that a trade mark shall not be registered:
　　'if it is contrary to public policy or to accepted principles of
　　morality'.
This section is akin to section 11 of the 1938 Act but arguably is wider in so far as section 11 was restricted to certain specified grounds of public policy whereas section 3(3)(a) embraces all grounds of public policy. Public policy undoubtedly was the rationale behind the old section 11 but was not specifically mentioned. The express reference to public policy in the 1994 Act potentially opens up a much wider enquiry. It will be for the courts to determine the scope of public policy and the principles of morality applicable in relation to the registration of trade marks. There is no reason to think that the principles governing decisions under the old section 11 will not

continue to be applied and, as was stated by Greene MR in relation
to the old section 11, it is to be remembered that the section is one
which exists 'not merely for the benefit of traders but for the benefit
of the public at large'.[1]

One would also have thought that it would be contrary to public
policy to register a mark which was contrary to accepted principles
of morality and, therefore, the second limb of section 3(3)(a) may be
redundant. In addition, the fact that section 3(3)(a) embraces all
grounds of public policy would also suggest that there will be a
substantial overlap with section 3(3)(b).

1   *Livron* (1937) 54 RPC 161.

2.13   Deception of the public, s3(3)(b)   Section 3(3)(b) of the
1994 Act provides that a trade mark shall not be registered if it is:
   'of such a nature as to deceive the public (for instance as to the
   nature, quality or geographical origin of the goods or service)'.
The examples provided in section 3(3)(b) are clearly not exhaustive
and this provision will cover any other feature or character of the
goods or services including their function or intended purpose or
any of the other attributes referred to in section 3(1)(c).

As with all other grounds for refusal, the relevant time of
deception (an issue under the 1938 Act) would appear to be the date
of the decision whether or not to register and not the date of
application. This follows from the wording 'shall not be registered'
which is used throughout sections 3, 4 and 5.

This sub-section is substantially similar to the first limb of section
11 of the 1938 Act although it is limited to trade marks which of their
nature deceive the public and does not apply to trade marks which
merely cause confusion. As stated above, one would have thought
that deceiving the public (and indeed possibly confusing the public)
would be contrary to public policy and therefore the trade mark
would also be refused under section 3(3)(a).

This sub-section may also overlap to some extent with the
relative grounds for refusal[1] in so far as a mark which is identical
with or similar to an earlier trade mark[2] could deceive the public as
to the origin of the goods or services.

The point could also be taken that this sub-section can be
construed so as to require actual deception and not merely the
likelihood of deception. Such an argument derives from the
omission of the word 'likely' (which appeared in the old section 11).

Accordingly, if this is right, and if there is no evidence of actual deception, the trade mark should not be refused under section 3(3)(b). Alternatively, the fact that the enquiry under section 3(3)(b) focuses on the 'nature' of the trade mark can be construed as giving the Registrar and the courts the right to take into account, if not actually assess, the likelihood of deception.

1 See section 5 and paragraphs 2.17 to 2.27.
2 See definition in section 6, and paragraph 2.17.

2.14 Trade marks the use of which is prohibited by law, s3(4) Section 3(4) of the 1994 Act provides that a trade mark shall not be registered if or to the extent that:
'its use is prohibited in the United Kingdom by any enactment
or rule of law or by any provision of Community law'.
The prohibition referred to in section 3(4) must relate to the use of the trade mark in the United Kingdom. Use of the mark must be prohibited by any of the following:
(a) any enactment;
(b) any rule of law; or
(c) any provision of Community law.
Section 3(4) should be distinguished from section 5(4).[1] Section 3(4) is an absolute ground for refusal where the use of the trade mark applied for is actually prohibited in the United Kingdom by one or more of the aforementioned laws. Section 5(4) is a relative ground for refusal and applies where the law confers a right on a third party who in reliance upon such right may be able to prevent the use of the mark applied for (eg the law of passing off which does not prohibit the use of trade marks and which is therefore irrelevant for the purposes of section 3(4) but which does enable a third party to enjoin such use).

Thus, the application of section 3(4) is more limited than section 5(4) because there are only relatively few laws which actually prohibit the use of a trade mark per se as opposed to laws which confer rights on third parties which may be enforced to prevent the use of the applicant's trade mark. An example of the former is the Trade Descriptions Act 1968.

1 See paragraphs 2.24 to 2.26.

2.15 Specially protected emblems, ss3(5) and 4 Section 3(5) of the 1994 Act provides that a trade mark shall not be registered in the cases specified or referred to in section 4.[1] Section 3(5) adds nothing to section 4 itself other than to make it clear that section 4 is an absolute ground for refusal as distinct from a relative ground.

1 See chapter 15.

2.16   Bad faith, s3(6)   The 1994 Act provides that a trade mark shall not be registered if or to the extent that the application is made in bad faith.[1]

What will constitute 'bad faith'? Section 3(6) will certainly embrace the situation where an application has been made without any bona fide intention to use the mark because this would mean that the statement provided pursuant to section 32(3) would be untruthful.[2] In *Nerit*[3] it was stated that merely having an ulterior motive was not necessarily inconsistent with the requisite bona fide intention to use. However, for the purpose of section 3(6) of the 1994 Act, one could argue that an 'ulterior motive' may, in the circumstances of a particular case, constitute bad faith even though the statement provided pursuant to section 32(3) was not untrue.

Another example of bad faith would be the situation specifically provided for in section 60 where an unauthorised application is made by a person who is an agent or representative of the proprietor of the trade mark.[4]

An interesting issue is whether an unauthorised application to register a trade mark used by another undertaking exclusively outside of the United Kingdom would constitute an application made in bad faith. The argument could proceed on the basis that the applicant was at least engaging in a sharp practice and/or was not the rightful proprietor of the trade mark.[5] Against this is the fact that trade marks are registered on a territorial basis and thus (subject to the recognition of well known marks) one could argue that the only test should be whether the applicant is the first person in the United Kingdom to use and apply to register the sign as a trade mark for the relevant goods or services.

Kerly[6] canvasses this issue and suggests that United Kingdom trade mark law should be more cognisant of the rights of the owners of foreign trade marks. To a certain extent, under the 1994 Act, such rights have been recognised in so far as protection is afforded to 'well known' trade marks in accordance with Article 6*bis* of the Paris Convention.

What must be beyond dispute is that applications involving an element of fraud or any breach of duty such as may exist in any confidential, fiduciary, employer/employee or other similar relationship must constitute bad faith. So also it must be bad faith to apply to register a mark the use of which would infringe a third party's intellectual property rights.[7] However, the likely parameters of the concept of bad faith are unclear, particularly as the more liberal rules relating to the registrability, assignment and licensing of trade marks (and indeed the wider definition of 'trade mark' itself) as compared with the 1938 Act, mean that the criteria which will be applied in assessing whether an application has been made in bad faith are not easy to define in advance.

1 Section 3(6).
2 In this respect cases decided under section 26(1) of the 1938 Act in relation to the phrase 'bona fide' will provide some guidance as to what may be considered to be 'bad faith'. In *Electrolux Ltd v Electrix Ltd* (1954) 71 RPC 23 it was held that the phrase 'bona fide' meant 'genuine, judged by commercial standards'. See also *Concord* TM [1987] FSR 209.
3 *Imperial Group Ltd v Philip Morris & Co Ltd* [1982] FSR 72.
4 See chapter 8.
5 *Karo Step* TM [1977] RPC 255.
6 Kerly's *Law of Trade Marks and Trade Names* 12th Edition, paragraph 4.03.
7 See, for example, in the context of copyright: *Karo Step* TM supra and *Oscar* TM [1979] RPC 173.

Relative grounds for refusal

The first part of this chapter has been concerned with the absolute grounds for refusal which relate to the characteristics of the mark itself. By comparison, the relative grounds for refusal are based on protecting the prior conflicting rights of the proprietors of earlier trade marks or other earlier rights. The relative grounds are now dealt with under headings corresponding to the five sub-sections of section 5. However, as sub-sections 5(1), (2) and (3) are all based on a conflict with an 'earlier trade mark', it is first necessary to consider the meaning of this phrase which is defined in section 6. The phrase 'earlier right' is only relevant in the context of section 5(4) and, therefore, is dealt with in paragraphs 2.24 and 2.25.

2.17 'Earlier trade mark', s6   The phrase 'earlier trade mark' is defined in section 6 as follows:
  '(a) a registered trade mark, international trade mark (UK)[1] or
      Community trade mark[2] which has a date of application

2.17 *Registrable trade marks*

for registration earlier than that of the trade mark in question, taking account (where appropriate) of the priorities claimed in respect of the trade marks;
(b) a Community trade mark which has a valid claim to seniority from an earlier registered trade mark or international trade mark (UK); or
(c) a trade mark which at the date of application for registration of the trade mark in question or (where appropriate) of the priority claimed in respect of the application, was entitled to protection under the Paris Convention as a well known trade mark.'[3]

It should be noted that an earlier trade mark will include an unregistered trade mark in respect of which an application for registration has been made provided that it would, if registered, be an earlier trade mark by virtue of section 6(1)(a) or (b).[4] Furthermore, an earlier trade mark falling within section 6(1)(a) or (b) whose registration expires will continue to be taken into account for a period of one year after expiry for the purpose of determining the registrability of a later mark unless the Registrar is satisfied that there was no bona fide use of the earlier trade mark during the two year period preceding the expiry of the registration.[5]

Bona fide use It is curious that the Registrar must be satisfied that there was no bona fide use of the earlier trade mark in order for him to disregard it in determining the registrability of a later mark. The ground on which the registration of a trade mark may be revoked under section 46 for non-use requires that the trade mark has not been put to 'genuine use' and therefore one would have thought that the tests should be phrased consistently. However, in practice, it is assumed that the two phrases must mean the same thing. Secondly, for the purposes of section 46, it will be sufficient if the trade mark in question has been used by the proprietor or 'with his consent'. Section 6(3) does not specify who must use the mark but presumably, consistent with section 46, it will be sufficient that the use has been either by the proprietor or with his consent, provided only that the use is *bona fide*.

1 See chapter 14.
2 See chapter 13.
3 For the meaning of 'well known trade mark' see paragraph 1.11.
4 Section 6(2).
5 Section 6(3).

30

2.18 Identical marks/identical goods or services, s5(1)

Section 5(1) of the 1994 Act prohibits the registration of a trade mark if it is:

'identical with an earlier trade mark and the goods or services for which the trade mark is applied for are identical with the goods or services for which the earlier trade mark is protected.'

This ground for refusal of registration is not remarkable but its extension to all earlier trade marks as defined in section 6 including well known trade marks[1] is one of the features of the 1994 Act in so far as under the 1938 Act registration could only be refused under section 12(1) on the basis of a prior conflicting registered trade mark. By contrast, a well known trade mark need not be registered.

The meaning of the word 'identical ' is unequivocal and any variance (subject to the de minimus rule) between the earlier trade mark and the mark applied for, and/or between the relevant goods or services, will necessarily result in a finding that the marks or the goods or services (as the case may be) are not identical. In such circumstances, the Registrar may still be able to refuse to register the mark under section 5(2) but this would also involve showing that there exists a likelihood of confusion as a result of the requisite similarity. Whereas, if a trade mark is identical with an earlier trade mark and if the application is made in respect of identical goods or services, then there is no need to establish the likelihood of confusion before refusing an application under section 5(1).

Although the meaning of this provision would appear to be straightforward, there may be practical difficulties in comparing certain trade marks such as non-visual marks. For example, would the registration of a series of musical notes be refused if an earlier sound trade mark comprised the same notes but played on a different instrument and at a different tempo so that aurally there was no identity? This may prove problematical where the registration of non-visual marks takes the form of a written description of the mark.[2]

1 See paragraph 2.17 above.
2 See examples in chapter 1, paragraph 1.04.

2.19 Section 5(2): Introduction

Scope and Effect Section 5(2) contains further grounds for the refusal of an application for registration where either the trade marks in question and/or the relevant goods or services are not 'identical' for the purposes of section 5(1). Thus, section 5(2) will apply where either:

(a)   (i) the trade mark applied for is *identical* with an earlier trade mark; and

     (ii) registration is sought in respect of goods or services which are *similar* to those for which the earlier trade mark is protected;

or

(b)   (i) the trade mark applied for is *similar* to an earlier trade mark; and

     (ii) registration is sought in respect of goods or services which are *identical* with those for which the earlier trade mark is protected;

or

(c)   (i) the trade mark applied for is *similar* to an earlier trade mark; and

     (ii) registration is sought in respect of goods or services which are *similar* to those for which the earlier trade mark is protected,

and

(d) in each case, there exists a likelihood of confusion on the part of the public, which includes the likelihood of association with the earlier trade mark, because of the identity/similarity of the trade marks and the goods or services in question.

The scope of section 5(2) is somewhat broader than the corresponding section 12(1) of the 1938 Act in so far as section 5(2) can apply where the mark applied for is either identical with or similar to any 'earlier trade mark', the definition of which embraces not only registered trade marks (which were the extent of the former enquiry under section 12(1)) but also international trade marks (UK), Community trade marks and well known trade marks.[1]

Issues The issues to be considered in relation to this section are as follows:

(a) in what circumstances will a trade mark be considered to be 'identical' with an earlier trade mark?

(b) in what circumstances will goods or services be considered to be 'identical' with each other?

(c) what are the rules of comparison which will be applied in determining whether a trade mark is 'similar' to an earlier trade mark?

(d) what are the rules of comparison which will be applied in determining whether the relevant goods or services are 'similar' to each other?

(e) what is the meaning and effect of the phrase 'likelihood of confusion on the part of the public, which includes the likelihood of association with the earlier trade mark'?

The first two issues have already been considered in the context of section 5(1) in paragraph 2.18 above. Issues (c), (d) and (e) are dealt with in turn in paragraphs 2.20 to 2.22 below.

1 See paragraph 2.17 and section 6.

2.20 Rules of comparison: similarity of trade marks, s5(2)

The corresponding provision of the 1938 Act prohibited the registration of a trade mark which 'nearly resembles' someone else's registered trade mark.[1]

It is certain that the change of wording from 'nearly resembles' to 'similar' was to reflect the wording of Article 4(1)(b) of the Directive and there is no substantive change in the law.

Accordingly, although there are certain general principles which can be derived from cases decided under earlier trade mark legislation, the bottom line is that, in the words of Lord Cranworth:[2]

'What degree of resemblance [similarity] is necessary . . . is from the nature of things incapable of definition a priori'.

The case law suggests that one has to:

(a) have regard to the mark as a whole and one should not divide the mark up and seek to distinguish a portion of it from a portion of the other mark;[3]

(b) have regard to the 'idea of the mark', the main idea left on the mind albeit that, when placed side by side, the two marks might have differences;[4]

(c) take account of the public's imperfect recollection of trade marks and remember also that the two marks in question will not always be seen by the public side by side;[5]

(d) compare the marks as they would be seen in actual use and not only in the form as they appear on the Register;[6] and

(e) in all other respects, consider all the circumstances of the trade in which the marks in question are used or to be used.[7]

There is no reason to believe that these principles should not be applied when comparing two marks to determine whether they are 'similar' for the purposes of section 5(2) (or for the purposes of section 10(2) in the context of infringement). However, as already stated, each case will always be decided on its own facts.

1 Section 12(1); provided that the relevant goods or services were also the same or of the same description etc.
2 *Seixo v Provezende* (1865) LR 1 Ch 192.
3 *Bailey (William) Limited's Application 'Erectico'* (1935) 52 RPC 136.
4 See the examples cited in paragraphs 17.08 and 17.09 of Kerly's *Law of Trade Marks and Trade Names* 12th Edition (including the Supplement).
5 *Sandow Limited's Application* (1914) 31 RPC 196, see Sargant J at 205.
6 *June* (1941) 58 RPC 147; *Ovax* (1946) 63 RPC 97.
7 See the definitive statement of Parker J in *Pianotist Co's Application (Pianola)* (1906) 23 RPC 774 at 777.

2.21 Rules of comparison: similarity of goods or services, s5(2) The corresponding provision of the 1938 Act prohibited the registration of a trade mark in respect of goods or services which were 'of the same description' or which were 'associated' with the goods or services covered by someone else's registration.[1]

Section 5(2) requires that the goods or services be 'similar'. Once again, the change in the wording is merely to reflect that adopted in Article 4(1)(b) of the Directive and should not produce any substantive change in the law.

Accordingly, as with the criteria to be applied in comparing two trade marks, each case will be decided on its own facts. However, the matters identified in *Panda*[2] as being relevant to the inquiry under section 12(1) of the 1938 Act should still be relevant in determining whether goods are 'similar', that is, one should have regard to:
(a) the nature and composition of the goods;
(b) the respective uses of the articles; and
(c) the trade channels through which the commodities respectively are bought and sold.[3]

These criteria do not, of course, apply in comparing two services, but the underlying principle will be the same. The practice of the Registry following the introduction of service mark registrations in 1986 was to treat services as being 'of the same description' if any two of the following four criteria were satisfied:
(a) the nature of the services is the same;
(b) the purpose of the services is the same;

(c) the users of the services are the same; and

(d) the normal business relationships are the same.

It can be argued that, if anything, the requirement of similarity will more easily be satisfied than the requirement that the goods or services be of the same description. That is, two products or services can be characterised as 'similar' even though one would not necessarily apply the same description to them.[4]

This will be particularly important in the case of trade marks which are not words or two-dimensional devices. It must therefore be right that a visual similarity, functional similarity or any other similarity as to the characteristics of the goods or services in question will always be prima facie relevant even though, from case to case, similarities may be weighted differently.

1 Section 12(1); provided that the trade marks in question were identical or nearly resembled each other etc.

2 *Jellinek's Application* (1946) 63 RPC 59, per Romer J; see also *Floradix* TM[1974] RPC 583.

3 See the examples of cases cited in paragraph 10.15 of Kerly's *Law of Trade Marks and Trade Names*, 12th Edition (including the Supplement).

4 Of course, this does not mean that goods or services will be found to be similar just because (to take an extreme example) the particular goods or services in question happen to be of a similar colour. There will thus be numerous similarities which, of themselves, will be irrelevant for the purposes of section 5(2) but which may add to or even detract from the overall impression of similarity when considered in the light of other characteristics of the goods or services.

2.22 Likelihood of confusion/likelihood of association, s5(2)

If registration is to be refused under section 5(2) it is necessary that, as a result of the identity/similarity of the trade marks and of the respective goods or services, there must exist:

'a likelihood of confusion on the part of the public, which includes the likelihood of association with the earlier trade mark.'

The wording of this phrase is ambiguous. There are at least two interpretations as to what must exist by reason of the identity/similarity of the trade marks and the goods or services in question.

(a) The likelihood of confusion must include the likelihood of association: that is, the likelihood of association is an additional requirement to the likelihood of confusion and it is therefore not sufficient merely to show a likelihood of confusion absent a likelihood of association with the earlier trade mark.

(b) A likelihood of confusion must exist but a likelihood of confusion is deemed to include the likelihood of association with the earlier trade mark, so that, even though there may not exist a likelihood of confusion in fact, it will be sufficient if there is a likelihood of association with the earlier trade mark.

Unfortunately, neither of these interpretations is satisfactory because the concept of likelihood of association is necessarily wider than the concept of likelihood of confusion. This means that it is unlikely (if not impossible) to conceive of a situation where one could establish a likelihood of confusion without there also being a likelihood of association with the earlier trade mark. Accordingly, the first interpretation is suspect because it is nonsensical to say that a likelihood of association is an additional requirement to the likelihood of confusion because, by establishing a likelihood of confusion, one must necessarily establish a likelihood of association with the earlier trade mark. If the first interpretation is adopted then the words 'which includes the likelihood of association' are redundant.

Similarly, if the second interpretation is adopted, then the words 'a likelihood of confusion on the part of the public' are redundant because, in effect, one only needs to establish the wider concept of the likelihood of association in order to establish the narrower concept of likelihood of confusion. This would not be a problem if the likelihood of association could be considered simply to be one example of a likelihood of confusion but, because the concept of the likelihood of association is wider than a likelihood of confusion, one cannot escape the conclusion that if there exists a likelihood of confusion (for whatever reason) there must also exist the likelihood of association with the earlier trade mark. Accordingly, the second interpretation also means that part of the phrase is redundant.

This wording, taken directly from Article 4(1)(b) of the Directive, not only poses the problems already stated but also raises the question as to what is meant by the phrase 'a likelihood of association' (regardless of whether it is an additional requirement or merely an example of likelihood of confusion).

Likelihood of association   It has been said[1] that the reference to the likelihood of association was included in the Directive in order to reflect the jurisprudence and case law of the Benelux Courts. Indeed, the following statement was entered into the minutes of the

meeting of the Council at which the Directive was adopted:
'the Council and the Commission note that "likelihood of association" is a concept which in particular has been developed by Benelux case law.'
The Benelux Court of Justice has, in a series of cases, established the proposition that under Benelux law, the test of infringement will be satisfied if the public are likely to associate the later trade mark with the earlier trade mark even if they are not confused in fact as to the origin of the product (indeed, confusion does not play a role under Benelux trade mark law).[2] For example, the trade mark ANTI-MONOPOLY was held to be likely to be associated with the trade mark MONOPOLY when used in relation to a board game, even though the public were not confused in fact as to the origin of the products.[3]

Finally, it must be remembered that the trade mark applied for may be refused if there exists merely a 'likelihood' of confusion on the part of the public and it will be of only marginal assistance for the applicant to adduce evidence that any particular individual or group of individuals have not in fact been confused nor have associated the applicant's trade mark with the earlier trade mark.

1 See 'Harmonisation of Trade Mark Law in Europe' [1992] 8 EIPR 262, Charles Gielen; see also 'Selected Benelux Cases', Marius Knijff, Trademark World, July/August 1994.
2 *Union v Union Soleure*, Case Number A 82/5, 20 May 1993.
3 For further examples see the articles referred to in note 1 above.

2.23   Trade marks of distinctive character or repute, s5(3)

Section 5(3) provides a new ground for refusing to register a trade mark where the applicant's trade mark might dilute or otherwise take unfair advantage of or be detrimental to the character or repute of an earlier trade mark.[1] Section 5(3), like section 5(2), applies where the applicant's trade mark is identical with or similar to an earlier trade mark. However, unlike section 5(2), section 5(3) will apply where the applicant seeks to register his trade mark for goods or services which are *not* similar to those for which the earlier trade mark is protected.

The application of the section is limited to the situation where:
(a) the earlier trade mark has a reputation in the United Kingdom; and
(b) the use of the applicant's mark without due cause would either:
    (i) take unfair advantage of; or
    (ii) be detrimental to,

the distinctive character or the repute of the earlier trade mark. The elements of section 5(3) are considered below.

Scope of protection   The first question to consider is the scope of the protection of the earlier trade mark as section 5(3) is only relevant where the goods or services covered by the application are outside the scope of that protection.

The scope of protection of any given earlier trade mark will need to be assessed in the circumstances of each case. For example, the goods or services for which a registered trade mark will be protected are those goods or services set out in the specification as well as 'similar' goods or services. However, it may be more difficult to assess the scope of protection in the case of an earlier trade mark which is a well known trade mark, especially where the well known trade mark is unregistered.

Of course, if the goods or services are 'similar' to those for which the earlier trade mark is protected then section 5(2) will apply (all other elements being satisfied). Therefore, although this is a somewhat academic exercise, it must nonetheless be carried out in order to determine whether section 5(2) or section 5(3) is to apply (if at all). No doubt the two grounds will usually be relied upon in the alternative by those concerned.

A reputation in the United Kingdom   This section is only applicable where there is an earlier trade mark which has 'a reputation' in the United Kingdom. This limitation is rightly imposed because the definition of earlier trade mark in section 6 embraces trade marks which may, in fact, have no reputation in the United Kingdom. For example, even a trade mark on the United Kingdom Register may have no reputation in the United Kingdom. One assumes, however, that a trade mark which qualifies as a well known trade mark under section 56 will necessarily have 'a reputation' for the purposes of section 5(3). The requirement of 'a reputation in the United Kingdom' is therefore included in order to limit the category of relevant earlier trade marks.

The 1994 Act does not specify either the nature or extent of the reputation which the earlier trade mark must possess in the United Kingdom. Strictly, any degree of reputation will suffice. However, in practice, if the nature and extent of the reputation is not real and substantive, then registration is unlikely to be refused under section 5(3) because the applicant's mark would not take unfair advantage of or be detrimental to the character or the repute of the earlier trade mark. But, one assumes that the requisite reputation need not extend to the goods or services applied for as it is possible for the use of the later trade mark either to take unfair advantage of or be detrimental to the distinctive character or the repute of the earlier trade mark even though the actual reputation of the earlier trade mark does not extend to those goods or services.

'Without due cause' The phrase 'without due cause' qualifies the whole of section 5(3). This would suggest that there may be circumstances in which the applicant's trade mark will not be refused registration under section 5(3) even though its use might either take unfair advantage of or be detrimental to the distinctive character or the repute of the earlier trade mark. It is difficult to foresee such circumstances arising other than perhaps:

(a) in the event that such use is authorised by the proprietor of the earlier trade mark;

(b) where the applicant is relying upon honest concurrent user rights as provided for in section 7; or

(c) where the applicant is in a position to claim proprietorship of the mark in the United Kingdom.

'Unfair advantage of/or detrimental to' The fact that a trade mark can be refused registration because it takes 'unfair advantage of' an earlier trade mark (all other requirements being satisfied) and the fact that the same phrase appears in section 10(3) in the context of infringement, arguably suggests that, for the first time in the United Kingdom, the concept of unfair competition (well known in other jurisdictions) has been introduced, albeit in the limited circumstances prescribed in sections 5(3) and 10(3).

The phrase 'take unfair advantage of' would appear to be directed at the situation where the use of the applicant's mark would benefit from the goodwill attaching to the earlier trade mark whereas the phrase 'detrimental to' must involve some form of diminution in or damage to the value of the goodwill attaching to the earlier trade mark.

Perhaps some guidance as to the meaning of these phrases can be found in decisions in passing off cases where the likelihood of damage was in issue. For example, there is authority for the proposition that any unauthorised appropriation of or profit from another's business goodwill or professional reputation will be detrimental to the character or repute of an earlier trade mark in so far as it deprives the proprietor of the earlier trade mark of the opportunity fully to exploit his trade mark himself.[2] Certainly, it will be detrimental to both the character and the repute of the earlier trade mark for a similar trade mark to be used on goods of a quality which is inferior to that associated with the earlier trade mark.

Finally, even though section 5(3) only applies where the applicant seeks to register a mark for goods or services outside the scope of the protection of the relevant earlier trade mark, there is no conceptual problem in the proposition that the use of a later mark can benefit from or damage the distinctive character or the reputation of an earlier trade mark even though that character or repute does not extend to the goods or services which are the subject of the application. In any event, the greater the 'reputation' of the earlier trade mark in the United Kingdom the more likely it must be that either or both of these requirements will be established.

1   As to the meaning of 'earlier trade mark', see section 6 and paragraph 2.17.
2   *Lego v Lego M Lemelstritch* [1983] FSR 155.

2.24   **Unregistered trade marks and signs, s5(4)(a)**   The applicant's trade mark will not be registered if, or to the extent that, its use in the United Kingdom is liable to be prevented by virtue of any rule of law which protects unregistered trade marks or other signs used in the course of trade.[1]

Section 5(4)(a) specifically cites the law of passing off as an example.[2] Unregistered trade marks or signs may also be works within the definition of the Copyright, Designs and Patents Act 1988, and thus may be protected by copyright which would also enable the owner to prevent the use of the trade mark if it constituted a breach of his copyright. However, the law of copyright would not generally be described as a rule of law which protects unregistered trade marks, but this is academic because section 5(4)(b) specifically refers to the law of copyright, as to which, see the following paragraph.

In practice, the problem with this ground for refusal is that it begs the question in each case as to whether the law of passing off would be available to prevent the use of the applicant's mark; the principle that such marks should be refused registration is, however, incontrovertible.

1 See section 5(4)(a).
2 See section 2(2) which states that nothing in the 1994 Act affects the law relating to passing-off, although no proceedings lie under the 1994 Act to prevent or recover damages for infringement of an unregistered trade mark as such.

2.25 Other 'earlier rights', s5(4)(b) The applicant's trade mark will be refused registration if, or to the extent that, its use in the United Kingdom is liable to be prevented by virtue of any other earlier right, not being an earlier trade mark for the purposes of section 5(1)–(3) nor a rule of law protecting unregistered trade marks or signs under section 5(4)(a).

Section 5(4)(b) specifically cites the law of copyright, design right and registered designs but will include any other earlier right which could be relied upon to prevent the use of the trade mark in the United Kingdom.

2.26 Comment on section 5(4) The grounds for refusal specified in section 5(4) raise the possibility of the Registrar having to interpret rules of law, decide questions of fact and examine rights conferred by statute and the common law beyond the scope of his normal remit.

Of course, any conflict with such earlier rights is more likely to be raised in opposition proceedings and applications for declarations of invalidity rather than by the Registrar on examination. This will not avoid the problem, however, as all opposition proceedings must initially be brought before the Registrar who will therefore be called upon to decide these issues even if they are not raised by him on examination.

2.27 Consent, s5(5) Finally, it should be noted that all objections to registration based on the relative grounds for refusal contained within section 5 can be overcome by obtaining the consent of the proprietor of the earlier trade mark or, in the case of section 5(4)(b), the proprietor of the earlier right. This reflects the shift in policy away from seeking to protect the public from being confused or misled by the use of similar trade marks towards being more concerned with the relative rights and interests of trade mark owners themselves. Thus, whereas under the 1938 Act a letter of consent from the proprietor of a cited registration could be ignored by the Registrar on the grounds of protecting the public interest, the Registrar must, under the 1994 Act, withdraw any citations of earlier trade marks or other earlier rights if the proprietor of the earlier trade mark or earlier right consents to the registration of the applicant's mark. Where the proprietor of an earlier trade mark or earlier right is approached by an applicant who is seeking his consent to registration it will be for the proprietor to determine the consequences of providing such consent and to take such action as he may consider appropriate to maintain the value and distinctiveness of his trade mark or right.

3 Registration: practice and procedure

3.01 Introduction Having considered in chapters 1 and 2 those trade marks which can be registered under the 1994 Act, this chapter examines:

(a) the formal procedure for applying for registration;
(b) the examination and registration procedure;
(c) the procedure for hearings before the Registrar;
(d) appeals from the Registrar; and
(e) certain specific matters relevant to trade mark proceedings in the court.

This first involves describing the administrative framework which exists within the Registry;[1] all of which is dealt with in Part III of the 1994 Act.

As this chapter relates substantially to matters of procedure, it is worth noting at the outset that any irregularity in procedure before the Registrar or in the Registry can always be rectified on such terms as the Registrar directs.[2] Furthermore, in the case of an irregularity or prospective irregularity which consists of a failure to comply with any times or periods specified by the 1994 Act or in the Rules and where the failure is attributable wholly or in part to an error, default or omission on the part of the Registry or the Registrar, the Registrar can alter the time or period in question in such a way as he thinks fit.[3]

---

1 ie: the Trade Marks Registry at the Patent Office: rule 2(1); referred to in the Rules as 'the Office'.
2 Rule 60(1).
3 Rule 60(2); see also paragraph 3.03 and rules 61 and 62.

3.02   The Registry   The Registry has its Head Office in Newport, Gwent[1] but retains a London office.[2]

There is a video-link between the London and Newport offices and hearings can be conducted using this facility; inter partes hearings are more usually conducted in either London or Newport.

The Manchester Branch; the Cutlers' Company   In the past, the Registry maintained a branch in Manchester at which applications relating to textile goods could be filed. Similarly, applications for metal goods could have been filed by traders in the Sheffield area through the Cutlers' Company. The Mathys Report recommended that these filing facilities should be discontinued as they no longer served a useful purpose.[3] These recommendations have now been implemented and therefore all filings must now be lodged with the Registry in either London or Newport.[4]

1   Cardiff Road, Newport, Gwent, NP9 1RH.
2   25 Southampton Buildings, London, WC2A 1AY.
3   Mathys Report paragraphs 213 and 218.
4   For the purposes of the transitional provisions, the old Sheffield Register will be treated as part of the Register kept under the 1938 Act and applications made to the Cutlers' Company which were pending as at 31 October 1994 will be treated as if they had been made to the Registrar: Schedule 3, paragraph 20.

3.03   The Registrar, s62   The Registrar is the Comptroller-General of Patents, Designs and Trade Marks.[1]

Maintenance of the Register   The Registrar is responsible for maintaining the Register of Trade Marks[2] and in this regard he has certain delegated powers and duties.[3] However, the Registrar and his officers will not be liable in respect of the exercise of his powers and the performance of his duties in so far as they are authorised by the 1994 Act.[4]

Examination, s37(1)   Apart from maintaining the Register, the Registrar's primary function is to examine applications for the registration of trade marks as required by section 37(1).[5]

Discretion as to time limits, r62   Subject to the exceptions referred below, any time or period which is prescribed in the Rules or specified by the Registrar can be extended by the Registrar as he thinks fit.[6] A person wanting to apply for an extension must do so to the Registrar[7] prior to the expiration of the time or period in question.[8]

However, the Registrar does have a discretion to grant an extension even after the time or period has expired.[9] If a request for an extension is made after the expiration of the relevant time or period, the Registrar may extend the period if he is satisfied with the applicant's explanation for the delay in requesting the extension and provided that the Registrar is satisfied that any such extension would not disadvantage any other person or party affected by the extension.[10]

Where the Registrar does extend any time or period, then any other person or party affected by the extension will be notified accordingly.[11]

In certain circumstances, the period within which a party to any proceedings before the Registrar must file evidence will begin upon the expiry of a preceding period in which the other party to the proceedings had to file his evidence. In the event that the latter party notifies the Registrar that he does not intend to file any such evidence, the Registrar may then direct that the relevant period within which the former party must file his evidence is to begin on such a date as he will notify to each of the parties to the proceedings.[12]

Exceptions, r62(3) The only instances in which the Registrar cannot extend the time or periods prescribed in the Rules are:

(a) rule 10(6), that is, the two-month period which one has in order to file an address for service;

(b) rule 11, that is, the two-month period which one has in order to correct deficiencies in an application;

(c) rule 13(1), that is, the three-month period which one has in order to file an opposition to registration;

(d) rule 13(2), that is, the three-month period which one has in order to file a counter-statement to an opposition to registration;

(e) rule 29, that is, the six-month period for late renewal applications to be made; and

(f) rule 30, that is, the six-month period for applying for the restoration of a removed registration.[13]

Discretion as to documentation, rr63 and 66 Rules require from time to time the filing of applications, notices and other documents by sending them by post or hand delivery. However, the Registrar is also given a discretion to permit all such documents to be filed by electronic means, subject to any terms or conditions which the

Registrar may specify.[14] It is clearly intended that the Registry, one day, will offer the facility for filing documents electronically and this will considerably improve the filing procedure.

On a different but related subject, it may be noted that where a document (or part thereof) which is not in English is sent to the Registrar, the Registrar is entitled to require an English translation to be furnished which must be verified to the satisfaction of the Registrar as corresponding to the original text.[15]

The Registrar retains a discretion to refuse to accept any translation which in his opinion is inaccurate and to require another verified translation of the document to be furnished.[16]

Forms and directions, s66 Many of the procedural matters in which the Registrar is involved relating to the registration of trade marks can only be initiated if the proper TM Form is used.[17] Section 66 permits the Registrar to require the use of such TM Forms as he may direct for any purpose relating to the registration of a trade mark or any other proceeding before the Registrar.

All TM Forms together with the Registrar's directions as to their use are published in the Journal[18] and a list of TM Forms can be found in schedule 4 to this book.

In most instances a fee is also payable in conjunction with the filing of the TM Form which is prescribed in the Rules.[19]

The Trade Marks Journal, s81 and r65 The 1994 Act provides for the continuation of the practice by the Registrar of publishing a journal containing particulars of applications for the registration of trade marks, together with a representation of the mark itself, as well as other information relating to the trade mark as the Registrar thinks fit.[20]

The journal will continue to be called 'The Trade Marks Journal' and will be published weekly.

Appearance in court, s74 In certain proceedings before the court,[21] the Registrar is entitled to appear and be heard and must appear if directed to do so by the court.[22]

1 Section 62.
2 Section 63(1); see also section 71 in relation to the Registrar's annual report.
3 eg: section 66(1): the power to require the use of specified forms for the registration of a trade mark; section 67(1): the duty to provide certain information concerning applications and registered trade marks.
4 Section 70(2) and (3).

5 See paragraphs 3.24 et seq.
6 Rule 62(1); see also rule 61 as to the effect of interruptions caused by postal services or in the Registry.
7 Using Form TM 9.
8 Rule 62(4).
9 Rule 62(5).
10 Rule 62(5).
11 Rule 62(1).
12 Rule 62(6).
13 Rule 62(3).
14 Rule 63.
15 Rule 66(1).
16 Rule 66(2).
17 Or a replica or such other form as is acceptable to the Registrar: rule 3(2).
18 Rule 3(1); see the Journal dated 31 October 1994.
19 Rule 4.
20 Section 81; rule 65.
21 As to which, see section 74(1).
22 Section 74(1); unless directed by the court he may choose to submit a written statement in accordance with section 74(2); see also paragraph 3.51.

3.04 The Register, s63 The Register is maintained by the Registrar[1] and references in the 1994 Act and in this book to 'registration' mean registration in the Register. The Register need not be kept in a documentary form[2] and this again confirms that it is the clear intention that the Register will one day be open for electronic filings of applications, notices and other documents.[3]

The Registrar will enter in the Register details of:

(a) registered trade marks;[4]

(b) prescribed particulars of registrable transactions affecting a registered trade mark;[5] and

(c) such other matters relating to registered trade marks as may be prescribed,[6] for example, any disclaimer or limitation affecting the registration,[7] but no notice of any trust (express, implied or constructive) will be entered.[8]

There is no division of the Register under the 1994 Act into Part A and Part B. All registered trade marks will therefore be in one unified Register. There is also no requirement and therefore no procedure for trade marks registered under the 1994 Act to be:

(a) 'associated' with another registered trade mark;[9] nor

(b) registered subject to a condition,[10]

accordingly, such matters cannot be entered in the 1994 Register.

Inspection of the Register The Register is available for public inspection[11] at the Registry during its hours of business.[12]

Furthermore, copies or extracts of entries in the Register can be obtained from the Registrar on request.[13] This right of inspection will not be affected if the Register is kept in an electronic form.[14]

Amendments to the Register, s64(4) and r38   Substantive amendments to any entry in the Register are dealt with elsewhere in this book.[15] For present purposes it may be noted that certain details not relating to substance can always be changed on request; thus:

(a)   the proprietor of a registered trade mark or a licensee (or any person having an interest in or charge on a registered trade mark which has been registered under rule 34) can notify the Registrar[16] of any change in his name or address;[17] and

(b)   anyone who has furnished an address for service pursuant to rule 10 can change that address.[18]

Rectification or correction of the Register, s64 and r31   Errors or omissions in the Register can be rectified or corrected pursuant to section 64. Rectification under section 64 does not relate to matters affecting the validity of the registration of the trade mark: these matters are covered by sections 46 and 47.[19] Thus, rectification must relate only to errors or omissions which do not affect the validity of the registration.

The effect of any rectification of the Register is that the error or omission in question is deemed never to have been made.[20] The Registrar or the court may, however, direct otherwise if the circumstances of the case so require.

Application for rectification, s64(2) and r31   An application for rectification can be made by 'any person having a sufficient interest' and may be made either to the Registrar or to the court.[21] However, if proceedings concerning the trade mark in question are already pending in the court, then the application for the declaration must be made to the court.[22] If the application is made to the Registrar, then he may at any stage of the proceedings refer the application to the court.[23]

An application for rectification under section 64 which is made to the Registrar[24] must be submitted together with a statement of the grounds on which the application is made.[25]

Where the application is made other than by the proprietor, the Registrar will send a copy of the application together with the statement of grounds to the proprietor.[26] The proprietor then has three months from the date on which the Registrar sends the application to him within which to file a counter-statement[27] and the Registrar will send a copy of the counter-statement to the party seeking rectification.

Thereafter, the provisions of Rule 13 will apply to the proceedings in the same way as if the proceedings were in respect of an opposition to the registration of a trade mark.[28]

Intervention in rectification proceedings, r31(5) There is also the option for any person, other than the registered proprietor, who claims to have an interest in the rectification proceedings to apply to the Registrar[29] for leave to intervene. The intervener must state the nature of his interest and the Registrar may either refuse leave to intervene or grant leave upon appropriate terms or conditions as he thinks fit, which may include an undertaking as to costs.[30] As always, the parties are entitled to request a hearing in relation to the issue as to whether leave to intervene should be either refused or granted.

If the application for leave to intervene is granted, the intervener will be treated as a party for the purposes of the application for rectification and the provisions of Rule 13 will apply to the intervener, subject only to any terms or conditions which the Registrar has imposed in respect of the intervention.[31]

Registrar's decision When the Registrar has made a decision in relation to the application for rectification and/or the application to intervene, he will send to the applicant, the proprietor and the intervener (if any) written notice of his decision, including the reasons for his decision.[32] In the event that there is any appeal from the Registrar's decision, then the date when the notice of his decision is sent to the parties will be taken to be the date of his decision.

Transitional provisions, schedule 3 An application by a registered proprietor under section 34 of the 1938 Act for the rectification or correction of the 1938 Register which is pending as at 31 October 1994 will be dealt with under the old law and any consequent rectification/correction will be entered in the 1994 Register.[33]

Removal of matter from the Register, s64(5) and r39 The Registrar is given the power to remove from the Register any matter which appears to him to have ceased to have effect.[34] The Rules set out the procedure for the Registrar to follow before removing any matter from the Register. Accordingly, where it appears to the Registrar that any matter in the Register has ceased to have effect he must, before removing it, first notify in writing any person who may be affected by its removal. The person concerned can then submit written representations of any objections which he has to the removal of the matter.[35] If the person concerned chooses to make written representations, he must do so within three months of the date of the Registrar's notice and the Registrar will give him the opportunity to be heard if he so requests.[36] The Registrar may then only remove the matter in question if either:

(a) there has not been a response to the Registrar's notice; or

(b) where representations have been made, the Registrar remains of the view after considering the representations that the matter nonetheless has ceased to have effect.[37]

1 Section 63(1).
2 Rule 32; see also rule 36(2).
3 As to which, see rule 63 and paragraph 3.02.
4 The Rules specify the particulars of each trade mark which will be entered in the Register: see rule 33; trade marks registered under the 1938 Act as at 31 October 1994 (whether in Part A or in Part B) will be transferred to the 1994 Register and will have effect as if registered under the 1994 Act: Schedule 3, paragraph 2(1); but the fact that such marks may have been 'associated' with other marks or were registered subject to a condition will cease to be relevant: Schedule 3, paragraphs 2(3), 3(1) and 10(3).
5 See section 25(1) and rule 34; see also chapter 10.
6 Section 63(2)(c).
7 Section 13 and rule 24.
8 The Registrar will not be affected by notice of any such trust: section 26(1).
9 ie: there is no equivalent to Section 23(2) of the 1938 Act.
10 ie: there is no exact equivalent to Section 14 of the 1938 Act.
11 Section 63(3)(a) and rule 36(1).
12 The Registry's business hours are specified by the Registrar pursuant to section 80 and are published in the Journal (31.10.94) pursuant to rule 64.
13 Section 63(3)(b); the request must be made using Form TM 31R: rule 37.
14 Rule 36(2).
15 See chapter 5 as to revocation and invalidity.
16 Using Form TM 21.
17 Section 64(4) and rule 38(1).
18 Using Form TM 33: rule 38(2).
19 See chapter 5.
20 Section 64(3).
21 Section 64(1) and (2).
22 Section 64(2)(a).
23 Section 64(2)(b).
24 Using Form TM 26.
25 Rule 31(1).

26 Rule 31(2).
27 Using Form TM 8.
28 Rule 31(4); subject to rule 31(2), (6) and (7).
29 Using Form TM 27.
30 Rule 31(5).
31 Rule 31(6).
32 Rule 31(7).
33 Schedule 3, paragraph 18(1).
34 Section 64(5); this relates to matter which was entered in the Register in error and thus rectification is effected by removing such matter.
35 Rule 39(1); the Registrar will also publish his intention to remove the matter where he considers it appropriate.
36 Rule 39(2); where the Registrar has published his intention to remove the matter, then third parties can file a notice of opposition using Form TM 7; in either case, rule 13 will apply.
37 Rule 39(3) and (4).

The application procedure

3.05 The application for registration, s32 and r5 The formalities governing the filing of applications for registration are set out in section 32 of the 1994 Act and in rule 5.

The application must be made to the Registrar[1] and lodged at the Registry.

The application must contain the particulars set out in section 32(2), being:

(a) a request for registration of the trade mark;

(b) the name and address of the applicant;

(c) a statement of the goods or services in relation to which it is sought to register the trade mark as well as a specification of the class in Schedule 4 of the Rules to which it relates;[2] and

(d) a representation of the trade mark.

Supplying these particulars is of more than procedural importance because it dictates the date on which the proprietor's exclusive rights take effect under section 9. This is because it is not until everything required by section 32(2) has been furnished to the Registrar that the application is given its 'date of filing'.[3] The date of filing of an application for registration is also deemed to be the date of registration,[4] assuming, of course, that the application proceeds to registration. The proprietor's exclusive rights will then take effect from the date of registration.[5] Thus, somewhat unnecessarily, three phrases are used in the 1994 Act to refer to the same date:

(a) the 'date of filing of the application': being the date on which

51

everything is furnished to the Registrar in accordance with section 32(2);[6]

(b)   the 'date of application for registration': which is deemed to be the 'date of filing of the application' (see (a) above);[7] and

(c)   the 'date of registration', which is deemed to be the date of filing of the application for registration (see (a) and (b) above).[8]

1   Section 32(1); using Form TM 3.
2   As to which, see paragraph 3.08. NB: the need to file separate applications for separate classes is no longer necessary and it is now possible to file multi-class applications, see paragraph 3.09.
3   Section 33(1).
4   Section 40(3).
5   Section 9(3).
6   Section 33(1).
7   Section 33(2).
8   Section 40(3).

3.06   Address for service, r10   Every applicant must file an address for service in the United Kingdom.[1] The address for service must be filed together with the application itself.[2]

Anything sent to the applicant at his address for service is deemed to be 'properly sent' for any purpose under the 1994 Act or the Rules.[3]

If an applicant fails to file an address for service, the Registrar will treat the application as having been abandoned.[4] Alternatively, the Registrar is entitled to treat the applicant's trade or business address as his address for service provided that it is in the United Kingdom.[5]

Upon the registration of a trade mark the applicant's address for service becomes the address for service of the registered proprietor.[6]

1   Rule 10(1)(a).
2   ie: on Form TM 3: rule 10(3).
3   Rule 10(4).
4   Rule 10(6)(a).
5   Rule 10(4).
6   Rule 10(2).

3.07   Fees, r5   As one would expect, the application is subject to the payment of certain fees:

(a)   the prescribed application fee; and

(b)   such other class fees as may be appropriate.[1]

The trade mark will not be registered unless such fees are paid within the prescribed period and, in default, the application is deemed to be withdrawn.[2] There is no 'prescribed period' as such but rule 5 states that the application is 'subject to' the payment of the fees.

1 Section 32(4) and rule 5.
2 Section 40(2); see also rule 11(b).

3.08 Statement of use, s32(3) The application must be supported by a statement that the trade mark is being used by the applicant (or with his consent) in relation to the goods or services for which he is seeking registration. Alternatively, the application will have to be supported by a statement that the applicant has a bona fide intention that the trade mark will be so used.[1]

It is significant that, where the applicant does not himself intend to use the trade mark, it is sufficient if the trade mark is used (or it is intended that it will be used) by a third party merely with the applicant's consent. It is therefore not even strictly necessary, for the purpose of complying with this requirement, for the third party user to have a formal licence, let alone for the user to be recorded as a registered user (for which there is indeed no procedure under the 1994 Act). Of course, any formal licence will be a registrable transaction for the purpose of section 25(2)[2] and it will almost invariably be preferable for the owner to enter into a formal licence with any third party user rather than relying simply on a bare consent.

A false statement as to use/intended use will constitute bad faith for the purpose of section 3(6) and thus would constitute an absolute ground for refusal of registration.[3]

1 Section 32(3).
2 See chapter 10.
3 It may also be an offence under section 94(1).

3.09 Multi-class application, r8 One of the important practical advantages under the 1994 Act is the new procedure allowing an applicant to file a single multi-class application without having to lodge separate applications for each class,[1] but separate class fees will still be payable.[2]

Where a multi-class application is filed the relevant statement of goods and/or services will have to:

(a) list the relevant classes in consecutive numerical order; and
(b) group the goods and/or services by reference to the numbers of the classes as specified.[3]

Adding a class, r8(3) It has already been noted that a multi-class application must include a statement of the goods and services grouped by reference to the numbers of the classes in relation to which it is sought to register the trade mark. If any goods or services are incorrectly grouped, in the sense that they are grouped by reference to the wrong class numbers, then those wrongly grouped goods/services will need to be re-grouped under the correct class number. This will not be a problem if the original application already includes other goods or services which fall within the correct class number. But if the incorrectly grouped goods or services do not fall within any class to which the original application relates, then the applicant will have to apply for the addition to his application of the appropriate class(es),[4] which will be subject to the payment of additional class fees as may be appropriate.[5]

1 Rule 8.
2 Rule 5.
3 Rule 8(2).
4 Using Form TM 3A.
5 Rule 8(3).

3.10 Correction of a deficiency in the application, r11
It is possible for the applicant to correct certain procedural irregularities relating to his application. Rule 11 applies in the situation where the Registrar considers that the application fails to comply with any of the requirements set out in:

(a) section 32(2), (3) or (4), concerning the requirements as to the application itself;

(b) rule 5, also concerning the requirements as to the application itself; and

(c) rule 8(2), concerning the requirements as to the specification of class(es).

If the applicant has failed to comply with any of these requirements, the Registrar will notify the applicant accordingly and the applicant then has two months within which to remedy the deficiency so as to meet each of the requirements. If the applicant fails to remedy the deficiency it will be treated:

(a) as never having been made in the case of a deficiency under section 32(2); or

(b) as abandoned, in the case of any other deficiency covered by rule 11.[1]

1 Rule 11(a) and (b).

3.11 Division of an application, s41(1)(a) and r19 At any time before registration[1] the applicant may request the Registrar[2] to divide his application into two or more separate applications (referred to as 'divisional applications'). Requests for a division will have to specify the goods or services to which each divisional application will apply and thereafter each divisional application is treated as a separate application for registration, although the original filing date will be retained.[3]

This is a new procedure which was not available under the 1938 Act, although UK patent applications and trade mark applications in many other countries have been divisible for many years. It will be most useful where objections are raised by the Registrar or an opposition is filed by a third party which relate to only some of the goods or services covered by the applicant's original application. In order to side-step the objections/opposition the applicant may be able to divide his application so that he can obtain registration in respect of those goods or services which are not the subject of the objection or opposition.[4] Until now, any objections/oppositions would have delayed an application until all were overcome (which could have been years), or the applicant would either have had to remove elements of his mark or limit the specification of his goods or services. If the applicant had wished to persevere in an attempt to obtain registration for either the elements of the mark or the goods or services removed, he would have had to file a fresh application with a new and later filing date. It may now be possible to avoid this situation by dividing-up the original application in order that the unobjectionable parts of the application can proceed without delay and so that the objectionable parts do not lose their priority date (assuming, of course, that the objections/opposition can be overcome).

1 Thus, even after acceptance, but see rule 19(2).
2 Using Form TM 12 and upon payment of the prescribed fee.
3 Rule 19(1).
4 Provided that he does so prior to the publication of the application, as otherwise any such objection/opposition to the original application will be taken to apply to each divisional application: rule 19(2).

3.12 Merger of an application, s41(1)(b) and r20 An applicant who has made separate applications for the registration of a trade mark may, at any time before preparations for the publication of any of his original applications have been completed by the Registry, request the Registrar[1] to merge the separate applications into a single application.[2]

The stipulation as to the time by which a request to merge can be made may lead to some uncertainty. For example, how will the applicant know when all the 'preparations' (whatever they may consist of) have been completed? The stipulation is also different to that specified (unambiguously) in rule 19 for the purpose of requesting the division of an application.[3]

That aside, the request to merge may only be made in respect of applications which:

(a) are in respect of the same trade mark;

(b) bear the same date of application; and

(c) are, at the time of the request, in the name of the same applicant.

If the Registrar is satisfied that these conditions are present then he has no discretion and must comply with the applicant's request.[4]

This is a new procedure which was not available under the 1938 Act. It will be most useful in reducing renewal fees where the applicant can merge two or more applications[5] into one, thus resulting in one registration and hence one renewal fee in the future. The merger of applications will also simplify the administration of large trade mark portfolios.

1 Using Form TM 17 and upon payment of the prescribed fee.
2 Rule 20(1).
3 As to which, see paragraph 3.11.
4 Rule 20(2).
5 Or, indeed, registrations: see paragraph 3.37.

3.13 Series applications, s41(1)(c) and r21   A 'series of trade marks' is defined as a collection of trade marks which resemble each other in their material particulars and which differ only as to matters of a non-distinctive character. Any such differences between the marks must not substantially affect the overall identity of the trade mark.[1]

This definition embodies the same concept of a series of marks as was provided for in section 21(2) of the 1938 Act, although the actual wording of the 1994 Act is more general in that it does not attempt to specify the 'matters of a non-distinctive character' which are allowed to differ between the trade marks in the series. However, in the absence of any wording in the 1994 Act to suggest otherwise, it is assumed that the Registrar's practice under the 1938

Act in relation to applications for a series of trade marks will continue unchanged.[2]

The procedure for applying for the registration of a series of trade marks is the same as applying for a single trade mark,[3] except that a representation of each trade mark in the series must be incorporated in the application.[4]

In order to overcome an objection to the registration of the series the applicant may:

(a) at any time before preparations for publication of the application have been completed, request the Registrar[5] to divide the application into separate applications in respect of one or more marks in the series;[6] and/or

(b) at any time request the Registrar to delete a mark in the series.[7]

1 Section 41(2).
2 Trade marks registered as a series under the 1938 Act as at 31 October 1994 (whether in Part A or Part B) will be transferred to the 1994 Register and will have effect as if registered under the 1994 Act: Schedule 3, paragraph 2(2).
3 ie: the application is made on Form TM 3 and the fee will be the same.
4 Rule 21(1).
5 Using Form TM 12.
6 Rule 21(2) subject to compliance with section 41(2); and any such division will be subject to the payment of additional application and divisional fees: rule 21(4).
7 Rule 21(3); the Registrar has no discretion in relation to such a request.

3.14 Classification of goods and services, s34 and r7 All goods and services are classified according to the system embodied in the Nice Agreement. There are 34 goods classes and 8 service classes, making 42 in total. Applicants filing multi-class applications must specify which classes their goods or services fall within.[1] Any question as to which is the proper class will be decided by the Registrar.[2]

The Nice classification system is found in Schedule 4 of the Rules and replaces the old classification system which is found in Schedule 3 of the Rules. Rule 7 confirms that trade marks which were registered prior to 27 July 1938 will be classified in accordance with Schedule 3 of the Rules, except where the specification of goods has already been converted to Schedule 4 of the Rules under either the 1938 Act or rule 40.

For trade marks registered on or after 27 July 1938 (and any prior registrations which have been converted under the 1938 Act) the goods and services will be classified in accordance with Schedule 4.

1 Rule 8(2).
2 Section 34(2); there is no appeal from the Registrar's decision.

3.15 Re-classification of goods, s65 and r40 The Registrar may on his own initiative amend an entry in the Register for the purpose of re-classifying the specification of any registered trade mark either:

(a) from Schedule 3 to Schedule 4; or

(b) so as to reflect any amendment to Schedule 4 itself,[1]

provided that the re-classification does not extend the rights conferred by the original registration.

If, however, compliance with this proviso would involve undue complexity and where the extension would not be substantial and would not adversely affect the rights of any person, then the re-classification can proceed even though it may involve extending the proprietor's rights.[2] The Registrar began the re-classification of Schedule 3 registrations prior to the commencement of the 1994 Act.

Notification and objection, r40 The Registrar must first notify the proprietor of the proposed re-classification[3] and the proprietor is given the opportunity to object in writing within three months.[4] Thereafter, if the proprietor does not object, the proposed re-classification will be published in the Journal[5] and thereafter can only be opposed by a third party.[6]

If the proprietor does object to the Registrar's proposed re-classification, the Registrar will consider those objections and will then publish his proposals either as originally notified to the proprietor or as amended in light of the proprietor's objection.[7]

Opposition, r41 Specific provision is made in the Rules for third parties to oppose the proposed re-classification which will no doubt be exercised where the third party's rights are affected adversely by the re-classification.[8]

A third party notice of opposition to the re-classification must be made[9] within three months of the publication of the Registrar's proposals. The notice must state the grounds of opposition and, in particular, how the re-classification would be contrary to section 65(3), that is, why it would extend the proprietor's rights conferred by the original registration and why the extension adversely affects the rights of the third party.[10]

Amendment by the proprietor Section 65(4) enables the Rules to empower the Registrar to require the proprietor himself to file a proposal for the amendment of the classification of his own trade mark. However, the Rules at present do not so provide.

Transitional provisions, schedule 3 Trade marks registered under the 1938 Act may not conform to the classification system prescribed by section 34 of the 1938 Act, that is, the Nice classification system.[11]

The Registrar may exercise his powers under rule 40 in order to bring any such 'old law' registrations into line with the Nice system.[12] This will be particularly relevant in the case of old law registrations which were classified according to the pre-1938 classification system set out in Schedule 3 to the Trade Marks and Service Marks Rules 1986.

1 Rule 40(1); pursuant to section 65(1) and (2).
2 Section 65(3).
3 Rule 40(2).
4 Rule 40(2)(a).
5 Rule 40(2)(b) and see rule 40(3).
6 Section 65(5); rule 41.
7 Rule 40(4); the Registrar's decision is final and there is no right of appeal.
8 See rule 41.
9 Using Form TM 7 and upon payment of any prescribed fee.
10 Rule 41(1); as to the opposition procedure see rule 41(2) and (3).
11 See paragraph 3.14.
12 Schedule 3, paragraph 12.

3.16 Claim to priority: Convention application, s35 and r6

In ordinary circumstances the crucial date for the purpose of assessing the registrability of the applicant's trade mark and for determining when the proprietor's exclusive rights will have effect is the actual date of filing of the application for registration.

However, there are two bases[1] on which an applicant may be able to claim a right to priority, that is, the right to rely on an earlier date than the actual filing of the application. The first arises by virtue of an earlier application filed in a Convention country (as to which, see below); the second will arise if an Order in Council is made by Her Majesty conferring a right to priority in respect of applications filed in certain overseas territories with which the United Kingdom has entered into a convention for the reciprocal protection of trade marks (as to which, see paragraph 3.17).

Convention applications In accordance with the Paris Convention, an applicant who has duly filed[2] an application in a

Convention country[3] (or his successor in title) has a right to priority for the purposes of registering his trade mark under the 1994 Act in the United Kingdom. The right to priority lasts only for a period of six months from the date of filing of the first Convention application and the applicant's subsequent United Kingdom application must be in respect of some or all of the same goods or services as the first Convention application.[4]

Particulars   The right to priority must be claimed in accordance with the Rules.[5] Rule 6(1) prescribes that either:
(a) particulars of the claim must be made at the time of the filing of the United Kingdom application indicating the relevant Convention country (or countries) and the date(s) of filing in that country; or
(b) the application must be accompanied by a certificate of the type referred to in rule 6(2).

Certificate   Rule 6(2) requires the filing of a certificate issued by the registering or other competent authority of the relevant Convention country certifying or verifying:
(a) the date of the filing of the first Convention application;
(b) the country of registering or competent authority;
(c) a representation of the mark; and
(d) the goods or services covered by the Convention application.
The certificate must be filed either with the application itself or within three months of the application being filed.

Effect of claim to priority   If the right to priority conferred by section 35(1) is validly claimed by the applicant in accordance with the Rules, the relevant date for the purposes of establishing which rights take precedence will be the date of filing of the first Convention application.[6] In certain circumstances a subsequent Convention application will be treated as the first Convention application where, for example, the first Convention application is withdrawn, abandoned or refused.[7] The reference to rights taking 'precedence' reflects the potential existence of competing rights and will be relevant in determining questions of registrability under section 5. However, a claim to priority does not backdate the deemed date of registration, which will remain the actual date of filing of the application in the United Kingdom.

Registrability of applicant's mark   If the right to priority is validly claimed as described above, the question of the registrability of the applicant's trade mark will not be affected by any use of the mark in the United Kingdom in the period between the date of the first Convention application and the date of his subsequent corresponding United Kingdom application. That is, the applicant cannot rely on any use of his trade mark in this period in support of his application.[8] If the registrability of the applicant's trade mark is to be assessed as at the date of filing of the applicant's first Convention application, then it is right that the applicant should have to show that his mark is entitled to registration in the United Kingdom as of the earlier date without relying on use subsequent to the filing of the Convention application.

1 Strictly, there are three bases, as an application which has been filed prior to 31 October 1994 for the protection of a trade mark in a relevant country within the meaning of section 39(A) of the 1938 Act can also confer a right to priority for the purposes of registering the same trade mark under the 1994 Act: see schedule 3, paragraph 14. A right to priority based on a section 39(A) application must be claimed within six months of that application and therefore this right of priority will not be available after 30 April 1995.
2 See section 35(3) which refers to and defines a 'regular national filing' as giving rise to the right of priority.
3 ie: a country other than the United Kingdom which is a party to the Paris Convention: section 55(1)(b).
4 Section 35(1); it matters not that the Convention application may have been made before the commencement of the 1994 Act: schedule 3, paragraph 13.
5 Section 35(5).
6 Section 35(2)(a).
7 See section 35(4).
8 Section 35(2)(b).

3.17 Claim to priority: reciprocal protection, s36 and r6

The second basis on which an applicant may be able to claim a right to priority is in respect of an earlier application filed in:

(a) any of the Channel Islands or a colony; or

(b) any other country or territory with which the United Kingdom has entered into a convention for the reciprocal protection of trade marks.[1]

Section 36 empowers Her Majesty by Order in Council to confer a right to priority on a person who has filed an application for protection of his trade mark in one of the countries, territories or colonies referred to above.

As is the case under section 35, the right to priority (once conferred) will only be available for the purpose of registering in the

United Kingdom the same trade mark for some or all of the same goods or services as has already been registered in the relevant country, territory or colony. No period is specified within which the right must be claimed, but it may be assumed that it is likely to be six months or such other period as may be stated in the relevant convention.

1 Section 36(1).

3.18 Withdrawal of an application, s39(1) Should an applicant not wish to pursue his application for any reason, he may withdraw it at any time.[1] In the event that his application has already been accepted and advertised at the date of the withdrawal, then the Registrar will publish an appropriate notice in the Journal.

A withdrawn application cannot be restored.

1 Section 39(1).

3.19 Disclaimers and limitations, s13 and r24 An applicant faced with objections raised by the Registrar or a third party opposition (or even for his own reasons) may voluntarily:
(a) disclaim any right to the exclusive use of any specified element of his trade mark; or
(b) agree that the rights conferred by any consequent registration will be subject to a specified territorial or other limitation.[1]
In the event that the application is accepted and the trade mark proceeds to registration, the exclusive rights conferred by registration[2] will be restricted by the terms of the disclaimer and/or the limitation.[3]

All disclaimers and limitations will be entered in the Register and published in the Journal.[4]

This provision allowing for voluntary disclaimers is to be distinguished from section 14 of the 1938 Act which enabled the Registrar to require disclaimers in respect of non-distinctive matter as a condition of registration. The 1994 Act does not empower the Registrar to require or even request disclaimers or limitations.[5]

1 Section 13(1).
2 ie: pursuant to section 9.
3 Section 13(1).
4 Rule 24.
5 See also chapter 7 in relation to the implication of disclaimers and limitations under the 1994 Act with respect to infringement actions.

3.20 Restrictions on an application, s39 In addition, or as an alternative to volunteering a disclaimer or limitation, an applicant may at any time restrict the goods or services covered by his application.[1] In the event that his application has already been accepted and advertised at the date of the restriction, then the Registrar will publish an appropriate notice in the Journal.

1 Section 39(1).

3.21 Amending an application, s39(2) and r17 Apart from the option of withdrawing his application or restricting the goods or services covered by his application an applicant may, in respect of limited matters, apply to amend his application.[1]

Permitted amendments Amendments to an application may only be made in order to correct:
(a) the name or address of the applicant;
(b) errors of wording or of copying; or
(c) obvious mistakes,
and provided that the correction does not substantially affect the identity of the trade mark or extend the goods or services covered by the original application.[2]

An amendment which is made after the application has been accepted and published and which affects either the representation of the trade mark or the goods or services covered by the original application will be open to opposition by any person claiming to be affected by the amendment.[3] In any event, the application as amended will be published by the Registrar to show the amendment.[4]

Comparison with section 17(7) 1938 Act Section 39(2) is more limited than the right of amendment provided for in the 1938 Act. Section 17(7) of the 1938 Act gave the Registrar the discretion to allow the applicant to amend his application upon 'such terms as the Registrar . . . may think fit'. When read in conjunction with Rule 121[5] the Registrar's former discretion could have extended to allowing an amendment of any drawing or other representation of the trade mark.

1 Section 39(2); the application to amend should be made using Form TM 21: rule 17.
2 Section 39(2).

3.22   Opposition to an amendment, s39(3) and r18(2) and (3)

Any person claiming to be affected by an amendment to an application which affects either:

(a)   the representation of the trade mark; or

(b)   the goods or services covered by the original application,

may give notice of opposition to the proposed amendment.

The procedure for giving notice of opposition and the grounds of opposition are dealt with in chapter 4.

3.23   Conversion of a 1938 Act application, schedule 3 and r68

An application for the registration of a trade mark under the 1938 Act which is pending as of 31 October 1994 will be dealt with under the old law and if the mark proceeds to registration it will be treated for the purposes of the transitional provisions as an existing registered mark.[1]

However, in the case of a pending application under the 1938 Act which has not been advertised[2] as of 31 October 1994, the applicant is entitled to give notice to the Registrar requesting to have the registrability of his trade mark determined in accordance with the provisions of the 1994 Act.[3]

As has already been noted in chapter 2, for the majority of trade marks it will often be easier to obtain registration under the 1994 Act and therefore applicants should strongly consider this option where available. If an applicant wishes to convert his pending application, then he must give notice to the Registrar[4] within six months of the commencement of the 1994 Act, that is, the request must be made on or before 30 April 1995.[5]

Once a request has been made for the conversion of a pending application the applicant cannot reverse his decision. The effect of making a request for conversion is that the original application will be treated as if it had been made immediately after the commencement of the 1994 Act, viz 31 October 1994.[6]

1   Schedule 3, paragraph 10(1).
2   ie: under section 18 of the 1938 Act.
3   Schedule 3, paragraph 11(1).
4   Using Form TM 15 set out in schedule 2 to the Rules: rule 68.
5   Schedule 3, paragraph 11(2).
6   Schedule 3, paragraph 11(3).

The examination and registration procedure

3.24 Examination, s37 Applications for the registration of a trade mark will be examined by the Registrar to determine whether the requirements of the 1994 Act are satisfied.[1]

Those requirements can be listed conveniently as follows:

(a) that the application is in respect of a 'trade mark', as defined in section 1(1);[2]

(b) that there are no absolute or relative grounds for refusing registration under sections 3, 4 or 5;[3]

(c) that the formalities specified in section 32 and in the Rules have been complied with;[4] and

(d) that any claim to priority is valid in accordance with section 35 or 36.[5]

Accordingly the Registrar must, inter alia, carry out a search to determine whether there is a conflict with earlier trade marks.[6] As the phrase 'earlier trade marks' is defined[7] to include marks which may not be registered, viz, well known trade marks protected (but not necessarily registered) under the Paris Convention, this task may prove difficult to fulfil in practice, although the search need only be carried out to the extent to which the Registrar considers necessary.

If the requirements for registration are met, the Registrar must accept the application.[8] He has no overriding discretion to refuse registration. The application will then be published in the Journal and will be open to third party oppositions for three months.[9]

1 Section 37(1); which requirements will include any imposed by the Rules.
2 As to which, see chapter 1.
3 As to which, see chapters 2 and 15.
4 As to which, see this chapter.
5 As to which, see paragraphs 3.16 and 3.17.
6 Section 37(2).
7 Section 6.
8 Section 37(5).
9 See chapter 4.

3.25 Representations by the applicant, s37(3) If the Registrar takes the view that the requirements for registration are not met, he must inform the applicant of his objections and give him an opportunity (within a period specified by the Registrar) either to make representations or to amend his application[1] so as to comply with the requirements.[2]

If the applicant's representations fail to overcome the objections raised by the Registrar or if he does not amend his application so as to meet the requirements within the specified period, the Registrar will have no option but to refuse the application.[3]

1 ie: pursuant to section 39(2), as to which, see paragraph 3.21.
2 Section 37(3).
3 Section 37(4).

3.26 Disclaimers and limitations, s13 and r24 It should be recalled at this point that an applicant faced with objections raised by the Registrar may voluntarily:

(a) disclaim any right to the exclusive use of any specified element of his trade mark; or

(b) agree that the rights conferred by any consequent registration will be subject to a specified territorial or other limitation.[1]

1 Section 13(1) and see paragraph 3.19.

3.27 Publication (advertisement), s38(1) and r12 If the Registrar accepts the application for registration, he will publish the application in the Journal.[1] This is to give interested third parties the opportunity to oppose the registration of the trade mark.[2]

There is no equivalent procedure to that under the proviso to section 18(1) of the 1938 Act whereby the Registrar could have advertised an application prior to acceptance. This is because the proviso to section 18(1) related only to a trade mark accepted pursuant to section 9(1)(e) of the 1938 Act for which there is no equivalent section in the 1994 Act.

1 Section 38(1) and rule 12.
2 As to which, see paragraph 3.28.

3.28 Notice of opposition, s38(2) and r13 Following publication of the application in the Journal any person may, within three months[1] of the date on which the application was published, give notice of opposition to the registration of the trade mark.[2]

The procedure for giving notice of opposition and the grounds of opposition are dealt with in chapter 4.

1 This period cannot be extended, unlike the equivalent one month period under the 1938 Act.
2 Section 38(2) and rule 13(1).

3.29 Observations, s38(3) and r15 A new provision has been introduced into the 1994 Act enabling any person, at any time after the date of publication but before the registration of the trade mark, to make observations in writing to the Registrar as to whether the trade mark should be registered.[1]

The procedure for making observations and the subject matter of such observations are dealt with in chapter 4.

1 Section 38(3).

3.30 Freedom of information, s67 and rr42–45 The 1994 Act provides for confidentiality to be maintained by the Registrar prior to the publication of an application (subject to four exceptions) and thereafter for freedom of information following publication.

Confidentiality prior to publication Prior to the publication of an application the Registrar must keep confidential all documents and information constituting or relating to the application,[1] except:

(a) the application itself[2] (and any amendments made to it);

(b) any particulars of a registrable transaction given to the Registrar under rule 35;[3]

(c) in the case of a person who has received notice that an application for registration of a trade mark has been made and that the applicant will, if the application is granted, rely on the subsequent registration of the trade mark to bring proceedings against that person in respect of that person's conduct after publication of the application. In such circumstances, the person receiving the notice may make a request under section 67(1) (which otherwise is applicable only once an application has been advertised) to inspect any documents held by the Registrar relating to the relevant application as though the application had already been published;[4] or

(d) with the applicant's consent.[5]

Freedom of information, s67(1) and r44 Upon publication of an application, the Registrar is obliged to provide to any member of the public who so requests[6] any information held by the Registrar relating to that application and/or the registration resulting from the application. Furthermore, the public are also entitled to inspect for themselves any documents held by the Registrar relating to that application and/or registration.[7]

The Registrar's obligation as stated above is only qualified to the extent that he need not provide access to the public to any document which he requires in order to complete the registration procedure or any of his other tasks.[8]

Any requests for information pursuant to section 67(1) must comply with the Rules which are quite specific in terms of which documents will not be made available: see rule 44(3) and (4). Furthermore, there is no appeal from a decision of the Registrar made under rule 44(4).[9]

Direction as to confidentiality, r45   A person filing a document at the Registry may, at the time of filing or within fourteen days afterwards, request that the document be treated as confidential. Reasons for claiming confidentiality must be stated and the Registrar is given a discretion to direct that the document (or part of it) should be treated as confidential. If the Registrar makes such a direction, then the document will not be open to public inspection[10] without the consent of the Registrar.[11] In any event, while the question of confidentiality is being determined by the Registrar, the document in question will not be open to public inspection. A direction as to confidentiality can also be made unilaterally by the Registrar in respect of documents issued by the Registry.[12]

A direction as to confidentiality can only be withdrawn by the Registrar after consulting with the person who made the original request under rule 45(1), unless such a consultation is not reasonably practical.[13]

1 Section 67(2).
2 Rule 43.
3 Rule 43.
4 Section 67(3).
5 Section 67(2)(b).
6 Using Form TM 31C.
7 Section 67(1) and rule 44(1); as to the opening hours of the Registry, see rule 64.
8 Rule 44(2).
9 Rule 44(5).
10 Rule 45(1).
11 Rule 45(2).
12 Rule 45(4).
13 Rule 45(3).

3.31 Registration, s40   Where an application has been accepted by the Registrar pursuant to section 37(5) and either:
(a) no notice of opposition has been given within three months of

the date of publication of the application; or
(b) all opposition proceedings have been withdrawn or dismissed,
the Registrar must register the trade mark,[1] except only where it
appears to him that the application was accepted in error.[2] In this
regard, the exception only applies where matters have come to the
Registrar's notice since he accepted the application, which would
include information received by way of written observations made
pursuant to section 38(3).[3]

One presumes that if the Registrar decides at this stage that the
application was accepted in error, then the applicant will be given
the opportunity to make representations or to amend his application
in accordance with section 37(3).[4]

Transitional provisions, Schedule 3 Trade marks registered under
the 1938 Act as at 31 October 1994 (whether in Part A or Part B)
will be transferred to the 1994 Register and will have effect as if
registered under the 1994 Act.[5]

1 Provided that any prescribed registration fee is paid within the prescribed period:
   section 40(2).
2 Section 40(1).
3 As to which, see paragraph 3.29.
4 As to which, see paragraph 3.25.
5 Schedule 3, paragraph 2(1); but the fact that such marks may have been
   'associated' with other marks or were registered subject to a condition will cease
   to be relevant: schedule 3, paragraphs 2(3), 3(1) and 10(3).

3.32 Date of registration, s40(3)

The effective date of
registration is the date of filing of the application for registration,[1]
which is the date on which everything required by section 32(2) is
furnished to the Registrar.[2]

The date of registration is crucial because it is from that date that
the proprietor's exclusive rights in his trade mark have effect.[3]

1 Section 40(3).
2 Section 33(1).
3 Section 9(3).

3.33 Advertisement of registration, s40(4) and r16

On
the registration of a trade mark the Registrar will publish the
registration, specifying the date upon which the trade mark was
entered in the Register.[1] This is purely a formality for the record.
The date on which the trade mark is entered in the Register is not
the date from which the proprietor's exclusive rights have effect,[2]

but it may be significant, for example in relation to assigning and licensing trade marks.[3]

Upon registration of the mark the Registrar will issue the Certificate of Registration to the proprietor.[4]

1 Section 40(4) and rule 16.
2 See paragraph 3.32.
3 See chapter 10.
4 Section 40(4).

3.34 Duration of registration, s42 The period of registration is now ten years. This period applies both to the initial period and to any renewal of the registration.[1] This replaces the respective periods of seven years and fourteen years under the 1938 Act and brings the United Kingdom into line with the majority of its trading partners.[2]

1 Section 42.
2 All registrations under the 1938 Act (including registrations in consequence of an application filed under the 1938 Act) will continue to remain in force until the end of their respective 7 or 14 year periods and will thereafter be renewed for 10 year periods: schedule 3, paragraph 15.

3.35 Renewal of registration, s43 and rr27–29 The registration of a trade mark may be renewed at the request of the proprietor. The request can only be made within six months prior to the expiry of the registration.[1] To this end, not earlier than six months and not later than one month before the expiration of the registration the Registrar will notify the proprietor that his registration is approaching expiration.[2]

The trade mark will only be renewed if the prescribed renewal fee is paid.[3] Both the request for renewal and the payment of the fee must be made before the registration expires[4] but the renewal will only take effect from the expiry of the previous registration[5] and will be published accordingly.[6]

If the period of registration expires and the renewal fee has not been paid the Registrar will advertise that fact in the Journal.[7]

Six months' grace A six month 'grace period' following the expiration of the registration may assist a tardy proprietor. Provided that a request for renewal[8] is filed within the grace period together with both the renewal fee and an additional renewal fee, the Registrar will nonetheless renew the registration without removing the trade mark from the Register.[9]

If renewal is not effected either prior to the expiry of the registration or within the grace period, the Registrar will remove the trade mark from the Register.[10] Even so, the proprietor may still be able to restore his registration.[11]

Registration after renewal, r29(4) In some cases, particularly those where there has been a third party opposition, the applicant's trade mark may not find its way onto the Register until more than ten years after the date on which the application for registration was filed. Because the rights conferred by registration date back to the date of the filing of the application, one therefore may encounter the situation of a trade mark not being put on the Register until after the date when the registration will have become due for renewal. In such circumstances the proprietor must pay a renewal fee within six months of the date on which the trade mark is actually entered in the Register.[12] Provided that the renewal fee is paid within six months of the actual date of registration, the registration will be renewed notwithstanding the fact that the payment of the renewal fee may have been more than six months after the renewal date calculated by reference to the filing date.

1 Section 43(1) and rule 28; using Form TM 11.
2 Section 43(2) and rule 27.
3 Section 43(1).
4 Section 43(3).
5 Section 43(4).
6 Section 43(6).
7 Rule 29(1).
8 Using Form TM 11.
9 Section 43(3) and rule 29(3).
10 Section 43(5) and rule 29(2); the Registrar will publish any removal of a trade mark from the Register: rule 29(5) and section 43(6).
11 As to which, see paragraph 3.36.
12 Rule 29(4).

3.36 Restoration of registration, s43(5) and r30 In the event that the trade mark is not renewed[1] and it is accordingly removed,[2] it is nonetheless possible, in certain circumstances, to restore the registration.

Rule 30(1) sets out the conditions applying to restoration. An application for restoration must be filed[3] within six months of the date of removal (which will be before the publication of the removal) and must be accompanied by the appropriate renewal and restoration fees. The Registrar has a discretion to restore a removed trade mark to the Register and renew the registration if, in the circumstances of the failure to renew, the Registrar is satisfied that restoration would be just.[4]

There was no time limit for restoration under the 1938 Act and it was possible in certain circumstances to obtain the restoration of a registration long after the period of six months from the date of removal.[5] It is now increasingly important for the Register accurately to reflect all trade mark registrations because applications, not only under the 1994 Act but also for Community trade marks and under the Madrid Protocol, may be examined in the light of the United Kingdom Register.

1 ie: in accordance with section 43 and rules 28 or 29.
2 ie: pursuant to section 43(5) and rule 29(2).
3 Using Form TM 13.
4 All restorations will be published, showing the date of restoration: section 43(6) and rule 30(2).
5 Rule 68 of the Trade Marks and Service Marks Rules 1986.

3.37 Merger of a registration, s41 and r20(3)–(6) A proprietor of two or more registrations of a trade mark can request the Registrar[1] to merge each of his registrations into one single registration. The only requirement is that the registrations must be in respect of the same trade mark. If so, the Registrar has no discretion and must comply with the proprietor's request.[2]

Of course, any disclaimer or limitation[3] relating to a trade mark to be merged will apply also to the merged registration.[4]

The date of registration of the merged registrations will be the latest date of registration of the previously separate registrations; of course, this is only relevant where the previously separate registrations bear different dates.[5]

Particulars relating to the grant of any licence or any security interest which relates to a trade mark which is to be merged will be entered in the Register in relation to the merged registration.[6]

1 Using Form TM 17.
2 Rule 20(3).
3 As to which, see paragraph 3.19.
4 Rule 20(4).
5 Rule 20(6).
6 Rule 20(5).

3.38 Alteration of a registered trade mark, s44 and r25
The proprietor of a registered trade mark can request the Registrar[1]

to alter his trade mark provided that the alteration:

(a) is limited to altering the proprietor's name or address which must appear in the trade mark itself; and

(b) does not substantially affect the identity of the mark.[2]

Any other requested alteration will be refused.[3]

The permitted grounds for altering a registered trade mark under the 1994 Act are narrower than the corresponding provision of the 1938 Act.[4] Under the 1938 Act, alterations were allowed even in respect of essential particulars of the trade mark (including adding to or altering the trade mark in any manner) so long as the identity of the trade mark was not substantially affected.[5]

A request for alteration pursuant to section 44(2) may need to be supported by evidence as to the circumstances in which the application is made.[6]

All permitted alterations will be published in the Journal[7] so as to allow third parties the opportunity to oppose the alteration.

Opposition to an alteration, r25(3)   Any person claiming to be affected by the alteration may file with the Registrar a notice of opposition[8] to the alteration. The procedure for giving notice of opposition and the grounds of opposition are dealt with in chapter 4.

1   Using Form TM 25.
2   Section 44(2).
3   Section 44(1).
4   ie: section 35.
5   The transitional provisions of the 1994 Act permit all applications under section 35 of the 1938 Act for the alteration of a registered trade mark which are pending as at 31 October 1994 to be dealt with under the old law and any consequent alteration will be entered in the 1994 Register: schedule 3, paragraph 16.
6   Rule 25(1).
7   Rule 25(2).
8   Using Form TM 7.

3.39   Surrender of registrations, s45 and r26   The proprietor of a trade mark may surrender his trade mark in respect of some or all of the goods or services for which it is registered.[1]

A proprietor who wishes to surrender his trade mark as above must notify the Registrar using:

(a) form TM 22, if the surrender is in respect of all the goods or services for which the mark is registered; or

(b) form TM 23, if the surrender is in respect of some only of those goods or services.[2]

The proprietor's notice will only be effective if he:

(a) supplies the name and address of any person having a registered interest in the mark (such as a licensee or a co-proprietor); and

(b) certifies that any such person:
   (i) has been given not less than three months' notice of the proprietor's intention to surrender his trade mark; or
   (ii) is not affected or, if affected, consents to the proprietor's surrender.[3]

Upon the surrender taking effect, the Registrar will make the appropriate entry in the Register and publish the surrender in the Journal[4] which, in the case of a surrender in respect of all goods or services for which the trade mark is registered, presumably means that the trade mark will be removed from the Register.[5]

1 Section 45(1).
2 Rule 26(1).
3 Rule 26(2).
4 Rule 26(3).
5 ie: pursuant to and in accordance with the procedure in rule 39.

Proceedings before the Registrar

3.40 Powers of the Registrar, s69(b) and (c) and r52 The Registrar has all the powers of an Official Referee of the Supreme Court in relation to the examination of witnesses on oath and the discovery and production of documents.[1] Accordingly, the rules which apply to the attendance of witnesses before an Official Referee will apply to the attendance of witnesses before the Registrar.[2] That is, witnesses may be subpoenaed and it will be a contempt of court for any witness not to attend in accordance with the subpoena.

1 Rule 52(1).
2 Rule 52(2).

3.41 Natural justice, r48 The Rules require the Registrar to give any party to any proceedings before him an opportunity to be heard before he takes any decision on any matter under the 1994

Act which is or may be adverse to that party.[1] The Registrar must indeed give such a party at least fourteen days' notice of when the hearing will take place.[2]

1 Rule 48(1).
2 Rule 48(2); unless the party consents to shorter notice.

3.42 Evidence in proceedings before the Registrar, s69(a) and rr49-51 Evidence in proceedings before the Registrar may be given either:

(a) by filing a statutory declaration or an affidavit;[1] or
(b) orally, either in lieu of or in addition to a statutory declaration and/or an affidavit.[2]

In either case, the Registrar must, unless he otherwise directs, allow any witness to be cross-examined on his statutory declaration, affidavit or oral evidence.[3]

The Rules stipulate precisely how a statutory declaration or an affidavit must be made and subscribed.[4] In the United Kingdom this must be before a Justice of the Peace or a Commissioner or other officer authorised by law to administer an oath for the purpose of legal proceedings.[5] Separate provisions deal with the situation outside the United Kingdom.[6]

In addition to such evidence the Registrar may, at any stage of proceedings before him, direct that certain other documents, information or evidence as he may require shall be filed within a time limit which he will specify.[7]

1 Rule 49(1).
2 Rule 49(2).
3 Rule 49(2).
4 Rule 50(1).
5 Rule 50(1)(a); and see rule 50(2).
6 See rule 50(1)(b) and (c); and see rule 50(2).
7 Rule 51.

3.43 Hearings before the Registrar, rr53 and 56 All hearings before the Registrar of any dispute between two or more parties relating to an application for the registration of a trade mark or a registered trade mark will be in public, unless the Registrar directs otherwise following a consultation with the parties.[1]

Following any hearing before the Registrar, including any proceedings based on written submissions, the Registrar will send notice of his decision in writing to each party.[2] If the notice of the

Registrar's decision does not include a statement of his reasons then, any party may, within one month of notice of the Registrar's decision being sent to him, request[3] the Registrar to state in writing the grounds for his decision.[4] In which case, the date on which the Registrar's written statement is sent becomes the effective date of his decision for the purpose of any appeal.[5]

1 Rule 53(1).
2 Rule 56(1).
3 Using Form TM 5.
4 Rule 56(2).
5 Rule 56(2); and see paragraph 3.46 in relation to appeals.

3.44 Costs, s68(1) and (2) and r54 The Registrar has the power to award costs to any party in any proceedings before him under the 1994 Act. Any award for costs is within the discretion of the Registrar as he may consider reasonable. The Registrar may furthermore direct how and by what parties the costs are to be paid.[1]

In the exercise of the Registrar's discretion he might have regard to whether proceedings could have been avoided if reasonable notice had first been given to the applicant or to the registered proprietor (as the case may be) before any notice of opposition or application for revocation, declaration of invalidity or rectification was filed.

The Registrar's costs order can be enforced in the same way as an order of the High Court.[2]

1 Rule 54.
2 Section 68(2)(a); in Scotland, the order is enforced in the same way as a decree for expenses granted by the Court of Session: section 68(2)(b).

3.45 Security for costs, s68(3) and r55 The Registrar has the power to require any person who is a party to any proceedings before him under the 1994 Act to give security for costs in relation to those proceedings. Furthermore, the Registrar may also require security to be given for the costs of any appeal from his decision.[1]

If the party who is directed to give security does not comply with the direction the Registrar may treat the party in default as having withdrawn his application, opposition, objection or intervention (as the case may be).[2]

1 Rule 55(1).
2 Rule 55(2); so may an appointed person under section 76 in the case of an appeal.

Appeals

3.46 Appeals from the Registrar, s76 and r57 An appeal lies from any decision of the Registrar under the 1994 Act.[1] In this regard, a 'decision' of the Registrar will include any act of the Registrar in the exercise of any discretion vested in him by the 1994 Act or the Rules.[2]

The appeal must be made either:

(a) to the Court;[3] or

(b) to an 'appointed person'.[4]

---

1 Section 76; except as provided in the Rules, for example, from a decision of the Registrar made under rules 40 or 41 (dealing with the re-classification of goods).
2 Section 76(1).
3 In England and Wales, the High Court: section 75(a); in Scotland, the Court of Session: section 75(b).
4 Section 76(2), as to which, see paragraph 3.47.

3.47 Appeals to appointed persons, ss76 and 77 and rr57 and 59 All appeals to an 'appointed person'[1] must be sent by the appellant to the Registrar (not to the appointed person) within one month of the date of the Registrar's decision which is the subject of the appeal.[2] That date will be the date on which the Registrar's statement of the grounds for his decision is sent to the appellant.[3] The notice of appeal must be accompanied by a written statement of the grounds for the appeal and the appellant's case in support of his appeal.[4]

The Registrar will then send the notice of appeal and the appellant's statement of grounds to the appointed person[5] as well as to any other party to the decision from which the appeal is made.[6]

An appeal to an appointed person (which is not referred to the Court)[7] will be heard and determined by the appointed person and his decision is final.[8] The hearing of the appeal by the appointed person is governed by rule 59. The appointed person must give at least fourteen days' notice[9] of the time and place appointed for the hearing of the appeal[10] and the notice must be sent:

(a) where no person other than the appellant was a party to the proceedings which are the subject of the appeal, to the Registrar and the appellant; or

(b) in all other cases, to the Registrar and to each person who was a party to the original proceedings.[11]

The rules of evidence,[12] the powers of the Registrar,[13] the conduct of the hearings[14] and the provisions as to costs and security for costs[15] will apply to all appeals to an appointed person as they apply to proceedings before the Registrar.[16]

After hearing the appeal the appointed person will then send a copy of his decision with a statement of his reasons to the Registrar, and to each person who is a party to the proceedings before him.[17]

1 ie: a person appointed by the Lord Chancellor to hear and decide appeals under the 1994 Act: section 77(1); see also the rules of eligibility and terms of appointment of appointed persons: section 77(2) and (3).
2 Rule 57(1).
3 Rule 56(2).
4 Rule 57(1).
5 Rule 57(2).
6 Rule 57(3).
7 As to which, see paragraph 3.48.
8 Section 76(4).
9 Rule 59(2).
10 Rule 59(1).
11 Rule 59(1).
12 Section 69 and rr49–51; as to which, see paragraph 3.42.
13 Rule 52; as to which, see paragraph 3.40.
14 Rule 53; as to which, see paragraph 3.43.
15 Section 68 and rr54 and 55; as to which, see paragraphs 3.44 and 3.45.
16 Rule 59(2).
17 Rule 59(3).

3.48   Referral of the appeal to the court, s76(3) and r57

An appeal to an appointed person may be referred by him to the court if:

(a) it appears to the appointed person that a point of general legal importance is involved;[1]

(b) the Registrar requests that the appeal be referred to the court;[2] or

(c) a specific request is made by any party to the proceedings before the Registrar in which the decision appealed against was made.[3]

However, before referring any appeal to the court, the appointed person must give the appellant and any other party to the appeal an opportunity to make representations as to whether the appeal should be referred to the court.[4]

1 Section 76(3)(a) and see rule 58(5) and (6).
2 Section 76(3)(b) and see rule 58(1)(a), (2) and (4).
3 Section 76(3)(c) and see rule 58(1)(b), (3) and (4).
4 Section 76(3).

Proceedings in the court

3.49 Practice and procedure The practice and procedure of
the court will be governed by the Rules of the Supreme Court.[1]
However, there are certain additional matters specific to
proceedings relating to trade marks which are provided for in the
1994 Act and need to be mentioned for completeness.

1 The White Book.

3.50 Certificate of validity, s73 If the validity of a registered
trade mark is contested in proceedings before the court and it is
found that the trade mark is registered validly the court may issue a
certificate of validity.[1]

In the event that a certificate of validity has been issued by the
court and, in subsequent proceedings:

(a) the validity of the registration is again challenged; and
(b) the proprietor once again obtains a final order or judgment in
     his favour,

the proprietor will be entitled to his costs as between solicitor and
client, unless the court directs otherwise.[2]

Whether or not a certificate of validity has been issued, in all
legal proceedings relating to a registered trade mark the registration
of the trade mark will of itself be prima facie evidence of the validity
of the registration and of any subsequent assignment or transmission
of the registration.[3]

1 Section 73(1).
2 Section 73(2); however, this does not extend to the costs of an appeal in any
   such proceedings.
3 Section 72.

3.51 Appearance of the Registrar, s74 In proceedings
before the court involving an application for:

(a) the revocation of the registration of a trade mark;
(b) a declaration of invalidity; or
(c) the rectification of the Register,

the Registrar will be entitled to appear and be heard, and indeed
must appear if he is so directed by the court.[1]

Alternatively, the Registrar may, instead of appearing, submit to
the court a signed statement giving particulars of:

(a) any proceedings before him in relation to the matter in issue;

(b) the grounds of any decision given by him affecting that matter;
(c) the practice of the Patent Office in like cases; or
(d) such other matters as are relevant to the issues and within the Registrar's knowledge as he thinks fit.[2]

The Registrar's statement will become part of the evidence in the proceedings before the court.[3]

1 Section 74(1).
2 Section 74(2); the Registrar may not exercise this option if he is directed otherwise by the court.
3 Section 74(2).

3.52 Transitional provisions, schedule 3 Schedule 3 of the 1994 Act contains the transitional provisions. Many of the transitional provisions relate to matters which have been dealt with in this chapter and references have been included in the text or in footnotes.

By way of a summary, the more important transitional provisions which affect practice and procedure are:
(a) trade marks registered under the 1938 Act as at 31 October 1994 (whether in Part A or Part B) will be transferred to the 1994 Register and will have effect as if registered under the 1994 Act;[1]
(b) trade marks registered under the 1938 Act will continue to be registered:
    (i) subject to any former disclaimer or limitation;[2] and
    (ii) where relevant, as a series;[3]
(c) trade marks registered under the 1938 Act will not continue to be registered:
    (i) subject to any former condition(s) of registration;[4] nor
    (ii) where relevant, as an associated mark;[5]
(d) the rights of co-proprietors of a 1938 Act registration will be governed by section 23 of the 1994 Act;[6]
(e) applications pending under the 1938 Act as at 31 October 1994 but which had not been advertised may be converted into applications under the 1994 Act;[7]
(f) applications pending under the 1938 Act which had been advertised under section 18 of the 1938 Act will be dealt with under the old law;[8] and
(g) registrations under the 1938 Act will continue in force until the

end of their respective 7 or 14 year periods as the case may be. On renewal they will be registered for 10 year periods.[9]

1 Schedule 3, paragraph 2(1).
2 Schedule 3, paragraph 3(2).
3 Schedule 3, paragraph 2(2).
4 Schedule 3, paragraph 3(1).
5 Schedule 3, paragraph 2(3).
6 Schedule 3, paragraph 7.
7 Schedule 3, paragraph 11.
8 Schedule 3, paragraph 10.
9 Schedule 3, paragraph 15.

4 Oppositions and observations

4.01 Approach taken by the 1994 Act When an application for registration of a trade mark has been accepted by the Registrar,[1] he will publish the application in the Journal.[2] Following publication, there are two options open to a third party who believes that there are grounds for refusing the registration of the trade mark as advertised.

Opposition The first option is to give a formal notice of opposition to the Registrar pursuant to section 38(2). This procedure is substantially similar to giving notice of opposition under section 18 of the 1938 Act. The giving of a notice of opposition is dealt with in the first part of this chapter, which also deals with analogous oppositions relating to:
(a) applications by agents or representatives;
(b) amendments of an application;
(c) alterations of a registered trade mark; and
(d) applications for collective or certification marks.

Observations The second option is a new procedure which enables any person to send written observations to the Registrar stating why he believes the trade mark should not be registered.[3] The making of observations is dealt with in the second part of this chapter.

1 Pursuant to section 37(5).
2 Section 38(1); and see rule 12.
3 Section 38(3).

Opposition

4.02 Opposition procedure, s38(2) and r13

Notice of opposition Any person may, within three months of the
date on which an application is published, give notice of opposition
to the registration of the trade mark.[1] The notice of opposition has
to include a statement of the grounds of opposition, a copy of which
will be sent by the Registrar to the applicant.[2]

Importantly, the three month time limit cannot be extended,[3]
unlike the former one month time limit under the 1938 Act which
did not limit the number or length of extensions that could be
obtained with the Registrar's consent.[4]

Counter-statement Following receipt of the notice of opposition,
an applicant who wishes to pursue his application will have to file a
counter-statement at the Registry[5] within three months of the date
on which the notice of opposition was sent by the Registrar. Strictly,
the applicant need not file a counter-statement if he is sufficiently
confident that the opposition as filed cannot succeed in any event.
The Registrar will send a copy of any counter-statement to the
person opposing the application.

The three month period cannot be extended,[6] unlike the
corresponding two month period for filing a counter-statement
under the 1938 Act.[7]

Opponent's evidence Upon receiving the counter-statement, the
person opposing the application must, within three months of the
date on which the counter-statement was sent by the Registrar, file
the evidence he may wish to rely upon in support of his opposition.
The evidence must be by way of affidavit or statutory declaration
and copies of any evidence filed must be sent by the opponent to
the applicant.[8] Unlike the periods for filing notices of opposition and
counter-statements, the time for filing evidence in support of the
opposition (or other evidence in opposition proceedings) can be
extended by the Registrar.[9]

If the person opposing the application does not file any evidence
then, unless the Registrar directs otherwise, the opposition will be
deemed abandoned.[10]

Applicant's evidence Where either:
(a) evidence is filed in support of the opposition; or

(b) the Registrar has directed that no evidence in support of the
    opposition is required,
the applicant, if he wishes to file any evidence, must do so within
three months of the date on which either a copy of the opponent's
evidence or a copy of the direction of the Registrar is sent to him.
This evidence must be filed by way of affidavit or statutory
declaration and a copy of the evidence must be sent by the
applicant to the opponent.[11] The three month time limit for filing
this evidence may be extended.[12]

Reply evidence The opponent may file evidence in reply to the
applicant's evidence within three months of the date on which a
copy of the applicant's evidence is sent to the opponent. This
evidence, by way of affidavit or statutory declaration filed at the
Registry, must be confined to matters which are strictly in reply to
the applicant's evidence. A copy of the reply evidence, if any, must
be sent by the opponent to the applicant.[13] The three month time
limit for filing reply evidence may be extended.[14]

Additional evidence No further evidence may be filed in the
opposition proceedings unless the Registrar, at his discretion, gives
leave to either party at any time to file evidence upon such terms as
the Registrar thinks fit.[15] This gives the Registrar a general discretion
to allow additional evidence to be filed by either party at any time
prior to the determination of the opposition proceedings.

Hearing Once all the evidence accepted by the Registrar has been
filed, the Registrar will, if a hearing is requested by either party to
the opposition proceedings, send to the parties notice of the date for
a hearing.[16] There is no prescribed time limit within which such a
notice must be sent, nor as to when the hearing must take place.
    If no hearing is requested by either party to an opposition, then
the Registrar will determine the matter on the evidence filed
without a hearing.

Decision of the Registrar Where, following an opposition, the
Registrar has made a decision on the acceptability of an application
for registration he will send a written notice of his decision to the
applicant and the opponent stating the reasons for his decision.[17]

Appeal For the purpose of any appeal against the Registrar's
decision in opposition proceedings the date of the decision will be

taken to be the date when notice of the decision is sent to the applicant or, as the case may be, the person opposing the application.[18]

1 Using Form TM 7. This is also the procedure for applications for registration made under the 1938 Act which are advertised on or after 31 October 1994: rule 67.
2 Section 38(2) and rule 13(1).
3 Rule 62(3).
4 Trade Marks and Service Marks Rules 1986, rule 114.
5 Rule 13(2); the counter-statement should be accompanied by the required notice of counter-statement using Form TM 8.
6 See note 3 above.
7 Trade Marks and Service Marks Rules 1986, rule 48.
8 Rule 13(3); compare this with the six month period for filing evidence in support of an opposition under the 1938 Act. As to the making and subscribing of affidavits and statutory declarations see rule 50.
9 Rule 62(1).
10 Rule 13(4).
11 Rule 13(5); again, compare this with the six month period for filing evidence by the applicant under the 1938 Act.
12 Rule 62(1).
13 Rule 13(6); under the 1938 Act there was a six month extendible period for filing reply evidence.
14 Rule 62(1).
15 Rule 13(7); the terms may include an order as to costs pursuant to section 68(1) and rule 54.
16 Rule 13(8).
17 Rule 14(1).
18 Rule 14(2) and see chapter 3 in respect of the appeal procedure.

4.03 Who may oppose, s38(2) Section 38(2) provides that 'any person' may give notice of opposition to the registration of a trade mark.[1] Thus, as has been suggested in relation to the corresponding provision in the 1938 Act, although there is no express test of standing to bring opposition proceedings it must be arguable that the opposition procedure cannot be used by a mere bystander. However, an opponent will not be confined to basing his opposition on an interference with his earlier rights.

1 This is identical to the corresponding provision of the 1938 Act, section 18(2).

4.04 Grounds of opposition The grounds of opposition most likely to be relied upon by an opponent will be any of the following, namely that the trade mark applied for:
(a) is not a sign which is both:
    (i) capable of being represented graphically; and

(ii) capable of distinguishing the applicant's goods or services from those of other undertakings;[1]

(b) is devoid of any distinctive character;[2]

(c) consists exclusively of signs or indications which may serve in trade to designate the kind, quality, quantity, intended purpose, value, geographical origin, the time of production of goods or of rendering of services, or other characteristics of goods or services;[3]

(d) consists exclusively of signs or indications which have become customary in the current language or in the bona fide and established practices of the trade;[4]

(e) consists exclusively of either:
  (i) the shape which results from the nature of the goods themselves;
  (ii) the shape of goods which is necessary to obtain a technical result; or
  (iii) the shape which gives substantial value to the goods;[5]

(f) is contrary to public policy or to accepted principles of morality;[6]

(g) is of such a nature as to deceive the public (for instance as to the nature, quality or geographical origin of the goods or service);[7]

(h) cannot be used because its use is prohibited in the United Kingdom by any enactment or rule of law or by any provision of Community law;[8]

(i) is a specially protected emblem for the purposes of section 4;[9]

(j) was applied for in bad faith;[10]

(k) is identical with an 'earlier trade mark' as defined in section 6 and the goods or services for which the trade mark is applied for are identical with the goods or services for which the earlier trade mark is protected;[11]

(l) is identical with an earlier trade mark and is to be registered for goods or services similar to those for which the earlier trade mark is protected and there exists a likelihood of confusion on the part of the public, which includes the likelihood of association with the earlier trade mark;[12]

(m) is similar to an earlier trade mark and is to be registered for goods or services identical with or similar to those for which the earlier trade mark is protected and there exists a likelihood of confusion on the part of the public, which includes the likelihood of association with the earlier trade mark;[13]

(n) is identical with or similar to an earlier trade mark and, although it is to be registered for goods or services which are not similar to those for which the earlier trade mark is registered, would nevertheless take unfair advantage of, or be detrimental to, the distinctive character or the repute of the earlier trade mark for the purposes of section 5(3);[14]

(o) is liable to be prevented from being used by virtue of any rule of law protecting an unregistered trade mark or other sign used in the course of trade or any other earlier right;[15]

(p) is not being used by the applicant or with his consent in relation to the goods or services covered by the application, and the applicant does not have a bona fide intention that the mark should be so used;[16] or

(q) was not applied for in accordance with the procedural requirements of section 32 and Rule 11.[17]

1 See paragraph 2.02 and chapter 1.
2 See paragraph 2.03.
3 See paragraph 2.04.
4 See paragraph 2.05.
5 See paragraphs 2.07 to 2.11.
6 See paragraph 2.12.
7 See paragraph 2.13.
8 See paragraph 2.14.
9 See paragraph 2.15 and chapter 15.
10 See paragraph 2.16.
11 See paragraph 2.18.
12 See paragraphs 2.19 to 2.22.
13 Ibid.
14 See paragraph 2.23.
15 See paragraphs 2.24 to 2.26.
16 As an example of an application being made in 'bad faith' see paragraph 2.16.
17 See chapter 3.

4.05 Opposition to applications by agents or representatives, s60 Where an application for the registration of a trade mark is made by a person who is the agent or the representative of a person who is the proprietor of the trade mark in a Convention country,[1] the application will be refused if the proprietor opposes the application[2] unless, or to the extent that, the agent or the representative justifies his action.[3]

This provision reflects Article 6*septies* of the Paris Convention and will involve the potentially complicated issue of whether the person claiming to be the proprietor can establish proprietorship of the mark in a Convention country. This will necessarily require the

Registrar or courts to consider and determine questions of foreign trade mark law. Presumably, the production of a certificate of registration of the relevant trade mark in a Convention country will be prima facie evidence of proprietorship. However, it must remain open to the agent or representative to challenge the validity of the foreign registration or to put the question of proprietorship in issue generally. This determination under foreign law may be more difficult where the proprietor is seeking to rely upon his proprietorship of an unregistered mark in a Convention country.

Neither Article 6*septies* nor section 60(2) makes it clear whether an opposition under this section is to be treated in the same way as a notice of opposition under section 38, or whether this is a sui generis remedy. Section 60(1) suggests that the proprietor's right to oppose the application arises immediately upon the application for registration being filed by his representative or agent. This is inconsistent with section 38 in so far as a notice of opposition under that section can only be given after the publication of the application following its acceptance by the Registrar.[4]

Furthermore, the Rules do not make express reference to a proprietor opposing an application pursuant to section 60(2). This suggests that the proprietor of the mark whose agent or representative has filed an application merely needs to notify the Registrar of his opposition to the application and the Registrar will be obliged to refuse to register the trade mark unless, thereafter, he is satisfied that the agent or representative is justified in making the application for registration.

From a procedural point of view it is not clear whether the proprietor of the mark becomes a party to any proceedings by virtue of his opposition to the application. On the above analysis, he does not. Therefore, the procedure would be as follows:

(a)   the agent or representative files the application for registration;

(b)   the person claiming to be the proprietor of the mark opposes the application;

(c)   the Registrar has no option but to refuse to register the mark; and

(d)   the agent or representative may seek to justify the filing of the application, for example, on the ground that the person claiming to be the proprietor of the trade mark is not in fact the proprietor of the mark in a Convention country or perhaps that the proprietor authorised the making of the application.

The complication arises because it is not clear whether the

proprietor who opposes the application actually instigates formal opposition proceedings governed by rule 13. If not, the question of whether the agent or representative can justify his action may have to be determined in the absence of the person claiming to be the proprietor. Presumably, however, he will be given the opportunity to comment on the grounds sought to be relied upon by his agent or representative by way of justification.

1 ie: a country other than the United Kingdom which is a party to the Paris Convention; see schedule 1.
2 Section 60(1) and (2).
3 Section 60(5).
4 Section 38(1) and (2).

4.06 Opposition to amendment of an application, s39(3) and r18(2) Section 39(2) provides for the amendment of an application for the registration of a trade mark provided that the correction does not either substantially affect the identity of the trade mark or extend the goods or services covered by the original application.

Where the amendment is made after publication of the original application, the amendment will be published in the Journal. Thereafter, any person claiming to be affected by an amendment which affects the representation of the trade mark may give notice of opposition to the amendment. The notice of opposition must be sent to the Registrar[1] within one month of the date on which the application as amended was published in the Journal. The notice of opposition must include a statement of the grounds of objection and, in particular, a statement as to why the amendment is contrary to section 39(2).[2] This, in essence, means a statement as to how the amendment substantially affects the identity of the trade mark or as to how the goods or services covered by the original application have been extended. Accordingly, someone opposing an amendment cannot rely on the more general grounds of opposition which would be available in proceedings relating to the opposition to the registration of a trade mark under section 38(2) and rule 13. However, the proceedings relating to the opposition to the amendment are the same as the opposition proceedings relating to the registration of a trade mark generally.[3]

1 Using Form TM 7.
2 Rule 18(2).
3 ie: rule 13 applies; rule 18(3) and therefore the three month period in which the notice of opposition must be given cannot be extended: rule 62(3).

4.07 Opposition to alteration of a registered trade mark, s44(3) and r25(3) Section 44(2) provides for the alteration of a registered trade mark where the mark includes the proprietor's name or address and provided that the alteration is limited to that name or address and does not substantially affect the identity of the mark.

The alteration will be published by the Registrar in the Journal. Thereafter, any person claiming to be affected by the alteration can give notice of opposition to the alteration which must include a statement of the grounds of opposition.[1] This, in essence, means a statement as to how the alteration either affects elements of the trade mark other than the proprietor's name or address or as to how it affects the identity of the mark. Accordingly, someone opposing an alteration cannot rely on the general grounds of opposition which would be available in proceedings under section 38(2).

The notice of opposition must be sent to the Registrar[2] within three months of the date on which the alteration was published in the Journal. The Registrar will send a copy of the statement of the grounds of opposition to the applicant and thereafter the procedure will be the same as the opposition procedure relating to the registration of a trade mark.[3]

1 Rule 25(3).
2 Rule 25(3); using form TM 7.
3 See rules 13(2)–(6) and paragraph 4.02; and therefore the three month period for giving notice of opposition cannot be extended.

4.08 Opposition to applications for collective and certification marks, Schedules 1 and 2 The procedure for opposing an application for the registration of a collective mark or a certification mark is the same as for opposing an ordinary trade mark. The available grounds of opposition are also the same.[1] In addition, the opposition may relate specifically to the regulations governing the use of a collective mark[2] and a certification mark,[3] including opposition to any amendment of the regulations.[4]

1 Subject to adjustments which need to be taken into account: see chapters 11 and 12.
2 Schedule 1, paragraph 8.
3 Schedule 2, paragraph 9.
4 See rule 23(4).

4.09 Opposition to division of an application, s41(1) and r19(2) Rule 19 provides for the division of an application into two or more separate applications, referred to as 'divisional

applications'. Each divisional application will be treated by the
Registrar as a separate application for registration. Therefore,
where the division of the application is made after the acceptance
and publication of the original application, it should be borne in
mind that any opposition to the original application will be taken
to apply to each divisional application.[1]

1 Rule 19(2).

Observations

4.10 Observation procedure, s38(3) and r15 Following the
acceptance and publication of an application[1] any person may, at
any time before the registration of the trade mark, send written
observations to the Registrar as to why he believes the trade mark
should not be registered.[2] The Registrar will send a copy of any
documents containing the observations to the applicant.[3]

Neither the 1994 Act nor the Rules specify what is to happen
next. However, where an application has been accepted the
Registrar may still refuse to register the trade mark if it appears to
him, having regard to matters coming to his notice since he
accepted the application, that it was wrongly accepted.[4] Therefore,
the Registrar could refuse to register the trade mark if he receives
written observations after accepting the application which persuade
him to conclude that the application was accepted by him in error.

In any event, the person making the observations will not
become a party to any proceedings before the Registrar.[5] If the
person making the observations wishes to become a party then he
must formally give notice of opposition to the registration under
section 38(2).[6]

1 Pursuant to section 37(5) and 38(1).
2 Section 38(3).
3 Rule 15.
4 Section 40(1).
5 Section 38(3).
6 See paragraphs 4.02–4.04 above.

4.11 Who may make observations, s38(3) As in the case of
opposition proceedings, section 38(3) provides that 'any person'
may make observations to the Registrar.[1]

1 As to the meaning of 'any person' see paragraph 4.03 above.

4.12 Subject matter of observations As with opposition proceedings, neither the 1994 Act nor the Rules specify or limit the subject matter of the observations. The wording of section 38(3) would suggest that any issue relevant to the question of whether a trade mark should be registered could be the proper subject of written observations. This would include any of the grounds of opposition referred to in paragraph 4.04 above.

4.13 Observations in relation to collective and certification marks, Schedules 1 and 2 The procedure for making observations concerning the registration of a certification mark or a collective mark is the same as for making observations concerning the registration of an ordinary trade mark, as is the subject matter for such observations.[1] In addition, written observations may be made relating specifically to the regulations governing the use of a collective mark[2] or a certification mark,[3] or to any amendment of such regulations.[4]

1 Subject to adjustments which need to be taken into account: see chapters 11 and 12.
2 Schedule 1, paragraph 8.
3 Schedule 2, paragraph 9.
4 Rule 23(3).

4.14 Observations in relation to the division of an application, r19(2) Where an application is divided, any observations made to the Registrar in respect of the original application shall be taken to apply to each divisional application.[1]

1 See paragraph 4.09.

Comment

4.15 Comparison with Community trade mark system
The proposed Community trade mark system limits the grounds for giving notice of opposition to objections based on the 'relative grounds' for refusal.[1] Furthermore, only the owner of the earlier trade mark or other earlier right may bring an opposition under the proposed Community system.

Any party will be able to submit observations concerning absolute grounds,[2] but the person making observations will not become a party to any proceedings. Accordingly, the opposition and observation procedure under the 1994 Act is wider than will be available under the proposed Community system in so far as:

(a) an opposition under the 1994 Act is not restricted to the relative grounds for refusal and can be brought by a person who is not the proprietor of an earlier trade mark or earlier right; and

(b) observations are not restricted under the 1994 Act to the absolute grounds.

The White Paper[3] indicates that consideration was given to aligning the United Kingdom opposition procedure with that of the Community system in terms of the grounds which can be raised in an opposition. However, there was a consensus in favour of continuing to allow any ground of objection to be raised in opposition proceedings and the 1994 Act has been drafted accordingly.

1 ie: the grounds equivalent to section 5 of the 1994 Act.
2 ie: the grounds equivalent to sections 3 and 4 of the 1994 Act.
3 Paragraph 4.18 of the White Paper.

5 Revocation and invalidity

5.01 Approach taken by the 1994 Act The 1994 Act provides for a registered trade mark to be either revoked or declared invalid in certain prescribed circumstances.

Revocation, s46 In essence, the grounds for revocation under section 46 are:
(a) non-use of the trade mark for five years;[1]
(b) where the trade mark has become a common name in the trade;[2] or
(c) where the trade mark has become liable to mislead the public.[3]

Invalidity, s47 In addition, or as an alternative to revocation, the grounds for invalidity under section 47 are:
(a) where the trade mark was registered contrary to the provisions of section 3;[4] or
(b) where the trade mark was registered contrary to the provisions of section 5.[5]

The practical distinction between revocation and invalidity is that the grounds for revocation relate to matters occurring after the registration of a trade mark, whereas the grounds for invalidity are based on matters which affect the original registration itself.

Each of these grounds for revocation and invalidity will now be considered in turn. However, it should be noted that both revocation and invalidity are discretionary orders under the 1994 Act and therefore equitable principles governing the exercise of discretionary powers will be applicable.

1 See paragraphs 5.02 to 5.09.
2 See paragraph 5.10.
3 See paragraph 5.11.
4 See paragraph 5.16.
5 See paragraph 5.17.

Revocation

5.02 Non-use, s46(1)(a) and (b) The registration of a trade mark may be revoked for non-use if either:

(a) within five years following the date of the completion of the registration procedure the trade mark has not been put to genuine use in the United Kingdom, either by the proprietor or with his consent, in relation to the goods or services covered by the registration; or

(b) there has been genuine use for the purposes of (a) above but such use has since been suspended for an uninterrupted period of five years,

provided also that, in each case, the proprietor cannot give proper reasons for the non-use.

In determining whether a trade mark is liable to be revoked for non-use it will be necessary to consider in particular a number of key phrases which appear in section 46; some are similar to those which appeared in the corresponding section 26 of the 1938 Act, some are not.[1] These phrases are discussed in paragraphs 5.03 to 5.05.

1 As to pending applications for revocation under section 26 of the 1938 Act, see paragraph 5.15.

5.03 Calculation of non-use period Section 46 removes any doubt concerning the date from which the five year non-use period commences. Under the 1938 Act it was only recently decided that the non-use period was measured from the date when the mark was actually put on the Register,[1] and not from the effective date of registration which would have been the original filing date. This decision is reflected in Article 10(1) of the Directive which has been adopted in section 46(1)(a).

1 *Bon Martin Trade Mark* [1989] RPC 537.

5.04   Genuine use   The 1994 Act provides three specific instances of what constitutes 'use'. The first two instances apply only for the purposes of section 46(1), whereas the third is of general application. These three instances are considered first, followed by a consideration of the meaning of 'genuine use' for the purposes of section 46(1).

'Use'   In the first place, the proprietor of a trade mark can rely on any use of his trade mark even though the mark actually used differs from the precise form in which it is registered, provided that the differences do not alter the distinctive character of the mark as registered.[1]

Secondly, the concept of 'use in the United Kingdom' will include affixing the trade mark in the United Kingdom to goods or to their packaging notwithstanding that the goods are intended only for export.[2]

Thirdly, it must be remembered that all references in the 1994 Act to the use of a trade mark will include use otherwise than by means of a graphic representation of the trade mark.[3] Thus, the proprietor can rely on any non-visual use, such as oral use, of his trade mark to defend a non-use action (provided, of course, that such use is 'genuine').

'Genuine use'   Although the 1994 Act specifies these three instances of what will constitute 'use' for the purposes of section 46, the Act does not give any guidance as to what must be established in order to obtain the revocation of a trade mark on the grounds of a lack of 'genuine use'. Certainly, the proprietor has the onus of showing what actual use has in fact been made of his trade mark,[4] but the onus remains on the party seeking revocation to prove that that use has not been 'genuine'.

The corresponding provision of the 1938 Act was section 26(1)(b) which required the party seeking revocation to establish that there had been no 'bona fide use' of the trade mark. The White Paper asserts that the change to the use of the word 'genuine' in the new law will amount only to a clarification rather than a substantive change.[5] In *Electrix*[6] it was held that 'bona fide' meant genuine, judged by commercial standards. It must be likely that the test of 'genuine use' will be interpreted by the courts consistently with their interpretation of bona fide use under the 1938 Act. Thus, issues raised by mere isolated instances of use, de minimis use, ghost marks and the stockpiling of trade marks will need to be considered in the context of the facts of each case in order to determine whether the use has been genuine.[7]

Although the cases decided under section 26(1) of the 1938 Act may be of some guidance in construing the meaning of the phrase 'genuine use' in section 46(1) of the 1994 Act, one should bear in mind a potential argument which, if accepted, could mean that those cases decided under the 1938 Act may be distinguished. The argument is based on the fact that the definition of 'trade mark' in the 1938 Act[8] included the requirement that the mark be used for the 'purpose of indicating, or so as to indicate, a connection in the course of trade' between the goods and the proprietor or a registered user. Accordingly, the decisions under the 1938 Act started with the premise that a mark which was being used for any other purpose could not be a 'trade mark' for the purposes of the 1938 Act. Thus, Lawton LJ, in *Nerit*[9] considered that he was entitled to look at the purpose for which the trade mark had been used and concluded that the proprietor's use of NERIT was not a 'bona fide use' because it had the 'unreal qualities of the ghost mark'. Furthermore, His Lordship stated that, even if the trade mark did in fact indicate a connection between the proprietor and his goods, where that connection was incidental to the purpose for which it was used, then this would also not constitute bona fide use of the trade mark.

The definition of 'trade mark' in the 1994 Act, however, makes no reference to the purpose for which a sign must be used in order for it to constitute a 'trade mark'. The only relevant requirement is that the sign must be capable of distinguishing the proprietor's goods or services from those of other undertakings. It is therefore arguable that provided the sign is in fact distinctive of those goods or services then it should not matter that there may be other purposes, even another paramount purpose, for which the trade mark is used.

Put another way, Shaw LJ, in the *Nerit* case,[10] referred to the 'philosophical concept' of a trade mark as being something which derives from the use of words or marks in relation to a course of trade in goods giving rise to a goodwill connecting the trader with the goods by reason of the trade mark. His Lordship reasoned that where there is no such course of trading there could be no interest to be protected.[11] The 1994 Act does away with the concept of the requirement of 'connecting the trader with the goods' and this is

borne out by the more relaxed attitude towards the licensing of
trade marks.[12] The court in *Nerit* thought that ghost marks were not
merely outside the scope of the 1938 Act but were directly contrary
to its 'spirit and intent'. That is, because ghost marks are not
registered for the purpose of building up goodwill and so as to
indicate a connection in the course of trade, they could not be trade
marks. The point of distinction lies in the fact that not merely do the
express words of the 1994 Act differ from those of the 1938 Act but
also, arguably, so does its 'spirit and intent'. If this is correct, then it
will be much more difficult to establish that the use has not been
'genuine' merely because the use would not have satisfied the
requirements of section 68(1) of the 1938 Act.

1 Section 46(2).
2 Section 46(2).
3 Section 103(2).
4 Section 100.
5 Paragraph 4.29.
6 (1954) 71 RPC 23.
7 See, for example, cases under the 1938 Act: *Imperial Group Limited v Philip
  Morris & Co Limited* [1982] FSR 72 and *Huggars* [1979] FSR 310.
8 See section 68(1).
9 See note 7.
10 Supra.
11 See also *Concord* [1987] FSR 209, where it was held that the use was not bona fide
   because the use was only temporary and not part of a genuine attempt to establish
   trading under the mark.
12 See chapter 10.

5.05 Use 'in relation to' goods or services Not only must
the use of a trade mark be genuine, the trade mark must also have
been used 'in relation to' the actual goods or services for which it is
registered. The failure so to use a trade mark will expose its
registration to revocation.

The first, and easier, question is one of fact, that is, whether the
goods or services covered by the registration match the goods or
services for which the mark has actually been used. This will be a
matter of evidence which the proprietor will have to supply.[1]

The second issue is whether the phrase 'in relation to' will
embrace use of a trade mark in advertisements or other media which
does not involve physically affixing or applying the trade mark to the
goods themselves. As the phrase 'in relation to' must be construed
when referring to services as including use otherwise than physically
affixing or applying the trade mark to the service, it would seem

illogical to construe the phrase any differently when referring to goods. Furthermore, a narrow interpretation would appear to be inconsistent with the broad terms of sections 10(4) and 103(2).

Although, for the purposes of infringement, section 10(4) specifies certain acts or conduct which will amount to the use of a sign, it should be remembered that that provision only applies for the purposes of section 10 itself, not section 46. It can be argued by analogy, however, that the acts and conduct specified in section 10(4) should also constitute use of a trade mark for the purposes of section 46. That, however, may not necessarily be the case: the purpose of section 10(4) is to ensure that a wide range of acts and conduct will constitute infringement, but different considerations arguably apply where a proprietor is being put to proof as to what use he has made of his trade mark so as to justify maintaining the registration. On the other hand, can it be right that acts or conduct can constitute infringement of a trade mark but, when done by the proprietor (or with his consent), do not necessarily constitute use of his trade mark?

Of course, the fact that a trade mark is actually physically affixed to a particular product does not necessarily mean that it is being used 'in relation to' that product. For example, the use of KODAK on T-shirts was held, in the circumstances of the case, to be use in relation to photographic film and not in relation to the T-shirts themselves.[2]

1 Section 100.
2 *Kodak Trade Mark* [1990] FSR 49; cf *Cheetah* [1993] FSR 263, where the use of the mark on delivery notes and invoices was held to constitute use in relation to the goods which had been delivered.

5.06 Use in relation to similar goods or services; use of an associated mark The 1938 Act enabled the proprietor in a non-use action to rely upon any use of his trade mark which was in relation to goods or services 'of the same description' as those covered by the registration.[1]

Furthermore, account could also be taken under the 1938 Act of any use by the proprietor of an associated registered trade mark.[2] As it was also possible for trade marks for goods to be associated with trade marks for related services,[3] the association of related marks could potentially have provided a valuable defence to an attack against one or more of the associated marks based on non-use.

The 1994 Act does not provide expressly for account to be taken

5.06 *Revocation and invalidity*

of any use of the trade mark other than its use in relation to the actual goods or services for which it is registered and the procedure for the association of trade marks has been abolished altogether.[4] However, use which would have been the basis of a defence on either of these grounds under the 1938 Act will, nevertheless, arguably remain relevant in the exercise of the discretion to revoke the registration.

1 Section 26(1) proviso 1938 Act.
2 Section 30(1) 1938 Act.
3 Section 23(2)A 1938 Act.
4 Indeed, even associated trade marks registered under the 1938 Act will no longer be recorded as such when they are transferred to the 1994 Register: Schedule 3, paragraph 2(3).

5.07 Use after the five year period, s46(3) The registration of a trade mark will not be revoked on either of the grounds of non-use[1] if genuine use by or with the consent of the proprietor is either commenced or resumed before the application for revocation is made. It does not matter that such use commences or resumes after the expiry of the relevant five year period[2] because any genuine use prior to the filing of the application for revocation (subject to the proviso below) effectively overcomes the non-use.

Proviso However, no account will be taken of any use which commences or resumes within three months prior to the making of the application for revocation, unless the proprietor began his preparations for the commencement or resumption of the use of his trade mark prior to becoming aware that the application for revocation might be made.[3]

The effect of the proviso is that someone considering applying for revocation should put the proprietor of the trade mark on notice of his intention to apply at the earliest opportunity after the five year period, so that the proprietor cannot rely on any subsequent use which he commences or resumes within three months before the making of the application for revocation. Of course, the person applying for revocation must then make his application for revocation within three months after putting the proprietor on notice, as otherwise the proprietor may be able to rely on use which commences or resumes after receiving notice of the intended application but more than three months prior to the making of the application for revocation.

Example Thus, if there has been a relevant five year period of non-use between, for example, 1 November 1989 and 31 October 1994, an application for revocation will still fail if either:

(a) the proprietor commences or resumes using his trade mark at any time on or after 1 November 1994 and provided that such use commences or resumes more than three months before the making of an application for revocation; or

(b) the proprietor commences or resumes using his trade mark on or after 1 November 1994 and even though an application for revocation is made within three months of that date but, at the time when the preparations for the commencement or resumption began, the proprietor was unaware that the application for revocation might be made.

Comment Under the 1938 Act the equivalent proviso applied to a period of only one month prior to the making of the application for revocation but it was irrelevant that the proprietor may have had no notice of the intended application. Extending the period during which use of the trade mark will be disregarded will give the parties a better opportunity to negotiate, because the party alleging non-use will not be prejudiced by delaying the bringing of his application for a period of three months (at least) rather than just one month. Accordingly, the need for formal revocation proceedings may, in some instances, be avoided.[4]

1 See paragraph 5.02.
2 Section 46(3).
3 Section 46(3) proviso.
4 It was, however, always open to the parties to agree on a without prejudice extension to the one month period under the 1938 Act.

5.08 Use with the proprietor's consent, s46(1) The 1994 Act overcomes the issue which arose under the 1938 Act as to what use other than by the proprietor could be relied upon to defeat a non-use action. Strictly, the 1938 Act appeared only to permit use by the proprietor himself or a registered user to be taken into account[1] but case law suggested and the Registrar's practice was that use by other persons could also be considered to be use by the proprietor for the purposes of section 26.[2]

The 1994 Act makes it clear that any genuine use with the consent of the proprietor will be sufficient. This will therefore include use by a third party even though no formal licence arrangement is in place and even though the prescribed particulars of any licence which has been entered into have not been registered in accordance with section 25, provided only that the proprietor has consented to the use. Indeed, even though the trade mark may be being used under a licence which is deemed to be 'not effective',[3] that should not of itself negate the necessary consent for the purposes of section 46(1).

1   This conclusion followed from sections 26(1) and 28(2).
2   *Bostitch* [1963] RPC 183: use by a licensee; *Radiation Ltd* (1930) 46 RPC 37: use by a subsidiary; *Molyslip* [1978] RPC 211.
3   ie: because the licence is not in writing: section 28(2).

5.09   Proper reasons for non-use, s46(1)   The two grounds for revocation based on non-use[1] may be overcome if the proprietor can establish 'proper reasons' for not using his trade mark.

The first issue is whether the proper reasons must have related to the whole five year period of non-use or is it sufficient that the proper reasons existed during any part of the relevant five year period (subject, presumably, to a mere de minimus part of that period). Certainly, the proper reasons must have been the operative cause of the non-use and, therefore, the proprietor will not be able to rely on those reasons if, in any event, there would have been no use of his trade mark. This issue also arose under section 26(3) of the 1938 Act where non-use of a trade mark due to 'special circumstances in the trade . . .' could not be relied upon in support of a non-use action. The second issue is whether the period during which the proper reasons existed will be treated as a period of actual use or whether that period will simply be disregarded for all purposes. The new wording of section 46(1) does not remove the ambiguity altogether, but is more consistent with the interpretation that the party seeking revocation will not succeed if the proprietor can establish proper reasons for the non-use which relate to any period during the relevant period of non-use. Thus, any period of non-use which can be excused for proper reasons will mean that, for the purpose of calculating the relevant five year period, one will have to: .
(a)   stop counting as at the beginning of the period; and
(b)   start counting afresh as from the end of the period,
during which the proper reasons were responsible for the non-use. It will therefore be necessary to establish a full uninterrupted five

year period of non-use during which there have been no proper reasons for such non-use.

What then are 'proper reasons' for not using a trade mark? One assumes that the circumstances specified in section 26(3) of the 1938 Act would constitute proper reasons under the 1994 Act. Perhaps also the usual acts or events which constitute force majeure may constitute proper reasons if they are the proximate cause of the non-use. More complicated issues will arise where the non-use is for commercial reasons which the proprietor considers to be 'proper' on any subjective test, but which may be inconsistent with the wider public policy of not allowing statutory monopolies to subsist which are not exercised and which could therefore prevent lawful competition and the free movement of goods and services. For example, a pharmaceutical company may be delayed in putting a particular drug on the market because the necessary regulatory approval has not been forthcoming as quickly as anticipated by the company. This is a proper reason for not marketing the product, but is it a proper reason for not using the trade mark intended to be used in relation to the product?[2]

The phrase 'proper reasons' comes from Article 10 of the Directive and it remains to be seen how the courts will interpret and apply these words. In the *Bali* case[3] at first instance Ungoed-Thomas J, referring to the 'special circumstances' exception under section 26(3) of the 1938 Act, made the point that a trade mark is a commercial asset intended to be used commercially by businessmen and special circumstances have to be understood and applied in a business sense. That statement of principle must be equally apposite today and therefore the phrase 'proper reasons' should also be construed and applied in a business sense.

1 See paragraph 5.02.
2 See *Re Jellied Beef* [1993] FSR 484, a case where the ban on a product was considered to be a justification for non-use.
3 *Bali* [1966] RPC 387 at 406.

5.10 Common name in the trade, s46(1)(c) The second ground on which a registered trade mark can be revoked is that, in consequence of either the acts or inactivity of the proprietor, the trade mark has become the common name in the trade for the product or the service for which it is registered.[1]

It is well established that a mark which is generic or descriptive is the very antithesis of a registrable trade mark and a registered trade mark which becomes generic or descriptive is thus liable to revocation.

In chapter 10 reference is made to that fact that the requirements relating to the licensing of registered trade marks have been relaxed in the 1994 Act. Nonetheless, section 46(1)(c) should always be borne in mind when licensing a trade mark because the failure to control adequately and effectively the licensee's use of the trade mark may lead to it becoming generic or descriptive of the goods or services for which it is registered. It is ironic that this ground for revocation may arise because the product or service for which the trade mark is registered has become so successful that the public adopt the trade mark as a description of all competing products of a like nature or function. Thus, the proprietor by himself and through any licensee(s) must carefully control the manner in which he uses the trade mark so that it continues to identify and distinguish his particular products or services and not the like products or services of competitors.

Acts or inactivity of the proprietor   The section will apply only where the trade mark becomes a common name for a product or service in consequence of acts or inactivity of the proprietor. The reference to 'inactivity' will, in principle, encompass the failure by the proprietor to control effectively either the use of the trade mark by his licensee(s) and/or by a third party infringer, provided that the proprietor has notice (actual or constructive) of the infringing use by the third party. If such failure to control results in the trade mark becoming the common name in the trade for the goods or services for which it is registered, then it will be liable to revocation.

'Common name in the trade'   It is as yet uncertain whether the phrase 'common name in the trade' will be interpreted differently to the phrase 'well-known and established use of the word as the name or description of the article or a substance by a person carrying on a trade therein . . .' which appeared in the proviso to section 15(1) of the 1938 Act. On its face, the phrase in the 1994 Act is simply a more compact expression of the same concept.

It is interesting to note that the ground for rectification set out in the proviso to section 15(1) of the 1938 Act was by way of an exception to the general proposition that the registration of a trade mark would not become invalid only because the trade mark contained or consisted of a word which was the name or description of an article or substance. This was because it was recognised that trade marks which are regarded by the public as the name of an article will have significant commercial value and should not be invalidated unless they had become generic within the meaning of the proviso.

'For a product or service for which it is registered' An application for revocation under the 1994 Act on the ground that a trade mark has become a common name in the trade will only succeed if it has become a common name for the specific product or service for which the trade mark is registered.

The 1994 Act thus overcomes the problem for proprietors which arose under the 1938 Act whereby they could lose their registration through the use of their mark (particularly by third parties, including the public) on goods or services other than those covered by the registration and in a way which the proprietor could not police.[2]

1 Section 46(1)(c).
2 See *Daiquiri Rum* [1969] RPC 600.

5.11 'Liable to mislead the public', s46(1)(d) The third ground on which a registered trade mark can be revoked is that, in consequence of the use made of it by the proprietor or with his consent in relation to the goods or services for which it is registered, the trade mark is liable to mislead the public.[1] Particular examples of the way in which the public may be misled are cited, including as to the nature, quality, or geographical origin of the goods or services.[2]

Use made of it by the proprietor The cause of the trade mark being liable to mislead the public must be the actual use made of the mark by the proprietor or with his consent and not merely the inactivity of the proprietor.[3] Furthermore, any use of the trade mark by unauthorised third parties will not be relevant.

'Liable to mislead' The concept of misleading the public involves more than merely creating confusion. Section 11 of the 1938 Act provided a similar ground for rectification merely if the use of the trade mark was likely to cause confusion and thus the 1994 Act imposes a stricter test. This is consistent with the shift in the emphasis in the 1994 Act from protecting the interests of the public

5.11 *Revocation and invalidity*

to being more concerned with the rights of trade mark owners.

Having said this, however, it will not be necessary for the party seeking revocation under the 1994 Act to establish that the proprietor consciously or advertently set out to mislead the public. The only requirement is that this is the result in fact (the 'consequence') of the use made of the trade mark by the proprietor or with his consent.

The goods or services for which it is registered As with section 46(1)(c), the use of the trade mark which causes it to become liable to mislead the public must be use in relation to those specific goods or services for which it is registered. Thus, any use of the trade mark on any other goods or services will be disregarded for the purposes of section 46(1)(d).

1   Section 46(1)(d).
2   Section 46(1)(d).
3   cf section 46(1)(c).

5.12 Application for revocation, s46(4) and r31 An application for revocation can be made by 'any person'[1] either to the Registrar or to the court.[2] However, if proceedings concerning the trade mark in question are pending in the court, then the application for revocation must be made to the court. If the application is made to the Registrar, then he can at any stage of the proceedings refer the application to the court.[3]

An application for revocation under section 46 which is made to the Registrar[4] must be submitted together with a statement of the grounds on which the application is made.[5] The Registrar will then send a copy of the application for revocation together with the statement of grounds to the proprietor.[6] The proprietor then has three months from the date on which the Registrar sends the application to him within which to file a counter-statement[7] and the Registrar will send a copy of the counter-statement to the applicant for revocation. Where the application for revocation is based on the grounds of non-use (under section 46(1)(a) or (b)) the proprietor is obliged also to file the evidence on which he intends to rely of the use of his trade mark.[8] If the proprietor fails to file any such evidence the Registrar is entitled to treat his defence as having been withdrawn.[9]

Thereafter, the provisions of rule 13 will apply to the proceedings in the same way as if the proceedings were in respect of an opposition to the registration of a trade mark, except that an application for revocation for non-use will succeed automatically if no counter-statement is filed by the proprietor.[10]

Intervention   It should also be noted that any person, other than the registered proprietor, who claims to have an interest in the revocation proceedings can apply to the Registrar[11] for leave to intervene. The intervener must state the nature of his interest and the Registrar may either refuse leave to intervene or grant leave upon appropriate terms or conditions as he thinks fit, which may include an undertaking as to costs.[12] As always, the parties are entitled to request a hearing in relation to the issue as to whether leave to intervene should be either refused or granted.

If the application for leave to intervene is granted, the intervener will be treated as a party for the purposes of the application for revocation and the provisions of rule 13 will apply to the intervener, subject only to any terms or conditions which the Registrar has imposed in respect of the intervention.[13]

Registrar's decision   When the Registrar has made a decision in relation to the application for revocation and/or the application to intervene, he will send the applicant, the proprietor and the intervener (if any) written notice of his decision, including the reasons for his decision.[14] In the event that there is any appeal from the Registrar's decision then the date when the notice of his decision is sent to the parties will be taken to be the date of his decision.[15]

1 See paragraph 4.03.
2 An application for revocation for non-use under section 46(1)(a) or (b) can be made in relation to a trade mark registered under the 1938 Act at any time after 31 October 1994: Schedule 3, paragraph 17(2); as to pending non-use applications under section 26 of the 1938 Act see paragraph 5.15.
3 Section 46(4).
4 Using Form TM 26.
5 Rule 31(1).
6 Rule 31(2).
7 Together with Form TM 8; rule 31(3).
8 ie: pursuant to his obligation under section 100; the evidence of use must be filed within the same period as applies to the filing of the counter-statement.
9 Rule 31(3) proviso.
10 Rule 31(4).
11 Using Form TM 27; rule 31(5).
12 Rule 31(5).
13 Rule 31(6).
14 Rule 31(7).
15 Rule 31(7).

5.13 Partial revocation, s46(5) Where grounds for revocation under section 46 exist in respect of only some of the goods or services for which the trade mark is registered, revocation will relate only to those specific goods or services.[1]

1 Section 46(5).

5.14 Effective date of revocation, s46(6) Where the registration of a trade mark is revoked to any extent, the rights of the proprietor will (to the extent that it is revoked) be deemed to have ceased as from either:
(a) the date of the application for revocation; or
(b) if the Registrar or the court is satisfied that the grounds for revocation existed at an earlier date, from that earlier date.
In the case of revocation pursuant to a counterclaim in infringement proceedings it would therefore be logical for the defendant/applicant for revocation to seek an order that the proprietor's rights should be deemed to have ceased at least immediately prior to the alleged acts of infringement. However, this must depend on the actual grounds on which revocation can be established and the facts giving rise to those grounds. For example, revocation for non-use would only, at best, date back to the end of the relevant five year period and therefore revocation on this ground would not, of itself, affect the proprietor's rights prior to or even during the five year period.

5.15 Transitional provisions, schedule 3

Removal for non-use An application under section 26 of the 1938 Act for removal of a trade mark on the ground of non-use which is pending as at 31 October 1994 will be dealt with under the old law and any consequent alteration will be made to the 1994 Register.[1]

Expungement for breach of a condition Under the 1938 Act the Registrar could require the proprietor to accept certain conditions relating to the registration of his mark. Pursuant to section 33 of the 1938 Act the registration of a trade mark could have been expunged or varied on the ground of any contravention of or any failure to observe such a condition. There is no equivalent provision in the 1994 Act, but proceedings which are pending under section 33 of the 1938 Act as at 31 October 1994 will continue to be dealt with under the old law and any consequent alteration will be made to the 1994 Register.[2]

Entries wrongly remaining in the 1938 Act Register An application under section 32 of the 1938 Act for the expungement or variation of an entry which was 'wrongly remaining' in the 1938 Register and which application is pending as at 31 October 1994 will be dealt with under the old law and any consequent alteration will be made to the 1994 Register.[3]

1 Schedule 3, paragraph 17(1).
2 Schedule 3, paragraph 3(1), notwithstanding that the condition will have ceased to have effect under the 1994 Act: Schedule 3, paragraph 3(1).
3 Schedule 3, paragraph 18(1).

Invalidity

The first part of this chapter has been concerned with the grounds on which the registration of a trade mark can be revoked; they relate to matters which have occurred since registration. The second part of this chapter considers the grounds on which the original registration of the trade mark can be declared invalid.

5.16 Registration contrary to section 3, s47(1) The registration of a trade mark may be declared invalid on the ground that the trade mark was registered in breach of section 3 or any of the provisions referred to in section 3.[1]

However, even where the trade mark has been registered in breach of section 3(1)(b), (c) or (d), it will still not be declared invalid if, in consequence of the subsequent use which has been made of it, the trade mark has since registration acquired a distinctive character in relation to the goods or services for which it is registered.[2]

1 Section 47(1); see chapter 2.
2 Section 47(1) proviso; see also section 3(1) proviso.

5.17 Registration contrary to section 5, s47(2) The registration of a trade mark may also be declared invalid on the grounds that:
(a) there is an earlier trade mark in relation to which the conditions set out in section 5(1), (2) or (3) are satisfied;[1] or
(b) there is an earlier right in relation to which the condition set out in section 5(4) is satisfied,
unless the proprietor of the earlier trade mark or other earlier right (as the case may be) has consented to the registration.[2]

Honest concurrent use Although an applicant for registration may be able to rely on the honest concurrent use of his trade mark in order to overcome an objection to registrability raised by the Registrar based on the relative grounds for refusal (ie: those contained in section 5),[3] such honest concurrent use does not affect a third party application for a declaration of invalidity under section 47(2).[4]

1 As to the availability of this ground for invalidity of registrations obtained under the 1938 Act, see paragraph 5.25.
2 Section 47(2).
3 See section 7 and chapter 2.
4 Section 7(4)(b); but see section 48(1)(a) and paragraph 5.19.

5.18 Registrations obtained by agents and representatives, s60(3) Where an application for the registration of a trade mark is made by an agent or a representative of the proprietor of the mark in a Convention country,[1] the proprietor may (if he does not oppose the agent's/representative's application) apply for a declaration of invalidity of the registration.[2] Alternatively, the proprietor can apply for rectification of the Register so as to substitute his name as the registered proprietor for that of his agent/representative.[3] This may be a more practical remedy if the proprietor uses or intends to use his trade mark in the United Kingdom.

In any event, the proprietor must make his application (whether for invalidity or rectification) within three years of becoming aware of the registration of his mark by his agent/representative.[4]

1 ie: a country, other than the United Kingdom, which is a party to the Paris Convention: section 55(1) see schedule 1 to this book.
2 Section 60(3)(a).
3 Section 60(3)(b); as to rectification see chapter 3.
4 Section 60(6).

5.19 Effect of acquiescence, s48(1)(a) In the event that the proprietor of an earlier trade mark[1] or other earlier right[2] has acquiesced for a continuous period of five years in the use of a registered trade mark in the United Kingdom, he will lose his entitlement to apply for a declaration of invalidity based on any conflict with his earlier trade mark or earlier right.[3]

1 See section 6.
2 See section 5(4).
3 Section 48(1)(a); unless the registration was applied for in bad faith.

110

5.20 Application for declaration of invalidity, s47(3) and r31 An application for a declaration of invalidity can be made by 'any person',[1] and may be made either to the Registrar or to the court. However, if proceedings concerning the trade mark in question are already pending in the court then the application for the declaration must be made to the court. If the application is made to the Registrar then he may at any stage of the proceedings refer the application to the court.[2]

In the case of an application for a declaration of invalidity on the ground that the original application for registration was made in bad faith,[3] the Registrar himself may apply directly to the court for a declaration of invalidity.[4]

An application for a declaration under section 47 which is made to the Registrar[5] must be submitted together with a statement of the grounds on which the application is made.[6] The Registrar will then send a copy of the application together with the statement of grounds to the proprietor.[7] The proprietor then has three months from the date on which the Registrar sends the application to him within which to file a counter-statement,[8] and the Registrar will send a copy of the counter-statement to the applicant seeking the declaration.

Thereafter, the provisions of rule 13 will apply to the proceedings in the same way as if the proceedings were in respect of an opposition to the registration of a trade mark.[9]

Intervention It should also be noted that any person, other than the registered proprietor, who claims to have an interest in the invalidity proceedings can apply to the Registrar[10] for leave to intervene. The intervener must state the nature of his interest and the Registrar may either refuse leave to intervene or grant leave upon appropriate terms or conditions as he thinks fit, which may include an undertaking as to costs.[11] As always, the parties are entitled to request a hearing in relation to the issue of whether leave to intervene should be either refused or granted.

If the application for leave to intervene is granted, the intervener will be treated as a party for the purposes of the application for the declaration and the provisions of rule 13 will apply to the intervener, subject only to any terms and conditions which the Registrar has imposed in respect of the intervention.[12]

Registrar's decision When the Registrar has made a decision in relation to the application for the declaration of invalidity and/or the application to intervene, he will give the applicant, the proprietor and the intervener (if any) written notice of his decision, including the reasons for his decision.[13] In the event that there is any appeal from the Registrar's decision, then the date when the notice of his decision is sent to the parties will be taken to be the date of his decision.[14]

1 See paragraph 4.03.
2 Section 47(3).
3 ie: in breach of section 3(6) and therefore pursuant to section 47(1).
4 Section 47(4).
5 Using Form TM 26.
6 Rule 31(1).
7 Rule 31(2).
8 Together with Form TM 8; rule 31(3).
9 Rule 31(4).
10 Using Form TM 27.
11 Rule 31(5).
12 Rule 31(6).
13 Rule 31(7).
14 Rule 31(7).

5.21 Partial invalidity, s47(5) Where grounds for invalidity exist in respect of only some of the goods or services for which the trade mark is registered, the trade mark will be declared invalid as regards only those specific goods or services.[1]

1 Section 46(5).

5.22 Effective date of invalidity, s47(6) Where the registration of a trade mark is declared invalid to any extent, the registration will (to the extent that it is declared invalid) be deemed never to have been made,[1] that is, the registration is void ab initio.[2]

However, in order to prevent the unravelling of any dealings with the registered trade mark prior to the declaration of invalidity, the declaration of invalidity will not affect any transactions which are 'past and closed', that is, transactions which are not still executory.

1 Section 47(6).
2 See also paragraph 5.25 in relation to the retrospective effect of section 47 on 1938 Act registrations.

5.23 Deemed validity, s72 There is no equivalent provision in the 1994 Act corresponding to section 13 of the 1938 Act, which deemed the registration of a trade mark in Part A to be valid after seven years from the date of registration.[1] The 1994 Act does, however, state that in all legal proceedings relating to a registered trade mark (including proceedings for rectification) the registration of a person as the proprietor of a trade mark will be prima facie evidence of the validity of the original registration and of any subsequent assignment or other transmission of it.[2] The effect of this is to confirm that the party seeking the declaration of invalidity, including the Registrar himself, will have the onus of establishing that the registration is invalid on one or more of the grounds specified in section 47.

1 Unless the registration was obtained by fraud or the trade mark came within section 11 of the 1938 Act.
2 Section 72.

5.24 Certificate of validity, s73 Where the validity of the registration of a trade mark is contested in any court proceedings and it is held that the trade mark is validly registered, the court can give a certificate of validity.[1] The value of a certificate of validity is that if in any subsequent proceedings the validity of the registration is again questioned and the proprietor again obtains a final order/judgment in his favour, then he is entitled to his costs as between solicitor and client, unless the court directs otherwise. Normally, the successful proprietor would only be entitled to his costs on a party and party basis which is a significantly lower level of assessment.[2]

1 Section 73; this provision mirrors section 47 of the 1938 Act and any certificate of validity previously given under section 47 will continue to have effect as if it had been given under section 73 1994 Act: Schedule 3, paragraph 21.
2 This does not extend to the costs of any appeal from the proceedings.

5.25 Transitional provisions, schedule 3 For the purposes of any proceedings under section 47 in relation to trade marks registered under the 1938 Act, the provisions of the 1994 Act are deemed to have been in force at all material times. Thus, a declaration of invalidity under section 47 in relation to registrations under the 1938 Act will be retrospective, that is, it will take effect as from the date of registration under the 1938 Act.[1]

However, although the 1994 Act is deemed to have been in force at all material times for the purposes of proceedings under section 47, it is not possible to challenge the validity of a registration under the 1938 Act on the ground that the registration should have been refused pursuant to section 5(3) of the 1994 Act.[2] The ground for refusal of registration under section 5(3) applies in certain circumstances where there is a conflict between the mark applied for and an earlier trade mark even where the earlier trade mark in question is not protected for the goods or services in relation to which the applicant seeks the registration of his mark. This is a new ground for refusal which had no counterpart in the 1938 Act and thus it would be inappropriate for it now to apply retrospectively.

1 Schedule 3, paragraph 18(2).
2 Schedule 3, paragraph 18(2).

6 Rights conferred by registration: infringement

6.01 Approach taken by the 1994 Act The registration of a trade mark confers a personal property right on the proprietor[1] which gives him exclusive rights in the trade mark which are infringed by the unauthorised use of the trade mark in the United Kingdom.[2] However, the proprietor's exclusive rights are subject to:

(a) the qualified 'defence' provided for in section 10(6);

(b) the specific statutory limitations on the effect of registration set out in sections 11 and 12; and

(c) any voluntary disclaimers or limitations relating to the registration.[3]

These limits on the rights conferred by registration, in effect, are all defences to an action for infringement and are dealt with, together with other defences which may be available, in chapter 7.

Section 10 of the 1994 Act specifies the acts which constitute infringement of a registered trade mark and which are actionable by the proprietor of the trade mark.[4] Section 56(2) of the 1994 Act confers a remedy on the proprietor of a 'well known' mark[5] in circumstances which are analogous to infringement under section 10(2), notwithstanding that a well known mark need not be registered. Similarly, section 60(4) confers a remedy on the proprietor of a mark in respect of certain acts of his agents or representatives which he has not authorised. It is not necessary to consider either sections 56(2) or 60(4) in this chapter because neither involves establishing the infringement of a registered trade mark per se, and they are therefore dealt with in the context of remedies in chapter 8.

6.01 *Rights conferred by registration: infringement*

In addition to conferring rights on the proprietor, the 1994 Act also confers rights on licensees including, in certain circumstances, the right to commence proceedings in respect of acts which constitute infringement of the proprietor's registered trade mark.[6]

Transitional provisions The 1938 Act will continue to apply in relation to infringements committed before 31 October 1994, whereas sections 9–12 of the 1994 Act apply to infringements occurring after that date, including infringements of registrations under the 1938 Act.[7]

1 Sections 2(1) and 22. In respect of co-proprietors see section 23 and paragraph 6.11.
2 Section 9(1); see paragraph 6.03
3 ie pursuant to section 13(1); disclaimers or limitations relating to registrations under the 1938 Act will also continue to apply: Schedule 3, paragraph 3(2).
4 Note that the 1994 Act confers no right of action for the infringement of an unregistered trade mark: section 2(2).
5 See chapter 1.
6 Sections 30 and 31 and see paragraph 6.10.
7 Schedule 3, paragraph 4(1).

6.02 Title by registration, s2(1) The effect of section 2(1) is that the proprietor acquires his statutory rights by the registration of his trade mark. It is not a matter of the proprietor registering his existing rights.

6.03 Exclusive rights, s9 The exclusive rights conferred by registration are not defined as such. Instead, the 1994 Act specifies the acts which, if done without the consent of the proprietor, will constitute an infringement of those exclusive rights. The proprietor's exclusive rights are, therefore, to do, and to authorise others to do, any act which if done by an unauthorised third party would amount to an infringement.[1]

The rights of the proprietor take effect from the 'date of registration' which is deemed to be the date of the filing of the application for registration.[2] However, infringement proceedings cannot be commenced before the date on which the trade mark is in fact registered.[3]

Only acts committed in the United Kingdom can amount to an infringement of the proprietor's exclusive rights.[4]

1 See section 9(1).
2 Sections 9(3) and 40(3).
3 Section 9(3)(a).
4 Section 9(1).

Acts of infringement

The acts of infringement can be dealt with conveniently under three headings which correspond to the first three sub-sections of section 10. However, those sub-sections are substantially in the same terms as the first three sub-sections of section 5 and thus most of the issues which arise under section 10 have already been dealt with in chapter 2 in the context of registrability. One important difference between section 5 and section 10 will be that the onus of proof will be reversed, as to which, see paragraph 6.07.

6.04 Identical marks/identical goods or services, s10(1)

It is an act of infringement for a person to use in the course of trade a sign:

(a) which is identical with a registered trade mark; and
(b) in relation to goods or services which are identical with the goods or services for which the trade mark is registered.[1]

Elements of infringement under section 10(1) A consideration of the elements required to establish infringement under section 10(1) involves looking at the following issues:

(A) the meaning of the phrase 'uses a sign';
(B) the meaning of the phrase 'in the course of trade';
(C) whether the defendant's sign is identical to the proprietor's registered trade mark;
(D) the meaning of the phrase 'in relation to goods or services' and
(E) whether the defendant's goods or services are identical to the goods or services for which the proprietor's trade mark is registered.

These issues are now discussed in turn.

(A) 'USES A SIGN', s10(4) All acts of infringement involve the unauthorised use of a sign in the course of trade in the circumstances described in sections 10(1), (2) or (3). For the purposes of section 10, a person is deemed to use a sign if, in particular, he:

(a) affixes the sign to goods or their packaging;
(b) offers or exposes goods for sale under the sign;
(c) puts goods on the market under the sign;
(d) stocks goods for the purpose of offering or exposing the goods for sale or to put them on the market under the sign;

(e) offers or supplies services under the sign;
(f) imports or exports goods under the sign; or
(g) uses the sign on business papers or in advertising.[2]

The use of the phrase 'in particular' in section 10(4) makes it clear that this list of examples of what constitutes use of a sign is not exhaustive. Indeed, the Directive uses the words 'inter alia' rather than 'in particular'.[3]

The concept of 'use' is clearly intended to be very broad. This is apparent from the fact that, in direct contrast to the 1938 Act which limited the concept of 'use of a mark' to the use of a printed or other visual representation of the mark,[4] the 1994 Act provides specifically that use may be otherwise than by means of graphic representation.[5] This means that the oral or other non-visual use of a sign may constitute infringement if such use otherwise falls within section 10(1), (2) or (3).

A further departure from the 1938 Act is that, in order to constitute infringement, it will not be a requirement that the sign be used in what was referred to as 'a trade mark sense'. This issue has been discussed in chapter 1 in the context of the definition of a trade mark and the 1994 Act excludes, by implication, the notion of 'use in a trade mark sense' for the purpose of establishing infringement. This proposition derives from the fact that section 10 makes it clear that the use of a mere sign can constitute infringement.

The White Paper[6] identifies one of the objectives to be achieved by broadening the concept of use for infringement purposes as being to enable trade mark owners to prevent the use of their trade marks by third parties as business names. The concern was that under the 1938 Act a retailer could adopt a trade mark as the name of his retail outlet selling goods for which the mark was registered and yet, by refraining from using the mark on or near the goods, avoid infringing the registration.[7] The broader definition of 'use' in sections 10(4) and 103(2) will now enable a proprietor of a registered trade mark to prevent another trader from using his trade mark as the name of a business dealing in goods or services which are identical with or similar to those for which the mark is registered.

(B) 'IN THE COURSE OF TRADE' The phrase 'in the course of trade' was used in both the definition of 'trade mark' and as one of the elements of infringement under the 1938 Act.[8] The phrase does

not form part of the definition of 'trade mark' in the 1994 Act, but
the phrase is adopted in section 10, which provides that the use of
a sign can only constitute an infringement if the use is 'in the
course of trade'.[9] It is logical that the use of a sign will not
constitute an infringement if it is only being used in a domestic,
social or other non-trading manner. Cases under the 1938 Act
which considered the meaning of the phrase 'in the course of
trade' will still be relevant in construing this phrase as it appears
in the 1994 Act.[10]

(C) COMPARING THE DEFENDANT'S SIGN WITH THE REGISTERED TRADE MARK
The comparison for the purposes of section 10(1) will be governed
by the same principles as those relevant to the comparison carried
out pursuant to section 5(1) to determine whether there are grounds
for refusing registration based on a prior conflicting identical mark.
The relevant principles are discussed in chapter 2.[11]

(D) THE MEANING OF THE PHRASE 'IN RELATION TO GOODS OR SERVICES'
The requirement that the defendant must have used a sign 'in
relation to goods or services' for which the proprietor's trade mark
is registered is satisfied even though the defendant may not have
used his sign upon the goods or services themselves and it will be
sufficient if the sign has been used otherwise than by physically
affixing or applying it to the goods or services. This conclusion is
consistent with the interpretation of the same phrase which
appeared in section 4 of the 1938 Act and is the only sensible
interpretation given the wide definition of use in sections 10(4) and
103(2). The meaning of this phrase is also relevant to and
discussed in the context of revocation proceedings for non-use in
chapter 5.[12]

(E) COMPARING THE RELEVANT GOODS OR SERVICES   The final element
of infringement under section 10(1) involves establishing that the
defendant has used a sign in relation to goods or services which are
'identical' with those for which the proprietor's trade mark is
registered. The question as to whether the goods or services are
identical is a question of fact to be answered in the circumstances
of each case and has been considered in the context of
registrability.[13]

Likelihood of confusion   Unlike section 10(2), if the defendant's
use of a sign falls within section 10(1), the plaintiff does not have to

go on to establish a likelihood of confusion or any other element to
prove infringement.

1 Section 10(1).
2 Section 10(4).
3 Article 5(3).
4 See section 68(2) of the 1938 Act.
5 Section 103(2).
6 Paragraphs 3.26 and 3.27.
7 There was a degree of uncertainty under the 1938 Act as to whether such use
  would constitute an infringement: see, for example, the decision of Ploughman J
  in *Autodrome* [1969] RPC 564.
8 Sections 68(1) and 4(1) respectively.
9 'Trade' includes any business or profession and 'business' means 'a trade or
  profession': section 103(1).
10 For a discussion of the meaning of this phrase under the 1938 Act see Kerly, 12th
  edition paragraph 2.14.
11 See paragraph 2.18.
12 See paragraph 5.05.
13 See paragraph 2.18.

**6.05 Identical marks/similar goods or services, s10(2)(a);
similar marks/identical goods or services; similar
marks/similar goods or services, s10(2)(b)** If the defendant
uses a sign which is either not identical with the proprietor's
registered trade mark or if the sign is used in relation to goods or
services which are not identical with those for which the trade mark
is registered, the defendant's acts may nonetheless constitute an
infringement pursuant to sections 10(2) or (3).

For the purposes of section 10(2), the proprietor's exclusive rights
will be infringed by the unauthorised use in the course of trade of a
sign which is either:

(a) identical with the proprietor's registered trade mark, provided
     that the sign is used in relation to goods or services similar to
     those covered by the registration; or

(b) similar to the proprietor's registered trade mark, provided that
     the sign is used in relation to goods or services which are
     identical with or similar to those covered by the registration;
     and

in either case, the proprietor can establish a likelihood of confusion
on the part of the public.

This is a significant extension to the acts which constituted trade
mark infringement under the 1938 Act, in that it was not an
infringement under the 1938 Act to use a trade mark for goods or
services not covered by the registration even if they were of the

same description as the goods or services for which the mark was registered.[1]

Elements of infringement under section 10(2)   A consideration of the elements required to establish infringement under section 10(2) involves looking at the following issues:
(A)   the meaning of the phrase 'uses a sign';
(B)   the meaning of the phrase 'in the course of trade';
(C)   whether the defendant's sign is either identical with or similar to the proprietor's registered trade mark;
(D)   the meaning of the phrase 'in relation to goods or services',
(E)   whether the defendant's goods or services are either identical with or similar to the goods or services for which the proprietor's trade mark is registered; and
(F)   the likelihood of confusion, including the likelihood of association.

(A)   'USES A SIGN'   See the discussion of the meaning of this phrase in paragraph 6.04 above.

(B)   'IN THE COURSE OF TRADE'   See the discussion of the meaning of this phrase in paragraph 6.04 above.

(C)   COMPARING THE DEFENDANT'S SIGN WITH THE REGISTERED TRADE MARK Section 10(2) may apply where the defendant's sign is either identical with or similar to the proprietor's registered trade mark. The question of whether a sign is identical with or similar to the registered trade mark is considered in chapter 2 in relation to the relative grounds for refusing a registration as a result of a conflict with earlier trade mark rights.[2] The White Paper asserts that the test of similarity for the purposes of registrability and infringement is the same.[3]

(D)   THE MEANING OF THE PHRASE 'IN RELATION TO GOODS OR SERVICES' See the discussion of the meaning of this phrase in paragraph 6.04 above.

(E)   COMPARING THE RELEVANT GOODS OR SERVICES   Section 10(2) may apply where the defendant's sign is used in relation to goods or services which are either identical with or similar to those for which the proprietor's trade mark is registered. The question of whether goods or services can be considered to be either identical with or similar to other goods or services is considered in chapter 2 in the context of registrability.[4]

(F) ASSESSING THE LIKELIHOOD OF CONFUSION, INCLUDING THE LIKELIHOOD OF ASSOCIATION   Once again this phrase has been considered in chapter 2 in the context of registrability and, subject to the comments in paragraph 6.07 in relation to the onus of proof, there is no reason to believe that the phrase will not be given the same meaning as accorded to it in the context of section 5.

1 Such use may have amounted to an actionable passing-off.
2 See paragraphs 2.18 and 2.20.
3 Paragraph 3.16.
4 See paragraphs 2.18 and 2.21.

6.06 Identical or similar marks/dissimilar goods or services, s10(3)   Even where a person uses a sign in the course of trade in relation to goods or services which are not similar to those for which a trade mark is registered, he may nonetheless infringe the registration of a trade mark by virtue of section 10(3). In order to establish infringement under this section the proprietor will have to establish:
(a) that the defendant has used a sign in the course of trade:
  (i) which is either identical with or similar to his registered trade mark; and
  (ii) which is used in relation to goods or services which are not similar to those covered by his registration;
(b) that his trade mark has a 'reputation' in the United Kingdom;
(c) that the defendant has used the sign 'without due cause'; and
(d) that such use either:
  (i) takes unfair advantage of, or
  (ii) is detrimental to,
  the distinctive character or the repute of the proprietor's registered trade mark.[1]

Elements of infringement under section 10(3)   A consideration of the elements required to establish infringement under section 10(3) involves looking at the following issues:
(A) the meaning of the phrase 'uses a sign';
(B) the meaning of the phrase 'in the course of trade';
(C) whether the defendant's sign is identical with or similar to the proprietor's registered trade mark;
(D) the meaning of the phrase 'in relation to goods or services';
(E) whether the registered trade mark has the necessary 'reputation' in the United Kingdom;

(F) the concept of what constitutes using a sign 'without due cause';

(G) the meaning of the phrases 'takes unfair advantage of' and 'detrimental to'; and

(H) the meaning of the phrase 'distinctive character or the repute' when used in relation to a trade mark.

Section 10(3) is substantially identical to section 5(3). The issues identified in (A) to (D) above have already been raised in this chapter in the context of sections 10(1) and (2)[2] whereas the issues identified in (E) to (H) are considered in chapter 2 in the context of registrability.[3]

1 Section 10(3).
2 See paragraphs 6.04 and 6.05 and chapter 2.
3 See paragraph 2.23.

6.07 Onus of proof The point has already been made that section 10 is substantially in the same terms as section 5. However, under section 5, if the Registrar is validly to refuse an application for registration, the onus is on him[1] to establish all of the elements specified in section 5(1), (2) or (3) as the case may be.

In contrast, under section 10 the onus is on the plaintiff to establish the elements of infringement.

1 Or, in the context of an application under section 38, the onus will be on the opponent and, in the context of invalidity under section 47, the onus will be on the applicant seeking the declaration.

Secondary infringement

6.08 Parties to use of infringing material, s10(5) Section 10(5) provides that a person who applies a registered trade mark to material intended to be used:

(a) for labelling or packaging goods;

(b) as a business paper; or

(c) for advertising goods or services,

is deemed to be a party to any use of the material which infringes the registered trade mark provided that, when he applied the mark to the material, he knew or had reason to believe that the application of the mark was not authorised by the proprietor or a licensee.

This is a new provision (for which there was no equivalent under the 1938 Act) and it extends the scope of infringement to persons who may be described as accessories or secondary infringers.

The fact that this sub-section only applies to those who know or have reason to believe that the application of the mark was not duly authorised means that the innocent use of a trade mark for labelling, packaging, etc, is not caught by this sub-section. However, in relation to well known marks (whether they be well known for the purposes of section 56(1) or otherwise), it may be more difficult for the person in question to deny actual or constructive knowledge that the application of the mark was not duly authorised by the proprietor in circumstances where he is not dealing with the proprietor or his ostensible agent or licensee. It would therefore be prudent for printers, publishers, packaging manufacturers and others potentially exposed to liability under this section to make reasonable enquiries and/or obtain suitable warranties and indemnities.

Comparative advertising

6.09 Identifying the proprietor's goods or services, s10(6)

The effect of section 10(6) is that any use of a registered trade mark which may otherwise constitute infringement under section 10 will not infringe a registration where:

(a) the use is for the purpose of identifying the goods or services as those of the proprietor or a licensee of the trade mark; and

(b) the use for that purpose is in accordance with honest practices in industrial or commercial matters.

The types of use likely to fall within this section would include the use of a registered trade mark for the purposes of comparative advertising and use in relation to the supply of spare parts or accessories. This sub-section, including in particular the meaning of the phrase 'honest practices in industrial or commercial matters', is dealt with in the context of defences in chapter 7.

If such use of the mark is not in accordance with the relevant honest practices then it will nonetheless be treated as infringing the registered trade mark provided that the use is:

(a) 'without due cause'; and

(b) takes unfair advantage of, or is detrimental to, the distinctive character or repute of the trade mark.

The meaning of these phrases is considered in chapter 2 in the context of registrability. For present purposes it is merely noted for the sake of completeness; we question, however, why it is that the phrase 'distinctive character or repute' used in section 10(6) omits the definite article 'the' as it appears in sections 5(3) and 10(3): surely nothing will turn on this as it must be an oversight.

Licensees

6.10 Rights of licensees The 1994 Act confers rights and remedies on licensees in relation to the infringement of registered trade marks.[1] The scope of these rights and remedies is considered in two chapters:

(a) chapter 8 which deals with the rights and remedies of licensees; and

(b) chapter 10 which deals with the licensing of trade marks.

1 See sections 30 and 31.

Co-proprietors

6.11 Rights of co-proprietors, s23 Infringement proceedings may be brought by any co-proprietor of a registered trade mark. However, without the leave of the court, one co-proprietor may not proceed with an action unless each other co-proprietor is either joined as a plaintiff or added as a defendant, except in the case of an application for interlocutory relief. Where a co-proprietor is added as a defendant he will not be liable for any costs in the action unless he takes part in the proceedings.[1]

Transitional provisions The provisions of section 23 apply as from 31 October 1994, including in relation to trade marks registered under the 1938 Act where two or more persons were registered as joint proprietors.[2]

1 Section 23(5); in the event that the co-proprietor has rights and obligations as a trustee or a personal representative, such rights and obligations are not affected: section 23(6).
2 Schedule 3, paragraph 7.

Threats of infringement proceedings

6.12 Groundless threats, s21 The 1994 Act introduces for the first time into trade mark law in the United Kingdom a new cause of action in respect of groundless threats of infringement proceedings.[1] Accordingly, proprietors and licensees should consider the implications of threatening someone with infringement proceedings. The elements of this cause of action and the relief available are dealt with in chapter 9.

1 Section 21.

7 Limits on effect of registration: defences

7.01 Approach taken by the 1994 Act The proprietor's exclusive rights conferred by registration and the acts amounting to an infringement of these rights have been considered in chapter 6. However, it is necessary to have regard to the defences which may be available before forming a final view as to whether the proprietor's rights have been infringed. It is these defences which are the subject of this chapter.

The 1994 Act does not contain any provisions which are described as defences as such. There are, however, a number of sections which, in effect, provide the basis of a defence. They can broadly be described as:

(a) the statutory limitations on the effect of registration contained in section 11;

(b) the saving in section 10(6) for the use of a registered trade mark for the purpose of identifying goods or services as those of the proprietor;

(c) statutory acquiescence, section 48;

(d) the exhaustion of rights, section 12;

(e) voluntary disclaimers and limitations, section 13; and

(f) the rights conferred on co-proprietors, section 23.

These defences all assume that an act of infringement has otherwise occurred. It will, of course, always be open to the defendant to base his defence on an assertion that one or more of the elements necessary to constitute an infringement for the purposes of section 10 is missing from the plaintiff's case or to establish that the plaintiff's registered trade mark is liable to be revoked or declared invalid.[1]

Transitional provisions The 1938 Act will continue to apply in relation to infringements committed before 31 October 1994. The defences referred to above only apply, therefore, to infringements occurring after that date, including infringements of registrations under the 1938 Act.[2]

In particular, it is not an infringement of either:

(a) a registration under the 1938 Act; or

(b) a trade mark registered under the 1994 Act of which the distinctive elements are substantially the same as those of a trade mark registered under the 1938 Act and which is registered for the same goods or services,

to continue after 31 October 1994 any use of the mark which did not amount to infringement under the old law.[3]

1 ie pursuant to section 46 or 47 respectively: see chapter 5.
2 Schedule 3, paragraph 4(1).
3 Schedule 3, paragraph 4(2).

Statutory limits on the effect of registration

Section 11 contains three sub-sections, each of which specifies quite different circumstances in which a registered trade mark is deemed not to be infringed. It is therefore an absolute defence to an allegation of infringement if the defendant's acts or conduct fall within one or more of these sub-sections.

7.02 Use of a registered trade mark, s11(1) A registered trade mark cannot be infringed by the use of another validly[1] registered trade mark in relation to the goods or services for which the latter is registered.[2] Accordingly, both proprietors will have concurrent rights in the use of their respective trade marks. This provision, in effect, is substantially identical to the corresponding provision in the 1938 Act.[2]

1 See section 47 and chapter 5; if the registration of the trade mark is declared invalid it will be deemed never to have been made: section 47(6).
2 Section 11(1).
3 Section 4(4), 1938 Act.

7.03 Descriptive use, s11(2) Section 11(2) specifies three categories of use which might otherwise constitute infringement. In broad terms they can be summarised as follows:

(a) the use of one's own name or address;
(b) the use of descriptive indications; and
(c) the use of a trade mark to indicate the intended purpose of a product or service.

However, in each case such use may still constitute an infringement unless the use is in accordance with honest practices in industrial or commercial matters. This phrase also appears in section 10(6) which provides a defence where a trade mark is used for the purpose of identifying goods or services as those of the proprietor or a licensee, and the meaning of the phrase is considered in detail in the context of that defence.[1] Specific problems of interpretation will also be raised in the context of each of the defences provided for in section 11(2).

1 See paragraph 7.08.

7.04 'Use of one's own name or address' A registered trade mark is not infringed by someone using their own name or address provided that the use of the name or address is in accordance with honest practices in industrial or commercial matters.[1] This provision substantially mirrors section 8(a) of the 1938 Act which required such use to be bona fide.

The reference to 'honest practices in industrial or commercial matters' in the context of using one's own name or address further highlights one of the problems associated with interpreting and applying this phrase: what happens if there is no practice (honest or otherwise) of using one's own name or address in the defendant's relevant line of business? Presumably, the test will have to be applied by reference to general commercial practices.

1 Section 11(2)(a).

7.05 Use of descriptive indications, s11(2)(b) A registered trade mark is not infringed by someone using an indication concerning any characteristic of goods or services, including an indication of the kind, quality, quantity, intended purpose, value, geographical origin, or the time of production of goods or the rendering of services. Once again, however, the use of the indication must be in accordance with honest practices in industrial or commercial matters.[1] This provision has a certain similarity with the defence in section 8(b) of the 1938 Act[2] which referred to the use of bona fide descriptions of the character or quality of goods.

This limit on the rights conferred by registration is entirely consistent with the absolute grounds for refusing registration contained in section 3(1)(c) except that, per curiam, a registered trade mark will not be infringed by the use of 'indications' which are descriptive in the sense specified whereas the grounds for refusing the registration of a descriptive trade mark relate to 'signs or indications'. Strictly, therefore, the use of a descriptive 'sign' which is not also an 'indication' would not fall within the defence provided in section 11(2)(b). It is assumed that nothing will turn on the omission of the word 'sign' as the words 'sign' and 'indication' arguably are synonymous. After all, it is only the use of a sign which can infringe a registered trade mark[3] and, therefore, there would be no need specifically to exclude from infringement any use of an indication which is not also use of a sign. This is consistent with the words 'signs' and 'indications' being read interchangeably.

1 Section 11(2)(b); however, note the protection separately conferred on geographical indications and designations of origin by the Regulation of 14 July 1992, EEC No 2081/92.
2 Although section 8(b) contains a proviso which is not present in the 1994 Act.
3 Section 10.

7.06 Use of a trade mark to indicate intended purpose: accessories and spare parts, s11(2)(c) A registered trade mark is not infringed by the use of that trade mark where its use is necessary to indicate the intended purpose of a product or service. Once again, however, the use of the trade mark must be in accordance with honest practices in industrial or commercial matters.[1]

The object of this provision is clearly to enable traders in spare parts or accessories to use a registered trade mark so as to identify the goods or services for which their spare parts or accessories are to be used.

This defence is subject to the defendant being able to establish that:

(a) his use of the registered trade mark is *necessary* for the purpose of indicating the intended purpose of his products or services; and

(b) such use is in accordance with honest practices in industrial or commercial matters.

The first limb of this requirement will be difficult to satisfy as the defendant in the majority of cases will not, of necessity, have to use someone else's trade mark so as to identify the intended purpose of his own goods or services. That is, there would in most if not all cases be alternative methods of indicating the intended purpose of his products or services as accessories or spare parts through, for example, the use of descriptive wording or photographs.

However, a trader in spare parts or accessories may not have to rely upon section 11(2)(c). Section 11(2)(b) could instead be relied upon in so far as it also provides a defence in respect of the use of 'indications' concerning the intended purpose of goods or services. The question is whether the reference to 'indications' in section 11(2)(b) will be construed so as to encompass a registered trade mark. Logically, there is no reason why not, as a descriptive indication of the kind listed in section 11(2)(b) may clearly be registered as a trade mark on proof of factual distinctiveness.[2]

Finally, in any event, the defendant will have to establish that his use of the proprietor's trade mark is in accordance with honest practices in industrial or commercial matters. Apart from the issues discussed in paragraph 7.08, the requirement that use of someone else's registered trade mark be in accordance with honest practices will involve considering the issue of whether such use can ever be honest if, in the circumstances of the case, it may involve diluting or devaluing the reputation or goodwill attaching to the registered trade mark.

1 Section 11(2)(c).
2 See the proviso to section 3(1) and paragraph 2.06.

7.07 Use of an earlier right, s11(3) The use in the course of trade of an earlier right will not infringe a registered trade mark in certain circumstances.[1] For this purpose an 'earlier right' means either:

(a) an unregistered trade mark; or
(b) any other sign,

which has been continuously used[2] in relation to goods or services where such use commenced prior to whichever is the earlier of:

(a) the use of the registered trade mark; or

(b) the registration of that registered trade mark.

In essence, this means that someone can continue to use their unregistered trade mark or other sign where it has been used continuously since before both the use and registration of the registered trade mark without infringing that registration. However, the right to continue the use of the earlier right is restricted to use within the particular locality where the earlier right would be protected by virtue of any rule of law, in particular, the law of passing off.[3] The word 'locality' could therefore extend to the whole of the United Kingdom or any part of it.

The general principle which is reflected in sections 7 and 11(3) is that unregistered trade marks should neither be denied registration nor their use be prevented merely because they are similar to or even identical with a subsequently registered trade mark.

Indeed, it can be argued that section 11(3) is too strict, in that in order to constitute a defence it must be shown that the defendant's earlier right is protected by virtue of any rule of law (the 1994 Act specifically cites the law of passing off as an example). This is stricter than either section 7 of the 1994 Act or section 7 of the 1938 Act. Under section 7 of the 1994 Act the only requirement, in order for the applicant to secure registration, is that his use must have been 'honest'. Under section 7 of the 1938 Act, the defence based on the prior use of an unregistered trade mark was established merely by showing actual continuous use. Why, therefore, should section 11(3) require the defendant to establish that the prior use of his trade mark has been of such a nature and to such an extent that he would be able to protect his trade mark by means of a passing-off action or under any other rule of law? This requirement will mean that the defendant may have to adduce evidence, for example, of the reputation/goodwill which he would have to prove in a passing-off action.

It would seem that in so limiting this defence the 1994 Act will, to some extent, result in the United Kingdom becoming a 'first to register' rather than a 'first to use' system and it will be prudent to register one's mark rather than having to rely upon use, which may not always be sufficient to avoid infringement of a later registered trade mark.

1 Section 11(3).
2 Such use may either have been by the person claiming the right or his predecessor in title: section 11(3).
3 Section 11(3).

7.08 Use for the purpose of identifying proprietor's goods or services, s10(6)   The effect of section 10(6) is that any use of a registered trade mark which may otherwise constitute infringement under section 10 will not infringe a registration where:

(a)   the use is for the purposes of identifying the goods or services as those of the proprietor or a licensee of the trade mark; and

(b)   the use for that purpose is in accordance with honest practices in industrial or commercial matters.

The types of use likely to fall within this section would include the use of a registered trade mark for the purposes of comparative advertising and use in relation to the supply of spare parts or accessories.

If such use of the mark is not in accordance with the relevant honest practices, then it will nonetheless be treated as infringing the registered trade mark provided that the use is:

(a)   'without due cause'; and

(b)   takes unfair advantage of, or is detrimental to, the distinctive character or repute of the trade mark.

Honest practices in industrial or commercial matters   Although this phrase at first sight would appear to be rather vague and imprecise, it is assumed that the courts will apply a purposive interpretation so as to give effect to the clear intention of Parliament, namely that comparative advertising (and certain other acts which may otherwise constitute infringement) should be permitted provided that it makes fair use of a registered trade mark for the purpose of informing the public.[1]

Certainly, the phrase could be criticised because each case will have to be decided on its own facts in order to determine whether the use is in accordance with the relevant honest practices.

The word 'honest' is defined in Chambers Concise Dictionary as:

'Truthful; just; fair-dealing; free from fraud; candid; frank . . .'

There should, therefore, be no real difficulty in stating as a matter of principle that a practice will be considered to be honest if it meets these criteria.

What, however, is the situation where there is no relevant existing practice within a particular area of industry or commerce against which the use of the trade mark can be compared in order to judge whether it is either honest or dishonest? Strictly, if there is no existing practice (whether honest or otherwise), then the use will not come within this phrase.

Another issue may arise as to whether the use of the trade mark must be consistent with the honest practices of the industry or area of commerce in which the defendant is engaged. This may be relevant if different standards of honesty and/or different practices are applicable in different industries/areas of commerce.

In the context of comparative advertising there is also a necessary inconsistency created by the fact that such advertising was, effectively, precluded by section 4(1)(b) of the 1938 Act. Accordingly, because such advertising amounted to infringement, arguably it could never have been an honest practice to publish comparative advertisements using another party's registered trade mark. Comparisons using trade marks have, however, been made in many industries for some time, and therefore it may be possible to show that such practices are honest.

Although, as already stated, the meaning of this phrase may initially be somewhat unclear, the courts have always been able to give effect to words and phrases such as 'reasonable' and 'fair dealing' as well as equally imprecise equitable principles or maxims. There is no reason to believe that the courts will have any difficulty in applying the ordinary English words 'honest practice in industrial or commercial matters' to the facts of each case.

1 Per Lord Strathclyde, *Hansard*, House of Lords, Public Bill Committee, 18.1.94, col 42.

7.09 Acquiescence, s48 Statutory acquiescence applies to the situation where the proprietor of either an earlier trade mark[1] or earlier right[2] has acquiesced for a continuous period of five years in the use of a later registered trade mark in the United Kingdom. The proprietor will only be deemed to have acquiesced, however, if he was aware of that use.

In these circumstances the proprietor will not be entitled[3] on the basis of his earlier trade mark or other earlier right to oppose the use of the later registered trade mark in relation to the goods or services for which it has been used.[4]

This section operates as a shield not a sword, because the proprietor of the later registered trade mark will not, by virtue of the earlier proprietor's acquiescence, be entitled to oppose either:

(a) the use of the earlier trade mark; or

(b) the exploitation of the earlier right,
notwithstanding that the earlier proprietor may no longer be able to invoke his rights against the use of the later registered trade mark.[5]

The obvious, but key, point to make is that statutory acquiescence only applies where the acquiescence has been to the use of a registered trade mark. The question is thus one of notice. Section 48(1) uses the phrase 'being aware of that use' rather than 'being aware of that registration'. Presumably, therefore, the fact of registration in the Register will not constitute constructive notice of use for the purposes of establishing statutory acquiescence.

'Oppose the use' Statutory acquiescence only precludes the entitlement of the proprietor of the earlier trade mark/earlier right to 'oppose the use' of the later registered trade mark.[6] A narrow interpretation of this wording would suggest that the acquiescence only prevents the earlier proprietor from obtaining injunctive relief. Will the earlier proprietor also be prevented from claiming damages or other remedies if otherwise available? Surely, the narrow interpretation cannot be right as it would lead to the absurd result that the earlier proprietor would be entitled to seek damages (even on-going damages) while not being able to prevent the on-going use.

Presumably, the phrase 'oppose the use' will be interpreted so as to deny the earlier proprietor the right to commence any proceedings in respect of the use of the registered trade mark.

1 As defined in section 6.
2 As defined in section 5(4).
3 The entitlement is not lost if the trade mark was registered in bad faith: section 48(1).
4 Section 48(1)(b); the proprietor also ceases to be entitled to apply for a declaration of invalidity: section 48(1)(a).
5 Section 48(2).
6 Section 48(1)(b).

7.10 Equitable acquiescence and consent Clearly, section 48(1) does not purport to be an exhaustive statement of the law of acquiescence and, therefore, one assumes that equitable doctrines of acquiescence, delay and consent have not been excluded. In any event, anything done with the consent of the proprietor of the registered trade mark will not infringe his exclusive rights.[1]

1 Section 9(1).

7.11   Exhaustion of rights, s12   In accordance with Community law[1] and cases decided thereunder[2] a registered trade mark will not be infringed by the use of the trade mark in relation to goods which have been put on the market in the European Economic Area under that trade mark by the proprietor or with his consent.[3]

Although this principle is in accordance with Community law, it clearly does not purport to codify the substantial body of case law which has developed over the last 25 years. It is beyond the scope of this book to discuss the free circulation rules and other numerous contentious issues which abound in this area.

The practical effect of section 12(1) is that, subject to the proviso discussed below, a proprietor of a United Kingdom trade mark registration cannot rely upon that registration to prevent the importation into the United Kingdom of goods which have been circulated in the European Economic Area under that trade mark by him or with his consent.

The proviso   The exhaustion principle referred to above does not apply where the proprietor can establish that there are 'legitimate reasons' for him to oppose further dealings in the goods.[4] This is also consistent with Community law on this subject, which enables a proprietor to prevent the use of his trade mark where the original condition of the goods put on the market by him has been changed or impaired without his consent.

1   The EEC Treaty: Articles 30 and 34.
2   For example, *Terrapin v Terranova* [1976] 2 CMLR 482; *Merck v Stephar* [1981] 3 CMLR 463; *Hag II* [1991] FSR 99; *Revlon* [1980] FSR 80.
3   Section 12(1).
4   Section 12(2).

7.12   Disclaimers and limitations, s13   It will be a defence to an action for infringement if the defendant's use of a sign falls within any disclaimer or limitation to the rights conferred by the registration.[1]

1   See section 13(1).

7.13   Rights of co-proprietors, s23(3)   A co-proprietor can do anything which would otherwise amount to an infringement of the registered trade mark subject only to any agreement between the co-proprietors to the contrary.[1] Thus, each co-proprietor is entitled to do any act[2] which would otherwise amount to an infringement without obtaining the consent of, or even the need to account to, his co-proprietor(s).[3]

Transitional provisions In relation to joint proprietors under the 1938 Act, whose relationship is as described in section 63 of the 1938 Act, it is deemed that there is an agreement to exclude the operation of section 23(3) of the 1994 Act and, accordingly, such co-proprietors are only able to do acts which would otherwise amount to an infringement of their registered trade mark with the consent of their co-proprietor(s).[4]

1 Section 23(3).
2 A co-proprietor does, however, need to obtain the consent of his co-proprietor(s) in respect of licensing or assigning the trade mark: section 23(4).
3 Section 23(3): he may also appoint agents to do any such acts.
4 Schedule 3, paragraph 7.

8 Remedies for infringement

8.01 Approach taken by the 1994 Act In chapter 6 the acts constituting infringement under the 1994 Act were considered. This chapter now sets out the remedies which may be available to the proprietor in respect of an infringement of his registration.

An infringement of a registered trade mark[1] is actionable by the proprietor of the trade mark[2] and, upon proof of infringement, the proprietor is entitled to those remedies provided for in the 1994 Act.[3] Those remedies are:

(a) pursuant to section 14(2):
   (i) damages;
   (ii) an account of profits;
   (iii) injunctive relief; and
   (iv) any other relief which would be available in respect of the infringement of any other property right;
(b) pursuant to section 15(1), the erasure, removal or obliteration of an 'offending sign';
(c) pursuant to section 15(2), the destruction of infringing goods;
(d) pursuant to section 16, the delivery up of infringing goods, material or articles; and
(e) pursuant to section 19(1), the destruction or forfeiture of infringing goods, material or articles.

The 1994 Act also provides special remedies in the case of:
(a) the importation of infringing goods, material or articles in respect of which a section 89 notice has been given to Customs and Excise;[4]

(b) the misuse of well known trade marks;[5] and

(c) an agent or representative of the proprietor of a mark making an unauthorised application for the registration of the mark.[6]

Each of these remedies is considered in turn in this chapter including, at the end of the chapter, in the context of the special provisions relating to co-proprietors and licensees. Many of the remedies, however, are not peculiar to the infringement of a registered trade mark and therefore readers should also refer to specialist works on the subject of remedies.

The remedies available to the proprietor can be split into two categories:

(a) general remedies, which will be available in accordance with established common law and equitable principles;[7] and

(b) statutory remedies, the availability of which is governed specifically by the 1994 Act.[8]

1 No proceedings lie under the 1994 Act in respect of the infringement of an unregistered trade mark: section 2(2).
2 Section 14(1); or by an exclusive licensee: section 31(1) and (2) and see paragraph 8.21 et seq.
3 Section 2(1).
4 Section 89(2).
5 Section 56(2).
6 Section 60.
7 Section 14(2).
8 Sections 15, 16, 19, 56, 60 and 89.

General remedies

8.02 Damages, s14(2) The proprietor of a registered trade mark is entitled as of right to recover damages in respect of any infringement of his trade mark.[1]

His entitlement to and the assessment of such damages will be determined in accordance with the established principles governing any infringement of an intellectual property right. Damages are a common law remedy and the proprietor will be entitled to recover his damages on proof of infringement. The quantum of damages recoverable will be a matter for the court to determine[2] based upon the evidence adduced. Ultimately, damages for infringement of a registered trade mark are calculated on the basis that the objective is to put the proprietor into the position that he would have been in had the infringement not occurred. The court will therefore make an award based on the particular circumstances of the case in order to achieve this objective.

The proprietor may, as an alternative to recovering his damages, elect to seek an account of the profits made by the defendant as a result of the defendant's infringement.[3]

Examples of calculating damages The quantum of damages is often assessed by reference to the amount of money which would constitute a reasonable licence fee. In this context, a reasonable licence fee is the amount that objectively represents what a reasonable licensee would have been prepared to pay and what a reasonable licensor would have been prepared to accept, had a licence been negotiated in respect of the defendant's use of the proprietor's trade mark.

Alternatively, the proprietor may be able to show that the defendant's sales of infringing goods have resulted in lost sales for the proprietor and the proprietor can, in these circumstances, recover the profits which he would have made on the lost sales. However, it is very unlikely that every infringing sale will be credited to the plaintiff when assessing damages on a loss of sales basis.[4]

Furthermore, damages may also be awarded where the defendant's infringing goods are of an inferior quality to those of the proprietor. Damages are therefore awarded to compensate the proprietor for the injury to the goodwill attaching to his trade mark.

1 Section 14(2).
2 Usually assessed by a Master.
3 See paragraph 8.03.
4 See the discussion of this problem in *Dormeuil v Feraglow* [1990] RPC 449.

8.03 Account of profits, s14(2) An account of profits is an alternative remedy to damages. It is an equitable remedy and the order of an account will be governed by the usual equitable principles. In particular, any order will be at the discretion of the court. For example, the defendant's knowledge of the proprietor's registration may affect the making of the order for an account of profits and/or the quantum of the award. The court will also have regard to any delay by the proprietor in bringing the proceedings and/or any acquiescence to the defendant's conduct.[1]

The proprietor must elect either to recover his damages or to receive an account of the defendant's profits at the conclusion of the hearing as to liability. The court[2] will then hear evidence either as to the proprietor's damages[3] or as to the defendant's profits, and will make an award accordingly.

1 Including statutory acquiescence: section 48; or equitable acquiescence.
2 Usually a Master.
3 Referred to as an 'inquiry as to damages'.

8.04 Injunctions, s14(2) The 1994 Act refers in section 14(2) to 'injunctions' which must include both interim and final injunctions. An injunction can be obtained in addition to either an award of damages or an account of profits. Furthermore, an injunction can be sought prior to the commencement by the defendant of any actual acts constituting infringement, provided that there is some threat or likelihood that the infringing acts will be commenced, continued or repeated.

The grant of an injunction is also an equitable remedy and therefore, like an account of profits, will be subject to the usual equitable principles, including delay and acquiescence.[1]

In order to obtain an interim (or interlocutory) injunction, the proprietor must establish that he has a good arguable case and that the balance of convenience favours the grant of an injunction. That is, that the potential harm to the proprietor if the defendant's conduct is allowed to commence or continue outweighs the likely harm to the defendant if the injunction were wrongly to be granted and, subsequently at any full trial, discharged by the court.

A proprietor seeking an interim injunction will have to give the usual undertaking as to damages, which means that if the interim injunction is subsequently discharged he may have to compensate the defendant in respect of any damages suffered by the defendant during the period of and arising out of the injunction. The undertaking as to damages is therefore potentially extremely onerous as the grant of an interim injunction may have the effect of putting the defendant out of business. In some cases, the plaintiff seeking an interim injunction is required to fortify his undertaking by putting up security for the damage which the defendant may suffer.

A final injunction will only be granted if the defendant is found to have infringed the proprietor's trade mark following the hearing of all the evidence at the full trial. Of course, the issue of balance of convenience is irrelevant in issuing a final injunction, but other relevant factors which affect the grant of equitable relief will be applicable.

1 Including statutory acquiescence: section 48(2); and equitable acquiescence.

8.05   Any other relief, s14(2)   The 1994 Act, although expressly referring to damages, injunctions and an account of profits, does not limit the remedies available to the proprietor and confirms that he is entitled to all such other relief as is available in respect of the infringement of any other property right.[1]

This is clearly intended to be a 'catch-all' provision, although the most frequently sought and certainly the most practical remedies are those which have already been mentioned, namely damages or an account of profits and an injunction. Indeed, it is difficult to think of any other relief to which a proprietor would be entitled in respect of the infringement of another property right, except, of course, those expressly provided for elsewhere in the 1994 Act. These remedies are considered below.

1   Section 14(2).

Statutory remedies

8.06   Infringing goods, material and articles, s17   The remedies of erasure,[1] delivery up,[2] destruction and forfeiture,[3] and the giving of notice to Customs and Excise under section 89, are only available in respect of infringing goods, material or articles in the possession, custody or control of the defendant.[4]

Accordingly, it is necessary first to consider the meaning of each of the three terms:

(a) 'infringing goods', section 17(2);
(b) 'infringing material', section 17(4); and
(c) 'infringing articles', section 17(5).

'Infringing goods', s17(2)   Goods are 'infringing goods' if they (or their packaging) bear a sign which is identical with or similar to a registered trade mark and either:

(a) the application of the sign to the goods or to their packaging was itself an infringement of the trade mark; or
(b) the goods are proposed to be imported into the United Kingdom and the application of the sign to the goods or to their packaging would have been an infringement of the trade mark if the application had occurred in the United Kingdom;[5] or
(c) the use of the sign otherwise constitutes an infringement of the trade mark.[6]

'Infringing material', s17(4) Material is 'infringing material' if it bears a sign which is identical with or similar to a registered trade mark and either:

(a) the material is used:
  (i) for labelling or packaging goods;
  (ii) as a business paper; or
  (iii) for advertising goods or services,
  provided that the material is used in such a way as to infringe the trade mark;[7] or
(b) the material is intended to be so used and such use would infringe the registered trade mark.[8]

'Infringing articles', s17(5) Articles are 'infringing articles' if they:
(a) are specifically designed or adapted for making copies of a sign which is identical with or similar to a registered trade mark; and
(b) are in the possession, custody or control of a person who knows or has reason to believe that such articles either have been or are to be used to produce infringing goods or material.[9]

The requirement that the article be 'specifically designed or adapted' for the purpose of making copies of a sign will be too onerous for many trade mark owners as, for example, the tools of trade of a counterfeiter may have many uses other than the copying of trade marks.

1 Section 15; and see paragraph 8.07.
2 Section 16; and see paragraph 8.09.
3 Section 15; and see paragraph 8.08.
4 A notice under section 89 must be in respect of goods, material or articles but they need not be in the possession, custody or control of the defendant.
5 But this will not affect the importation of goods which are lawfully imported into the UK by virtue of an enforceable Community right: section 17(3). This must be a reference to traders' rights derived from the effect of Articles 30 and 34 of the EEC Treaty; as to the definition of United Kingdom see sections 107 and 108.
6 Section 17(2).
7 Section 17(4)(a).
8 Section 17(4)(b).
9 Section 17(5).

8.07 Erasure, removal or obliteration, s15(1)(a) Where the proprietor has established that the defendant has infringed his trade mark the court may make an order requiring the defendant to erase, remove or obliterate the offending sign from any infringing goods, material or articles which are in the defendant's possession, custody or control.[1]

If appropriate, the court may instead order that the infringing goods, material or articles be delivered up to a person nominated by the court for that person to erase, remove or obliterate the sign. Such an order can only be made if the original order for erasure, removal or obliteration has not been complied with by the defendant or if it appears to the court that it is likely that such an order will not be complied with by the defendant.[2]

1 Section 15(1)(a).
2 Section 15(2).

8.08 Destruction, s15(1)(b) If the remedy referred to above of erasure, removal or obliteration is, in the circumstances of the case, not reasonably practicable, the court may instead order the defendant to arrange for the destruction of the infringing goods, material or articles in question.[1]

Once again, where necessary, the court may instead order that the infringing goods, material or articles be delivered up to another person for destruction, but only if the defendant has not complied with the original order or if it appears to the court that the defendant is unlikely to comply with the order.[2]

This will be a useful (if not essential) remedy where the mark is integral to the goods, for example where the mark consists of the shape of the goods themselves.

1 Section 15(1)(b).
2 Section 15(2).

8.09 Delivery up, s16 Another alternative is for the proprietor to apply to the court[1] for an order for the delivery up of infringing goods, material or articles. However, such an order may only be granted in respect of infringing goods, material or articles which a person has in his possession, custody or control in the course of business[2] and provided that:

(a) the proprietor's application is made before the end of the statutory limitation period specified in section 18;[3] and

(b) the court also makes or there are grounds for making an order under section 19 for the disposal of the infringing goods, material or articles.[4]

The order for delivery up can be made against someone other than the person who has infringed the proprietor's trade mark, provided only that that person has infringing goods, material or articles in his possession, custody or control in the course of a business.

Furthermore, the court may order that the delivery up be made either to the proprietor or to any other person. Such an order can, however, only be made pursuant to a specific application made by the proprietor[5] and therefore the proprietor should consider whether it is appropriate to apply, in the alternative to an order for delivery up to himself, for an order for delivery up to 'such other person as the court may direct'. This may be appropriate if there is any reason for the court not to make an order for delivery up to the proprietor himself.

The infringing goods, material or articles which have been delivered up will become the property of the person to whom they are delivered up. That person may do with them as he likes subject to any order of the court and provided that he must retain them pending the making of an order for their disposal.[6]

1 In Scotland, the application may be brought in the sheriff court; in Northern Ireland, the application may be brought in the county court: section 20.
2 Section 16(1); 'business' includes any trade or profession: section 103(1).
3 Section 16(2); and see paragraph 8.10.
4 Section 16(2); and see paragraph 8.11.
5 This follows from the fact that section 16(1) confers the right on the proprietor and does not appear to confer an inherent right on the court itself to make the order: see section 16(1) and distinguish the wording from section 15(1).
6 Section 16(3); ie, an order under section 19, or pending a formal decision not to make any order under section 19; see also paragraph 8.11 in relation to orders under section 19.

8.10 Limitation period, s18 Any application for an order for delivery up under section 16 must be made within the statutory limitation period, which is a period of six years calculated from a date which may vary depending on whether one is seeking the delivery up of either goods or material or articles.[1]

Goods In the case of infringing goods, the six year period commences on the date on which the trade mark was applied to the goods or their packaging.[2]

Material In the case of infringing material, the period commences on the date on which the trade mark was applied to the material.[3]

Articles In the case of infringing articles, the period commences on the date on which they were made.[4]

Exceptions In each case these dates are subject to two specific exceptions. These exceptions apply where the proprietor of the registered trade mark, during the whole or part of the limitation period, is either:

(a) under a disability;[5] or

(b) prevented from discovering the facts entitling him to apply for an order for delivery up as the result of fraud or concealment.[6]

In either of these circumstances an application for delivery up may be made at any time before the end of the six year period calculated from the date on which the proprietor:

(a) ceased to be under the disability; or

(b) could with reasonable diligence have discovered the facts entitling him to apply for an order for delivery up,[7] as the case may be.

1 Section 18(1).
2 Section 18(1)(a).
3 Section 18(1)(b).
4 Section 18(1)(c).
5 Definition: see section 18(3).
6 Section 18(2).
7 Section 18(2).

8.11 Order as to disposal of infringing goods, material or articles, s19 Following the delivery up of infringing goods, material or articles pursuant to an order under section 16, a further application may be made to the court[1] for either:

(a) an order that they be either:

　(i) destroyed; or

　(ii) forfeited to such person as the court may think fit; or

(b) a formal decision that no order as to destruction or forfeiture be made,[2] in which case the person in whose possession, custody or control the goods, material or articles were before being delivered up will be entitled to their return.[3]

Thus the defendant can recover the goods, material or articles by making an application for a decision that no order be made for their destruction or forfeiture. In considering whether to make an order for their destruction or forfeiture, the court will have regard to whether other remedies are available which would be adequate to compensate and to protect the interests of the proprietor (and any licensee).[4]

Accordingly, if the court considers damages to be an adequate remedy, then it may decide to make no order as to destruction or forfeiture provided that the proprietor's interests are or will otherwise be protected. If so, the defendant will be entitled to the return of the goods, material or articles in question.[5]

1 In Scotland, the application may be made in the sheriff court; in Northern
   Ireland, the application may be made in the county court: section 20.
2 Section 19(1).
3 Section 19(5).
4 Section 19(2).
5 Section 19(5).

**8.12 Persons having an interest in the infringing goods,
material or articles, s19(3)** The 1994 Act enables rules of court
to be made to establish the procedure whereby persons having an
interest[1] in the infringing goods, material or articles:

(a) must be notified of; and

(b) will be entitled to appear and to appeal in respect of,

any proceedings for an order for their destruction or forfeiture.[2] Any
order under section 19 will not take effect until the end of the period
within which the person interested is entitled to appeal and, if an
appeal is made, the order will not take effect until the appeal is
finally disposed of.[3]

If more than one person is interested in the relevant goods,
material or articles, then the court will make an order as it thinks just.[4]

1 As to those persons who have such an interest see section 19(6).
2 Section 19(3).
3 Section 19(3).
4 Section 19(4).

Section 89 notice

**8.13 Importation of infringing goods, material or
articles, ss89 and 90** In order to try to stop the importation
of prohibited goods into the United Kingdom, the proprietor of
a registered trade mark (or his licensee) may notify the
Commissioners of Customs and Excise (Customs) in writing:

(a) that he is the proprietor (or, as the case may be, a licensee) of
     the trade mark; and

(b) that infringing goods, material or articles are expected to arrive
     in the United Kingdom either:

    (i) from outside the European Economic Area (EEA); or

    (ii) from within the EEA but not having been in free circulation
     in the EEA.

8.13 *Remedies for infringement*

The notice must specify the time and place of the expected arrival in the United Kingdom of the relevant infringing goods, material or articles. Provided that the proprietor can supply all of this information he may request Customs to treat the infringing goods, material or articles as 'prohibited goods'.[1] Prohibited goods may not be imported into the United Kingdom and are liable to forfeiture.[2]

Council Regulation (EEC) No 3842/86 A proprietor cannot lodge a section 89 notice with Customs where he is entitled to lodge an application under Article 3(1) of the Counterfeit Goods Regulation.[3] Article 3(1) of that Regulation reads as follows:

'In each Member State, a trade mark owner may lodge an application in writing with the competent authorities for suspension by the Customs authorities of the release of counterfeit goods entered for free circulation in that Member State where he has valid grounds for suspecting that the importation of such counterfeit goods is contemplated in that Member State.'

The Regulation will shortly be repealed and replaced with a new Regulation which will, when it comes into force, relate to both counterfeit goods and pirated goods. The present draft of Article 3(1) of the new Regulation (which may be amended before coming into force) reads as follows:

'In each Member State, an owner or holder of a right may lodge an application in writing with the competent authority for the release of counterfeit or pirated goods entered for free circulation or for export in that Member State to be refused by the Customs authorities or for the seizure of such goods where they are carried to that Member State under a transit procedure, where he has valid grounds for suspecting that the importation, exportation or carriage under a transit procedure of such counterfeit or pirated goods is contemplated in the Member State.'

For the purposes of this Article, 'entered for free circulation' and 'for export' mean entered on the basis of declarations made in writing or orally or by other means.

1 Section 89(1).
2 Section 89(2); no other penalty is applicable and the prohibition does not apply to goods imported for private or domestic use.
3 Council Regulation (EEC) No 3842/86 of 1 December 1986 published in the Official Journal on 18 December 1986, number L357/1, as amended or replaced: section 103(3).

8.14 Regulations, s90 Customs have been authorised under
section 90 to make regulations as to the giving of a section 89 notice.
The regulations may specify the evidence which Customs will
require in support of the section 89 notice[1] and may also deal with
matters such as:
(a) the fees to be paid by the proprietor for lodging the notice;
(b) the giving of security by the proprietor to cover Customs'
potential liability or expenses; and
(c) the giving of an indemnity by the proprietor.[2]
As at 31 October 1994 no such regulations had been made but it is
expected that they will be published in draft shortly.

1 Section 90(1).
2 Section 90(2).

Well known trade marks

8.15 Injunction, s56(2) The proprietor of a well known trade
mark[1] is entitled[2] to an injunction to restrain the use in the United
Kingdom of a trade mark which, or the essential part of which:
(a) is either identical with or similar to the proprietor's well known
trade mark; and
(b) is used in respect of identical or similar goods or services to
those for which the proprietor's well known trade mark is
entitled to protection (ie those for which it is well known),
provided that the use by the defendant is likely to cause confusion.[3]

The availability of an injunction under this provision is not
dependent upon establishing infringement as such but nonetheless
involves establishing what would constitute infringement under
section 10(1) or (2) of the 1994 Act. However, unlike an action for
infringement where the sign in question is identical with the
registered trade mark and is used in respect of identical goods or
services,[4] the proprietor of the well known mark must, even in such
circumstances, establish that the defendant's use of the mark is
likely to cause confusion. Strictly, this means that the proprietor of
the well known mark will be put to proof of the likelihood of
confusion even if the defendant is using an identical mark on
identical goods or services. Presumably, however, the likelihood of
confusion will be more easily established (or even inferred by the
court) in the case of the use of a mark which is identical with the

well known trade mark in relation to identical goods or services for which the well known mark is protected.

A trade mark   Section 56(2) enables the proprietor of a well known trade mark to obtain an injunction against the use in the United Kingdom of 'a trade mark'. Logically, the reference to a trade mark means that the mere use of a sign is not sufficient unless that sign falls within the definition of 'trade mark' in section 1(1). Limiting the remedy under section 56(2) to the use by the defendant of a trade mark is inconsistent with section 10, which makes it an infringement of a registered trade mark to use a 'sign' in any of the circumstances provided for in section 10.

Another point of interest arises because the reference to 'trade mark' must necessarily include registered trade marks. Hence, the position must be that the proprietor of a well known trade mark can enjoin the use of a registered trade mark if such use otherwise falls within section 56(2). This is confirmed by the proviso at the end of the sub-section which provides that the right to the injunction is subject to section 48[5] which only applies in relation to acquiescence in the use of a registered trade mark. However, the proprietor of the registered trade mark will not be able to rely on the defence afforded by section 11(1) because that defence is only available in an action for the infringement of a registered trade mark: an injunction under section 56(2) is not founded on such an action. This means that the proprietor of a well known trade mark takes priority over a registered trade mark in the event that there is a conflict and the proprietor of the registered trade mark cannot rely on his registration to defeat an application for an injunction based on a well known trade mark. Indeed, none of the statutory defences available to a defendant in an action for infringement are available to defeat such an application except for acquiescence and bona fide prior use.

Essential part of a trade mark   It is sufficient for the grant of an injunction under section 56(2) if the 'essential part' of the defendant's trade mark is either identical with or similar to the well known trade mark.[6] Presumably, the 'essential part' of the defendant's mark will be the distinctive element(s) of the mark which distinguish the goods or services to which it is applied. It may be the case that one or more elements of the well known trade mark can be identified as being the feature(s) which make the mark 'well known' for the purpose of comparing the well known trade mark with the defendant's mark. If the defendant's mark contains one or more of these elements, then it can be argued strongly that its 'essential part' is at least similar to that of the well known trade mark.

Likely to cause confusion   The wording of the requirement that the defendant's use must be 'likely to cause confusion' is similar but not identical to the requirement in section 10(2) where, in order to constitute an infringement of a registered trade mark, the use of the defendant's mark must give rise to 'a likelihood of confusion on the part of the public . . .'[7]

Exceptions   The entitlement of the proprietor of a well known trade mark to an injunction under section 56(2) is subject to two exceptions, namely:

(a) where there has been acquiescence by the proprietor of the well known trade mark;[8] and

(b) where there has been bona fide use of the mark by the defendant prior to 31 October 1994, being the date of the commencement of section 56.[9]

---

1 ie: a mark which is entitled to protection under the Paris Convention as a well known mark: see the definition in section 56(1); see also chapter 1.
2 Subject to any statutory acquiescence: section 48, as to which, see paragraph 8.16.
3 Section 56(2).
4 ie: an infringement under section 10(1).
5 ie: acquiescence by the proprietor.
6 Provided, of course, that the other elements are satisfied.
7 See paragraph 2.22 in relation to this phrase which also appears in sections 10(2) and 5(2).
8 As to which, see paragraph 8.16.
9 As to which, see paragraph 8.17.

8.16 Acquiescence, ss48 and 56(2)   Statutory acquiescence under section 48 applies to the proprietors of an 'earlier trade mark' which, by virtue of the definition in section 6, will include the proprietor of a well known trade mark. Thus, the proprietor of a well known trade mark will not be entitled to an injunction under section 56(2) to restrain the use of a registered trade mark where the proprietor:

(a) has acquiesced for a continuous period of five years to the use of the registered trade mark in the United Kingdom; and

(b) was aware of that use.

As an exception to the exception, the injunction will always be available, despite the proprietor's acquiescence, where the original registration of the trade mark was applied for in bad faith.[1]

1 Section 48(1)(b); see chapter 7 for further comments on statutory acquiescence.

8.17   Saving for existing bona fide use, s56(3)   An injunction will not be granted under section 56(2) to prevent the continuation of any bona fide use of a trade mark (whether registered or unregistered), provided that such use commenced prior to 31 October 1994, being the date on which section 56 came into force.[1] Section 100 makes it clear that the onus is on the proprietor of a registered trade mark to show the use to which the mark has been put and, presumably, the same onus will be on the proprietor of an unregistered trade mark who seeks to rely on the exception set out in section 56(3).

Contrast also the more appropriate requirement of prior 'bona fide' use with the requirement under section 11(3) where, to constitute a defence to infringement based on the use of an earlier right, the proprietor must be able to establish that the use of his earlier right is 'protected by virtue of any rule of law (in particular, the law of passing off)'.

1 Section 56(3).

Agents and representatives

8.18   Unauthorised acts of agents or representatives, s60
The proprietor of a trade mark in a Convention country,[1] in addition to being able to oppose an application for the registration of his trade mark made by his agent(s) or representative(s),[2] may also (where such an application has been made) obtain an injunction to restrain any unauthorised use of his trade mark in the United Kingdom. The injunction will not be granted, however, if either:
(a) the agent or representative can justify his action;[3] or
(b) the proprietor of the trade mark has acquiesced to the use of his mark in the United Kingdom for a continuous period of at least three years.[4]
The proprietor can enjoin the unauthorised use of his trade mark by any party but, curiously, the injunction can only be granted under section 60(4) once an application for registration of his trade mark has been made by either his agent(s) or representative(s).[5]

Section 60 of the 1994 Act is based on and purports to implement the terms of Article 6*septies* of the Paris Convention, which also requires an unauthorised application for registration to have been made by an agent or representative before the proprietor can obtain injunctive relief under Article 6*septies*.

1 ie: a country other than the United Kingdom which is a party to the Paris Convention: section 55(1).
2 Section 60(2); the proprietor may also apply for a declaration of invalidity of any subsequent registration or, alternatively, apply for rectification so as to substitute his name as the registered proprietor for that of his agent/representative: section 60(3); see chapter 5 as to invalidity and chapter 3 as to rectification.
3 Section 60(5); as to which, see paragraph 8.19.
4 Section 60(6).
5 Section 60(1).

8.19 Justification, s60(5) An injunction under section 60(4) will not be granted to the proprietor of the mark if, or to the extent that, the agent or representative justifies his action.[1]

A number of points need to be made concerning this proviso.

'Justifies his action' Obvious ways in which the agent or representative could seek to justify his action would be to rely on either:

(a) an express or implied authorisation, whether contractual or otherwise; or

(b) a claim to be the proprietor of the trade mark in the United Kingdom.

What is it, though, that the agent or representative must 'justify'? In the context of section 60(4), the injunction sought will be in respect of the use made of the proprietor's trade mark, and therefore the 'action' which the agent or representative must justify is his use of the trade mark. This will not be the case in the context of sections 60(2) and (3) where the 'action' which the agent or representative will need to justify is the making of the application for registration.

'Restrain any use' The injunction available to the proprietor under section 60(4) can extend to 'any use' of the proprietor's trade mark which is not authorised by him. Accordingly, the injunction can extend to third parties other than the proprietor's agents or representatives. The proviso in section 60(5), however, only expressly refers to the agents or representatives justifying their action and therefore does not apply for the benefit of such third parties. This may not be significant, however, as an injunction,

being an equitable remedy, arguably would not be granted by the court in any event if the defendant could justify his action, even though he would not be relying specifically on the statutory proviso.

1 Section 60(5).

Co-proprietors

8.20 Co-proprietors, s23 Co-proprietors, subject to any agreement between them to the contrary, are entitled to an equal undivided share in the registered trade mark.[1] Accordingly, any pecuniary remedy which co-proprietors may be awarded in respect of the infringement of their trade mark will be shared equally.

It will therefore be advisable for a co-proprietor who brings infringement proceedings by himself[2] to reach an agreement in advance with his co-proprietor(s) as to the apportionment of any pecuniary remedy which may be awarded in respect of the infringement.

1 Section 23(1).
2 ie: in accordance with section 23(5).

Licensees

8.21 Introduction, ss30 and 31 The position of a licensee in the context of considering remedies for infringement will depend upon whether:

(a) the licensee is the plaintiff suing for the infringement of his licensor's registered trade mark; or

(b) the licensor/proprietor is the plaintiff and the licensee has suffered or is likely to suffer loss.

Reference should also be made to chapter 10 on the subject of licensing in general.

8.22 Licensee as the plaintiff One further needs to distinguish between licensees generally and those exclusive licensees who have the rights and remedies of an assignee.

Licensees generally Licensees generally[1] are given a statutory entitlement[2] to bring proceedings in their own name if the proprietor[3] refuses or fails to do so within two months of being called upon by his licensee.[4]

In these circumstances, the licensee may bring proceedings in his own name as if he were the proprietor.[5] Therefore, he will have the same rights and remedies to which the proprietor would have been entitled had the proprietor himself commenced the proceedings. This does not mean, of course, that the licensee can recover damages suffered by the proprietor; the licensee will only be able to recover damages which he himself has suffered.

Exclusive licensees It is necessary to consider separately the position of exclusive licensees[6] who, pursuant to the terms of their exclusive licence,[7] have the same rights and remedies in respect of matters occurring after the grant of the licence as if the licence had been an assignment. Such exclusive licensees may bring infringement proceedings against any person (other than the proprietor) in their own name,[8] and their rights and remedies are deemed to be concurrent with those of the proprietor.[9] Some of the effects of 'concurrency' are that, in an action for infringement:

(a) the court, in assessing damages, will take into account:
   (i) the terms of the licence; and
   (ii) any pecuniary remedy already awarded or available to either of them in respect of the infringement;[10]
(b) no account of profits will be directed by the court if either:
   (i) an award of damages has been made; or
   (ii) an account of profits has been directed,
  in favour of the other of them in respect of the same infringement;[11] and
(c) the court will, if an account of profits is directed, apportion those profits between the proprietor and the exclusive licensee as the court considers just.[12]

These conditions apply to any action for infringement in respect of which the proprietor and an exclusive licensee have or had concurrent rights, regardless of whether they are both parties to the proceedings. If not, the court will make directions as it thinks fit as to how the party to the proceedings is to hold the proceeds of any pecuniary remedy on behalf of the other.

1 Including exclusive licensees not having the rights and remedies of an assignee under section 31(1), as well as sub-licensees in the case of an exclusive licensee having the rights and remedies of an assignee: section 30(7).
2 Section 30(2), subject to the terms of the licence.

3 Or an exclusive licensee who has the rights and remedies of an assignee: section 30(7).
4 Section 30(3).
5 Section 30(3); the proprietor himself will need to be joined as a plaintiff or added as a defendant: section 30(4); but not in the case of an application for interlocutory relief which can be made by the licensee alone: section 30(4).
6 Definition, see section 29(1).
7 Definition, see section 29(1).
8 Section 31(1); the proprietor himself will need to be joined as a plaintiff or added as a defendant: section 31(4), but not in the case of an application for interlocutory relief which can be made by the licensee alone: section 31(4).
9 Section 31(2).
10 Section 31(6)(a).
11 Section 31(6)(b).
12 Section 31(6)(c); subject to any agreement between the proprietor and the licensee: section 31(6)(c) and section 31(8).

8.23   Proprietor as the plaintiff   Once again, one must distinguish between licensees generally and those exclusive licensees who have the rights and remedies of an assignee.

Licensees generally   In infringement proceedings brought by the proprietor, any loss suffered or likely to be suffered by licensees[1] will be taken into account and the court will give directions as it thinks fit as to the extent to which the proprietor is to hold the proceeds of any pecuniary remedy on behalf of licensees.[2]

Exclusive licensees   The position of an exclusive licensee who has, pursuant to the terms of his licence, the rights and remedies of an assignee, is that if the proprietor and the exclusive licensee are not both parties to the proceedings, then the court will give directions as it thinks fit as to the extent to which the party to the proceedings is to hold the proceeds of any pecuniary remedy on behalf of the other.[3]

1 Including exclusive licensees not having the rights and remedies of an assignee under section 31(1), as well as sub-licensees in the case of an exclusive licensee having the rights and remedies of an assignee: section 30(7).
2 Section 30(6).
3 Section 31(6).

8.24   Remedy for groundless threats, s21   The 1994 Act introduces for the first time in trade mark legislation in the United Kingdom a remedy for groundless threats of infringement proceedings. However, this is not a remedy for the infringement of a registered trade mark and therefore is not dealt with in this chapter: see chapter 9.

9 Groundless threats of infringement proceedings

9.01 Introduction The 1994 Act introduces a new cause of action for certain threats of proceedings for infringement of a registered trade mark.[1] Similar causes of action are available in respect of threats of proceedings for infringement of other intellectual property rights. The corresponding provision relating to patents[2] is drafted in similar terms to section 21 of the 1994 Act and useful guidance as to the likely interpretation of certain phrases can be found in reported decisions of the courts concerning the action of unjustifiable threats of patent infringement.

1 Section 21(1); see also sections 52(3)(a)(i) and 54(3)(a) pursuant to which the Secretary of State may make regulations applying the provisions of section 21 to Community trade marks and international trade marks.
2 Patents Act 1977, section 70.

9.02 Cause of action, s21 Where someone threatens a third party with registered trade mark infringement proceedings, then any person aggrieved by the threat may bring proceedings for certain relief.[1] However, no right of action exists where the alleged infringement is said to arise out of :
(a) the application of the mark to goods or their packaging;
(b) the importation of goods to which, or to the packaging of which, the mark has been applied; or
(c) the supply of services under the mark.[2]

Threat It falls to consider what will constitute a threat for the purpose of this section. It has been held in the context of a threat of patent infringement proceedings that it is enough '. . . if the language used is such as would convey to any reasonable man that the person using the language intended to bring proceedings for infringement against the person said to be threatened'.[3] The question as to whether a communication constitutes a threat will be decided objectively.[4]

It should be noted that the mere notification that a trade mark is registered, or that an application for registration has been made, does not constitute a 'threat' and therefore is not actionable.[5]

Finally, there is no requirement that the threat be in writing, and an oral threat may therefore be actionable.

Person aggrieved   The cause of action is only conferred on a 'person aggrieved' by the threat of infringement proceedings. Elsewhere in the 1994 Act the right to bring proceedings is conferred on 'any person' in the case of opposition proceedings,[6] revocation proceedings,[7] and invalidity proceedings.[8] It is clearly appropriate that this new cause of action should only be available to persons actually affected by the threat.

The phrase 'person aggrieved' was the test for standing to bring proceedings under the 1938 Act for the removal of a registered trade mark on the basis of non-use[9] or for the rectification of the Register.[10] Under the 1938 Act the courts construed this phrase liberally and it has been suggested that any person in or connected with the goods or services concerned or any allied trade or service would be likely to have sufficient standing.[11]

Certainly, the person receiving the threat must be a person aggrieved. So, also, may be any manufacturer, supplier and/or distributor of the relevant goods or services. As decided in cases under earlier trade mark legislation, it is likely that the courts, in considering whether a person is a 'person aggrieved' under the 1994 Act, will require that the grievance is substantial and not merely fanciful.[12] In circumstances where the person claiming to be aggrieved is not the party threatened with the infringement proceedings, it will generally be necessary for that person to adduce evidence of the nature of his grievance.[13]

The defendant   It is clear that the cause of action will be against the person making the threat and thus proprietors and their legal advisers alike may be exposed to liability. Certainly, this has been the case under the corresponding provisions of patent legislation.

1 As to which, see paragraph 9.04.
2 Section 21(1).
3 *C & P Development Coy (London) LD v Sisabro Novelty Coy LD* (1953) 70 RPC 277 per Jenkins LJ.
4 See also the decisions of Clauson J in *Luna Advertising Company LD v Burnham & Company* (1928) 45 RPC 258 at 260 and Aldous J in *Bowden Controls Ltd v Acco Cable Controls Ltd and Anor* [1990] RPC 427 at 431. For a useful list of what has and has not been accepted as constituting a threat under patent law, see *Encyclopaedia of United Kingdom and European Patent Law*, paragraph 10-403.
5 Section 21(4).
6 Section 38(2).
7 Section 46(4).
8 Section 47(3).
9 Section 26(1) 1938 Act.
10 Section 32(1) 1938 Act.
11 Kerly, 12th edition, paragraph 11.07.
12 For example *Wright Crossley* (1898) 15 RPC 131 and at 377 (Ct.A).
13 See *Reymes-Cole v Elite Hosiery Company Limited* [1965] RPC 102 where the failure to adduce such evidence was held to be a fatal lacuna in the defendant's claim against the plaintiff under section 65(2) of the Patents Act 1949.

9.03 The exception or the rule? Logically, any threat of infringement proceedings must be based on an allegation that a person has infringed a registered trade mark on one or more of the grounds specified in section 10. An infringement under section 10 involves the alleged infringer using a sign, in particular, in one or more of the ways specified in section 10(4).

The cause of action in respect of a threat of infringement proceedings is specifically limited so that certain threats will not be actionable. Accordingly, certain alleged acts of infringement can be the subject of a threat of proceedings without the risk of the alleged infringer, or other aggrieved person, being able to obtain relief under section 21(1).

In order to identify which threats are potentially actionable one needs to cross-match those uses of a mark which can constitute infringement under section 10 with those uses of a mark which are specified in the exceptions to the cause of action listed in section 21(1). The table below shows that there are some strange anomalies. For example, it is not an actionable threat under section 21 if the threatened infringement proceedings are in respect of the *supply* of services, but it may be actionable under section 21 to make a threat of proceedings in respect of the *offer* of services under the mark.

9.03 *Groundless threats of infringement proceedings*

ACTIONABLE THREAT	NON-ACTIONABLE THREAT
Offers or exposes goods for sale	Affixes mark to goods; 21(1)(a)
Puts goods on the market	Affixes mark to packaging; 21(1)(a)
Offers services	Supplies services; 21(1)(c)
Exports goods	Imports goods; 21(1)(b)
Uses the mark on business papers	
Uses the mark in advertising	
Stocks goods for offering or exposing goods for sale	

Presumably, the reference in section 21(1)(a), (b) and (c) to 'the mark' must be construed as a reference to the mark, sign or indication being used by the alleged infringer. The alternative interpretation, that 'the mark' refers to the proprietor's registered trade mark, would limit the availability of the exceptions to situations where the threat of infringement proceedings refers specifically to the use of the registered trade mark. This would mean that a threat of infringement proceedings in respect of the use of a sign (where the sign is not the registered trade mark) can never come within the exceptions and, hence, any such threat will be actionable under section 21(1).[1]

1 It would have been more logical had the exceptions been drafted with reference to the use of 'a sign' rather than by reference to the use of 'the mark'.

9.04 Relief, s21(2) A person aggrieved by an actionable threat of infringement proceedings may apply for:
(a) a declaration that the threats are unjustifiable;
(b) an injunction against the continuance of the threats; and
(c) damages in respect of any loss he has sustained by the threats.[1]

1 Section 21(2).

9.05 Defence, s21(2) The applicant (person aggrieved) is entitled to the specified remedies unless the person making the threat establishes that the act(s) in respect of which proceedings were threatened actually constitutes an infringement of the registered trade mark in question.[1]

160

This defence will not be made out if the applicant (person aggrieved) establishes that the registration of the trade mark relied upon is either invalid[2] or liable to be revoked[3] in a relevant respect.[4]

1 Section 21(2).
2 Pursuant to section 47.
3 Pursuant to section 46.
4 Section 21(3).

9.06 Comment When drafting a letter before action threatening certain trade mark infringement proceedings, it will obviously be important to bear in mind the wording of section 21, in particular, because it may be possible to draft the letter in such a way that the threat is not actionable in any event.

It may be argued that in certain circumstances it would be better tactics not to write a letter before action but merely commence proceedings to ensure that the owner of the trade mark is a plaintiff in an infringement action rather than the defendant to a 'threats' action. The cost implications of proceeding in such a manner would have to be taken into account.

10 Dealings in trade marks: assignment and licensing

10.01 Approach taken by the 1994 Act The statutory provisions relating to the assignment and licensing of registered trade marks have become steadily less restrictive. This can be seen by comparing section 22 of the 1938 Act with section 22 of the 1905 Act and section 70 of the 1883 Act. Consistent with this more liberal attitude, the 1994 Act further simplifies the conditions and restrictions attaching to such dealings.

In relation to the assignment of registered trade marks there are four notable improvements to the 1938 Act:

(a) it is possible under the 1994 Act to assign partially a registered trade mark in relation to a particular manner of use or in relation to a particular locality[1] without having to seek the Registrar's approval;[2]

(b) there is no procedure under the 1994 Act for the Registrar to enter identical or similar marks on the Register as associated trade marks and thus such marks can be assigned independently of each other;[3]

(c) the assignment of a registered trade mark under the 1994 Act without the goodwill of the business in which it is used will take effect immediately, without the need to advertise the assignment;[4] and

(d) it is possible under the 1994 Act to assign a pending application for the registration of a trade mark independently of another registered trade mark.[5]

These amendments reflect the new policy underlying the 1994

162

Act, that is, to provide a legal framework which serves the requirements of modern business and industry. Applying this policy to the assignment and licensing of trade marks has meant that the rules which sought primarily to protect the public from being misled or deceived by the fact of two or more people using the same trade mark have been relaxed. Although the new policy rightly enables trade mark owners to deal more freely with their trade marks without the intervention of strict and even artificial rules, all trade mark owners will nonetheless have to be vigilant to ensure that:

(a) their dealings do not result in their trade marks becoming misleading, deceptive or even generic; and

(b) the goodwill attaching to their trade marks does not become diluted.

The 1994 Act deals with:

(a) the transmission (including the assignment) of trade marks in section 24;

(b) the licensing of trade marks in sections 28 and 29;

(c) the rights and remedies of licensees in sections 30 and 31;

(d) the registering of prescribed particulars of registrable transactions (of which assignments and licences are examples) in section 25; and

(e) the granting of security interests in respect of trade marks in section 24(4) and (5).

This chapter deals with each of these issues; (c) above is also considered in chapter 8.

1   Section 24(2).
2   cf section 22(6) 1938 Act.
3   cf section 23 1938 Act; but an assignment which renders the subsequent use of the trade mark likely to mislead the public may lead to the revocation of the registration pursuant to section 46(1)(d) 1994 Act.
4   cf section 22(7) 1938 Act; but the prescribed particulars of all assignments should still be registered pursuant to section 25 1994 Act.
5   cf section 22(3) 1938 Act.

Transmissions

10.02 Assignments and other transmissions, s24(1) A registered trade mark or an application for the registration of a trade mark[1] is transmissible:

(a) by assignment;[2]

(b) by testamentary disposition; or

(c) by operation of law,

in the same way as other personal or moveable property.[3]

The transmission may be made either in connection with the goodwill of a business or independently of such goodwill.[4] This provision is similar in substance to section 22(1) of the 1938 Act,[5] provided that, as already stated:

(a) there is no need to advertise an assignment which is without goodwill;[6] and

(b) applications for the registration of a trade mark may also be assigned independently of any registered trade mark.[7]

The freedom to transmit a registered trade mark or an application therefor is tempered by the risk that the subsequent use made of the mark may lead to possible revocation of the registration if the use is liable to mislead the public, particularly as to the nature, quality or geographical origin of the goods or services in relation to which it is registered.[8] This concern is all the more real in practice where the transmission is without the goodwill of the business in which the mark has been used, because the mark may no longer be used in relation to the goods or services for which it has become known. This point should also be borne in mind in relation to partial transmissions.

1 Section 27(1).
2 In the case of co-proprietors, subject to the consent of each: section 23(4)(b).
3 Section 24(1).
4 Section 24(1).
5 The 1938 Act will continue to apply in relation to transactions occurring prior to 31 October 1994 while section 24 of the 1994 Act will apply to transactions occurring on or after that date: schedule 3, paragraph 8(1).
6 ie: there is no equivalent to section 22(7) of the 1938 Act.
7 Section 27(1).
8 ie: pursuant to section 46(1)(d).

10.03 Partial assignments and other transmissions, s24(2)

An assignment or other transmission of a registered trade mark (or an application for the registration of a trade mark[1]) may be partial, that is, limited so that it applies only in relation to:

(a) some but not all of the goods or services for which the trade mark is registered; and/or

(b) the use of the trade mark in:

     (i) a particular manner; and/or

(ii) a particular locality.[2]

The option to assign partially a registered trade mark or an application therefor in a manner described in (b) above extends the scope of permissible dealings which, under the 1938 Act, absent the consent of the Registrar, were limited to those specified in (a) above.[3] Furthermore, the scope of permissible dealings under the 1938 Act did not extend to applications at all.

1 Section 27(1).
2 Section 24(2).
3 See section 24(2) 1994 Act and cf section 22(6) 1938 Act.

10.04 Transmissions subject to licences, ss28(3) and 29(2)

If a licence has been granted by the proprietor in respect of a registered trade mark which is then assigned or otherwise transmitted then, unless the licence otherwise provides:

(a) the licence will be binding on the successor in title to whom the mark has been assigned or otherwise transmitted;[1] and

(b) an exclusive licensee will have the same rights against the successor in title as he had against the proprietor.[2]

1 Section 28(3).
2 Section 29(2).

10.05 Requirement of writing, s24(3)

It is a mandatory requirement that both an assignment and an assent of a personal representative relating to either:

(a) a registered trade mark; or

(b) an application for the registration of a trade mark,

must be in writing and signed[1] by or on behalf of the assignor or, as the case may be, the personal representative.[2]

A purported assignment or assent which does not comply with these requirements is not effective.

1 The requirement of a signature may be satisfied by a body corporate affixing its seal (except in Scotland).
2 Section 24(3).

10.06 Operation of law, s24(1)

Apart from an assignment or a testamentary disposition, a registered trade mark (or an application therefor) is only transmissible by 'operation of law'. This phrase was not used in section 22 of the 1938 Act but will include any order of a court or other competent authority transferring the trade mark (or the application for registration) to another person.[1] Such a transmission is a registrable transaction for the purposes of section 25(2).[2]

1   eg: section 60(3)(b) pursuant to which the name of the proprietor can be substituted in certain circumstances.
2   As to which, see paragraph 10.18 et seq.

10.07   Assignment of unregistered trade marks, s24(6)

Nothing in the 1994 Act affects the assignment or other transmission of an unregistered trade mark as part of the goodwill of a business.[1] Thus, such an assignment will not be governed by section 24 and will stand or fall in accordance with the common law rules relating to unregistered trade marks. For example, it has been held that the sale of the goodwill of a business will, by implication, operate as an assignment to the purchaser of the business of the unregistered trade marks used in that business without any express assignment needed.[2] An assignment, by implication, could not occur in respect of a registered trade mark because the requirements of section 24(3) would not have been satisfied.

1   Section 24(6).
2   *Shipwright v Clements* (1871) 19WR 599; *Currie v Currie* (1898) 15RPC 339; *Western* [1968] RPC167 at 183.

10.08   Security and charges, s24(4) and (5)

The provisions relating to the transmission of a registered trade mark apply equally to an assignment by way of security.[1]

A registered trade mark (and an application for the registration of a trade mark) may be the subject of a charge[2] in the same way as other personal or moveable property.[3] Thus, the proprietor of a registered trade mark (or an application for registration) can, for example, secure any loan or other debt by granting a charge over his trade mark which may be fixed or floating.

1   Section 24(4).
2   In Scotland, the subject of security.
3   Section 24(5); in the case of co-proprietors, subject to the consent of each: section 23(4)(b).

10.09   Transitional provisions, schedule 3

Transactions occurring prior to 31 October 1994   The 1938 Act will continue to apply in relation to transactions occurring prior to

31 October 1994 while section 24 of the 1994 Act applies to transactions occurring on or after that date.[1]

Assignments and transmissions registered under the 1938 Act Entries in the 1938 Register under section 25 of the 1938 Act relating to assignments and transmissions which occurred prior to 31 October 1994 were transferred to the 1994 Register on 31 October 1994 and have effect as if made under section 25 of the 1994 Act.[2]

Applications under the 1938 Act An application under section 25 of the 1938 Act for the registration of an assignment or transmission which has occurred prior to 31 October 1994 will be dealt with under either:

(a) the 1938 Act, where the application has already been determined but not finally determined as at 31 October 1994;[3] or

(b) section 25 of the 1994 Act, where the application is pending as at 31 October 1994.[4]

Applications under the 1994 Act Where a person has become entitled prior to 31 October 1994 by virtue of an assignment or transmission to a registered trade mark under the 1938 Act but has not registered his title, any subsequent application for the registration of his title must be made under section 25 of the 1994 Act. Section 25(3) of the 1938 Act will, however, continue to apply as regards the consequences of his failure to register the assignment/transmission rather than section 25(3) and (4) of the 1994 Act.[5]

1 Schedule 3, paragraph 8(1).
2 Schedule 3, paragraph 8(2).
3 Schedule 3, paragraph 8(4); any subsequent registration will be transferred to the 1994 Register pursuant to paragraph 8(2).
4 Schedule 3, paragraph 8(3); in which case the application will proceed in accordance with section 25 of the 1994 Act, except that section 25(3) of the 1938 Act will continue to apply as regards the consequences of failing to register the assignment/transmission rather than section 25(3) and (4) of the 1994 Act.
5 Schedule 3, paragraph 8(5) and (6).

Licences

10.10 Introduction, ss28 and 29 A distinguishing feature of the 1994 Act is that it contains no registered user provisions, although it does provide for particulars of registrable transactions,[1] including licences,[2] to be entered in the Register.[3]

Importantly, there are no express requirements in the 1994 Act in relation to the substance of licence agreements as were found in section 28 of the 1938 Act[4] and the so-called 'anti-trafficking' provision[5] has no equivalent in the 1994 Act. Thus, the decision in *Holly Hobbie*[6] (as it relates to section 28(6)) will no longer be applicable, no doubt to the great relief of those involved in one form of merchandising or another and not least to Lord Bridge.

As with assignments, the policy is that trade mark owners should be free to license the use of their trade marks as they see fit and the only caveat is the proprietor's own interest in maintaining the distinctiveness and hence the value of his trade mark by, inter alia, asserting proper quality control over the goods or services for which it is licensed.

1 As to which, see paragraph 10.18 et seq.
2 Section 25(2)(b).
3 Section 25(1).
4 As to the transitional provisions relating to registered users recorded under the 1938 Act see paragraph 10.17.
5 ie: section 28(6).
6 [1984] RPC 329; [1984] 1 WLR 189; [1984] 1 All ER 426.

10.11 General and limited licences, s28(1) A licence to use a registered trade mark may be general or limited.[1] 'General' means that the licensee may use the trade mark throughout the United Kingdom in relation to all the goods or services for which the trade mark is registered; 'limited' means that the licensee may, for example, only be allowed to use the trade mark:
(a) in relation to some but not all of the goods or services covered by the registration; and/or
(b) in a particular manner or in a particular locality.[2]

Comparison with the 1938 Act Provided that the licence otherwise complied with the requirements of section 28 of the 1938 Act, a licensee could also have been granted either a 'general' or a 'limited' licence in the same terms as provided for in section 28 of the 1994 Act. However, unlike the 1938 Act, there is no express requirement in the 1994 Act that the Registrar must first be satisfied that the use of the trade mark by the licensee would not be contrary to the public interest.[3] Of course, under the 1994 Act, if a licensee's use of the trade mark results in it becoming generic or misleading to the public, then the registration of the trade mark may be revoked pursuant to section 46(1)(c) or (d).

1 Section 28(1).
2 Section 28(1); this is not an exhaustive list of the ways in which a licence can be limited.
3 See section 28(5) 1938 Act.

10.12 Requirement of writing, s28(2) A licence, whether general or limited, must be in writing and signed[1] by or on behalf of the licensor.[2]

A purported licence which does not comply with these requirements is 'not effective'.[3] This may create a problem when read in the context of section 46(1)(a) or (b) which provide that a trade mark may be revoked on the grounds of non-use. However, 'use' for the purposes of that section will include any use of the trade mark with the 'consent' of the proprietor. What then is the effect in this context of a licence which is 'not effective' because it does not comply with section 28(2)? It is assumed that the mere fact that a licence is not effective does not negate the proprietor's actual consent to the use of his trade mark by the licensee. More difficult questions may arise as to, for example:

(a) whether a licensor can sue to enforce royalty payments;
(b) whether a licensee can rely on the licence as a defence to an infringement action; and
(c) the rights of successors in title.

Certainly, a licence which is 'not effective' is not a registrable transaction for the purposes of section 25 and therefore the licensee will not have the rights and remedies prescribed in sections 30 and 31.

1 The requirement of a signature may be satisfied by a body corporate affixing its seal (except in Scotland).
2 Section 28(2).
3 Section 28(2).

10.13 Assignees subject to licensees, ss28(3) and 29(2)
Unless the licence provides otherwise it will be binding on any subsequent assignee (or other transferee) whose title will be subject to the terms of the licence[1] and therefore to the rights of the licensee.

Furthermore, an exclusive licensee has the same rights against a subsequent proprietor/assignee who is bound by the licence as he (the exclusive licensee) has against the licensor.[2]

1 Section 28(3).
2 Section 29(2).

10.14 Sub-licences, s28(4) The provisions of the 1994 Act relating to licences and licensees apply equally to sub-licences and to sub-licensees. However, the right to sub-license will not be implied. A licensee wishing to grant a sub-licence must obtain the express right to do so.[1]

1 Section 28(4).

10.15 Rights and remedies of licensees, ss30 and 31 The rights and remedies of a licensee will depend on whether the licensee is an exclusive licensee or a non-exclusive licensee and on the terms of the licence itself.

Exclusive licensees An exclusive licensee is a licensee who has been authorised to the exclusion of all other persons, including the licensor, to use a registered trade mark in the manner authorised by the terms of the licence.[1] Thus, a licensee may be an exclusive licensee even though he merely has a limited licence, provided that he is the only person who may use the trade mark in the limited manner prescribed by the licence. Any licensee not coming within the definition of an exclusive licensee must necessarily be a non-exclusive licensee.

In relation to an exclusive licensee, one must further distinguish between exclusive licensees who have and those who do not have the same rights and remedies in respect of matters occurring after the grant of the licence, as if the licence had been an assignment, that is, the rights and remedies of a proprietor. An exclusive licensee will only have such rights and remedies if, and to the extent that, the terms of the exclusive licence expressly so provide. If his exclusive licence does contain a provision to the effect that his rights and remedies are to be the same as if the licence had been an assignment, then his rights and remedies are governed by section 31;[2] absent such a provision, his rights and remedies will be governed by section 30.[3]

An exclusive licensee whose exclusive licence does contain such a provision will be treated as if he were the proprietor of the registered trade mark for the purposes of considering the rights and remedies of any sub-licensee. That is, a sub-licensee may exercise the same rights and remedies under section 30 vis-à-vis an exclusive licensee as a licensee may exercise vis-à-vis the proprietor/licensor.[4]

A decision therefore needs to be made as to whether an exclusive licence should expressly provide that the exclusive licensee is to have the rights and remedies, in respect of matters occurring after the grant of the licence, as if the licence were an assignment. The clear advantage for the licensee of so providing is that his rights and remedies will be concurrent with those of the proprietor.[5]

Non-exclusive licensees Non-exclusive licensees and sub-licensees (like those exclusive licensees whose rights and remedies are not governed by section 31) have the rights and remedies conferred by section 30.[6]

In the absence of any provisions in the licence to the contrary, section 30 enables the licensee to call on the proprietor to bring infringement proceedings in respect of any matter which affects the licensee's interests, but this right can be varied or even excluded by the terms of the licence. Accordingly, a proprietor who wishes to retain the sole discretion as to whether to institute infringement proceedings should exclude expressly in the licence the operation of section 30(2).

1 Section 29(1).
2 As to which, see paragraph 8.22.
3 As to which, see paragraph 8.22.
4 Sections 28(4) and 30(7).
5 Section 31(2).
6 As to which, see paragraph 8.22.

10.16 Drafting points The following questions need to be considered in drafting a trade mark licence under the 1994 Act.

1 Is it intended that the licence should be exclusive?
   If so, the licence must fall within the definition of an exclusive licence, see section 29(1) and go to question 2.
   If not, go to question 3.
2(a) Is it intended that the exclusive licensee should have the same rights and remedies, in respect of matters occurring after the grant of the licence, as if the licence had been an assignment, ie, is it intended that the licensee's rights and remedies should be

concurrent with those of the proprietor?

If so, the licence must expressly so provide, see section 31(1) and go to question 2(b).

If not, go to question (3).

2(b) Is it intended to vary or exclude the operation of any of subsections 31(4)–(7)?

If so, the licence must expressly so provide, see section 31(8).

If not, no action need be taken.

3   Is it intended that the licensee should be entitled to call upon the proprietor to bring infringement proceedings in respect of matters affecting the licensee's interests?

If so, such an entitlement will be deemed, see section 30(2).

If not, the entitlement must be expressly varied or excluded by the terms of the licence.

4   Is it intended that the licensee should be able to grant sublicences?

If so, the licence must expressly so provide, see section 28(4).

If not, the licence should simply stay silent on this issue.

10.17 Transitional provisions, schedule 3

Licences granted prior to 31 October 1994 The 1938 Act will continue to apply in relation to licences granted prior to 31 October 1994 while sections 28 and 29(2) of the 1994 Act apply to licences granted on or after that date.[1]

Registered users recorded under the 1938 Act Entries in the 1938 Register under section 28 of the 1938 Act relating to registered users were transferred to the 1994 Register on 31 October 1994 and have effect as if made under section 25 of the 1994 Act.[2]

Applications for the registration of registered users under the 1938 Act An application for the registration of a registered user will be dealt with under either:

(a) the 1938 Act, where the application has already been determined but not finally determined as at 31 October 1994;[3] or

(b) section 25 of the 1994 Act, where the application is pending as at 31 October 1994.[4]

Applications for the variation or cancellation of registered users An application for the variation or cancellation of a registered user pursuant to section 28(8) or (10) of the 1938 Act which is pending as at 31 October 1994 will be dealt with under the old law and any consequent alteration will be made to the 1994 Register.[5]

1 Schedule 3, paragraph 9(1).
2 Schedule 3, paragraph 9(2).
3 Schedule 3, paragraph 9(4); any subsequent registration will be transferred to the 1994 Register pursuant to paragraph 9(2).
4 Schedule 3, paragraph 9(3); in which case the application will proceed in accordance with section 25 of the 1994 Act.
5 Schedule 3, paragraph 9(5).

Registrable transactions

10.18 Introduction, s25 Like the 1938 Act (and others before it), the 1994 Act provides for the registration of certain dealings affecting trade marks, referred to in the 1994 Act as 'registrable transactions'. However, the 1994 Act merely enables prescribed particulars of registrable transactions to be entered in the Register. There are no substantive requirements imposed by the 1994 Act in terms of the content of the transactions themselves, although there are certain consequences if one does not apply for the registration of the prescribed particulars.

10.19 Registrable transactions, s25(2) The following are registrable transactions for the purposes of the 1994 Act:
(a) an assignment of a registered trade mark or any right in it;[1]
(b) the grant of a licence under a registered trade mark;[2]
(c) the granting of any security interest (whether fixed or floating) over a registered trade mark or any right in or under it;
(d) the making by personal representatives of an assent in relation to a registered trade mark or any right in or under it;
(e) an order of a court or other competent authority transferring a registered trade mark or any right in or under it;[3] or
(f) any of the transactions of the type specified in (a) to (e) above, in respect of an application for the registration of a trade mark.[4]
It is not clear whether this is intended to be an exhaustive list of registrable transactions; one assumes that it is, because sections 24 and 28 would appear to embody the provisions governing all

transactions which can affect a registered trade mark and these transactions are all included in (a) to (e) above.

1   As to entries and applications for entries under section 25 of the 1938 Act relating to transactions occurring before 31 October 1994 see paragraph 10.09.
2   As to entries and applications for entries under section 28 of the 1938 Act relating to registered users see paragraph 10.17.
3   Section 25(2).
4   Section 27(1); can one grant a licence under a mere application for the registration of a trade mark? Section 28 (which is not governed by section 27(1)) relates only to the granting of a licence in respect of registered trade marks. However, nothing in section 28 expressly prohibits the grant of such a licence and thus it should be possible to notify the Registrar of the particulars of a licence granted under an application for the registration of a trade mark: rule 35(4) assumes that this is the case.

10.20   Application for the registration of prescribed particulars, s25(1)   The Registrar will enter in the Register the prescribed particulars[1] of all registrable transactions upon receiving an application from either:

(a)   the person claiming to be entitled to an interest in or under a registered trade mark by virtue of a registrable transaction;[2] or
(b)   any other person claiming to be 'affected' by such a transaction.[3]

In the case of registrable transactions affecting or relating to applications for the registration of a trade mark one cannot apply to have the relevant particulars entered in the Register as such: instead, the applicant can notify the particulars to the Registrar[4] who will enter them in the Register upon the registration of the mark.[5]

1   See rules 34 and 35 and paragraph 10.21.
2   Section 25(1)(a).
3   Section 25(1)(b); this would include a proprietor, assignor or licensor.
4   Section 27(3).
5   Rule 35(4).

10.21   Prescribed particulars, rr34 and 35   Rules 34 and 35 set out the prescribed particulars which must be entered in the Register in respect of the various registrable transactions. These are set out below.

Assignments, r34   In the case of an assignment of a registered trade mark or any right in it, the particulars to be supplied are:
(a)   the name and address of the assignee;

(b) the date of the assignment; and
(c) where the assignment is only in respect of any right in the mark,[1] a description of the right assigned.
Form TM 16 should be used.[2]

Licences, r34 In the case of the grant of a licence under a registered trade mark, the particulars to be supplied are:
(a) the name and address of the licensee;
(b) the fact (if it is the case) that the licence is an exclusive licence;
(c) where the licence is limited, a description of the limitation;
(d) the duration of the licence, assuming that the duration is (or is ascertainable as) for a definite period.
Form TM 50 should be used to apply for the registration of the prescribed particulars. Form TM 51 should be used to amend or remove an entry relating to a licence granted under a registered trade mark.[3]

Security interests, r34 In the case of the grant of any security interest over a registered trade mark or any right in or under it, the particulars to be supplied are:
(a) the name and address of the grantee;
(b) the nature of the interest (whether fixed or floating); and
(c) the extent of the security and the right in or under the mark secured.
Form TM 24 should be used.[4]

Assent, r34 In the case of the making of any assent by a personal representative in relation to a registered trade mark or any right in or under it, the particulars to be supplied are:
(a) the name and address of the person in whom the mark (or any right) vests by virtue of the assent; and
(b) the date of the assent.
Form TM 24 should be used.[5]

Court orders, r34 In the case of a court or other competent authority transferring a registered trade mark or any right in or under it, the particulars to be supplied are:
(a) the name and address of the transferee;
(b) the date of the order; and
(c) where the transfer is only in respect of any right in the mark, a description of the right.
Form TM 24 should be used.[6]

Applications for the registration of prescribed particulars, r35
In each case, the prescribed particulars will only be entered in
the Register if:
(a) in the case of assignments, the application is signed by or on
     behalf of the parties;[7]
(b) in the case of the grant of a licence or any security interest
     (including any amendment or termination of same), the
     application is signed by the grantor of the licence or the
     security interest;[8] or
(c) the Registrar is otherwise satisfied with the documentary evi-
     dence of the transaction;[9] and, in any event,
(d) any stamp duty payable on the transaction has been paid.[10]
The date on which the entry is made will also be entered in the
Register.[11]

Applications for the registration of a trade mark, r35 Section 25
provides for the registration of prescribed particulars relating to
registrable transactions which affect registered trade marks.
Pursuant to section 27(1) and (3) it is also possible to give notice to
the Registrar of particulars of a transaction affecting an application
for the registration of a trade mark.[12] Logically, the particulars of
such a transaction are the same particulars as are required to be
given under rule 34 in relation to transactions affecting registered
trade marks, as otherwise the Registrar would not be able to
register those particulars upon the subsequent registration of the
trade mark.[13]

The same TM forms must also be used for the purpose of
notifying the Registrar of transactions affecting an application for
the registration of a trade mark.

1 ie: a partial assignment pursuant to section 24(2).
2 Rule 35(1)(a).
3 Rule 35(1)(b) and (c).
4 Rule 35(1)(d).
5 Rule 35(1)(e).
6 Rule 35(1)(e).
7 Rule 35(2)(a).
8 Rule 35(2)(b).
9 Rule 35(2).
10 Rule 35(3).
11 Rule 34.
12 In the event that the applicant divides his original application pursuant to section
    41 and rule 19, then the particulars of any relevant licence or security interest will
    be deemed to apply to each divisional application: rule 19(3).
13 Rule 35(4).

10.22 Consequences of the failure to register prescribed particulars of a registrable transaction, s25(3) and (4)

There are three direct consequences of failing to register the prescribed particulars of a registrable transaction.

In the first place, until such time as an application has been made for the registration of the relevant prescribed particulars, the transaction will be ineffective against someone who acquires, in ignorance of the registrable transaction, a conflicting interest in or under the registered trade mark.[1]

Does this mean that the subsequent application for the registration of the prescribed particulars will cure the omission? The wording of section 25(3) would seem to suggest that once the application has been made for the registration of the particulars the transaction will then become effective against a person who acquires a conflicting interest even if that interest was acquired in ignorance of the transaction. This follows from the use of the word 'until' at the beginning of the section. But was this the intention of the legislature? Surely the object was to protect the interests of third parties who acquire an interest in a trade mark without notice (either actual or constructive) of an earlier registrable transaction affecting that mark, the particulars of which had not been supplied to the Registrar.

Secondly, and in addition to the above, until such time as an application has been made for the registration of the relevant prescribed particulars, a licensee will not have the rights and remedies in relation to any infringement of the trade mark as are prescribed by sections 30 and 31 and which would otherwise be available to him.[2] Once again, it would seem that the licensee can cure the omission and thus become entitled to the rights and remedies conferred by sections 30 and 31 by applying to register the relevant particulars.

Finally, where a person becomes either the subsequent proprietor or licensee of a registered trade mark by virtue of a registrable transaction, he will not be entitled to damages or to an account of profits in respect of any infringement of the trade mark which occurs after the date of the transaction but before the prescribed particulars of the transaction are entered in the Register, unless:

(a) an application for the registration of the prescribed particulars of the transaction is made within six months of the date of the transaction;[3] or

(b) the court is satisfied that it was not practicable for such an application to be made within six months and that an application was made as soon as practicable thereafter.[4]

The intention behind section 25 is clearly to try to ensure that the Register records as accurately as possible all interests in or under registered trade marks. The consequences of failing to register the particulars of a registrable transaction are a strong incentive for assignees and licensees (in particular) to treat this section as tantamount to a mandatory requirement.

1   Section 25(3)(a).
2   Section 25(3)(b).
3   Section 25(4)(a).
4   Section 25(4)(b).

11 Certification marks

11.01 Introduction It has been noted on a number of occasions that a trade mark must serve to distinguish the proprietor's goods or services from those of other undertakings.[1] There are, however, two important exceptions to this rule and they are:

(a) certification marks, which are discussed in this chapter; and

(b) collective trade marks, which are discussed in chapter 12.

Readers will be familiar with certification marks which were registrable under the 1938 Act.[2]

1 Section 1(1); see chapter 1.
2 Section 37; and under section 62 of the 1905 Act.

11.02 Definition of certification mark, s50 A certification mark is a mark which indicates that the goods or services in respect of which the mark is used have been 'certified' by the proprietor of the mark[1] to comply with certain objective standards.[2] The proprietor's certification of the goods or services may be in respect of a number of characteristics of the relevant goods or services, namely:

(a) the origin of the goods or services;

(b) the material (or composition) of the goods;

(c) the mode of manufacture of the goods;

(d) the performance of the services;

(e) the quality of the goods or services;

(f) the accuracy of the goods or services; or

(g) any 'other characteristics' of the goods or services.[3]

These are the same characteristics as were specified in section 37(1) of the 1938 Act.[4]

The reference to 'other characteristics' means that the list is not exhaustive. Furthermore, the proprietor of a certification mark may, if he wishes, choose only to certify one or more of these characteristics.

1   Section 50(1).
2   Which must be filed as part of the regulations which accompany an application for a certification mark: see paragraph 11.08.
3   Section 50(1).
4   Except for the additional reference to certifying the performance of the services as there was no provision for certification of service marks.

11.03   Application of the 1994 Act, ss1(2), 50(2) and schedule 2   All references in the 1994 Act to a 'trade mark' include references to a certification mark[1] but one must look to schedule 2 of the 1994 Act to ascertain the necessary adjustments which must be taken into account when applying the Act to certification marks.[2] The remainder of this chapter considers those adjustments; in all other respects the 1994 Act, the Rules (where relevant) and the other relevant chapters of this book apply equally to certification marks as they do to ordinary trade marks.

1   Section 1(2).
2   Section 50(2).

Schedule 2, 1994 Act

11.04   Signs of which a certification mark may consist, paragraph 2   The definition of 'trade mark' in section 1(1) of the 1994 Act cannot be applied literally to certification marks. The second limb of the definition requires a trade mark to be 'capable of distinguishing goods or services of one undertaking from those of other undertakings'. But this is not the purpose of a certification mark which can be applied to the goods or services of numerous undertakings. A certification mark will therefore never serve to distinguish uniquely the goods or services of one undertaking. Accordingly, the second limb of the definition must be construed, for the purposes of certification marks, as a reference to distinguishing the goods or services which are certified from those which are not certified.[1]

1   Schedule 2, paragraph 2.

11.05 Registrability: nature of proprietor's business, paragraph 4 A certification mark cannot be registered if the proprietor/applicant carries on a business which involves the supply of goods or services of the kind which he certifies or proposes to certify.[1]

This prohibition mirrors the proviso set out in section 68(1) of the 1938 Act. Of course, one can easily side-step paragraph 4 by setting up two companies, one to certify and to own the certification mark and the other to carry on the business of supplying the goods or services under the trade mark.

1 Schedule 2, paragraph 4.

11.06 Registrability: indications of geographical origin, paragraph 3 An absolute ground for refusing the registration of an ordinary trade mark is that it consists exclusively of a sign which indicates the geographical origin of the proprietor's goods or services.[1]

Geographical signs can be registered as certification marks.[2] The registration of a geographical sign does not, however, entitle the proprietor to prevent the use of the sign by a third party provided that the use is in accordance with 'honest practices in industrial or commercial matters'.[3]

1 Section 3(1)(c); see paragraph 2.04.
2 Schedule 2, paragraph 3(1); subject to the EC Regulation on the Protection of Geographical Indications and Designations of Origin for Agricultural Products and Foodstuffs No 2081/92 dated 14 July 1992.
3 Schedule 2, paragraph 3(2); as to the meaning of the phrase 'honest practices in industrial or commercial matters' see paragraph 7.08 in the context of defences to infringement of a trade mark.

11.07 Grounds for refusal of registration: misleading as to character or significance, paragraph 5(1) In addition to the absolute grounds for refusing the registration of an ordinary trade mark,[1] a certification mark cannot be registered if the public is liable to be misled in relation to the character or significance of the mark.[2]

1 ie: under section 3, see chapter 2.
2 Schedule 2, paragraph 5(1); and compare this with section 3(3)(b).

11.08 The regulations, paragraphs 6 and 7 Regulations governing the use of the certification mark must be filed by the applicant within nine months of the date on which the application for registration is made.[1] A failure to file the regulations on time will result in the application being treated as having been withdrawn.[2]

The regulations must include a statement as to:

(a) who is authorised to use the certification mark;

(b) the characteristics to be certified by the mark;

(c) how the certifying body is to test those characteristics and to supervise the use of the certification mark;

(d) the fees (if any) to be paid in connection with the operation of the mark; and

(e) the procedures for resolving disputes.[3]

The certification mark will not be registered unless the regulations comply with these requirements and provided also that they are not contrary to public policy nor to accepted principles of morality.[4]

Furthermore, the Registrar is obliged to refuse the application for a certification mark if the applicant is not competent to certify the relevant goods or services.[5] This would appear to involve the Registrar in having to assess the competence or otherwise of the applicant.

Transitional provisions Regulations governing the use of a certification mark the registration of which was obtained under the 1938 Act[6] are treated as if they had been filed under paragraph 6 of schedule 2.[7]

1 Rule 22; schedule 2, paragraph 6(1); Form TM 35 must be used and a fee will be payable; the regulations will be open to public inspection in the same way as the Register: schedule 2, paragraph 10.
2 Schedule 2, paragraph 7(2).
3 Schedule 2, paragraph 6(2).
4 Schedule 2, paragraph 7(1)(a).
5 Schedule 2, paragraph 7(1)(b).
6 ie: pursuant to section 37.
7 Schedule 3, paragraph 19(1).

11.09 Approval of the regulations, paragraph 8 If the Registrar is satisfied that all the requirements for registration of a certification mark are met (including the requirements relating to the regulations), he will accept the application and the procedure set out in section 38 will be followed as regards publication, opposition proceedings and observations.[1]

The regulations will also be published and, again, notice of opposition can be given and observations made.[2]

If the Registrar is not satisfied that the regulations comply with paragraph 7(1), then the procedure set out in paragraph 8(2) and (3)

will be followed. That is, the Registrar will inform the applicant of the objections and give him the opportunity:
(a) to make representations; and/or
(b) to file amended regulations,
in order to try to overcome the objections. The Registrar will refuse the application altogether if the applicant does not overcome the objections.

1 Schedule 2, paragraph 8(4); see also chapters 3 and 4.
2 Schedule 2, paragraph 9.

11.10 Amendment, paragraph 11 and rule 23 The regulations can only be amended in accordance with paragraph 11 and rule 23[1] which involves the Registrar first accepting the amendments and possibly also publishing them for opposition and/or observations if the Registrar thinks it appropriate.[2]

Transitional provisions A request for the amendment of the regulations relating to a certification mark registered under the 1938 Act which is pending as at 31 October 1994 will be dealt with under the old law.[3]

1 The application for amendment must be filed on Form TM 36.
2 See the procedure set out in rule 23; any notice of opposition must be filed within three months of publication and Form TM 7 must be used; see also chapter 4.
3 Schedule 3, paragraph 19(2).

11.11 Assignment of a registered certification mark, paragraph 12 The Registrar's consent is required in order to assign or otherwise transmit a registered certification mark.

11.12 Rights of authorised users, paragraphs 13 and 14
An authorised user of a registered certification mark is put in a similar position to that of a licensee of an ordinary trade mark. That is, sections 10(5), 19(2) and 89 of the 1994 Act will apply for the benefit of authorised users.[1]

Any loss or potential loss suffered by authorised users will be taken into account in any infringement proceedings commenced by the proprietor of the certification mark[2] provided that the infringement was committed after 31 October 1994.[3]

1 Schedule 2, paragraph 13.
2 Schedule 2, paragraph 14.
3 Schedule 3, paragraph 6(2).

11.13   **Revocation and invalidity, paragraphs 15 and 16**

Revocation   In addition to the grounds for revocation which apply to an ordinary trade mark,[1] a registered certification mark can also be revoked on the ground that:

(a)   the proprietor has begun to carry on a business involving the supply of goods or services of the kind certified;

(b)   the manner in which the mark has been used by the proprietor has caused it to become liable to mislead the public as regards its character or significance;

(c)   the proprietor has failed to observe, or to secure the observance of, the regulations;

(d)   an amendment of the regulations has been made so that they no longer comply with the requirements of paragraph 6(2) or such that the regulations are contrary to public policy or to accepted principles of morality; or

(e)   the proprietor is no longer competent to certify the relevant goods or services.

Invalidity   Furthermore, in addition to the grounds for invalidity which apply to an ordinary trade mark,[2] a registered certification mark can be declared invalid on the ground that it was registered in breach of paragraphs 4, 5(1) or 7(1).[3]

1   ie: under section 46; see also chapter 5.
2   ie: under section 47; see also chapter 5.
3   Schedule 2, paragraph 16.

12 Collective marks

12.01 Introduction The 1994 Act introduces for the first time the concept of a 'collective mark'. In chapter 1 the requirement that a trade mark must serve to distinguish the proprietor's goods or services from those of other undertakings[1] was considered. There are, however, two important exceptions to this rule and they are:

(a) certification trade marks, which have already been discussed in chapter 11; and

(b) collective trade marks, which are discussed in this chapter.

1 Section 1(1).

12.02 Definition of collective mark, s49 A collective mark is owned by an association of members, not by a single undertaking. Thus, a collective mark is a mark which distinguishes the goods or services of the members of the association from those of other undertakings.[1]

1 Section 49(1).

12.03 Application of the 1994 Act, ss1(2), 49(2) and schedule 1 References in the 1994 Act to a 'trade mark' include a collective mark[1] but one must look to schedule 1 of the 1994 Act to ascertain the necessary adjustments which must be taken into account when applying the Act to collective marks.[2] The remainder of this chapter addresses those adjustments; in all other respects the 1994 Act, the Rules (where relevant) and the other relevant chapters of this book apply equally to collective marks as they do to ordinary trade marks.

1 Section 1(2).
2 Section 49(2).

Schedule 1, 1994 Act

12.04 Signs of which a collective mark may consist, paragraph 2 The definition of 'trade mark' in section 1(1) of the 1994 Act cannot be applied literally to collective marks. The second limb of the definition requires a trade mark to be 'capable of distinguishing goods or services of one undertaking from those of other undertakings'. But this is not the purpose of a collective mark which is usually applied to the goods or services of numerous 'undertakings'. A collective mark will therefore never serve to distinguish uniquely the goods or services of one undertaking. Accordingly, the second limb of the definition must be construed, for the purposes of collective marks, as a reference to distinguishing the goods or services of the members of the particular association which is the proprietor of the mark from those of other undertakings which are not members of the association.[1]

1 Schedule 1, paragraph 2.

12.05 Registrability: indications of geographical origin, paragraph 3 An absolute ground for refusing the registration of an ordinary trade mark is that it consists exclusively of a sign which indicates the geographical origin of the proprietor's goods or services.[1]

Geographical signs can be registered as collective marks.[2] The registration of a geographical sign does not, however, entitle the proprietor to prevent the use of the sign by a third party provided that the use is in accordance with 'honest practices in industrial or commercial matters'.[3]

1 Section 3(1)(c); see paragraph 2.04.
2 Schedule 1, paragraph 3(1); subject to the EC Regulation on the Protection of Geographical Indications and Designations of Origin for Agricultural Products and Foodstuffs No 2081/92 dated 14 July 1992.
3 Schedule 1, paragraph 3(2); as to the meaning of the phrase 'honest practices in industrial or commercial matters', see paragraph 7.08 in the context of defences to infringement of a trade mark.

12.06   Grounds for refusal of registration: misleading as to character or significance, paragraph 4(1)   In addition to the absolute grounds for refusing the registration of an ordinary trade mark,[1] a collective mark cannot be registered if the public is liable to be misled in relation to the character or significance of the mark.[2]

1 ie: under section 3; see chapter 2.
2 Paragraph 4(1); and compare this with section 3(3)(b).

12.07   The regulations, paragraphs 5 and 6   Regulations governing the use of the collective mark must be filed by the applicant within nine months of the date on which the application for registration is made.[1] A failure to file the regulations on time will result in the application being treated as having been withdrawn.[2]

The regulations must include a statement as to:
(a)   who is authorised to use the collective mark;
(b)   the conditions of membership of the association; and
(c)   where they exist, the conditions of use of the collective mark, including any sanctions against misuse.[3]

The collective mark will not be registered unless the regulations comply with these requirements and provided also that they are not contrary to public policy nor to accepted principles of morality.[4]

1 Rule 22; schedule 1, paragraph 5(1); Form TM 35 must be used and a fee will be payable; the regulations will be open to public inspection in the same way as the Register: schedule 1, paragraph 9.
2 Schedule 1, paragraph 6(2).
3 Schedule 1, paragraph 5(2).
4 Schedule 1, paragraph 6(1).

12.08   Approval of the regulations, paragraph 7   If the Registrar is satisfied that all the requirements for registration of a collective mark are met (including the requirements relating to the regulations), he will accept the application and the procedure set out in section 38 will be followed as regards publication, opposition proceedings and observations.[1]

The regulations will also be published and, again, notice of opposition can be given and observations made.[2]

If the Registrar is not satisfied that the regulations comply with paragraph 6(1), then the procedure set out in paragraph 7(2) and (3) will be followed. That is, the Registrar will inform the applicant of

the objections and give him the opportunity:
(a) to make representations; and/or
(b) to file amended regulations,
in order to try to overcome the objections. The Registrar will refuse the application altogether if the applicant does not overcome the objections.

1   Schedule 1, paragraph 7(4); see also chapters 3 and 4.
2   Schedule 1, paragraph 8.

12.09   Amendment, paragraph 10 and rule 23   The regulations can only be amended in accordance with paragraph 10 and rule 23,[1] which involves the Registrar first accepting the amendments and possibly also publishing them for opposition and/or observations if the Registrar thinks it appropriate.[2]

1   The application for amendment must be filed on Form TM 36.
2   See the procedure set out in rule 23; any notice of opposition must be filed within three months of publication; Form TM 7 should be used; see also chapter 4.

12.10   Rights of authorised users, paragraphs 11 and 12
An authorised user of a registered collective mark is put in a similar position to that of a licensee of an ordinary trade mark. That is, sections 10(5), 19(2) and 89 of the 1994 Act will apply for the benefit of authorised users.[1]

Any loss or potential loss suffered by authorised users will be taken into account in any infringement proceedings commenced by the proprietor of the collective mark.[2]

1   Schedule 1, paragraphs 11 and 12; see in particular paragraph 12 in relation to the manner in which provisions corresponding to section 30 will apply to an authorised user of a registered collective mark in infringement cases.
2   Schedule 1, paragraph 12(6).

12.11   Revocation and invalidity, paragraphs 13 and 14

Revocation   In addition to the grounds for revocation which apply to an ordinary trade mark,[1] a registered collective mark can also be revoked on the ground that:
(a) the manner in which the mark has been used by the proprietor has caused it to become liable to mislead the public as regards its character or significance;
(b) the proprietor (ie the association of members) has failed to observe, or to secure the observance of, the regulations; or

(c) an amendment to the regulations has been made such that they no longer comply with the requirements of paragraph 5(2) or such that the regulations are contrary to public policy or to accepted principles of morality.

Invalidity Furthermore, in addition to the grounds for invalidity which apply to an ordinary trade mark,[2] a registered collective mark can be declared invalid on the ground that it was registered in breach of paragraphs 4(1) or 6(1).[3]

1 ie: under section 46; see also chapter 5.
2 ie: under section 47; see also chapter 5.
3 Schedule 1, paragraph 14.

13 Community trade mark

13.01 Introduction The 1994 Act confers upon the Secretary of State the power to make provision in connection with the implementation of the Community Trade Mark Regulation (the Regulation). As yet, no provision has been made.

The two relevant sections of the 1994 Act (sections 51 and 52), therefore, have no immediate effect and it will be early 1996 before trade mark owners can take advantage of the EC-wide registration system that will become available through the introduction of the Community trade mark system.

This chapter does not purport to give the reader a complete summary of the Regulation. Indeed, the Regulation is far more extensive and detailed than the Directive, consisting as it does of some 143 Articles compared with just 17 Articles of the Directive. Instead, the more important provisions of the Regulation have been selected and briefly summarised in order to provide an overview of how the Community trade mark system is likely to operate in the future.

References in this chapter to Articles are to the Articles of the Regulation.

13.02 The Regulation, EC No 40/94 The Regulation was issued on 20 December 1993, published in the Official Journal on 14 January 1994 and came into force on 15 March 1994. The Regulation is a freestanding supranational instrument which is legally and directly binding in all Member States of the EC.[1]

1 Article 189 EEC Treaty.

13.03 Unitary nature of the Community trade mark, Article 1(2) The Regulation does not replace national trade mark law nor the national systems for the registration of trade marks. Rather, it provides an alternative system. An applicant seeking to protect his trade mark in the EC will have several options:

(a) to file a national application in any one or more of the Member States;

(b) to file a single Community trade mark application, either at the Community Trade Mark Office (CTMO)[1] or with an individual Member State's national trade mark registry, which will then transmit the application to the CTMO; or

(c) to do both (a) and (b).[2]

The registration of a mark as a Community trade mark will result in that mark having equal effect throughout the entire EC. This means that a Community trade mark can only be:

(a) registered;

(b) transferred;

(c) surrendered; or

(d) revoked or declared invalid,

in respect of the whole of the EC.

The application for a Community trade mark must stand or fall for the entire EC. Thus, for example, if a successful opposition is encountered on the basis of an earlier trade mark in a single EC country, the Community trade mark application will be rejected *in toto*. Also, once a Community trade mark registration is obtained, the registration as a whole will be revoked if it is attacked successfully on the basis of an earlier trade mark in a single Member State. However, if a Community trade mark registration or application is revoked or is rejected for this reason, the Community trade mark may be converted into a series of individual national trade mark rights.[3]

1 The CTMO's formal designation is 'The Office for Harmonisation in the Internal Market (Trade Marks and Designs)'.
2 See also chapter 14 in relation to the possible filing of an application for an international registration.
3 See paragraph 13.10.

13.04 Who can own a Community trade mark registration, Article 5 Nationals of Member States can naturally apply for a Community trade mark;[1] so also may non-EC nationals provided that they are nationals of countries which are

party to the Paris Convention.[2] Furthermore, companies and other
entities domiciled in, or which have their seat or a real and effective
industrial or commercial establishment within either the EC or a
state which is a party to the Paris Convention, can own Community
trade marks.[3]

Finally, other trade mark owners not falling within the above
categories will be able to obtain a Community trade mark
registration on the basis of reciprocity.[4]

Applications for a Community trade mark will be filed at the
CTMO. Applications will be received at the CTMO as from 1
January 1996. However, applications filed within three months
prior to that date will be deemed to have been filed on that date.[5]

1   Article 5.1(a).
2   Article 5.1(b).
3   Article 5.1(c).
4   Article 5.1(d).
5   Article 143(3) and (4).

13.05   Basis of rights, Article 6   Rights are created under
the Regulation by registration alone.[1] Registrations will subsist
for ten years from the date of filing and are renewable for periods
of ten years, without the necessity of proving use at the time of
renewal.[2]

1   Article 6.
2   Article 46; see Article 47 as to renewal of registration.

13.06   The Community Trade Mark Office (CTMO)   The
location of the CTMO has now been decided. It is to be in
Alicante, Spain.

In addition to deciding whether to accept applications for the
registration of a Community trade mark, the CTMO will handle
revocation and invalidation actions. Oppositions are also filed with
the CTMO. Thus, the CTMO will consider questions of
distinctiveness, descriptiveness, similarity, non-use and earlier trade
mark rights.

13.07   What is registrable as a Community trade mark?
The definition of 'Community trade mark' mirrors that of 'trade
mark' in section 1(1) of the 1994 Act.[1] Similarly, the absolute and
relative grounds for refusal of registration are substantially

identical to sections 3, 4 and 5 of the 1994 Act.[2]

1   Article 4; see also chapter 1.
2   Articles 7 and 8; see also chapter 2.

13.08   Rights of owners of prior conflicting marks ('earlier trade marks'), Article 8   A mark will not be registered as a Community trade mark if its registration is successfully opposed on the ground that it is identical with or confusingly similar to an 'earlier trade mark' which is protected in respect of identical or similar goods or services. 'Earlier trade marks' are defined in Article 8 as including the following marks and earlier applications for such marks:

(a)   a Community trade mark;
(b)   a mark registered in a Member State and a mark registered under international arrangements with effect in a Member State; and
(c)   a mark that is well known according to the definition of that term in Article 6*bis* of the Paris Convention.

Not included within the definition of 'earlier trade mark', but also constituting a valid ground for the refusal of a Community trade mark, are:

(a)   marks applied for by an agent or a representative without the proprietor's consent, where the proprietor objects and the agent or representative cannot justify his action;[1] and
(b)   unregistered marks where prior use has been of more than mere local significance and where national law confers a right on the proprietor of the unregistered mark to prohibit the use of a subsequent trade mark.[2]

In each case, the mark applied for will only be refused if the proprietor of the mark referred to opposes the registration.

Under Article 8(5), even where the goods or services in respect of which the trade mark is to be registered are not similar to the goods or services in respect of which an identical or similar mark is registered, the later mark may still be refused registration as a Community trade mark in certain circumstances. These are where the proprietor of the earlier trade mark who opposes registration can show a reputation in the EC or the Member State concerned and that use without due cause of the mark applied for would take unfair advantage of, or be detrimental to, the distinctive character or the repute of the earlier trade mark.

In essence, the rights of proprietors of earlier trade marks are protected by Article 8 as they are by section 5 of the 1994 Act. The significant difference is that the Registrar may himself object under section 5 to the registration of a trade mark under the 1994 Act on the grounds of a conflict with an earlier trade mark, whereas the registration of a Community trade mark will only be refused under Article 8 if the proprietor of the earlier trade mark formally opposes the registration of the mark applied for.

1 Article 8(3).
2 Article 8(4).

13.09 Examination, searches and opposition, Articles 36, 39 and 42

Examination The provisions for official examination are dealt with in Article 36. The CTMO is to check that the application complies with the Regulation and that the appropriate fees have been paid. The applicant is given a chance to remedy any deficiencies. Unlike the examination procedure in the United Kingdom Registry under the 1994 Act, the CTMO will only examine whether there are absolute grounds for refusal of registration under Article 7.

Searches Under Article 39, once official examination is completed, the CTMO will draw up a search report citing any prior conflicting Community trade mark registrations or applications. The CTMO will not conduct an official search covering the national registers because costs would be prohibitive. National registries can search their own records for conflicting national registrations and applications but they are not obliged to do so. However, every regular national filing will be recognised as giving rise to a right of priority.[1]

Results of searches of the Community trade mark register and of any national registers will be sent to the applicant by the CTMO who must then decide whether or not to proceed with his application. The owner of an earlier cited Community trade mark registration or application is likewise informed of the application upon publication.

Opposition After a search of Community trade mark references and any search conducted by national registries, the Community trade mark application is then published (to the extent that it has not been refused).[2] Not more than three months following publication, a proprietor of or licensee under an earlier trade mark[3] and other persons with an interest in the mark[4] can give notice of opposition to the Community trade mark application. An opposition may only be brought on the basis of any or all of the earlier rights referred to above,[5] not on the absolute grounds for refusal under Article 7 which is a matter for the CTMO.

Third parties may also submit written observations to the CTMO stating the grounds on which the mark applied for should not be registered. Such parties will not be parties to the proceedings before the CTMO but observations will be communicated to the applicant who may comment upon them.[6]

1   Articles 29 and 30.
2   Article 40.
3   As defined in Article 8(2).
4   Under Article 8(3) or (4).
5   Article 42.
6   Article 41.

13.10   Conversion into a national application, Article 108

An application for a Community trade mark which is refused, or a Community trade mark which ceases to have effect (but only to that extent) can be converted into one or more national trade mark applications. A Community trade mark cannot be converted if it is cancelled for non-use or if the specific grounds for revocation or invalidity apply in the particular Member State concerned. An example of where such grounds apply (and where conversion would not therefore be allowed) in a particular country is where there exists a conflict between a prior national registration and the Community trade mark in the country in which the prior national registration is in force.[1]

The term 'conversion' as used in the Regulation means that a Community trade mark application is transformed into a national trade mark application. It will enjoy the same date of filing and priority as the Community trade mark application or the same seniority as the registered Community trade mark. Requests for conversion must be made with a conversion fee at the CTMO. If the conditions are satisfied the request will then be sent to the relevant national trade mark registries, which will examine the converted application as a national application.[2]

Converted Community applications and registrations are not subjected to any formal requirements of national law which are different from, or in addition to, those provided by the Regulation.[3] However, the national registry can request the payment of an official national fee, the submission of a translation of the converted application, an indication of an address for service, and representations of the mark.[4] This would appear to enable an applicant to avoid national requirements for registration which are more onerous than those of the Regulation. For example, under the 1994 Act, the United Kingdom Registry will raise objections based on earlier trade mark rights. However, under the Regulation, earlier trade mark rights are merely notified to the proprietor. Accordingly, a Community trade mark application which is converted to a United Kingdom national application will not be subject in the United Kingdom to objections from the Registrar based on earlier trade mark rights.

1 Article 108.
2 Article 109.
3 Article 110(2).
4 Article 110(3).

13.11 Infringement An infringement action is brought in the Member State where the defendant has his domicile or, if he has no such domicile, where he has an establishment.[1] If he has neither, the action is to be brought in the country of the plaintiff's domicile or establishment.[2] If neither the plaintiff nor the defendant has such a domicile or establishment, the action is to be brought in the courts of Spain, being the country where the CTMO has its seat. In either case, the court[3] has exclusive jurisdiction regardless of where the infringement occurred.

A decision involving a Community trade mark in a particular Member State will have effect throughout the whole EC. The exception to this is where an infringement action is brought in the Member State where the infringement occurred. In these circumstances, the court shall have jurisdiction only in respect of acts committed or threatened within the territory of that Member State.[4] Parties are free to agree, however, to another forum.[5]

No special courts are established to handle infringement cases involving a Community trade mark. Each Member State is to designate a limited number of existing national courts to handle

Community trade mark cases. A national court is also to be
designated to hear appeals from decisions of the trial court. All these
courts are called Community trade mark courts although they
remain national courts.[6]

Community trade mark courts have exclusive jurisdiction for
Community trade mark matters and any related counterclaims
arising under the Regulation. Counterclaims include revocation and
invalidity actions.[7] Such counterclaims may be based on non-use,
the assertion of earlier trade mark rights or allegations that a mark
was wrongly registered because, for example, it is descriptive or
generic. Thus, national courts will rule on a very large number of
issues involving the Regulation.

1   Article 93(1).
2   Article 93(2).
3   Definition, see Article 91.
4   Article 94(2).
5   Article 93(4).
6   Article 91.
7   Article 92.

**13.12   Relation of national law to Community trade
marks**   The Regulation will co-exist with national trade mark laws.
This has several consequences. The Regulation does not affect the
rights of owners of prior national trade marks to prevent the use
under national law (where such national law so provides) of a
Community trade mark.[1]

In a particular country, the same proprietor may own both Community trade mark and national trade mark registrations. He may
commence simultaneously an infringement action on the basis of
national and Community trade mark rights. However, where
successive actions involving identical marks for identical goods or
services are commenced in different countries, the court where the
later action is commenced may decline jurisdiction in favour of the
court where the first proceedings were commenced, or stay proceedings if jurisdiction is contested.[2]

Also, a court hearing an infringement case brought on the basis
of a Community trade mark must dismiss the action if there is a final
decision on the merits regarding the same cause of action between
the same parties on the basis of an identical national trade mark in
force for identical goods or services. Similarly, a court hearing an
infringement action based on a national trade mark must dismiss the

case if such a decision has already been made on the basis of an identical Community trade mark valid for identical goods or services.[3] These rules are intended to avoid contradictory decisions, but do not apply to interlocutory proceedings.[4]

1 Article 106.
2 Article 105(1)(a).
3 Article 105(2) and (3).
4 Article 105(4).

13.13 Seniority based on a national registration, Article 34
A proprietor of a national trade mark registration will not be prejudiced in so far as he will be able to retain the 'seniority' of his earlier identical national trade mark registration for the purpose of his later Community trade mark registration.[1] This provision only applies, however, where the proprietor surrenders his national trade mark registration or allows it to lapse; it does not apply if his national registration is revoked or invalidated[2] or liable to have been revoked or invalidated before surrender or lapse.[3]

1 Article 34(1).
2 Article 34(2) and (3).
3 ie: pursuant to Article 14 of the Directive.

13.14 Use requirements, Article 15   Rights to a Community trade mark can be lost for non-use during any five year period following registration.[1] The use required must be 'genuine use', which should eliminate token use, and includes affixing the Community trade mark to goods or packaging in the EC solely for export purposes.[2] Commencement or resumption of genuine use cures the defect of prior non-use,[3] provided that this is not within three months preceding the filing of an application to revoke or counterclaim, and that such preparations do not occur only after the proprietor becomes aware that the application or counterclaim may be filed.

The genuine use must be in the EC and thus use in a single Member State only will be sufficient. This is a significant advantage of the Community trade mark system over national trade mark systems. Under existing national systems if a mark is registered in several Member States as a national mark but is used in only one of those States it can be revoked in the others due to non-use.

Another important feature of the Community trade mark use requirement is that non-use can be raised by the applicant as a defence to an opposition.[4] The proprietor of an earlier Community trade mark who is opposing an application can be obliged at the request of the applicant to provide proof of genuine use of his mark in the last five years, or proper reasons for non-use, or else the opposition will fail. Potential opponents will therefore have to think carefully about launching an opposition since they could lose their own registration.

It is not necessary to record licences in order for permitted use by the licensee to accrue to the benefit of the licensor.[5]

1 Article 15.
2 Article 15(2).
3 Article 50(1).
4 Article 43(2).
5 This being the effect of Article 15(3).

13.15 Grounds for invalidity, Article 51 The registration of a Community trade mark may be declared invalid on the ground that it should not have been registered in the first place or because the sign applied for is not a registrable mark, or where the applicant was acting in bad faith when he filed the application for the Community trade mark.[1] The Regulation refers to such grounds as 'absolute grounds for invalidity'.[2] However, such a mark may not be declared invalid if, in consequence of the use made of it, it has after registration acquired a distinctive character in relation to the goods or services for which it is registered.[3]

The registration of a Community trade mark may also be declared invalid because the mark conflicts with earlier rights of third parties.[4] The Regulation refers to such grounds as 'relative grounds for invalidity'. However, if the proprietor has, in good faith, used a Community trade mark for more than five years without this use being objected to and with the knowledge of the proprietor of the earlier mark, the owner of that earlier mark is barred from applying for a declaration that the later Community trade mark is invalid and from opposing the use of the later mark in respect of goods or services for which it is being used, unless the registration of the later Community trade mark was applied for in bad faith.[5]

1 Article 51.
2 Article 51.
3 Article 51(2).
4 Article 52.
5 Article 53.

13.16   Assignments, Article 17   Since the Community trade mark stands or falls for the whole EC, a Community trade mark cannot be assigned for individual Member States.

Assignments need not include the goodwill of the assignor.[1] However, an important safeguard is that the transfer must not be likely to mislead the public.[2]

All assignments must be made in writing and signed by all parties (except where it is the result of a judgment), otherwise the assignment is void.[3]

Note that stamp duty will not be chargeable on assignments (and other instruments) relating to a Community trade mark by reason only of the fact that the Community trade mark has legal effect in the United Kingdom.[4]

1   Article 17(1).
2   Article 17(4).
3   Article 17(3).
4   Section 61 of the 1994 Act.

13.17   Appeals, Articles 57 to 63   Decisions of departments of the CTMO may be appealed.[1] Notice of appeal is filed with the CTMO and referred to the particular office where the application was made. If the decision is not then rectified within one month the appeal must be remitted to the Board of Appeal.[2] Finally, an appeal from the Board of Appeal may be brought before the European Court of Justice in Luxembourg.[3]

1   Article 57.
2   Article 60(2).
3   Article 63(1)

13.18   Comment   Once the CTMO commences operation, trade mark owners will have the option of filing individual national applications in each Member State, a single application for a Community trade mark, or both.

There are several potential advantages of the Community trade mark system. In the first place, it has been said publicly that the CTMO will apply the Regulation and the rules under it in a liberal manner.

Secondly, applicants should also be able to save money by filing a single Community trade mark application. Presumably, official CTMO filing fees will initially be lower than the aggregate of the national filing fees for each of the Member States. Moreover, agents' fees should also be reduced. This is because, at least at the time of filing, only one agent is required to deal with one application governed by only one law.

Perhaps the most important advantage of a Community trade mark registration is that the use of a Community trade mark in any part of the EC will protect the registration from attack for non-use. Also, the rule that a single infringement action in one country decides the question of infringement for the entire EC is an advantage if the trade mark owner is successful. (Of course, it would be a distinct disadvantage if the owner is unsuccessful.)

The Community trade mark system arguably should result in more certainty and clarity for trade mark owners, should they choose to use it. However, it must be borne in mind that there may be considerable competition from the international registration system under the Madrid Protocol and this is considered in chapter 14.

14 The Madrid Protocol

14.01 Introduction The 1994 Act confers upon the Secretary of State the power to make provision to give effect in the United Kingdom to the provisions of the Madrid Protocol relating to 'international registrations'. The relevant sections of the 1994 Act are sections 53 and 54 which in themselves, like sections 51 and 52 relating to the Community trade mark, have no immediate effect.

14.02 The Madrid Agreement Since the end of the 19th century a system has been in place whereby a so-called 'international registration' of a trade mark can be secured covering all or any of the Contracting States to the Madrid Agreement.[1] There are notable exceptions from the current list of contracting states including the United States of America, Japan, the United Kingdom, and three other EC countries: namely, Ireland, Denmark and Greece.

The phrase 'international registration' is perhaps something of a misnomer as it tends to suggest that there is a single registration which has equal effect in each of the countries covered by the registration. It is more accurate to describe the procedure as an international application which leads to separate registrations within the nominated countries.

Who may apply Under the Madrid Agreement, only the owner of a national registration in a contracting state (in which the owner has a real and effective place of business) can apply for an international registration. Therefore, although the United Kingdom is not a contracting state, this does not necessarily preclude a United Kingdom based company from applying for such a registration if it can show that it has a real and effective industrial or commercial establishment in one of the contracting states.

Requirement of home national registration   It is necessary for an application for an international registration to be based upon an existing national registration in the applicant's country. The goods to be covered by an application for an international registration must be goods which fall within the national registration.

Scope of registration   An international registration does not extend to the country of origin as the mark is protected in that country by virtue of the national registration. The protection afforded by an international registration extends only to those countries nominated in the application or to which an extension is subsequently sought.

Procedure   An application for an international registration is filed with the national registry of the country of the applicant. The details of the application are then forwarded to the International Bureau of the World Intellectual Property Organisation (WIPO) in Geneva. The International Bureau must satisfy itself that the mark is recorded in the national register in the name of the applicant company and that such national registration covers all the goods or services for which the international registration is being sought. When the International Bureau is in receipt of an application which complies with the requirements of the Agreement, it assigns a serial number to the application and publishes the mark in its bulletin 'Les Marques Internationales'. The acceptance of the application is notified to the registries of the nominated countries.

Each national registry has a period of twelve months within which to accept or refuse registration of the mark in its country. In the absence of notification by a registry of refusal within the one year period, registration is deemed to have been accepted in that country.

In some contracting states a mark which has been accepted by the International Bureau is subjected to a national administrative examination and, in certain cases, may be refused. Such refusal may be provisional (which may be overcome by argument) or final.

Duration of registration   The initial duration of an international registration is twenty years, renewable indefinitely thereafter for further twenty year terms.

Dependency on national registration The registration within each of the nominated contracting states remains dependent upon the validity of the original national registration for a period of five years. Therefore, if the national registration is attacked and declared invalid or allowed to lapse within this five year period, the registration in each relevant contracting state is automatically invalidated. It is, therefore, important to ensure that proper commercial use of the mark in the applicant's home country is made within the relevant period. On the expiration of the five year period the international registration becomes independent in each of the nominated contracting states where registration was accepted and is, therefore, no longer susceptible to central attack.

1 Madrid Agreement Concerning the International Registration of Marks, of 14 April 1891; see schedule 2 for list of Contracting States as at 1 January 1994.

14.03 Limitations of the Madrid Agreement The Madrid Agreement in its original form is very well suited to those countries where there is little or no examination of a trade mark application prior to registration. The registration procedure in countries where there is a substantive examination will inevitably take longer and the requirement of a home national registration would place companies based in such countries at a disadvantage when seeking to benefit from the international registration system.

Other perceived deficiencies of the Madrid Agreement (in so far as a United Kingdom company and the United Kingdom Registry is concerned) include having French as the only official language and a fixed low-fee structure which again unfairly prejudices those countries where, through substantive examination procedures, official fees are maintained at a higher level. Many of the countries refusing to join the Madrid Agreement were also concerned that the principle of central attack resulting in the invalidity of the registration in each country is unduly harsh.

14.04 Madrid Protocol The International Bureau established a Protocol relating to the Madrid Agreement[1] with a view to overcoming the limitations of the Agreement in an attempt to attract other countries to become contracting states to the Protocol. The main advantages of the Protocol are set out below:

(a) The Protocol provides that an application for an international registration can be based not only on a national registration but also on a national application. This addresses to some degree the concern that countries with long application procedures are unfairly disadvantaged under the Agreement.

(b) The time limit within which each national Registry may notify the International Bureau of refusal may be extended to eighteen months, again in recognition of the concerns voiced by some countries that the period of twelve months was considered too short. The White Paper states that the provisions implementing the Protocol in the United Kingdom will extend the time limit to eighteen months at the appropriate time in accordance with Article 5(2)(b) of the Protocol.[2]

(c) In response to the strong objection to the central attack possibility the Protocol provides for the conversion of an international registration or application into a series of national registrations or applications in any of the nominated contracting states in the event that the home national registration or application ceases to have effect within five years[3] or is cancelled. The original priority date of the international registration will, however, be maintained.[4]

(d) In addition to French, the Protocol also nominates English as an official language.

(e) The Protocol also provides for inter-governmental organisations to become a party to the Protocol and it is therefore conceivable, and indeed likely, that the Community trade mark system will be linked into the international registration system.

(f) Registration of a mark at the International Bureau is effected for ten years, renewable thereafter for further ten year periods.[5]

1 Protocol relating to the Madrid Agreement Concerning the International Registration of Marks of 28 June 1989.
2 Paragraph 5.11 of the White Paper.
3 See Article 6(3) of the Protocol.
4 Article 9 *quinquies.*
5 Articles 6(1) and 7(1).

14.05 Current status of the Protocol As at 1 September 1994 only Spain had ratified the Madrid Protocol, although twenty-eight countries, including the United Kingdom, had signed the Protocol.[1] The 1994 Act provides a mechanism for implementing the Protocol, thereby enabling the United Kingdom to ratify. The value of the Protocol to a United Kingdom company will, of course, depend upon the wide scale acceptance of the Protocol. Indeed, the Protocol will not actually come into force until such time as it has been ratified by at least four countries.

1   See schedule 3 for a list of signatories to the Protocol as at 1 January 1994.

14.06   Comment   Within the next few years companies based in the United Kingdom will have the choice of filing either:
(a)   national applications in countries of interest;
(b)   an international application pursuant to the Madrid Protocol;
(c)   an application for a Community trade mark;[1] or
(d)   a combination of the above.

The decision at the end of the day will require careful consideration and the factors that will determine which route is preferable in each instance will include the nature and importance of the mark, the countries for which registration is required, and the cost.

1   See chapter 13.

15 Emblems

15.01 Specially protected emblems By virtue of section 3(5) of the 1994 Act, it is an absolute ground for refusal of registration if the applicant's trade mark consists of or contains one or more of the various emblems which are protected by section 4.

Special remedies are also conferred for the benefit of the owners of protected emblems and these remedies are also considered in this chapter.

The 1938 Act contained an express provision proscribing the use of the Royal Arms (etc)[1] but did not specifically refer to other protected emblems. It was a part of the Registrar's general discretion under the 1938 Act to be able to refuse registration on the ground that the applicant's mark contained or consisted of a specially protected emblem. As the Registrar retains no general discretion under the 1994 Act it has been necessary to codify the grounds for refusal of registration based on conflicts with such emblems.

1 Section 61 1938 Act; see also the 1986 Rules.

15.02 Royal arms, s4(1) The applicant's trade mark will be refused registration if it consists of or contains either:
(a) the Royal arms,[1] or any insignia or device which so nearly resembles the Royal arms as to be likely to be mistaken for them or it;[2]
(b) a representation of the Royal crown or any of the Royal flags;[3]
(c) a representation of Her Majesty or any member of the Royal

family, or any colourable imitation thereof;[4] or

(d) words, letters or devices likely to lead people to think that the applicant either has or recently has had Royal patronage or authorisation,[5]

unless the consent of Her Majesty or the relevant member of the Royal family has been obtained by the applicant.

1 Including any of the principal armorial bearings of the Royal arms.
2 Section 4(1)(a).
3 Section 4(1)(b).
4 Section 4(1)(c).
5 Section 4(1)(d).

15.03   National flags, s4(2)   A trade mark which consists of or contains a representation of either:

(a) the Union Jack;[1] or

(b) the flag of England, Wales, Scotland, Northern Ireland or the Isle of Man,[2]

can be refused registration but only if it appears to the Registrar that the use of the applicant's trade mark would be misleading or grossly offensive.

For example, it can easily be imagined that the use of national flags could imply an official status or endorsement which may not exist. However, if the use of the flag merely indicates the nationality or domicile of the applicant or the origin of the applicant's goods or services then that should not of itself cause the trade mark to be refused registration under this section.

1 Section 4(2)(a).
2 Section 4(2)(b).

15.04   Emblems of Convention countries, ss4(3), 57 and 59
A trade mark which consists of or contains either:

(a) the flag;

(b) the armorial bearings or any other state emblem; or

(c) an official sign or hallmark,

of, or adopted by, a Convention country[1] will not be registered unless certain conditions are satisfied. The relevant conditions for registration differ slightly in each case and are set out below.

Flags, s57(1)   In relation to the flags of a Convention country, a trade mark which consists of or contains such a flag will only be registered with the authorisation of the competent authorities of the relevant country, unless it appears to the Registrar that the applicant's use of the flag is permitted without any authorisation.[2]

Armorial bearings and state emblems, s57(2) In relation to the armorial bearings or any other state emblem of a Convention country which are protected under the Paris Convention,[3] a trade mark which consists of or contains such bearings or such an emblem will only be registered with the authorisation of the competent authorities of the relevant country and there is no exception to this condition.[4]

Signs and hallmarks, s57(3) In relation to official signs or hallmarks adopted by a Convention country which indicate control and warranty and which are protected under the Paris Convention,[5] trade marks which consist of such signs or hallmarks will not be registered where the applicant seeks registration in relation to goods or services of the same, or a similar kind, as those in relation to which the sign or hallmark indicates control and warranty. Registration can only be obtained with the authorisation of the competent authorities of the country concerned.[6]

Imitations, s57(4) It should also be noted that the ground for refusal of registration relating to national flags, armorial bearings and other state emblems and official signs or hallmarks applies equally to anything which, from a heraldic point of view, is an imitation of any such flags, bearings or other state emblems or signs or hallmarks.[7]

Authorised use, s57(5) The grounds for refusal of registration under section 57 do not apply to applications lodged by a national of a country who is authorised to make use of the emblem, sign or hallmark of that country and notwithstanding that it may be similar to that of another country.[8]

1 'A Convention country' means a country, other than the United Kingdom, which is a party to the Paris Convention: section 55(1).
2 Section 57(1).
3 An emblem, official sign or hallmark is regarded as protected under the Paris Convention only if, or to the extent that:
   (a) the country in question has notified the United Kingdom in accordance with Article 6*ter*(3) of the Convention that it desires to protect that emblem, sign or hallmark;
   (b) the notification remains in force; and
   (c) the United Kingdom has not objected to it in accordance with Article 6*ter*(4) or any such objection has been withdrawn: section 59(1). Note also that notification under Article 6*ter*(3) of the Convention shall have effect only in

relation to applications for registration made more than two months after the receipt of the notification: section 59(3). The Registrar keeps and makes available for public inspection a list of emblems, signs and hallmarks which are for the time being protected under the Convention by virtue of notification under Article 6*ter*(3): section 59(4)(a).

4 Section 57(2).
5 See note 3.
6 Section 57(3).
7 Section 57(4).
8 Section 57(5).

15.05 Injunction, s57(6) Section 57(6) provides a remedy for the authorities of a Convention country to restrain by injunction any use of a mark in the United Kingdom which could not be registered without their consent by reason of section 57.

15.06 Emblems of international organisations, ss4(3), 58 and 59 A trade mark will be refused registration if it consists of or contains either:

(a) an armorial bearing, flag or other emblem; or

(b) the abbreviation or name,

of an international intergovernmental organisation of which one or more Convention countries[1] are members and which are protected under the Paris Convention.[2]

Authorisation, s58(2) Where the applicant's trade mark consists of or contains any such emblem, abbreviation or name which is protected under the Paris Convention, it may still be registered provided that the authorisation of the international organisation concerned is first obtained. Furthermore, the trade mark may yet be registered even without such authorisation if the Registrar is satisfied that the applicant's proposed use of the emblem, abbreviation or name:

(a) is not such as to suggest to the public that a connection exists between the organisation concerned and the applicant's trade mark; or

(b) is not likely to mislead the public as to the existence of a connection between the use and the organisation concerned.[3]

Imitations, s58(3) It should also be noted that the ground for refusal of registration in relation to armorial bearings, flags and other emblems of an international organisation applies equally to anything which, from a heraldic point of view, is an imitation of any such emblem.[4]

Bona fide use, s58(5) The ground for refusal of registration under section 58 does not affect the rights of a person whose bona fide use of the trade mark in question began before 4 January 1962.[5]

1 See paragraph 15.04, note 1.
2 Emblems, abbreviations and names of an international organisation are regarded as protected under the Paris Convention only if, or to the extent that:
   (a) the organisation in question has notified the United Kingdom in accordance with Article 6*ter*(3) of the Convention that it desires to protect that emblem, abbreviation or name;
   (b) the notification remains in force; and
   (c) the United Kingdom has not objected to it in accordance with Article 6*ter*(4) or any such objection has been withdrawn: section 59(2). Note also that notification under Article 6*ter*(3) of the Convention shall have effect only in relation to applications for registration made more than two months after the receipt of the notification: section 59(3). The Registrar keeps and makes available for public inspection a list of emblems, abbreviations and names of international organisations which are for the time being protected under the convention by virtue of notification under Article 6*ter*(3): section 59(4)(b).
3 Section 58(2).
4 Section 58(3).
5 Being the date on which the relevant provisions of the Paris Convention entered into force in relation to the United Kingdom: section 58(5).

15.07 Injunction, s58(4) Section 58(4) confers upon international organisations the right to restrain by injunction any use of a trade mark in the United Kingdom which could not be registered without their authorisation by reason of section 58.

15.08 Grant of arms, s4(4) and r9 Pursuant to section 4(4), rule 9 prohibits the registration of a trade mark which consists of or contains either:

(a) arms to which a person is entitled by virtue of a grant of arms by the Crown; or

(b) insignia so nearly resembling such arms as to be likely to be mistaken for them,

unless it appears to the Registrar that the person entitled to the arms has given his consent to the registration (and not merely to the use of the arms).

In any event, where such a mark is registered, neither its registration nor anything else in the 1994 Act can be relied on as authorising the use of that mark which would be contrary to the laws of arms.[1]

1 As to which, see Halsbury's Volume 48 pp 6 and 95.

16 Trade mark agents

16.01 Approach taken by the 1994 Act The 1994 Act contains several specific provisions relating to trade mark agents. These are found in sections 82–88 as supplemented by rules 46 and 47.

These provisions deal with the following matters:

(a) the recognition of agents, sections 82 and 88;
(b) the register of trade mark agents, section 83;
(c) the regulation of 'registered trade mark agents', section 83;
(d) proscribing unregistered persons from calling themselves 'registered trade mark agents', sections 84 and 85;
(e) the use of the term 'trade mark attorney', section 86;
(f) privilege in relation to communications with a trade mark agent, section 87.

16.02 Recognition of agents, ss82 and 88 Section 82 of the 1994 Act substantially reproduces section 65 of the 1938 Act. Thus, subject to the provisions referred to below, an agent may, on behalf of his principal, do any act which is required or authorised by the 1994 Act to be done by the principal in connection with the registration of a trade mark or any procedure relating to a trade mark. Similarly, any act which is required or authorised by the 1994 Act to be done to the principal may be done to the agent.[1] In this regard, the agent may be authorised by his principal either orally or in writing.[2] It should be noted that the reference to an agent is not restricted to a 'registered trade mark agent' as defined in section 83. Therefore, any person may act as an agent for the purposes of, inter alia, filing and prosecuting trade mark applications on behalf of an applicant. However, communications with an agent who is not a registered trade mark agent will not be the subject of privilege under section 87; similarly, neither can an agent who is not a registered trade mark agent call himself a trade mark attorney pursuant to section 86.

There are circumstances in which an agent's capacity to act on behalf of his principal may not be recognised by the Registrar. These circumstances arise under rules made pursuant to sections 82 and 88.

Rule 46(2), made pursuant to section 82, is purely procedural and applies where a person has become a party to proceedings before the Registrar and thereafter he either appoints an agent for the first time or substitutes one agent for another. In either case, the agent must file Form TM 33 and until he does so he may not act on behalf of his principal.

Rule 47, made pursuant to section 88(1), is substantive and enables the Registrar to refuse to recognise certain agents on the grounds that:

(a) the person has been convicted of an offence under section 84 (that is to say, a person who wrongly uses the description of 'registered trade mark agent');

(b) the person is an individual whose name is currently removed from the register of trade mark agents on the grounds of misconduct;

(c) the person, whose name has not been in the register of trade mark agents, has been guilty of such conduct as would have rendered him liable to have had his name erased from the register on the grounds of misconduct; or

(d) in the case of a partnership or body corporate, one of the partners or directors is a person whom the Registrar could refuse to recognise by virtue of either (a), (b) or (c) above.

Furthermore, the Registrar may refuse to recognise an agent on the grounds specified in rule 14(5) of the Trade Marks and Service Marks Rules 1986 as amended.[3] Rule 14(5) operates in parallel with rule 47 of the Rules pursuant to paragraph 22(2) of Schedule 3.

Additional rules can be made under section 88(2) prescribing the circumstances in which a person is to be taken to have been guilty of misconduct.

1 Section 82.
2 Section 82; the Registrar may require the personal signature or presence of either the agent or his principal: rule 46(1); and the Registrar may, by notice in writing sent to the agent, require him to produce evidence of authority: rule 46(3).
3 See SI 1990 No 1459.

16.03   The register of trade mark agents, s83   Section 83(1) of the 1994 Act enables the Secretary of State to make rules in relation to the keeping of a register of persons who act as trade mark agents.[1] Anyone whose name is entered in the register is entitled to be referred to as a 'registered trade mark agent'.[2]

At the date of enactment no rules had been made pursuant to section 83. In due course, however, such rules may be made which contain provisions regulating the registration of trade mark agents.[3] In the meantime, the transitional provisions set out in schedule 3 of the 1994 Act will apply. Thus, the rules made pursuant to section 282 of the Copyright, Designs and Patents Act 1988 will continue in force and have effect as if they had been made under section 83 of the 1994 Act.[4]

1 Section 83(1); the rules may delegate the keeping of the register to another person: section 83(3).
2 Section 83(1).
3 Section 83(2).
4 Schedule 3, paragraph 22(1); notwithstanding that section 282 is repealed by the 1994 Act: schedule 5.

16.04   Registered trade mark agents, ss84 and 85   The permissible use of the term 'registered trade mark agent' has to be considered in the separate context of an individual, a partnership and a body corporate.

Individuals   Only an individual who is a registered trade mark agent may:
(a) carry on a business (otherwise than in partnership) under any name or other description which contains the words 'registered trade mark agent'; or
(b) in the course of business otherwise describe or hold himself out, or permit himself to be described or held out, as a 'registered trade mark agent'.[1]

Partnerships   A partnership is only entitled:
(a) to carry on a business under any name or other description which contains the words 'registered trade mark agent'; or
(b) in the course of a business otherwise to describe or hold itself out, or permit itself to be described or held out, as a firm of registered trade mark agents;
provided that either:
(a) all the partners are registered trade mark agents; or

(b) the partnership satisfies the conditions as may be prescribed for the purposes of section 84.²

Bodies corporate   A body corporate is only entitled:
(a) to carry on a business (otherwise than in partnership) under any name or other description which contains the words 'registered trade mark agent'; or
(b) in the course of a business otherwise to describe or hold itself out, or permit itself to be described or held out, as a registered trade mark agent;
provided that either:
(a) all the directors of the body corporate are registered trade mark agents; or
(b) the body satisfies the conditions as may be prescribed for the purposes of section 84.³

1 Section 84(1).
2 Section 84(2); the conditions will be prescribed in rules to be made pursuant to section 85.
3 Section 84(3); the conditions shall be prescribed in rules to be made pursuant to section 85.

16.05 Mixed partnerships and bodies corporate, s85   As already stated, partnerships and bodies corporate may only make use of the words 'registered trade mark agent' if all the partners or all the directors as the case may be are either:
(a) registered trade mark agents; or
(b) members of a partnership or body corporate satisfying conditions prescribed in rules to be made pursuant to section 85.
Although section 85 enables the Secretary of State to make rules prescribing these conditions, no such rules had been made at the date of enactment. Accordingly, pursuant to the transitional provisions in Schedule 3 of the 1994 Act, the rules in force under section 283 of the Copyright, Designs and Patents Act 1988 governing those persons entitled to describe themselves as registered trade mark agents will continue in force and will have effect as if they had been made under section 85 of the 1994 Act.¹

1 Schedule 3, paragraph 22(1): section 85 of the 1994 Act substantially reproduces section 283 of the Copyright, Designs and Patents Act 1988, which is repealed by the 1994 Act.

16.06 Offences, s84(4)   It is an offence for a person (including a partnership or body corporate) to use the words 'registered trade mark agent' contrary to the provisions of section 84. On summary conviction an offender is liable to a fine not exceeding level 5 on the standard scale.[1] It will also be an offence to contravene any requirement imposed by any rules which may be made pursuant to section 85(1).[2] In the meantime, it will continue to be an offence to contravene the rules made under section 283 of the Copyright, Designs and Patents Act.[3]

1   Section 84(4): proceedings for such an offence must be commenced within a year from the date of the offence; in Scotland, see the supplementary provisions as to summary proceedings: section 96.
2   Section 85(3).
3   Schedule 3, paragraph 22(1).

16.07   Trade mark attorney, s86   Prior to the implementation of section 86 it was an offence under section 21 of the Solicitor's Act 1974,[1] in certain circumstances, for any person not qualified to act as a solicitor to use the term 'attorney'. Section 86 now provides that it will not be an offence to use the term 'trade mark attorney' in reference to a registered trade mark agent. This section removes the inconsistency in the use of the term 'attorney' by patent agents and some overseas trade mark agents who already describe themselves as patent attorneys and trade mark attorneys respectively.

1   In Scotland: section 31 Solicitor's (Scotland) Act 1980; in Northern Ireland: article 22 Solicitor's (Northern Ireland) Order 1976.

16.08   Privilege, s87   Section 87 of the 1994 Act governs privilege attaching to certain communications with registered trade mark agents. This section substantially reproduces section 284 of the Copyright, Designs and Patents Act 1988 which is repealed by the 1994 Act.[1]

Scope of the communication   Privilege will attach to any communication:
(a)   between a person and his trade mark agent;[2] or
(b)   for the purpose of obtaining, or in response to a request for, information which a person is seeking for the purpose of instructing his trade mark agent,
provided that the communication relates to any matter involving the protection of any design or trade mark or involving passing-off.[3]

The word 'protection' must include the prosecution of a trade mark application as well as matters concerning the infringement of registered trade mark rights. Arguably, it may also encompass many circumstances in relation to dealings with trade marks, including, in particular, the assignment and licensing of trade marks. For example, a communication between a trade mark agent and his client relating to the quality control provisions to be incorporated in a trade mark licence should be privileged on the basis that such advice relates to the protection of the validity of the trade mark. However, communications which relate to other aspects of a deal involving trade marks may not be privileged if they do not relate to the 'protection' of the trade marks as such. Of course, such communications may be confidential, but confidentiality is not the same as privilege.[4]

Section 87(2)(b) will confer privilege upon relevant communications between parties other than the applicant and/or his trade mark agent provided that they relate to the obtaining of information required by the applicant for the purpose of instructing his trade mark agent.

Scope of the privilege   Communications which fall within the scope of section 87(1) and (2) are privileged from[5] disclosure in legal proceedings in the same way as a communication would be if it had been made between a person and his solicitor or, as the case may be, for the purpose of instructing his solicitor.[6]

1   Schedule 5 of the 1994 Act.
2   As to the meaning of 'trade mark agent', see section 87(3), the effect of which is that registered trade mark agents, partnerships and bodies corporate entitled to describe themselves as registered trade mark agents under sections 84 and 85 are 'trade mark agents' for the purpose of privilege.
3   Section 87(1) & (2).
4   Confidential communications in writing would still be discoverable, whereas privileged communications in writing are not.
5   In Scotland: 'protected against'.
6   Section 87(2).

17 Offences

17.01 Approach taken by the 1994 Act The 1994 Act sets out certain criminal offences specifically relating to trade marks. These are:

(a) the unauthorised use of a trade mark, section 92;[1]

(b) the falsification of the Register and related offences, section 94;[2] and

(c) the making of false representations that a trade mark is registered, section 95.[3]

The 1994 Act also lays down the penalties in respect of these offences and provides for the forfeiture of counterfeit goods.[4]

This chapter describes these offences in turn together with the relevant penalties and the availability of any defences specifically provided for in the 1994 Act.

1 See paragraph 17.02.
2 See paragraph 17.06.
3 See paragraph 17.09.
4 In England, Wales or Northern Ireland see section 97; in Scotland see section 98.

Unauthorised use of a trade mark

17.02 Elements of the offence, s92(1)–(4) It is an offence for a person who with a view to gain for himself or another, or with intent to cause loss to another, and without the consent of the proprietor:

(a) applies to goods or their packaging a sign identical to, or likely

218

to be mistaken for, a registered trade mark;[1]

(b) sells or lets for hire, offers or exposes for sale or hire or distributes goods which bear, or the packaging of which bears, such a sign;[2]

(c) has in his possession, custody or control in the course of a business any such goods with a view to the doing of anything, by himself or another, which would be an offence under paragraph (b);[3]

(d) applies a sign identical to, or likely to be mistaken for, a registered trade mark to material intended to be used:

   (i) for labelling or packaging goods;

   (ii) as a business paper in relation to goods; or

   (iii) for advertising goods;[4]

(e) uses in the course of a business material bearing such a sign for labelling or packaging goods, as a business paper in relation to goods, or for advertising goods;[5]

(f) has in his possession custody or control in the course of a business any such material with a view to the doing of anything, by himself or another, which would be an offence under paragraph (e);[6]

(g) makes an article specifically designed or adapted for making copies of a sign identical to, or likely to be mistaken for, a registered trade mark;[7] or

(h) has such an article specified in (g) above in his possession, custody or control in the course of a business.[8]

In the case of (g) and (h), the offence is only committed if the offender knew or had reason to believe that the article has been, or is to be, used:

   (i) to produce goods; or

   (ii) to produce material for labelling or packaging goods; or

   (iii) as a business paper in relation to goods; or

   (iv) for advertising goods.

In the case of all offences referred to in (a)–(h), the offence is only committed under section 92 if:

   (i) the relevant goods are goods in respect of which the trade mark is registered; or

   (ii) the trade mark has a reputation in the United Kingdom and the use of the sign takes or would take unfair advantage of, or is or would be detrimental to, the distinctive character or the repute of the trade mark.[9]

In any event, no offence under section 92 is committed by anything done before the date of publication of the registration.[10]

1 Section 92(1)(a).
2 Section 92(1)(b).
3 Section 92(1)(c).
4 Section 92(2)(a).
5 Section 92(2)(b).
6 Section 92(2)(c).
7 Section 92(3)(a).
8 Section 92(3)(b).
9 Section 92(4); the requirement in section 92(4)(b) appears in section 10(3): see comments in paragraph 6.06.
10 Section 9(3)(b).

17.03 Defence, s92(5) It will be a complete defence for a person charged with an offence under section 92 to show that he believed on reasonable grounds that the use of the sign in the manner in which it was used, or was to be used, was not an infringement of the registered trade mark.[1]

1 Section 92(5); as to the question of infringement see chapter 6.

17.04 Enforcement, s93 All local weights and measures authorities have a statutory duty to enforce, within their respective area, the provisions of section 92.[1] For this purpose certain provisions of the Trade Descriptions Act 1968, namely sections 27, 28, 29 and 33 will apply in relation to the enforcement of section 92.[2]

Furthermore, the Trade Descriptions Act 1968 applies as if section 92 of the 1994 Act were contained within it for the purposes of any other Act which authorises the disclosure of information to facilitate the enforcement of the Trade Descriptions Act.[3]

1 Section 93(1); in Northern Ireland it is the duty of the Department of Economic Development to enforce section 92: section 93(3).
2 Section 93(2); in Northern Ireland references in the Trade Descriptions Act 1968 to a local weight and measures authority and any officer of such an authority must be read as references to the Department of Economic Development and any of its officers: section 93(3).
3 Section 93(4).

17.05 Penalties, s92(6) A person guilty of an offence under section 92 is liable:
(a) on summary conviction, to imprisonment for a term not exceeding six months or a fine not exceeding the statutory maximum, or both; or

(b) on conviction on indictment, to a fine or imprisonment for a term not exceeding ten years, or both.[1]

1 Section 92(6); in Scotland see the supplementary provisions as to summary proceedings: section 96.

Falsification of the Register and related offences

17.06 Elements of the offence, s94(1) & (2) Section 94 creates various offences relating to the Register.

In the first place, it is an offence to make, or cause to be made, a false entry in the Register knowing or having reason to believe that it is false.[1]

Secondly, it is also an offence to:
(a) make or cause to be made anything falsely purporting to be a copy of an entry in the Register; or
(b) to produce or tender or cause to be produced or tendered in evidence any such thing,

knowing or having reason to believe that it is false.[2]

1 Section 94(1).
2 Section 94(2).

17.07 Defences There are no statutory defences to an offence under section 94.

17.08 Penalties, s94(3) A person guilty of an offence under section 94(3) is liable:
(a) on summary conviction, to imprisonment for a term not exceeding six months or a fine not exceeding the statutory maximum, or both; or
(b) on conviction on indictment, to imprisonment for a term not exceeding two years or a fine, or both.[1]

1 Section 94(3); in Scotland, see the supplementary provisions as to summary proceedings: section 96.

False representations

17.09 Elements of the offence, s95 It is an offence for a person:
(a) falsely to represent that a mark is a registered trade mark; or

(b) to make a false representation as to the goods or services for
which a trade mark is registered,

knowing or having reason to believe that the representation is false.

The use in the United Kingdom of the word 'registered', or any
other word or symbol (presumably including an encircled 'R' device)
importing an express or implied reference to registration in relation
to a trade mark, is deemed to be a representation as to registration
under the 1994 Act.[1]

1 Section 95(2).

17.10 Defences, s95(2)   A defence will be available where the
defendant can show that the use of the word or symbol is a
reference to registration in a country other than in the United
Kingdom and that, in fact, the trade mark is registered in that other
country for the goods or services in question.[1]

1 Section 95(2).

17.11 Penalty, s95(3)   A person guilty of an offence under
section 95 is liable on summary conviction to a fine not exceeding
level 3 on the standard scale.[1]

1 Section 95(3); in Scotland see the supplementary provisions as to summary
proceedings: section 96.

Forfeiture

17.12 Introduction   The 1994 Act provides for an application
to be made for an order for the forfeiture of goods, material or
articles. Section 97 deals with the making of an application for
forfeiture in England, Wales and Northern Ireland while section 98
deals with the position in Scotland. The substantive provisions
relating to forfeiture in Scotland are similar to those in England,
Wales and Northern Ireland. Accordingly, this chapter sets out the
forfeiture provisions as they apply in England, Wales and Northern
Ireland with appropriate footnote references to the corresponding
provisions which apply in Scotland.

17.13 Application for forfeiture, s97(1)–(4)   An application
may be made for an order for the forfeiture of relevant goods,
material or articles which have come into the possession of any

person in connection with the investigation or prosecution of a
relevant offence. A 'relevant offence'[1] is:
(a) an offence under section 92 of the 1994 Act;
(b) an offence under the Trade Descriptions Act 1968; or
(c) any offence involving dishonesty or deception.
The relevant goods, material or articles are respectively:
(a) goods which, or the packaging of which, bears a sign identical
to or likely to be mistaken for a registered trade mark;
(b) material bearing such a sign and intended to be used for
labelling or packaging goods, as a business paper in relation to
goods, or for advertising goods; and
(c) articles specifically designed or adapted for making copies of
such a sign.[2]
Where proceedings have been brought in any court for a relevant
offence relating to some or all of the goods, material or articles, the
application for forfeiture should be made to that court. However,
where no such proceedings have been brought, the application for
forfeiture should be made by way of complaint to a Magistrates' Court.[3]

The court will only make an order for forfeiture of any goods,
material or articles if it is satisfied that a relevant offence has been
committed in relation to relevant goods, material or articles.[4]
However, a court may infer that such an offence has been
committed if it is satisfied that such an offence has been committed
in relation to goods, material or articles which are representative of
them (which may be by reason of their being of the same design or
part of the same consignment or batch, or otherwise).[5]

1 Section 97(8); in Scotland: section 98(14).
2 Section 97(1); in Scotland: section 98(1).
3 Section 97(2); in Scotland: section 98(2); as to 'the court' in Scotland, see section 98(14).
4 Section 97(3); in Scotland: section 98(3).
5 Section 97(4); in Scotland: section 98(4).

17.14 Appeals, s97(5) Any person who is aggrieved by:
(a) an order for forfeiture made under section 97 by a Magistrates' Court; or
(b) a decision of a Magistrates' Court not to make an order for forfeiture,
may appeal against the order or the decision (as the case may be).
The appeal in England and Wales will be to the Crown Court and
in Northern Ireland to the County Court.[1]

Any order made by a magistrate under section 97 may provide that the order will not come into force pending the making and determination of any appeal.[2]

1 Section 97(5); appeal includes an application under section 111 of the Magistrates' Courts Act 1980 or Article 146 of the Magistrates' Courts (Northern Ireland) Order 1981 (statement of case); in Scotland see the procedure for any person interested appearing at the hearing of the application for forfeiture: section 98(5),(6),(7),(8) and (9).
2 Section 97(5); in Scotland: section 98(10) and (11).

17.15 Destruction or release, s97(6) & (7) Any goods, material or articles which are forfeited pursuant to an order under section 97 will be destroyed in accordance with the directions of the court.[1] However, at the discretion of the court it may instead order that the goods, material or articles be released to a person specified by the court on condition that the person to whom they are released:

(a) causes the offending sign to be erased, removed or obliterated; and

(b) complies with any order to pay costs which has been made against him in the proceedings for the order for forfeiture.[2]

1 Section 97(6); in Scotland: section 98(12).
2 Section 97(7); in Scotland: section 98(13).

Appendix

Index to appendix

The Trade Marks Act 1994

1994 CHAPTER 26

An Act to make new provision for registered trade marks, implementing Council Directive No 89/104/EEC of 21 December 1988 to approximate the laws of the Member States relating to trade marks; to make provision in connection with Council Regulation (EC) No 40/94 of 20 December 1993 on the Community trade mark; to give effect to the Madrid Protocol Relating to the International Registration of Marks of 27 June 1989, and to certain provisions of the Paris Convention for the Protection of Industrial Property of 20 March 1883, as revised and amended; and for connected purposes.

Annotations

Council Directive No 89/104/EEC: OJ No L40, 11.2.89, p 1.
Council Regulation (EC) No 40/94: OJ No L11, 14.1.94, p 1.

[21 July 1994]

BE IT ENACTED by the Queen's most Excellent Majesty, by and with the advice and consent of the Lords Spiritual and Temporal, and Commons, in this present Parliament assembled, and by the authority of the same, as follows: –

Part I
Registered Trade Marks
Introductory

1 Trade Marks

(1) In this Act a 'trade mark' means any sign capable of being represented graphically which is capable of distinguishing goods or services of one undertaking from those of other undertakings.

A trade mark may, in particular, consist of words (including personal names), designs, letters, numerals or the shape of goods or their packaging.

(2) References in this Act to a trade mark include, unless the context otherwise requires, references to a collective mark (see section 49) or certification mark (see section 50).

Annotations

Date in force: 31 October 1994.

Commencement order: SI 1994 No 2550.

2 Registered trade marks

(1) A registered trade mark is a property right obtained by the registration of the trade mark under this Act and the proprietor of a registered trade mark has the rights and remedies provided by this Act.

(2) No proceedings lie to prevent or recover damages for the infringement of an unregistered trade mark as such; but nothing in this Act affects the law relating to passing off.

Annotations

Date in force: 31 October 1994.

Commencement order: SI 1994 No 2550.

Grounds for refusal of registration

3 Absolute grounds for refusal of registration

(1) The following shall not be registered –
   (a) signs which do not satisfy the requirements of section 1(1),
   (b) trade marks which are devoid of any distinctive character,
   (c) trade marks which consist exclusively of signs or indications which may serve, in trade, to designate the kind, quality, quantity, intended purpose, value, geographical origin, the time of production of goods or of rendering of services, or other characteristics of goods or services,
   (d) trade marks which consist exclusively of signs or indications which have become customary in the current language or in the bona fide and established practices of the trade:
   Provided that, a trade mark shall not be refused registration by virtue of paragraph (b), (c) or (d) above if, before the date of application for registration, it has in fact acquired a distinctive

character as a result of the use made of it.

(2) A sign shall not be registered as a trade mark if it consists exclusively of –

(a) the shape which results from the nature of the goods themselves,

(b) the shape of goods which is necessary to obtain a technical result, or

(c) the shape which gives substantial value to the goods.

(3) A trade mark shall not be registered if it is –

(a) contrary to public policy or to accepted principles of morality, or

(b) of such a nature as to deceive the public (for instance as to the nature, quality or geographical origin of the goods or service).

(4) A trade mark shall not be registered if or to the extent that its use is prohibited in the United Kingdom by any enactment or rule of law or by any provision of Community law.

(5) A trade mark shall not be registered in the cases specified, or referred to, in section 4 (specially protected emblems).

(6) A trade mark shall not be registered if or to the extent that the application is made in bad faith.

Annotations

Date in force: 31 October 1994.

Commencement order: SI 1994 No 2550.

4 Specially protected emblems

(1) A trade mark which consists of or contains –

(a) the Royal arms, or any of the principal armorial bearings of the Royal arms, or any insignia or device so nearly resembling the Royal arms or any such armorial bearing as to be likely to be mistaken for them or it,

(b) a representation of the Royal crown or any of the Royal flags,

(c) a representation of Her Majesty or any member of the Royal family, or any colourable imitation thereof, or

(d) words, letters or devices likely to lead persons to think that the applicant either has or recently has had Royal patronage or authorisation,

shall not be registered unless it appears to the registrar that consent has been given by or on behalf of Her Majesty or, as the case may be, the relevant member of the Royal family.

(2) A trade mark which consists of or contains a representation of –
  (a) the national flag of the United Kingdom (commonly known as the Union Jack), or
  (b) the flag of England, Wales, Scotland, Northern Ireland or the Isle of Man,

shall not be registered if it appears to the registrar that the use of the trade mark would be misleading or grossly offensive.

  Provision may be made by rules identifying the flags to which paragraph (b) applies.

(3) A trade mark shall not be registered in the cases specified in –
section 57 (national emblems, &c of Convention countries), or section 58 (emblems, &c of certain international organisations).

(4) Provision may be made by rules prohibiting in such cases as may be prescribed the registration of a trade mark which consists of or contains –
  (a) arms to which a person is entitled by virtue of a grant of arms by the Crown, or
  (b) insignia so nearly resembling such arms as to be likely to be mistaken for them,

unless it appears to the registrar that consent has been given by or on behalf of that person.

  Where such a mark is registered, nothing in this Act shall be construed as authorising its use in any way contrary to the laws of arms.

Annotations

Date in force: 31 October 1994 (sub-ss(1)–(3), sub-s(4) certain purposes); 29 September 1994 (sub-s(4), remaining purposes).

Commencement order: SI 1994 No 2550.

5 Relative grounds for refusal of registration

(1) A trade mark shall not be registered if it is identical with an earlier trade mark and the goods or services for which the trade mark is applied for are identical with the goods or services for which the earlier trade mark is protected.

(2) A trade mark shall not be registered if because –
  (a) it is identical with an earlier trade mark and is to be registered for goods or services similar to those for which

the earlier trade mark is protected, or

(b) it is similar to an earlier trade mark and is to be registered for goods or services identical with or similar to those for which the earlier trade mark is protected,

there exists a likelihood of confusion on the part of the public, which includes the likelihood of association with the earlier trade mark.

(3) A trade mark which –

(a) is identical with or similar to an earlier trade mark, and

(b) is to be registered for goods or services which are not similar to those for which the earlier trade mark is protected,

shall not be registered if, or to the extent that, the earlier trade mark has a reputation in the United Kingdom (or, in the case of a Community trade mark, in the European Community) and the use of the later mark without due cause would take unfair advantage of, or be detrimental to, the distinctive character or the repute of the earlier trade mark.

(4) A trade mark shall not be registered if, or to the extent that, its use in the United Kingdom is liable to be prevented –

(a) by virtue of any rule of law (in particular, the law of passing off) protecting an unregistered trade mark or other sign used in the course of trade, or

(b) by virtue of an earlier right other than those referred to in subsections (1) to (3) or paragraph (a) above, in particular by virtue of the law of copyright, design right or registered designs.

A person thus entitled to prevent the use of a trade mark is referred to in this Act as the proprietor of an 'earlier right' in relation to the trade mark.

(5) Nothing in this section prevents the registration of a trade mark where the proprietor of the earlier trade mark or other earlier right consents to the registration.

Annotations

Date in force: 31 October 1994.

Commencement order: SI 1994 No 2550.

6   Meaning of 'earlier trade mark'

(1) In this Act an 'earlier trade mark' means –

(a) a registered trade mark, international trade mark (UK) or

Community trade mark which has a date of application for registration earlier than that of the trade mark in question, taking account (where appropriate) of the priorities claimed in respect of the trade marks,

(b) a Community trade mark which has a valid claim to seniority from an earlier registered trade mark or international trade mark (UK), or

(c) a trade mark which, at the date of application for registration of the trade mark in question or (where appropriate) of the priority claimed in respect of the application, was entitled to protection under the Paris Convention as a well known trade mark.

(2) References in this Act to an earlier trade mark include a trade mark in respect of which an application for registration has been made and which, if registered, would be an earlier trade mark by virtue of subsection 1(a) or (b), subject to its being so registered.

(3) A trade mark within subsection (1)(a) or (b) whose registration expires shall continue to be taken into account in determining the registrability of a later mark for a period of one year after the expiry unless the registrar is satisfied that there was no bona fide use of the mark during the two years immediately preceding the expiry.

Annotations

Date in force: 31 October 1994.

Commencement order: SI 1994 No 2550.

7 Raising of relative grounds in case of honest concurrent use

(1) This section applies where on an application for the registration of a trade mark it appears to the registrar –

(a) that there is an earlier trade mark in relation to which the conditions set out in section 5(1), (2) or (3) obtain, or

(b) that there is an earlier right in relation to which the condition set out in section 5(4) is satisfied,

but the applicant shows to the satisfaction of the registrar that there has been honest concurrent use of the trade mark for which registration is sought.

(2) In that case the registrar shall not refuse the application by

reason of the earlier trade mark or other earlier right unless objection on that ground is raised in opposition proceedings by the proprietor of that earlier trade mark or other earlier right.

(3) For the purposes of this section 'honest concurrent use' means such use in the United Kingdom, by the applicant or with his consent, as would formerly have amounted to honest concurrent use for the purposes of section 12(2) of the Trade Marks Act 1938.

(4) Nothing in this section affects –
   (a) the refusal of registration on the grounds mentioned in section 3 (absolute grounds for refusal), or
   (b) the making of an application for a declaration of invalidity under section 47(2) (application on relative grounds where no consent to registration).

(5) This section does not apply when there is an order in force under section 8 below.

Annotations
Date in force: 31 October 1994.
Commencement order: SI 1994 No 2550.

8 Power to require that relative grounds be raised in opposition proceedings

(1) The Secretary of State may by order provide that in any case a trade mark shall not be refused registration on a ground mentioned in section 5 (relative grounds for refusal) unless objection on that ground is raised in opposition proceedings by the proprietor of the earlier trade mark or other earlier right.

(2) The order may make such consequential provision as appears to the Secretary of State appropriate –
   (a) with respect to the carrying out by the registrar of searches of earlier trade marks, and
   (b) as to the persons by whom an application for a declaration of invalidity may be made on the grounds specified in section 47(2) (relative grounds).

(3) An order making such provision as is mentioned in subsection (2)(a) may direct that so much of section 37 (examination of application) as requires a search to be carried out shall cease to have effect.

(4) An order making such provision as is mentioned in subsection (2)(b) may provide that so much of section 47(3) as provides that any person may make an application for a declaration of invalidity shall have effect subject to the provisions of the order.

(5) An order under this section shall be made by statutory instrument, and no order shall be made unless a draft of it has been laid before and approved by a resolution of each House of Parliament.

No such draft of an order making such provision as is mentioned in subsection (1) shall be laid before Parliament until after the end of the period of ten years beginning with the day on which applications for Community trade marks may first be filed in pursuance of the Community Trade Mark Regulation.

(6) An order under this section may contain such transitional provisions as appear to the Secretary of State to be appropriate.

Annotations
Date in force: 31 October 1994.
Commencement order: SI 1994 No 2550.

Effects of registered trade mark

9 Rights conferred by registered trade mark

(1) The proprietor of a registered trade mark has exclusive rights in the trade mark which are infringed by use of the trade mark in the United Kingdom without his consent.

The acts amounting to infringement, if done without the consent of the proprietor, are specified in section 10.

(2) References in this Act to the infringement of a registered trade mark are to any such infringement of the rights of the proprietor.

(3) The rights of the proprietor have effect from the date of registration (which in accordance with section 40(3) is the date of filing of the application for registration):

Provided that –

(a) no infringement proceedings may be begun before the date on which the trade mark is in fact registered; and

(b) no offence under section 92 (unauthorised use of trade

mark, &c in relation to goods) is committed by anything
done before the date of publication of the registration.

Annotations

Date in force: 31 October 1994.
Commencement order: SI 1994 No 2550.

10   Infringement of registered trade mark

(1) A person infringes a registered trade mark if he uses in the
course of trade a sign which is identical with the trade mark in
relation to goods or services which are identical with those for
which it is registered.

(2) A person infringes a registered trade mark if he uses in the
course of trade a sign where because –
  (a) the sign is identical with the trade mark and is used in
relation to goods or services similar to those for which the
trade mark is registered, or
  (b) the sign is similar to the trade mark and is used in relation
to goods or services identical with or similar to those for
which the trade mark is registered,
there exists a likelihood of confusion on the part of the public,
which includes the likelihood of association with the trade
mark.

(3) A person infringes a registered trade mark if he uses in the
course of trade a sign which –
  (a) is identical with or similar to the trade mark, and
  (b) is used in relation to goods or services which are not similar
to those for which the trade mark is registered,
where the trade mark has a reputation in the United Kingdom
and the use of the sign, being without due cause, takes unfair
advantage of, or is detrimental to, the distinctive character or
the repute of the trade mark.

(4) For the purposes of this section a person uses a sign if, in
particular, he –
  (a) affixes it to goods or the packaging thereof;
  (b) offers or exposes goods for sale, puts them on the market or
stocks them for those purposes under the sign, or offers or
supplies services under the sign;
  (c) imports or exports goods under the sign; or
  (d) uses the sign on business papers or in advertising.

(5) A person who applies a registered trade mark to material intended to be used for labelling or packaging goods, as a business paper, or for advertising goods or services, shall be treated as a party to any use of the material which infringes the registered trade mark if when he applied the mark he knew or had reason to believe that the application of the mark was not duly authorised by the proprietor or a licensee.

(6) Nothing in the preceding provisions of this section shall be construed as preventing the use of a registered trade mark by any person for the purpose of identifying goods or services as those of the proprietor or a licensee.

But any such use otherwise than in accordance with honest practices in industrial or commercial matters shall be treated as infringing the registered trade mark if the use without due cause takes unfair advantage of, or is detrimental to, the distinctive character or repute of the trade mark.

Annotations

Date in force: 31 October 1994.

Commencement order: SI 1994 No 2550.

11 Limits on effect of registered trade mark

(1) A registered trade mark is not infringed by the use of another registered trade mark in relation to goods or services for which the latter is registered (but see section 47(6) (effect of declaration of invalidity of registration)).

(2) A registered trade mark is not infringed by –
   (a) the use by a person of his own name or address,
   (b) the use of indications concerning the kind, quality, quantity, intended purpose, value, geographical origin, the time of production of goods or of rendering of services, or other characteristics of goods or services, or
   (c) the use of the trade mark where it is necessary to indicate the intended purpose of a product or service (in particular, as accessories or spare parts),

   provided the use is in accordance with honest practices in industrial or commercial matters.

(3) A registered trade mark is not infringed by the use in the course of trade in a particular locality of an earlier right which applies only in that locality.

For this purpose an 'earlier right' means an unregistered trade mark or other sign continuously used in relation to goods or services by a person or a predecessor in title of his from a date prior to whichever is the earlier of –

(a) the use of the first-mentioned trade mark in relation to those goods or services by the proprietor or a predecessor in title of his, or

(b) the registration of the first-mentioned trade mark in respect of those goods or services in the name of the proprietor or a predecessor in title of his;

and an earlier right shall be regarded as applying in a locality if, or to the extent that, its use in that locality is protected by virtue of any rule of law (in particular, the law of passing off).

Annotations
Date in force: 31 October 1994.
Commencement order: SI 1994 No 2550.

12   Exhaustion of rights conferred by registered trade mark

(1) A registered trade mark is not infringed by the use of the trade mark in relation to goods which have been put on the market in the European Economic Area under that trade mark by the proprietor or with his consent.

(2) Subsection (1) does not apply where there exist legitimate reasons for the proprietor to oppose further dealings in the goods (in particular, where the condition of the goods has been changed or impaired after they have been put on the market).

Annotations
Date in force: 31 October 1994.
Commencement order: SI 1994 No 2550.

13   Registration subject to disclaimer or limitation

(1) An applicant for registration of a trade mark, or the proprietor of a registered trade mark, may –

(a) disclaim any right to the exclusive use of any specified element of the trade mark, or

(b) agree that the rights conferred by the registration shall be

subject to a specified territorial or other limitation;
and where the registration of a trade mark is subject to a disclaimer or limitation, the rights conferred by section 9 (rights conferred by registered trade mark) are restricted accordingly.

(2) Provision shall be made by rules as to the publication and entry in the register of a disclaimer or limitation.

Annotations

Date in force: 31 October 1994 (sub-s(1), sub-s(2) certain purposes); 29 September 1994 (sub-s(2), remaining purposes).

Commencement order: SI 1994 No 2550.

Infringement proceedings

14 Action for infringement

(1) An infringement of a registered trade mark is actionable by the proprietor of the trade mark.

(2) In an action for infringement all such relief by way of damages, injunctions, accounts or otherwise is available to him as is available in respect of the infringement of any other property right.

Annotations

Date in force: 31 October 1994.

Commencement order: SI 1994 No 2550.

15 Order for erasure, &c of offending sign

(1) Where a person is found to have infringed a registered trade mark, the court may make an order requiring him –
   (a) to cause the offending sign to be erased, removed or obliterated from any infringing goods, material or articles in his possession, custody or control, or
   (b) if it is not reasonably practicable for the offending sign to be erased, removed or obliterated, to secure the destruction of the infringing goods, material or articles in question.

(2) If an order under subsection (1) is not complied with, or it appears to the court likely that such an order would not be complied with, the court may order that the infringing goods, material or articles be delivered to such person as the court may

direct for erasure, removal or obliteration of the sign, or for destruction, as the case may be.

Annotations
Date in force: 31 October 1994.
Commencement order: SI 1994 No 2550.

16   Order for delivery up of infringing goods, material or articles

(1) The proprietor of a registered trade mark may apply to the court for an order for the delivery up to him, or such other person as the court may direct, of any infringing goods, material or articles which a person has in his possession, custody or control in the course of a business.

(2) An application shall not be made after the end of the period specified in section 18 (period after which remedy of delivery up not available); and no order shall be made unless the court also makes, or it appears to the court that there are grounds for making, an order under section 19 (order as to disposal of infringing goods, &c).

(3) A person to whom any infringing goods, material or articles are delivered up in pursuance of an order under this section shall, if an order under section 19 is not made, retain them pending the making of an order, or the decision not to make an order, under that section.

(4) Nothing in this section affects any other power of the court.

Annotations
Date in force: 31 October 1994.
Commencement order: SI 1994 No 2550.

17   Meaning of 'infringing goods, material or articles'

(1) In this Act the expressions 'infringing goods', 'infringing material' and 'infringing articles' shall be construed as follows.

(2) Goods are 'infringing goods', in relation to a registered trade mark, if they or their packaging bear a sign identical or similar to that mark and –
   (a) the application of the sign to the goods or their packaging was an infringement of the registered trade mark, or
   (b) the goods are proposed to be imported into the United

Kingdom and the application of the sign in the United Kingdom to them or their packaging would be an infringement of the registered trade mark, or

    (c) the sign has otherwise been used in relation to the goods in such a way as to infringe the registered trade mark.

(3) Nothing in subsection (2) shall be construed as affecting the importation of goods which may lawfully be imported into the United Kingdom by virtue of an enforceable Community right.

(4) Material is 'infringing material', in relation to a registered trade mark, if it bears a sign identical or similar to that mark and either –

    (a) it is used for labelling or packaging goods, as a business paper, or for advertising goods or services, in such a way as to infringe the registered trade mark, or

    (b) it is intended to be so used and such use would infringe the registered trade mark.

(5) 'Infringing articles', in relation to a registered trade mark, means articles –

    (a) which are specifically designed or adapted for making copies of a sign identical or similar to that mark, and

    (b) which a person has in his possession, custody or control, knowing or having reason to believe that they have been or are to be used to produce infringing goods or material.

Annotations

Date in force: 31 October 1994.

Commencement order: SI 1994 No 2550.

18 Period after which remedy of delivery up not available

(1) An application for an order under section 16 (order for delivery up of infringing goods, material or articles) may not be made after the end of the period of six years from –

    (a) in the case of infringing goods, the date on which the trade mark was applied to the goods or their packaging,

    (b) in the case of infringing material, the date on which the trade mark was applied to the material, or

    (c) in the case of infringing articles, the date on which they were made,

except as mentioned in the following provisions.

(2) If during the whole or part of that period the proprietor of the registered trade mark –
   (a) is under a disability, or
   (b) is prevented by fraud or concealment from discovering the facts entitling him to apply for an order,
   an application may be made at any time before the end of the period of six years from the date on which he ceased to be under a disability or, as the case may be, could with reasonable diligence have discovered those facts.

(3) In subsection (2) 'disability' –
   (a) in England and Wales, has the same meaning as in the Limitation Act 1980;
   (b) in Scotland, means legal disability within the meaning of the Prescription and Limitation (Scotland) Act 1973;
   (c) in Northern Ireland, has the same meaning as in the Limitation (Northern Ireland) Order 1989.

Annotations

Date in force: 31 October 1994.

Commencement order: SI 1994 No 2550.

19 Order as to disposal of infringing goods, material or articles

(1) Where infringing goods, material or articles have been delivered up in pursuance of an order under section 16, an application may be made to the court –
   (a) for an order that they be destroyed or forfeited to such person as the court may think fit, or
   (b) for a decision that no such order should be made.

(2) In considering what order (if any) should be made, the court shall consider whether other remedies available in an action for infringement of the registered trade mark would be adequate to compensate the proprietor and any licensee and protect their interests.

(3) Provision shall be made by rules of court as to the service of notice on persons having an interest in the goods, material or articles, and any such person is entitled –
   (a) to appear in proceedings for an order under this section, whether or not he was served with notice, and
   (b) to appeal against any order made, whether or not he appeared;

and an order shall not take effect until the end of the period within which notice of an appeal may be given or, if before the end of that period notice of appeal is duly given, until the final determination or abandonment of the proceedings on the appeal.

(4) Where there is more than one person interested in the goods, material or articles, the court shall make such order as it thinks just.

(5) If the court decides that no order should be made under this section, the person in whose possession, custody or control the goods, material or articles were before being delivered up is entitled to their return.

(6) References in this section to a person having an interest in goods, material or articles include any person in whose favour an order could be made under this section or under section 114, 204 or 231 of the Copyright, Designs and Patents Act 1988 (which make similar provision in relation to infringement of copyright, rights in performances and design right).

Annotations

Date in force: 31 October 1994.

Commencement order: SI 1994 No 2550.

20 Jurisdiction of sheriff court or county court in Northern Ireland

Proceedings for an order under section 16 (order for delivery up of infringing goods, material or articles) or section 19 (order as to disposal of infringing goods, &c) may be brought –

(a) in the sheriff court in Scotland, or

(b) in a county court in Northern Ireland.

This does not affect the jurisdiction of the Court of Session or the High Court in Northern Ireland.

Annotations

Date in force: 31 October 1994.

Commencement order: SI 1994 No 2550.

21 Remedy for groundless threats of infringement proceedings

(1) Where a person threatens another with proceedings for infringement of a registered trade mark other than –

(a) the application of the mark to goods or their packaging,

(b) the importation of goods to which, or to the packaging of which, the mark has been applied, or

(c) the supply of services under the mark,

any person aggrieved may bring proceedings for relief under this section.

(2) The relief which may be applied for is any of the following –

(a) a declaration that the threats are unjustifiable,

(b) an injunction against the continuance of the threats,

(c) damages in respect of any loss he has sustained by the threats; and the plaintiff is entitled to such relief unless the defendant shows that the acts in respect of which proceedings were threatened constitute (or if done would constitute) an infringement of the registered trade mark concerned.

(3) If that is shown by the defendant, the plaintiff is nevertheless entitled to relief if he shows that the registration of the trade mark is invalid or liable to be revoked in a relevant respect.

(4) The mere notification that a trade mark is registered, or that an application for registration has been made, does not constitute a threat of proceedings for the purposes of this section.

Annotations
Date in force: 31 October 1994.
Commencement order: SI 1994 No 2550.

Registered trade mark as object of property

22   Nature of registered trade mark

A registered trade mark is personal property (in Scotland, incorporeal moveable property).

Annotations
Date in force: 31 October 1994.
Commencement order: SI 1994 No 2550.

23   Co-ownership of registered trade mark

(1) Where a registered trade mark is granted to two or more persons jointly, each of them is entitled, subject to any agreement to the contrary, to an equal undivided share in the registered trade mark.

243

(2) The following provisions apply where two or more persons are co-proprietors of a registered trade mark, by virtue of subsection (1) or otherwise.

(3) Subject to any agreement to the contrary, each co-proprietor is entitled, by himself or his agents, to do for his own benefit and without the consent of or the need to account to the other or others, any act which would otherwise amount to an infringement of the registered trade mark.

(4) One co-proprietor may not without the consent of the other or others –
  (a) grant a licence to use the registered trade mark, or
  (b) assign or charge his share in the registered trade mark (or, in Scotland, cause or permit security to be granted over it).

(5) Infringement proceedings may be brought by any co-proprietor, but he may not, without the leave of the court, proceed with the action unless the other, or each of the others, is either joined as a plaintiff or added as a defendant.

  A co-proprietor who is thus added as a defendant shall not be made liable for any costs in the action unless he takes part in the proceedings.

  Nothing in this subsection affects the granting of interlocutory relief on the application of a single co-proprietor.

(6) Nothing in this section affects the mutual rights and obligations of trustees or personal representatives, or their rights and obligations as such.

Annotations
Date in force: 31 October 1994.
Commencement order: SI 1994 No 2550.

24 Assignment, &c of registered trade mark

(1) A registered trade mark is transmissible by assignment, testamentary disposition or operation of law in the same way as other personal or moveable property.

  It is so transmissible either in connection with the goodwill of a business or independently.

(2) An assignment or other transmission of a registered trade mark may be partial, that is, limited so as to apply –
  (a) in relation to some but not all of the goods or services for which the trade mark is registered, or

(b) in relation to use of the trade mark in a particular manner or a particular locality.

(3) An assignment of a registered trade mark, or an assent relating to a registered trade mark, is not effective unless it is in writing signed by or on behalf of the assignor or, as the case may be, a personal representative.

Except in Scotland, this requirement may be satisfied in a case where the assignor or personal representative is a body corporate by the affixing of its seal.

(4) The above provisions apply to assignment by way of security as in relation to any other assignment.

(5) A registered trade mark may be the subject of a charge (in Scotland, security) in the same way as other personal or moveable property.

(6) Nothing in this Act shall be construed as affecting the assignment or other transmission of an unregistered trade mark as part of the goodwill of a business.

Annotations

Date in force: 31 October 1994.

Commencement order: SI 1994 No 2550.

25 Registration of transactions affecting registered trade mark

(1) On application being made to the registrar by –

(a) a person claiming to be entitled to an interest in or under a registered trade mark by virtue of a registrable transaction, or

(b) any other person claiming to be affected by such a transaction,

the prescribed particulars of the transaction shall be entered in the register.

(2) The following are registrable transactions –

(a) an assignment of a registered trade mark or any right in it;

(b) the grant of a licence under a registered trade mark;

(c) the granting of any security interest (whether fixed or floating) over a registered trade mark or any right in or under it;

(d) the making by personal representatives of an assent in relation to a registered trade mark or any right in or under it;

(e) an order of a court or other competent authority transferring a registered trade mark or any right in or under it.

(3) Until an application has been made for registration of the prescribed particulars of a registrable transaction –

(a) the transaction is ineffective as against a person acquiring a conflicting interest in or under the registered trade mark in ignorance of it, and

(b) a person claiming to be a licensee by virtue of the transaction does not have the protection of section 30 or 31 (rights and remedies of licensee in relation to infringement).

(4) Where a person becomes the proprietor or a licensee of a registered trade mark by virtue of a registrable transaction, then unless –

(a) an application for registration of the prescribed particulars of the transaction is made before the end of the period of six months beginning with its date, or

(b) the court is satisfied that it was not practicable for such an application to be made before the end of that period and that an application was made as soon as practicable thereafter,

he is not entitled to damages or an account of profits in respect of any infringement of the registered trade mark occurring after the date of the transaction and before the prescribed particulars of the transaction are registered.

(5) Provision may be made by rules as to –

(a) the amendment of registered particulars relating to a licence so as to reflect any alteration of the terms of the licence, and

(b) the removal of such particulars from the register –

(i) where it appears from the registered particulars that the licence was granted for a fixed period and that period has expired, or

(ii) where no such period is indicated and, after such period as may be prescribed, the registrar has notified the parties of his intention to remove the particulars from the register.

(6) Provision may also be made by rules as to the amendment or removal from the register of particulars relating to a security

interest on the application of, or with the consent of, the person entitled to the benefit of that interest.

Annotations

Date in force: 31 October 1994 (sub-ss(1), (5), (6) certain purposes, sub-ss(2)–(4)); 29 September 1994 (sub-ss(1), (5), (6), remaining purposes).

Commencement order: SI 1994 No 2550.

26   Trusts and equities

(1)   No notice of any trust (express, implied or constructive) shall be entered in the register; and the registrar shall not be affected by any such notice.

(2)   Subject to the provisions of this Act, equities (in Scotland, rights) in respect of a registered trade mark may be enforced in like manner as in respect of other personal or moveable property.

Annotations

Date in force: 31 October 1994.

Commencement order: SI 1994 No 2550.

27   Application for registration of trade mark as an object of property

(1)   The provisions of sections 22 to 26 (which relate to a registered trade mark as an object of property) apply, with the necessary modifications, in relation to an application for the registration of a trade mark as in relation to a registered trade mark.

(2)   In section 23 (co-ownership of registered trade mark) as it applies in relation to an application for registration, the reference in subsection (1) to the granting of the registration shall be construed as a reference to the making of the application.

(3)   In section 25 (registration of transactions affecting registered trade marks) as it applies in relation to a transaction affecting an application for the registration of a trade mark, the references to the entry of particulars in the register, and to the making of an application to register particulars, shall be construed as references to the giving of notice to the registrar of those particulars.

Annotations

Date in force: 31 October 1994.

Commencement order: SI 1994 No 2550.

Licensing

28 Licensing of registered trade mark

(1) A licence to use a registered trade mark may be general or limited. A limited licence may, in particular, apply –
    (a) in relation to some but not all of the goods or services for which the trade mark is registered, or
    (b) in relation to use of the trade mark in a particular manner or a particular locality.
(2) A licence is not effective unless it is in writing signed by or on behalf of the grantor.
    Except in Scotland, this requirement may be satisfied in a case where the grantor is a body corporate by the affixing of its seal.
(3) Unless the licence provides otherwise, it is binding on a successor in title to the grantor's interest.
    References in this Act to doing anything with, or without, the consent of the proprietor of a registered trade mark shall be construed accordingly.
(4) Where the licence so provides, a sub-licence may be granted by the licensee; and references in this Act to a licence or licensee include a sub-licence or sub-licensee.

Annotations
Date in force: 31 October 1994.
Commencement order: SI 1994 No 2550.

29 Exclusive licenses

(1) In this Act an 'exclusive licence' means a licence (whether general or limited) authorising the licensee to the exclusion of all other persons, including the person granting the licence, to use a registered trade mark in the manner authorised by the licence.
    The expression 'exclusive licensee' shall be construed accordingly.
(2) An exclusive licensee has the same rights against a successor in title who is bound by the licence as he has against the person granting the licence.

Annotations
Date in force: 31 October 1994.
Commencement order: SI 1994 No 2550.

30 General provisions as to rights of licensees in case of infringement

(1) This section has effect with respect to the rights of a licensee in relation to infringement of a registered trade mark.

The provisions of this section do not apply where or to the extent that, by virtue of section 31(1) below (exclusive licensee having rights and remedies of assignee), the licensee has a right to bring proceedings in his own name.

(2) A licensee is entitled, unless his licence, or any licence through which his interest is derived, provides otherwise, to call on the proprietor of the registered trade mark to take infringement proceedings in respect of any matter which affects his interests.

(3) If the proprietor –
(a) refuses to do so, or
(b) fails to do so within two months after being called upon, the licensee may bring the proceedings in his own name as if he were the proprietor.

(4) Where infringement proceedings are brought by a licensee by virtue of this section, the licensee may not, without the leave of the court, proceed with the action unless the proprietor is either joined as a plaintiff or added as a defendant.

This does not affect the granting of interlocutory relief on an application by a licensee alone.

(5) A proprietor who is added as a defendant as mentioned in subsection (4) shall not be made liable for any costs in the action unless he takes part in the proceedings.

(6) In infringement proceedings brought by the proprietor of a registered trade mark any loss suffered or likely to be suffered by licensees shall be taken into account; and the court may give such directions as it thinks fit as to the extent to which the plaintiff is to hold the proceeds of any pecuniary remedy on behalf of licensees.

(7) The provisions of this section apply in relation to an exclusive licensee if or to the extent that he has, by virtue of section 31(1), the rights and remedies of an assignee as if he were the proprietor of the registered trade mark.

Annotations

Date in force: 31 October 1994.

Commencement order: SI 1994 No 2550.

31 Exclusive licensee having rights and remedies of assignee

(1) An exclusive licence may provide that the licensee shall have, to such extent as may be provided by the licence, the same rights and remedies in respect of matters occurring after the grant of the licence as if the licence had been an assignment.

Where or to the extent that such provision is made, the licensee is entitled, subject to the provisions of the licence and to the following provisions of this section, to bring infringement proceedings, against any person other than the proprietor, in his own name.

(2) Any such rights and remedies of an exclusive licensee are concurrent with those of the proprietor of the registered trade mark; and references to the proprietor of a registered trade mark in the provisions of this Act relating to infringement shall be construed accordingly.

(3) In an action brought by an exclusive licensee by virtue of this section a defendant may avail himself of any defence which would have been available to him if the action had been brought by the proprietor of the registered trade mark.

(4) Where proceedings for infringement of a registered trade mark brought by the proprietor or an exclusive licensee relate wholly or partly to an infringement in respect of which they have concurrent rights of action, the proprietor or, as the case may be, the exclusive licensee may not, without the leave of the court, proceed with the action unless the other is either joined as a plaintiff or added as a defendant.

This does not affect the granting of interlocutory relief on an application by a proprietor or exclusive licensee alone.

(5) A person who is added as a defendant as mentioned in subsection (4) shall not be made liable for any costs in the action unless he takes part in the proceedings.

(6) Where an action for infringement of a registered trade mark is brought which relates wholly or partly to an infringement in respect of which the proprietor and an exclusive licensee have or had concurrent rights of action –
  (a) the court shall in assessing damages take into account –
    (i) the terms of the licence, and
    (ii) any pecuniary remedy already awarded or available to either of them in respect of the infringement;

(b) no account of profits shall be directed if an award of damages has been made, or an account of profits has been directed, in favour of the other of them in respect of the infringement; and

(c) the court shall if an account of profits is directed apportion the profits between them as the court considers just, subject to any agreement between them.

The provisions of this subsection apply whether or not the proprietor and the exclusive licensee are both parties to the action; and if they are not both parties the court may give such directions as it thinks fit as to the extent to which the party to the proceedings is to hold the proceeds of any pecuniary remedy on behalf of the other.

(7) The proprietor of a registered trade mark shall notify any exclusive licensee who has a concurrent right of action before applying for an order under section 16 (order for delivery up); and the court may on the application of the licensee make such order under that section as it thinks fit having regard to the terms of the licence.

(8) The provisions of subsections (4) to (7) above have effect subject to any agreement to the contrary between the exclusive licensee and the proprietor.

Annotations

Date in force: 31 October 1994.

Commencement order: SI 1994 No 2550.

Application for registered trade mark

32   **Application for registration**

(1) An application for registration of a trade mark shall be made to the registrar.

(2) The application shall contain –

(a) a request for registration of a trade mark,

(b) the name and address of the applicant,

(c) a statement of the goods or services in relation to which it is sought to register the trade mark, and

(d) a representation of the trade mark.

(3) The application shall state that the trade mark is being used, by the applicant or with his consent, in relation to those goods or services,

or that he has a *bona fide* intention that it should be so used.

(4) The application shall be subject to the payment of the application fee and such class fees as may be appropriate.

Annotations

Date in force: 31 October 1994.

Commencement order: SI 1994 No 2550.

33 Date of filing

(1) The date of filing of an application for registration of a trade mark is the date on which documents containing everything required by section 32(2) are furnished to the registrar by the applicant.

If the documents are furnished on different days, the date of filing is the last of those days.

(2) References in this Act to the date of application for registration are to the date of filing of the application.

Annotations

Date in force: 31 October 1994.

Commencement order: SI 1994 No 2550.

34 Classification of trade marks

(1) Goods and services shall be classified for the purposes of the registration of trade marks according to a prescribed system of classification.

(2) Any question arising as to the class within which any goods or services fall shall be determined by the registrar, whose decision shall be final.

Annotations

Date in force: 31 October 1994 (sub-s(1) certain purposes, sub-s(2)); 29 September 1994 (sub-s(1), remaining purposes).

Commencement order: SI 1994 No 2550.

Priority

35 Claim to priority of Convention application

(1) A person who has duly filed an application for protection of a trade mark in a Convention country (a 'Convention application'), or his successor in title, has a right to priority, for

the purposes of registering the same trade mark under this Act for some or all of the same goods or services, for a period of six months from the date of filing of the first such application.

(2) If the application for registration under this Act is made within that six-month period –

(a) the relevant date for the purposes of establishing which rights take precedence shall be the date of filing of the first Convention application, and

(b) the registrability of the trade mark shall not be affected by any use of the mark in the United Kingdom in the period between that date and the date of the application under this Act.

(3) Any filing which in a Convention country is equivalent to a regular national filing, under its domestic legislation or an international agreement, shall be treated as giving rise to the right of priority.

A 'regular national filing' means a filing which is adequate to establish the date on which the application was filed in that country, whatever may be the subsequent fate of the application.

(4) A subsequent application concerning the same subject as the first Convention application, filed in the same Convention country, shall be considered the first Convention application (of which the filing date is the starting date of the period of priority), if at the time of the subsequent application –

(a) the previous application has been withdrawn, abandoned or refused, without having been laid open to public inspection and without leaving any rights outstanding, and

(b) it has not yet served as a basis for claiming a right of priority. The previous application may not thereafter serve as a basis for claiming a right of priority.

(5) Provision may be made by rules as to the manner of claiming a right to priority on the basis of a Convention application.

(6) A right to priority arising as a result of a Convention application may be assigned or otherwise transmitted, either with the application or independently.

The reference in subsection (1) to the applicant's successor in title shall be construed accordingly.

Annotations

Date in force: 31 October 1994 (sub-ss(1)–(4), (6), sub-s(5) certain purposes); 29 September 1994 (sub-s(5), remaining purposes).

Commencement order: SI 1994 No 2550.

36 Claim to priority from other relevant overseas application

(1) Her Majesty may by Order in Council make provision for conferring on a person who has duly filed an application for protection of a trade mark in –

  (a) any of the Channel Islands or a colony, or

  (b) a country or territory in relation to which Her Majesty's Government in the United Kingdom have entered into a treaty, convention, arrangement or engagement for the reciprocal protection of trade marks,

a right to priority, for the purpose of registering the same trade mark under this Act for some or all of the same goods or services, for a specified period from the date of filing of that application.

(2) An Order in Council under this section may make provision corresponding to that made by section 35 in relation to Convention countries or such other provision as appears to Her Majesty to be appropriate.

(3) A statutory instrument containing an Order in Council under this section shall be subject to annulment in pursuance of a resolution of either House of Parliament.

Annotations

Date in force: 31 October 1994.

Commencement order: SI 1994 No 2550.

Registration procedure

37 Examination of application

(1) The registrar shall examine whether an application for registration of a trade mark satisfies the requirements of this Act (including any requirements imposed by rules).

(2) For that purpose he shall carry out a search, to such extent as he considers necessary, of earlier trade marks.

(3) If it appears to the registrar that the requirements for registration are not met, he shall inform the applicant and give him an opportunity, within such period as the registrar may specify, to make representations or to amend the application.

(4) If the applicant fails to satisfy the registrar that those

requirements are met, or to amend the application so as to meet them, or fails to respond before the end of the specified period, the registrar shall refuse to accept the application.

(5) If it appears to the registrar that the requirements for registration are met, he shall accept the application.

Annotations
Date in force: 31 October 1994.
Commencement order: SI 1994 No 2550.

38 Publication, opposition proceedings and observations

(1) When an application for registration has been accepted, the registrar shall cause the application to be published in the prescribed manner.

(2) Any person may, within the prescribed time from the date of the publication of the application, give notice to the registrar of opposition to the registration.

The notice shall be given in writing in the prescribed manner, and shall include a statement of the grounds of opposition.

(3) Where an application has been published, any person may, at any time before the registration of the trade mark, make observations in writing to the registrar as to whether the trade mark should be registered; and the registrar shall inform the applicant of any such observations.

A person who makes observations does not thereby become a party to the proceedings on the application.

Annotations
Date in force: 31 October 1994 (sub-ss(1), (2) certain purposes, sub-s(3)); 29 September 1994 (sub-ss(1), (2), remaining purposes).
Commencement order: SI 1994 No 2550.

39 Withdrawal, restriction or amendment of application

(1) The applicant may at any time withdraw his application or restrict the goods or services covered by the application.

If the application has been published, the withdrawal or restriction shall also be published.

(2) In other respects, an application may be amended, at the

request of the applicant, only by correcting –
(a) the name or address of the applicant,
(b) errors of wording or of copying, or
(c) obvious mistakes,
and then only where the correction does not substantially affect
the identity of the trade mark or extend the goods or services
covered by the application.
(3) Provision shall be made by rules for the publication of any
amendment which affects the representation of the trade mark,
or the goods or services covered by the application, and for the
making of objections by any person claiming to be affected by it.

Annotations

Date in force: 31 October 1994 (sub-ss(1), (2), sub-s(3) certain purposes); 29
September 1994 (sub-s(3), remaining purposes).

Commencement order: SI 1994 No 2550.

40   Registration

(1) Where an application has been accepted and –
(a) no notice of opposition is given within the period referred
to in section 38(2), or
(b) all opposition proceedings are withdrawn or decided in
favour of the applicant,
the registrar shall register the trade mark, unless it appears to
him having regard to matters coming to his notice since he
accepted the application that it was accepted in error.
(2) A trade mark shall not be registered unless any fee prescribed
for the registration is paid within the prescribed period.
    If the fee is not paid within that period, the application shall
be deemed to be withdrawn.
(3) A trade mark when registered shall be registered as of the date
of filing of the application for registration; and that date shall be
deemed for the purposes of this Act to be the date of registration.
(4) On the registration of a trade mark the registrar shall publish
the registration in the prescribed manner and issue to the
applicant a certificate of registration.

Annotations

Date in force: 31 October 1994 (sub-ss(1)–(3), sub-s(4) certain purposes); 29
September 1994 (sub-s(4), remaining purposes).

Commencement order: SI 1994 No 2550.

41   Registration: supplementary provisions

(1) Provision may be made by rules as to –

(a) the division of an application for the registration of a trade mark into several applications;

(b) the merging of separate applications or registrations;

(c) the registration of a series of trade marks.

(2) A series of trade marks means a number of trade marks which resemble each other as to their material particulars and differ only as to matters of a non-distinctive character not substantially affecting the identity of the trade mark.

(3) Rules under this section may include provision as to –

(a) the circumstances in which, and conditions subject to which, division, merger or registration of a series is permitted, and

(b) the purposes for which an application to which the rules apply is to be treated as a single application and those for which it is to be treated as a number of separate applications.

Annotations

Date in force: 31 October 1994 (sub-ss(1), (3) certain purposes, sub-s(2)); 29 September 1994 (sub-ss(1), (3) remaining purposes).

Commencement order: SI 1994 No 2550.

Duration, renewal and alteration of registered trade mark

42   Duration of registration

(1) A trade mark shall be registered for a period of ten years from the date of registration.

(2) Registration may be renewed in accordance with section 43 for further periods of ten years.

Annotations

Date in force: 31 October 1994.

Commencement order: SI 1994 No 2550.

43   Renewal of registration

(1) The registration of a trade mark may be renewed at the request of the proprietor, subject to payment of a renewal fee.

(2) Provision shall be made by rules for the registrar to inform the proprietor of a registered trade mark, before the expiry of the registration, of the date of expiry and the manner in which the registration may be renewed.

(3) A request for renewal must be made, and the renewal fee paid, before the expiry of the registration.

Failing this, the request may be made and the fee paid within such further period (of not less than six months) as may be prescribed, in which case an additional renewal fee must also be paid within that period.

(4) Renewal shall take effect from the expiry of the previous registration.

(5) If the registration is not renewed in accordance with the above provisions, the registrar shall remove the trade mark from the register.

Provision may be made by rules for the restoration of the registration of a trade mark which has been removed from the register, subject to such conditions (if any) as may be prescribed.

(6) The renewal or restoration of the registration of a trade mark shall be published in the prescribed manner.

Annotations

Date in force: 31 October 1994 (sub-ss(1), (4), sub-ss(2), (3), (5), (6) certain purposes); 29 September 1994 (sub-ss(2), (3), (5), (6), remaining purposes).

Commencement order: SI 1994 No 2550.

44 Alteration of registered trade mark

(1) A registered trade mark shall not be altered in the register, during the period of registration or on renewal.

(2) Nevertheless, the registrar may, at the request of the proprietor, allow the alteration of a registered trade mark where the mark includes the proprietor's name or address and the alteration is limited to alteration of that name or address and does not substantially affect the identity of the mark.

(3) Provision shall be made by rules for the publication of any such alteration and the making of objections by any person claiming to be affected by it.

Annotations

Date in force: 31 October 1994 (sub-ss(1), (2), sub-s(3) certain purposes); 29 September 1994 (sub-s(3), remaining purposes).

Commencement order: SI 1994 No 2550.

Surrender, revocation and invalidity

45 Surrender of registered trade mark

(1) A registered trade mark may be surrendered by the proprietor in respect of some or all of the goods or services for which it is registered.

(2) Provision may be made by rules –

    (a) as to the manner and effect of a surrender, and

    (b) for protecting the interests of other persons having a right in the registered trade mark.

Annotations

Date in force: 31 October 1994 (sub-s(1), sub-s(2) certain purposes); 29 September 1994 (sub-s(2), remaining purposes).

Commencement order: SI 1994 No 2550.

46 Revocation of registration

(1) The registration of a trade mark may be revoked on any of the following grounds –

    (a) that within the period of five years following the date of completion of the registration procedure it has not been put to genuine use in the United Kingdom, by the proprietor or with his consent, in relation to the goods or services for which it is registered, and there are no proper reasons for non-use;

    (b) that such use has been suspended for an uninterrupted period of five years, and there are no proper reasons for non-use;

    (c) that, in consequence of acts or inactivity of the proprietor, it has become the common name in the trade for a product or service for which it is registered;

    (d) that in consequence of the use made of it by the proprietor or with his consent in relation to the goods or services for which it is registered, it is liable to mislead the public, particularly as to the nature, quality or geographical origin of those goods or services.

(2) For the purposes of subsection (1) use of a trade mark includes use in a form differing in elements which do not alter the distinctive character of the mark in the form in which it was registered, and use in the United Kingdom includes affixing the trade mark to goods or to the packaging of goods in the United Kingdom solely for export purposes.

(3) The registration of a trade mark shall not be revoked on the ground mentioned in subsection (1)(a) or (b) if such use as is referred to in that paragraph is commenced or resumed after the expiry of the five year period and before the application for revocation is made:

   Provided that, any such commencement or resumption of use after the expiry of the five year period but within the period of three months before the making of the application shall be disregarded unless preparations for the commencement or resumption began before the proprietor became aware that the application might be made.

(4) An application for revocation may be made by any person, and may be made either to the registrar or to the court, except that –
   (a) if proceedings concerning the trade mark in question are pending in the court, the application must be made to the court; and
   (b) if in any other case the application is made to the registrar, he may at any stage of the proceedings refer the application to the court.

(5) Where grounds for revocation exist in respect of only some of the goods or services for which the trade mark is registered, revocation shall relate to those goods or services only.

(6) Where the registration of a trade mark is revoked to any extent, the rights of the proprietor shall be deemed to have ceased to that extent as from –
   (a) the date of the application for revocation, or
   (b) if the registrar or court is satisfied that the grounds for revocation existed at an earlier date, that date.

Annotations

Date in force: 31 October 1994.

Commencement order: SI 1994 No 2550.

47 Grounds for invalidity of registration

(1) The registration of a trade mark may be declared invalid on he ground that the trade mark was registered in breach of section 3 or any of the provisions referred to in that section (absolute grounds for refusal of registration).

   Where the trade mark was registered in breach of subsection (1)(b), (c) or (d) of that section, it shall not be declared invalid if, in consequence of the use which has been made of it, it has after registration acquired a distinctive character in relation to the goods or services for which it is registered.

(2) The registration of a trade mark may be declared invalid on the ground –

   (a) that there is an earlier trade mark in relation to which the conditions set out in section 5(1), (2) or (3) obtain, or

   (b) that there is an earlier right in relation to which the condition set out in section 5(4) is satisfied,

unless the proprietor of that earlier trade mark or other earlier right has consented to the registration.

(3) An application for a declaration of invalidity may be made by any person, and may be made either to the registrar or to the court, except that –

   (a) if proceedings concerning the trade mark in question are pending in the court, the application must be made to the court; and

   (b) if in any other case the application is made to the registrar, he may at any stage of the proceedings refer the application to the court.

(4) In the case of bad faith in the registration of a trade mark, the registrar himself may apply to the court for a declaration of the invalidity of the registration.

(5) Where the grounds of invalidity exist in respect of only some of the goods or services for which the trade mark is registered, the trade mark shall be declared invalid as regards those goods or services only.

(6) Where the registration of a trade mark is declared invalid to any extent, the registration shall to that extent be deemed never to have been made:

Provided that this shall not affect transactions past and closed.

Annotations

Date in force: 31 October 1994.

Commencement order: SI 1994 No 2550.

48 Effect of acquiescence

(1) Where the proprietor of an earlier trade mark or other earlier right has acquiesced for a continuous period of five years in the use of a registered trade mark in the United Kingdom, being aware of that use, there shall cease to be any entitlement on the

basis of that earlier trade mark or other right –
(a) to apply for a declaration that the registration of the later trade mark is invalid, or
(b) to oppose the use of the later trade mark in relation to the goods or services in relation to which it has been so used,
unless the registration of the later trade mark was applied for in bad faith.
(2) Where subsection (1) applies, the proprietor of the later trade mark is not entitled to oppose the use of the earlier trade mark or, as the case may be, the exploitation of the earlier right, notwithstanding that the earlier trade mark or right may no longer be invoked against his later trade mark.

Annotations

Date in force: 31 October 1994.

Commencement order: SI 1994 No 2550.

Collective marks

49   Collective marks

(1) A collective mark is a mark distinguishing the goods or services of members of the association which is the proprietor of the mark from those of other undertakings.
(2) The provisions of this Act apply to collective marks subject to the provisions of Schedule 1.

Annotations

Date in force: 31 October 1994 (sub-s(1), sub-s(2) certain purposes); 29 September 1994 (sub-s(2), remaining purposes).

Commencement order: SI 1994 No 2550.

Certification marks

50   Certification marks

(1) A certification mark is a mark indicating that the goods or services in connection with which it is used are certified by the proprietor of the mark in respect of origin, material, mode of manufacture of goods or performance of services,

quality, accuracy or other characteristics.

(2) The provisions of this Act apply to certification marks subject to the provisions of Schedule 2.

Annotations

Date in force: 31 October 1994 (sub-s(1), sub-s(2) certain purposes); 29 September 1994 (sub-s(2), remaining purposes).

Commencement order: SI 1994 No 2550.

Part II
Community Trade Marks and International Matters

Community trade marks

51   Meaning of 'Community trade mark'

In this Act –

'Community trade mark' has the meaning given by Article 1(1) of the Community Trade Mark Regulation; and

'the Community Trade Mark Regulation' means Council Regulation (EC) No 40/94 of 20 December 1993 on the Community trade mark.

Annotations

Date in force: 31 October 1994.

Commencement order: SI 1994 No 2550.

Council Regulation (EC) No 40/94: OJ No L11, 14.1.94, p 1.

52   Power to make provision in connection with Community Trade Mark Regulation

(1) The Secretary of State may by regulations make such provision as he considers appropriate in connection with the operation of the Community Trade Mark Regulation.

(2) Provision may, in particular, be made with respect to –

(a) the making of applications for Community trade marks by way of the Patent Office;

(b) the procedures for determining *a posteriori* the invalidity, or liability to revocation, of the registration of a trade mark from which a Community trade mark claims seniority;

(c) the conversion of a Community trade mark, or an

application for a Community trade mark, into an
application for registration under this Act;

(d) the designation of courts in the United Kingdom having
jurisdiction over proceedings arising out of the Community
Trade Mark Regulation.

(3) Without prejudice to the generality of subsection (1), provision
may be made by regulations under this section –

(a) applying in relation to a Community trade mark the
provisions of –

(i) section 21 (remedy for groundless threats of infringement proceedings);

(ii) sections 89 to 91 (importation of infringing goods,
material or articles); and

(iii) sections 92, 93, 95 and 96 (offences); and

(b) making in relation to the list of professional representatives
maintained in pursuance of Article 89 of the Community
Trade Mark Regulation, and persons on that list, provision
corresponding to that made by, or capable of being made
under, sections 84 to 88 in relation to the register of trade
mark agents and registered trade mark agents.

(4) Regulations under this section shall be made by statutory
instrument which shall be subject to annulment in pursuance of
a resolution of either House of Parliament.

Annotations

Date in force: 31 October 1994.

Commencement order: SI 1994 No 2550.

The Madrid Protocol

International registration

53   The Madrid Protocol

In this Act –

'the Madrid Protocol' means the Protocol relating to the
Madrid Agreement concerning the International
Registration of Marks, adopted at Madrid on 27 June 1989;

'the International Bureau' has the meaning given by Article 2(1)
of that Protocol; and

'international trade mark (UK)' means a trade mark which
is entitled to protection in the United Kingdom under
that Protocol.

Annotations

Date in force: 31 October 1994.

Commencement order: SI 1994 No 2550.

54 Power to make provision giving effect to Madrid Protocol

(1) The Secretary of State may by order make such provision as he
thinks fit for giving effect in the United Kingdom to the
provisions of the Madrid Protocol.

(2) Provision may, in particular, be made with respect to –

    (a) the making of applications for international registrations by
way of the Patent Office as office of origin;

    (b) the procedures to be followed where the basic United
Kingdom application or registration fails or ceases to be
in force;

    (c) the procedures to be followed where the Patent Office
receives from the International Bureau a request for
extension of protection to the United Kingdom;

    (d) the effects of a successful request for extension of protection
to the United Kingdom;

    (e) the transformation of an application for an international
registration, or an international registration, into a national
application for registration;

    (f) the communication of information to the International Bureau;

    (g) the payment of fees and amounts prescribed in respect of
applications for international registrations, extensions of
protection and renewals.

(3) Without prejudice to the generality of subsection (1), provision
may be made by regulations under this section applying in
relation to an international trade mark (UK) the provisions of –

    (a) section 21 (remedy for groundless threats of infringement
proceedings);

    (b) sections 89 to 91 (importation of infringing goods, material
or articles); and

    (c) sections 92, 93, 95 and 96 (offences).

(4) An order under this section shall be made by statutory

instrument which shall be subject to annulment in pursuance of a resolution of either House of Parliament.

Annotations
Date in force: 31 October 1994.
Commencement order: SI 1994 No 2550.

The Paris Convention
Supplementary provisions

55 The Paris Convention

(1) In this Act –
   (a) 'the Paris Convention' means the Paris Convention for the Protection of Industrial Property of 20 March 1883, as revised or amended from time to time, and
   (b) a 'Convention country' means a country, other than the United Kingdom, which is a party to that Convention.
(2) The Secretary of State may by order make such amendments of this Act, and rules made under this Act, as appear to him appropriate in consequence of any revision or amendment of the Paris Convention after the passing of this Act.
(3) Any such order shall be made by statutory instrument which shall be subject to annulment in pursuance of a resolution of either House of Parliament.

Annotations
Date in force: 31 October 1994.
Commencement order: SI 1994 No 2550.

56 Protection of well-known trade marks: Article 6*bis*

(1) References in this Act to a trade mark which is entitled to protection under the Paris Convention as a well known trade mark are to a mark which is well-known in the United Kingdom as being the mark of a person who –
   (a) is a national of a Convention country, or
   (b) is domiciled in, or has a real and effective industrial or commercial establishment in, a Convention country,
whether or not that person carries on business, or has any goodwill, in the United Kingdom.

References to the proprietor of such a mark shall be construed accordingly.

(2) The proprietor of a trade mark which is entitled to protection under the Paris Convention as a well known trade mark is entitled to restrain by injunction the use in the United Kingdom of a trade mark which, or the essential part of which, is identical or similar to his mark, in relation to identical or similar goods or services, where the use is likely to cause confusion.

This right is subject to section 48 (effect of acquiescence by proprietor of earlier trade mark).

(3) Nothing in subsection (2) affects the continuation of any *bona fide* use of a trade mark begun before the commencement of this section.

Annotations
Date in force: 31 October 1994.
Commencement order: SI 1994 No 2550.

57   National emblems, &c of Convention countries: Article 6*ter*

(1) A trade mark which consists of or contains the flag of a Convention country shall not be registered without the authorisation of the competent authorities of that country, unless it appears to the registrar that use of the flag in the manner proposed is permitted without such authorisation.

(2) A trade mark which consists of or contains the armorial bearings or any other state emblem of a Convention country which is protected under the Paris Convention shall not be registered without the authorisation of the competent authorities of that country.

(3) A trade mark which consists of or contains an official sign or hallmark adopted by a Convention country and indicating control and warranty shall not, where the sign or hallmark is protected under the Paris Convention, be registered in relation to goods or services of the same, or a similar kind, as those in relation to which it indicates control and warranty, without the authorisation of the competent authorities of the country concerned.

(4) The provisions of this section as to national flags and other state emblems, and official signs or hallmarks, apply equally to anything which from a heraldic point of view imitates any such

flag or other emblem, or sign or hallmark.

(5) Nothing in this section prevents the registration of a trade mark on the application of a national of a country who is authorised to make use of a state emblem, or official sign or hallmark, of that country, notwithstanding that it is similar to that of another country.

(6) Where by virtue of this section the authorisation of the competent authorities of a Convention country is or would be required for the registration of a trade mark, those authorities are entitled to restrain by injunction any use of the mark in the United Kingdom without their authorisation.

Annotations

Date in force: 31 October 1994.

Commencement order: SI 1994 No 2550.

58   Emblems, &c of certain international organisations: Article 6*ter*

(1) This section applies to –
   (a)   the armorial bearings, flags or other emblems, and
   (b)   the abbreviations and names,
   of international intergovernmental organisations of which one or more Convention countries are members.

(2) A trade mark which consists of or contains any such emblem, abbreviation or name which is protected under the Paris Convention shall not be registered without the authorisation of the international organisation concerned, unless it appears to the registrar that the use of the emblem, abbreviation or name in the manner proposed –
   (a)   is not such as to suggest to the public that a connection exists between the organisation and the trade mark, or
   (b)   is not likely to mislead the public as to the existence of a connection between the user and the organisation.

(3) The provisions of this section as to emblems of an international organisation apply equally to anything which from a heraldic point of view imitates any such emblem.

(4) Where by virtue of this section the authorisation of an international organisation is or would be required for the registration of a trade mark, that organisation is entitled to restrain by injunction any use of the mark in the United Kingdom without its authorisation.

(5) Nothing in this section affects the rights of a person whose *bona fide* use of the trade mark in question began before 4 January 1962 (when the relevant provisions of the Paris Convention entered into force in relation to the United Kingdom).

Annotations

Date in force: 31 October 1994.

Commencement order: SI 1994 No 2550.

59 Notification under Article 6*ter* of the Convention

(1) For the purposes of section 57 state emblems of a Convention country (other than the national flag), and official signs or hallmarks, shall be regarded as protected under the Paris Convention only if, or to the extent that –
   (a) the country in question has notified the United Kingdom in accordance with Article 6*ter*(3) of the Convention that it desires to protect that emblem, sign or hallmark,
   (b) the notification remains in force, and
   (c) the United Kingdom has not objected to it in accordance with Article 6*ter*(4) or any such objection has been withdrawn.
(2) For the purposes of section 58 the emblems, abbreviations and names of an international organisation shall be regarded as protected under the Paris Convention only if, or to the extent that –
   (a) the organisation in question has notified the United Kingdom in accordance with Article 6*ter*(3) of the Convention that it desires to protect that emblem, abbreviation or name,
   (b) the notification remains in force, and
   (c) the United Kingdom has not objected to it in accordance with Article 6*ter*(4) or any such objection has been withdrawn.
(3) Notification under Article 6*ter*(3) of the Paris Convention shall have effect only in relation to applications for registration made more than two months after the receipt of the notification.
(4) The registrar shall keep and make available for public inspection by any person, at all reasonable hours and free of charge, a list of –
   (a) the state emblems and official signs or hallmarks, and
   (b) the emblems, abbreviations and names of international organisations,

which are for the time being protected under the Paris Convention by virtue of notification under Article 6*ter*(3).

Annotations
Date in force: 31 October 1994.
Commencement order: SI 1994 No 2550.

60 Acts of agent or representative: Article 6*septies*

(1) The following provisions apply where an application for registration of a trade mark is made by a person who is an agent or representative of a person who is the proprietor of the mark in a Convention country.
(2) If the proprietor opposes the application, registration shall be refused.
(3) If the application (not being so opposed) is granted, the proprietor may –
    (a) apply for a declaration of the invalidity of the registration, or
    (b) apply for the rectification of the register so as to substitute his name as the proprietor of the registered trade mark.
(4) The proprietor may (notwithstanding the rights conferred by this Act in relation to a registered trade mark) by injunction restrain any use of the trade mark in the United Kingdom which is not authorised by him.
(5) Subsections (2), (3) and (4) do not apply if, or to the extent that, the agent or representative justifies his action.
(6) An application under subsection (3)(a) or (b) must be made within three years of the proprietor becoming aware of the registration; and no injunction shall be granted under subsection (4) in respect of a use in which the proprietor has acquiesced for a continuous period of three years or more.

Annotations
Date in force: 31 October 1994.
Commencement order: SI 1994 No 2550.

Miscellaneous

61 Stamp duty

Stamp duty shall not be chargeable on an instrument relating to a Community trade mark or an international trade mark (UK), or an application for any such mark, by reason only of the fact that such a mark has legal effect in the United Kingdom.

Annotations
Date in force: 31 October 1994.
Commencement order: SI 1994 No 2550.

Part III
Administrative and other Supplementary Provisions
The registrar

62 The registrar

In this Act 'the registrar' means the Comptroller-General of Patents, Designs and Trade Marks.

Annotations
Date in force: 31 October 1994.
Commencement order: SI 1994 No 2550.

The register

63 The register

(1) The registrar shall maintain a register of trade marks.
    References in this Act to 'the register' are to that register; and references to registration (in particular, in the expression 'registered trade mark') are, unless the context otherwise requires, to registration in that register.

(2) There shall be entered in the register in accordance with this Act –
    (a) registered trade marks,
    (b) such particulars as may be prescribed of registrable transactions affecting a registered trade mark, and
    (c) such other matters relating to registered trade marks as may be prescribed.

(3) The register shall be kept in such manner as may be prescribed, and provision shall in particular be made for –
    (a) public inspection of the register, and

(b) the supply of certified or uncertified copies, or extracts, of entries in the register.

Annotations

Date in force: 31 October 1994 (sub-s(1), sub-ss(2), (3) certain purposes); 29 September 1994 (sub-ss(2), (3), remaining purposes).

Commencement order: SI 1994 No 2550.

64 Rectification or correction of the register

(1) Any person having a sufficient interest may apply for the rectification of an error or omission in the register:

Provided that an application for rectification may not be made in respect of a matter affecting the validity of the registration of a trade mark.

(2) An application for rectification may be made either to the registrar or to the court, except that –

(a) if proceedings concerning the trade mark in question are pending in the court, the application must be made to the court; and

(b) if in any other case the application is made to the registrar, he may at any stage of the proceedings refer the application to the court.

(3) Except where the registrar or the court directs otherwise the effect of rectification of the register is that the error or omission in question shall be deemed never to have been made.

(4) The registrar may, on request made in the prescribed manner by the proprietor of a registered trade mark, or a licensee, enter any change in his name or address as recorded in the register.

(5) The registrar may remove from the register matter appearing to him to have ceased to have effect.

Annotations

Date in force: 31 October 1994 (sub-ss(1)–(3), (5), sub-s(4) certain purposes); 29 September 1994 (sub-s(4), remaining purposes).

Commencement order: SI 1994 No 2550.

65 Adaptation of entries to new classification

(1) Provision may be made by rules empowering the registrar to do such things as he considers necessary to implement any amended or substituted classification of goods or services for

the purposes of the registration of trade marks.

(2) Provision may in particular be made for the amendment of existing entries on the register so as to accord with the new classification.

(3) Any such power of amendment shall not be exercised so as to extend the rights conferred by the registration, except where it appears to the registrar that compliance with this requirement would involve undue complexity and that any extension would not be substantial and would not adversely affect the rights of any person.

(4) The rules may empower the registrar –
   (a) to require the proprietor of a registered trade mark, within such time as may be prescribed, to file a proposal for amendment of the register, and
   (b) to cancel or refuse to renew the registration of the trade mark in the event of his failing to do so.

(5) Any such proposal shall be advertised, and may be opposed, in such manner as may be prescribed.

Annotations

Date in force: 31 October 1994 (sub-ss(1), (3)–(5) certain purposes, sub-s(2)); 29 September 1994 (sub-ss(1), (3)–(5), remaining purposes).

Commencement order: SI 1994 No 2550.

Powers and duties of the registrar

66 Power to require use of forms

(1) The registrar may require the use of such forms as he may direct for any purpose relating to the registration of a trade mark or any other proceeding before him under this Act.

(2) The forms, and any directions of the registrar with respect to their use, shall be published in the prescribed manner.

Annotations

Date in force: 31 October 1994 (certain purposes); 29 September 1994 (remaining purposes).

Commencement order: SI 1994 No 2550.

67 Information about applications and registered trade marks

(1) After publication of an application for registration of a trade mark, the registrar shall on request provide a person with such

information and permit him to inspect such documents relating to the application, or to any registered trade mark resulting from it, as may be specified in the request, subject, however, to any prescribed restrictions.

Any request must be made in the prescribed manner and be accompanied by the appropriate fee (if any).

(2) Before publication of an application for registration of a trade mark, documents or information constituting or relating to the application shall not be published by the registrar or communicated by him to any person except –
   (a) in such cases and to such extent as may be prescribed, or
   (b) with the consent of the applicant;
   but subject as follows.

(3) Where a person has been notified that an application for registration of a trade mark has been made, and that the applicant will if the application is granted bring proceedings against him in respect of acts done after publication of the application, he may make a request under subsection (1) notwithstanding that the application has not been published and that subsection shall apply accordingly.

Annotations

Date in force: 31 October 1994 (sub-ss(1), (2) certain purposes, sub-s(3)); 29 September 1994 (sub-ss(1), (2), remaining purposes).

Commencement order: SI 1994 No 2550.

68 Costs and security for costs

(1) Provision may be made by rules empowering the registrar, in any proceedings before him under this Act –
   (a) to award any party such costs as he may consider reasonable, and
   (b) to direct how and by what parties they are to be paid.

(2) Any such order of the registrar may be enforced –
   (a) in England and Wales or Northern Ireland, in the same way as an order of the High Court;
   (b) in Scotland, in the same way as a decree for expenses granted by the Court of Session.

(3) Provision may be made by rules empowering the registrar, in such cases as may be prescribed, to require a party to proceedings before him to give security for costs, in relation to

those proceedings or to proceedings on appeal, and as to the consequences if security is not given.

Annotations

Date in force: 31 October 1994 (sub-ss(1), (3) certain purposes, sub-s(2)); 29 September 1994 (sub-ss(1), (3), remaining purposes).

Commencement order: SI 1994 No 2550.

69 Evidence before registrar

Provision may be made by rules –

(a) as to the giving of evidence in proceedings before the registrar under this Act by affidavit or statutory declaration;

(b) conferring on the registrar the powers of an official referee of the Supreme Court as regards the examination of witnesses on oath and the discovery and production of documents; and

(c) applying in relation to the attendance of witnesses in proceedings before the registrar the rules applicable to the attendance of witnesses before such a referee.

Annotations

Date in force: 31 October 1994 (certain purposes); 29 September 1994 (remaining purposes).

Commencement order: SI 1994 No 2550.

70 Exclusion of liability in respect of official acts

(1) The registrar shall not be taken to warrant the validity of the registration of a trade mark under this Act or under any treaty, convention, arrangement or engagement to which the United Kingdom is a party.

(2) The registrar is not subject to any liability by reason of, or in connection with, any examination required or authorised by this Act, or any such treaty, convention, arrangement or engagement, or any report or other proceedings consequent on such examination.

(3) No proceedings lie against an officer of the registrar in respect of any matter for which, by virtue of this section, the registrar is not liable.

Annotations

Date in force: 31 October 1994.

Commencement order: SI 1994 No 2550.

71 Registrar's annual report

(1) The Comptroller-General of Patents, Designs and Trade Marks shall in his annual report under section 121 of the Patents Act 1977, include a report on the execution of this Act, including the discharge of his functions under the Madrid Protocol.

(2) The report shall include an account of all money received and paid by him under or by virtue of this Act.

Annotations

Date in force: 31 October 1994.

Commencement order: SI 1994 No 2550.

Legal proceedings and appeals

72 Registration to be prima facie evidence of validity

In all legal proceedings relating to a registered trade mark (including proceedings for rectification of the register) the registration of a person as proprietor of a trade mark shall be prima facie evidence of the validity of the original registration and of any subsequent assignment or other transmission of it.

Annotations

Date in force: 31 October 1994.

Commencement order: SI 1994 No 2550.

73 Certificate of validity of contested registration

(1) If in proceedings before the court the validity of the registration of a trade mark is contested and it is found by the court that the trade mark is validly registered, the court may give a certificate to that effect.

(2) If the court gives such a certificate and in subsequent proceedings –
    (a) the validity of the registration is again questioned, and
    (b) the proprietor obtains a final order or judgment in his favour,
he is entitled to his costs as between solicitor and client unless the court directs otherwise.

   This subsection does not extend to the costs of an appeal in any such proceedings.

Annotations

Date in force: 31 October 1994.

Commencement order: SI 1994 No 2550.

74 Registrar's appearance in proceedings involving the register

(1) In proceedings before the court involving an application for –
   (a) the revocation of the registration of a trade mark,
   (b) a declaration of the invalidity of the registration of a trade mark, or
   (c) the rectification of the register,
   the registrar is entitled to appear and be heard, and shall appear if so directed by the court.

(2) Unless otherwise directed by the court, the registrar may instead of appearing submit to the court a statement in writing signed by him, giving particulars of –
   (a) any proceedings before him in relation to the matter in issue,
   (b) the grounds of any decision given by him affecting it,
   (c) the practice of the Patent Office in like cases, or
   (d) such matters relevant to the issues and within his knowledge as registrar as he thinks fit;
   and the statement shall be deemed to form part of the evidence in the proceedings.

(3) Anything which the registrar is or may be authorised or required to do under this section may be done on his behalf by a duly authorised officer.

Annotations
Date in force: 31 October 1994.
Commencement order: SI 1994 No 2550.

75 The court

In this Act, unless the context otherwise requires, 'the court' means –
   (a) in England and Wales and Northern Ireland, the High Court, and
   (b) in Scotland, the Court of Session.

Annotations
Date in force: 31 October 1994.
Commencement order: SI 1994 No 2550.

76 Appeals from the registrar

(1) An appeal lies from any decision of the registrar under this Act, except as otherwise expressly provided by rules.

For this purpose 'decision' includes any act of the registrar in exercise of a discretion vested in him by or under this Act.

(2) Any such appeal may be brought either to an appointed person or to the court.

(3) Where an appeal is made to an appointed person, he may refer the appeal to the court if –

(a) it appears to him that a point of general legal importance is involved,

(b) the registrar requests that it be so referred, or

(c) such a request is made by any party to the proceedings before the registrar in which the decision appealed against was made.

Before doing so the appointed person shall give the appellant and any other party to the appeal an opportunity to make representations as to whether the appeal should be referred to the court.

(4) Where an appeal is made to an appointed person and he does not refer it to the court, he shall hear and determine the appeal and his decision shall be final.

(5) The provisions of sections 68 and 69 (costs and security for costs; evidence) apply in relation to proceedings before an appointed person as in relation to proceedings before the registrar.

Annotations

Date in force: 31 October 1994 (sub-s(1) certain purposes, sub-ss(2)–(5)); 29 September 1994 (sub-s(1), remaining purposes).

Commencement order: SI 1994 No 2550.

77 Persons appointed to hear and determine appeals

(1) For the purposes of section 76 an 'appointed person' means a person appointed by the Lord Chancellor to hear and decide appeals under this Act.

(2) A person is not eligible for such appointment unless –

(a) he has a 7 year general qualification, within the meaning of section 71 of the Courts and Legal Services Act 1990;

(b) he is an advocate or solicitor in Scotland of at least 7 years' standing;

(c) he is a member of the Bar of Northern Ireland or solicitor of the Supreme Court of Northern Ireland of at least 7 years' standing; or

(d) he has held judicial office.

(3) An appointed person shall hold and vacate office in accordance with his terms of appointment, subject to the following provisions –
   (a) there shall be paid to him such remuneration (whether by way of salary or fees), and such allowances, as the Secretary of State with the approval of the Treasury may determine;
   (b) he may resign his office by notice in writing to the Lord Chancellor;
   (c) the Lord Chancellor may by notice in writing remove him from office if –
      (i) he has become bankrupt or made an arrangement with his creditors or, in Scotland, his estate has been sequestrated or he has executed a trust deed for his creditors or entered into a composition contract, or
      (ii) he is incapacitated by physical or mental illness,
      or if he is in the opinion of the Lord Chancellor otherwise unable or unfit to perform his duties as an appointed person.
(4) The Lord Chancellor shall consult the Lord Advocate before exercising his powers under this section.

Annotations
Date in force: 31 October 1994.
Commencement order: SI 1994 No 2550.

Rules, fees, hours of business, &c

78   **Power of Secretary of State to make rules**

(1) The Secretary of State may make rules –
   (a) for the purposes of any provision of this Act authorising the making of rules with respect to any matter, and
   (b) for prescribing anything authorised or required by any provision of this Act to be prescribed,
   and generally for regulating practice and procedure under this Act.
(2) Provision may, in particular, be made –
   (a) as to the manner of filing of applications and other documents;
   (b) requiring and regulating the translation of documents and the filing and authentication of any translation;
   (c) as to the service of documents;
   (d) authorising the rectification of irregularities of procedure;

(e) prescribing time limits for anything required to be done in connection with any proceeding under this Act;

(f) providing for the extension of any time limit so prescribed, or specified by the registrar, whether or not it has already expired.

(3) Rules under this Act shall be made by statutory instrument which shall be subject to annulment in pursuance of a resolution of either House of Parliament.

Annotations

Date in force: 31 October 1994 (certain purposes); 29 September 1994 (remaining purposes).

Commencement order: SI 1994 No 2550.

79 Fees

(1) There shall be paid in respect of applications and registration and other matters under this Act such fees as may be prescribed.

(2) Provision may be made by rules as to –

(a) the payment of a single fee in respect of two or more matters, and

(b) the circumstances (if any) in which a fee may be repaid or remitted.

Annotations

Date in force: 31 October 1994 (certain purposes); 29 September 1994 (remaining purposes).

Commencement order: SI 1994 No 2550.

80 Hours of business and business days

(1) The registrar may give directions specifying the hours of business of the Patent Office for the purpose of the transaction by the public of business under this Act, and the days which are business days for that purpose.

(2) Business done on any day after the specified hours of business, or on a day which is not a business day, shall be deemed to have been done on the next business day; and where the time for doing anything under this Act expires on a day which is not a business day, that time shall be extended to the next business day.

(3) Directions under this section may make different provision for

different classes of business and shall be published in the prescribed manner.

Annotations

Date in force: 31 October 1994 (subss (1), (3) certain purposes, sub-s(2)); 29 September 1994 (sub-ss(1), (3), remaining purposes).
Commencement order: SI 1994 No 2550.

81   The trade marks journal

Provision shall be made by rules for the publication by the registrar of a journal containing particulars of any application for the registration of a trade mark (including a representation of the mark) and such other information relating to trade marks as the registrar thinks fit.

Annotations

Date in force: 31 October 1994 (certain purposes); 29 September 1994 (remaining purposes).
Commencement order: SI 1994 No 2550.

Trade mark agents

82   Recognition of agents

Except as otherwise provided by rules, any act required or authorised by this Act to be done by or to a person in connection with the registration of a trade mark, or any procedure relating to a registered trade mark, may be done by or to an agent authorised by that person orally or in writing.

Annotations

Date in force: 31 October 1994 (certain purposes); 29 September 1994 (remaining purposes).
Commencement order: SI 1994 No 2550.

83   The register of trade mark agents

(1)   The Secretary of State may make rules requiring the keeping of a register of persons who act as agent for others for the purpose of applying for or obtaining the registration of trade marks; and in this Act a registered trade mark agent means a person whose name is entered in the register kept under this section.

Appendix

(2) The rules may contain such provision as the Secretary of State thinks fit regulating the registration of persons, and may in particular –
  (a) require the payment of such fees as may be prescribed, and
  (b) authorise in prescribed cases the erasure from the register of the name of any person registered in it, or the suspension of a person's registration.
(3) The rules may delegate the keeping of the register to another person, and may confer on that person –
  (a) power to make regulations –
    (i) with respect to the payment of fees, in the cases and subject to the limits prescribed by the rules, and
    (ii) with respect to any other matter which could be regulated by the rules, and
  (b) such other functions, including disciplinary functions, as may be prescribed by the rules.

Annotations
Date in force: 31 October 1994.
Commencement order: SI 1994 No 2550.

84 Unregistered persons not to be described as registered trade mark agents

(1) An individual who is not a registered trade mark agent shall not –
  (a) carry on a business (otherwise than in partnership) under any name or other description which contains the words 'registered trade mark agent'; or
  (b) in the course of a business otherwise describe or hold himself out, or permit himself to be described or held out, as a registered trade mark agent.
(2) A partnership shall not –
  (a) carry on a business under any name or other description which contains the words 'registered trade mark agent'; or
  (b) in the course of a business otherwise describe or hold itself out, or permit itself to be described or held out, as a firm of registered trade mark agents,
unless all the partners are registered trade mark agents or the partnership satisfies such conditions as may be prescribed for the purposes of this section.

(3) A body corporate shall not –
  (a) carry on a business (otherwise than in partnership) under any name or other description which contains the words 'registered trade mark agent'; or
  (b) in the course of a business otherwise describe or hold itself out, or permit itself to be described or held out, as a registered trade mark agent,
  unless all the directors of the body corporate are registered trade mark agents or the body satisfies such conditions as may be prescribed for the purposes of this section.
(4) A person who contravenes this section commits an offence and is liable on summary conviction to a fine not exceeding level 5 on the standard scale; and proceedings for such an offence may be begun at any time within a year from the date of the offence.

Annotations
Date in force: 31 October 1994.
Commencement order: SI 1994 No 2550.

85   Power to prescribe conditions, &c for mixed partnerships and bodies corporate

(1) The Secretary of State may make rules prescribing the conditions to be satisfied for the purposes of section 84 (persons entitled to be described as registered trade mark agents) –
  (a) in relation to a partnership where not all the partners are qualified persons, or
  (b) in relation to a body corporate where not all the directors are qualified persons,
  and imposing requirements to be complied with by such partnerships or bodies corporate.
(2) The rules may, in particular –
  (a) prescribe conditions as to the number or proportion of partners or directors who must be qualified persons;
  (b) impose requirements as to –
    (i) the identification of qualified and unqualified persons in professional advertisements, circulars or letters issued by or with the consent of the partnership or body corporate and which relate to its business, and
    (ii) the manner in which a partnership or body corporate is to organise its affairs so as to secure that qualified

persons exercise a sufficient degree of control over the activities of unqualified persons.

(3) Contravention of a requirement imposed by the rules is an offence for which a person is liable on summary conviction to a fine not exceeding level 5 on the standard scale.

(4) In this section qualified person means a registered trade mark agent.

Annotations
Date in force: 31 October 1994.
Commencement order: SI 1994 No 2550.

86 Use of the term 'trade mark attorney'

(1) No offence is committed under the enactments restricting the use of certain expressions in reference to persons not qualified to act as solicitors by the use of the term 'trade mark attorney' in reference to a registered trade mark agent.

(2) The enactments referred to in subsection (1) are section 21 of the Solicitors Act 1974, section 31 of the Solicitors (Scotland) Act 1980 and Article 22 of the Solicitors (Northern Ireland) Order 1976.

Annotations
Date in force: 31 October 1994.
Commencement order: SI 1994 No 2550.

87 Privilege for communications with registered trade mark agents

(1) This section applies to communications as to any matter relating to the protection of any design or trade mark, or as to any matter involving passing off.

(2) Any such communication –
   (a) between a person and his trade mark agent, or
   (b) for the purpose of obtaining, or in response to a request for, information which a person is seeking for the purpose of instructing his trade mark agent,

is privileged from, or in Scotland protected against, disclosure in legal proceedings in the same way as a communication between a person and his solicitor or, as the case may be, a communication for the purpose of obtaining, or in response to a request for, information which a person is seeking for the purpose of instructing his solicitor.

(3) In subsection (2) 'trade mark agent' means –
   (a) a registered trade mark agent, or
   (b) a partnership entitled to describe itself as a firm of registered trade mark agents, or
   (c) a body corporate entitled to describe itself as a registered trade mark agent.

Annotations
Date in force: 31 October 1994.
Commencement order: SI 1994 No 2550.

88 Power of registrar to refuse to deal with certain agents

(1) The Secretary of State may make rules authorising the registrar to refuse to recognise as agent in respect of any business under this Act –
   (a) a person who has been convicted of an offence under section 84 (unregistered persons describing themselves as registered trade mark agents);
   (b) an individual whose name has been erased from and not restored to, or who is suspended from, the register of trade mark agents on the ground of misconduct;
   (c) a person who is found by the Secretary of State to have been guilty of such conduct as would, in the case of an individual registered in the register of trade mark agents, render him liable to have his name erased from the register on the ground of misconduct;
   (d) a partnership or body corporate of which one of the partners or directors is a person whom the registrar could refuse to recognise under paragraph (a), (b) or (c) above.

(2) The rules may contain such incidental and supplementary provisions as appear to the Secretary of State to be appropriate and may, in particular, prescribe circumstances in which a person is or is not to be taken to have been guilty of misconduct.

Annotations
Date in force: 31 October 1994 (certain purposes); 29 September 1994 (remaining purposes).
Commencement order: SI 1994 No 2550.

Importation of infringing goods, material or articles

89   Infringing goods, material or articles may be treated as prohibited goods

(1)   The proprietor of a registered trade mark, or a licensee, may give notice in writing to the Commissioners of Customs and Excise –

    (a)   that he is the proprietor or, as the case may be, a licensee of the registered trade mark,

    (b)   that, at a time and place specified in the notice, goods which are, in relation to that registered trade mark, infringing goods, material or articles are expected to arrive in the United Kingdom –

        (i)   from outside the European Economic Area, or

        (ii)   from within that Area but not having been entered for free circulation, and

    (c)   that he requests the Commissioners to treat them as prohibited goods.

(2)   When a notice is in force under this section the importation of the goods to which the notice relates, otherwise than by a person for his private and domestic use, is prohibited; but a person is not by reason of the prohibition liable to any penalty other than forfeiture of the goods.

(3)   this section does not apply to goods entered, or expected to be entered, for free circulation in respect of which the proprietor of the registered trade mark, or a licensee, is entitled to lodge an application under Article 3(1) of Council Regulation (EEC) No 3842/86 laying down measures to prohibit the release for free circulation of counterfeit goods.

Annotations

Date in force: 31 October 1994.

Commencement order: SI 1994 No 2550.

Council Regulation (EEC) No 3842/86: OJ No L357, 18.12.86, p 1.

90   Power of Commissioners of Customs and Excise to make regulations

(1)   The Commissioners of Customs and Excise may make regulations prescribing the form in which notice is to be given

under section 89 and requiring a person giving notice –

(a) to furnish the Commissioners with such evidence as may be specified in the regulations, either on giving notice or when the goods are imported, or at both those times, and

(b) to comply with such other conditions as may be specified in the regulations.

(2) The regulations may, in particular, require a person giving such a notice –

(a) to pay such fees in respect of the notice as may be specified by the regulations;

(b) to give such security as may be so specified in respect of any liability or expense which the Commissioners may incur in consequence of the notice by reason of the detention of any goods or anything done to goods detained;

(c) to indemnify the Commissioners against any such liability or expense, whether security has been given or not.

(3) The regulations may make different provision as respects different classes of case to which they apply and may include such incidental and supplementary provisions as the Commissioners consider expedient.

(4) Regulations under this section shall be made by statutory instrument which shall be subject to annulment in pursuance of a resolution of either House of Parliament.

(5) Section 17 of the Customs and Excise Management Act 1979 (general provisions as to Commissioners receipts) applies to fees paid in pursuance of regulations under this section as to receipts under the enactments relating to customs and excise.

Annotations

Date in force: 31 October 1994 (certain purposes); 29 September 1994 (remaining purposes).

Commencement order: SI 1994 No 2550.

91   Power of Commissioners of Customs and Excise to disclose information

Where information relating to infringing goods, material or articles has been obtained by the Commissioners of Customs and Excise for the purposes of, or in connection with, the exercise of their functions in relation to imported goods, the Commissioners may authorise the disclosure of that information for the purpose of facilitating the exercise by any person of any function in connection

with the investigation or prosecution of an offence under section 92
below (unauthorised use of trade mark, &c in relation to goods) or
under the Trade Descriptions Act 1968.

Annotations

Date in force: 31 October 1994.

Commencement order: SI 1994 No 2550.

Offences

92 Unauthorised use of trade mark, &c in relation to goods

(1) A person commits an offence who with a view to gain for
himself or another, or with intent to cause loss to another, and
without the consent of the proprietor –
  (a) applies to goods or their packaging a sign identical to, or
likely to be mistaken for, a registered trade mark, or
  (b) sells or lets for hire, offers or exposes for sale or hire or
distributes goods which bear, or the packaging of which
bears, such a sign, or
  (c) has in his possession, custody or control in the course of a
business any such goods with a view to the doing of
anything, by himself or another, which would be an offence
under paragraph (b).

(2) A person commits an offence who with a view to gain for
himself or another, or with intent to cause loss to another, and
without the consent of the proprietor –
  (a) applies a sign identical to, or likely to be mistaken for, a
registered trade mark to material intended to be used –
    (i) for labelling or packaging goods,
    (ii) as a business paper in relation to goods, or
    (iii) for advertising goods, or
  (b) uses in the course of a business material bearing such a sign
for labelling or packaging goods, as a business paper in
relation to goods, or for advertising goods, or
  (c) has in his possession, custody or control in the course of a
business any such material with a view to the doing of
anything, by himself or another, which would be an offence
under paragraph (b).

(3) A person commits an offence who with a view to gain for himself or another, or with intent to cause loss to another, and without the consent of the proprietor –
  (a) makes an article specifically designed or adapted for making copies of a sign identical to, or likely to be mistaken for, a registered trade mark, or
  (b) has such an article in his possession, custody or control in the course of a business,
knowing or having reason to believe that it has been, or is to be, used to produce goods, or material for labelling or packaging goods, as a business paper in relation to goods, or for advertising goods.

(4) A person does not commit an offence under this section unless –
  (a) the goods are goods in respect of which the trade mark is registered, or
  (b) the trade mark has a reputation in the United Kingdom and the use of the sign takes or would take unfair advantage of, or is or would be detrimental to, the distinctive character or the repute of the trade mark.

(5) It is a defence for a person charged with an offence under this section to show that he believed on reasonable grounds that the use of the sign in the manner in which it was used, or was to be used, was not an infringement of the registered trade mark.

(6) A person guilty of an offence under this section is liable –
  (a) on summary conviction to imprisonment for a term not exceeding six months or a fine not exceeding the statutory maximum, or both;
  (b) on conviction on indictment to a fine or imprisonment for a term not exceeding ten years, or both.

Annotations
Date in force: 31 October 1994.
Commencement order: SI 1994 No 2550.

93 Enforcement function of local weights and measures authority

(1) It is the duty of every local weights and measures authority to enforce within their area the provisions of section 92 (unauthorised use of trade mark, &c in relation to goods).

(2) The following provisions of the Trade Descriptions Act 1968

apply in relation to the enforcement of that section as in relation to the enforcement of that Act –

section 27 (power to make test purchases),

section 28 (power to enter premises and inspect and seize goods and documents),

section 29 (obstruction of authorised officers), and

section 33 (compensation for loss, &c of goods seized).

(3) Subsection (1) above does not apply in relation to the enforcement of section 92 in Northern Ireland, but it is the duty of the Department of Economic Development to enforce that section in Northern Ireland.

For that purpose the provisions of the Trade Descriptions Act 1968 specified in subsection (2) apply as if for the references to a local weights and measures authority and any officer of such an authority there were substituted references to that Department and any of its officers.

(4) Any enactment which authorises the disclosure of information for the purpose of facilitating the enforcement of the Trade Descriptions Act 1968 shall apply as if section 92 above were contained in that Act and as if the functions of any person in relation to the enforcement of that section were functions under that Act.

(5) Nothing in this section shall be construed as authorising a local weights and measures authority to bring proceedings in Scotland for an offence.

Annotations

Date in force: 31 October 1994.

Commencement order: SI 1994 No 2550.

94 Falsification of register, &c

(1) It is an offence for a person to make, or cause to be made, a false entry in the register of trade marks, knowing or having reason to believe that it is false.

(2) It is an offence for a person –

(a) to make or cause to be made anything falsely purporting to be a copy of an entry in the register, or

(b) to produce or tender or cause to be produced or tendered in evidence any such thing,

knowing or having reason to believe that it is false.

(3) A person guilty of an offence under this section is liable –
  (a) on conviction on indictment, to imprisonment for a term not exceeding two years or a fine, or both;
  (b) on summary conviction, to imprisonment for a term not exceeding six months or a fine not exceeding the statutory maximum, or both.

Annotations
Date in force: 31 October 1994.
Commencement order: SI 1994 No 2550.

95   Falsely representing trade mark as registered

(1) It is an offence for a person –
  (a) falsely to represent that a mark is a registered trade mark, or
  (b) to make a false representation as to the goods or services for which a trade mark is registered
  knowing or having reason to believe that the representation is false.
(2) For the purposes of this section, the use in the United Kingdom in relation to a trade mark –
  (a) of the word registered, or
  (b) of any other word or symbol importing a reference (express or implied) to registration,
  shall be deemed to be a representation as to registration under this Act unless it is shown that the reference is to registration elsewhere than in the United Kingdom and that the trade mark is in fact so registered for the goods or services in question.
(3) A person guilty of an offence under this section is liable on summary conviction to a fine not exceeding level 3 on the standard scale.

Annotations
Date in force: 31 October 1994.
Commencement order: SI 1994 No 2550.

96   Supplementary provisions as to summary proceedings in Scotland

(1) Notwithstanding anything in section 331 of the Criminal Procedure (Scotland) Act 1975, summary proceedings in

Scotland for an offence under this Act may be begun at any time within six months after the date on which evidence sufficient in the Lord Advocate's opinion to justify the proceedings came to his knowledge.

For this purpose a certificate of the Lord Advocate as to the date on which such evidence came to his knowledge is conclusive evidence.

(2) For the purposes of subsection (1) and of any other provision of this Act as to the time within which summary proceedings for an offence may be brought, proceedings in Scotland shall be deemed to be begun on the date on which a warrant to apprehend or to cite the accused is granted, if such warrant is executed without undue delay.

Annotations
Date in force: 31 October 1994.
Commencement order: SI 1994 No 2550.

Forfeiture of counterfeit goods, &c

97 Forfeiture: England and Wales or Northern Ireland

(1) In England and Wales or Northern Ireland where there has come into the possession of any person in connection with the investigation or prosecution of a relevant offence –
   (a) goods which, or the packaging of which, bears a sign identical to or likely to be mistaken for a registered trade mark,
   (b) material bearing such a sign and intended to be used for labelling or packaging goods, as a business paper in relation to goods, or for advertising goods, or
   (c) articles specifically designed or adapted for making copies of such a sign,
   that person may apply under this section for an order for the forfeiture of the goods, material or articles.

(2) An application under this section may be made –
   (a) where proceedings have been brought in any court for a relevant offence relating to some or all of the goods, material or articles, to that court;
   (b) where no application for the forfeiture of the goods, material or articles has been made under paragraph (a), by way of complaint to a magistrates' court.

(3) On an application under this section the court shall make an order for the forfeiture of any goods, material or articles only if it is satisfied that a relevant offence has been committed in relation to the goods, material or articles.

(4) A court may infer for the purposes of this section that such an offence has been committed in relation to any goods, material or articles if it is satisfied that such an offence has been committed in relation to goods, material or articles which are representative of them (whether by reason of being of the same design or part of the same consignment or batch or otherwise).

(5) Any person aggrieved by an order made under this section by a magistrates' court, or by a decision of such a court not to make such an order, may appeal against that order or decision –

(a) in England and Wales, to the Crown Court;

(b) in Northern Ireland, to the county court;

and an order so made may contain such provision as appears to the court to be appropriate for delaying the coming into force of the order pending the making and determination of any appeal (including any application under section 111 of the Magistrates' Courts Act 1980 or Article 146 of the Magistrates' Courts (Northern Ireland) Order 1981 (statement of case)).

(6) Subject to subsection (7), where any goods, material or articles are forfeited under this section they shall be destroyed in accordance with such directions as the court may give.

(7) On making an order under this section the court may, if it considers it appropriate to do so, direct that the goods, material or articles to which the order relates shall (instead of being destroyed) be released, to such person as the court may specify, on condition that that person –

(a) causes the offending sign to be erased, removed or obliterated and

(b) complies with any order to pay costs which has been made against him in the proceedings for the order for forfeiture.

(8) For the purposes of this section a 'relevant offence' means an offence under section 92 above (unauthorised use of trade mark, &c in relation to goods) or under the Trade Descriptions Act 1968 or any offence involving dishonesty or deception.

Annotations

Date in force: 31 October 1994.

Commencement order: SI 1994 No 2550.

Appendix

98 Forfeiture: Scotland

(1) In Scotland the court may make an order for the forfeiture of any –
   (a) goods which bear, or the packaging of which bears, a sign identical to or likely to be mistaken for a registered trade mark,
   (b) material bearing such a sign and intended to be used for labelling or packaging goods, as a business paper in relation to goods, or for advertising goods, or
   (c) articles specifically designed or adapted for making copies of such a sign.

(2) An order under this section may be made –
   (a) on an application by the procurator-fiscal made in the manner specified in section 310 of the Criminal Procedure (Scotland) Act 1975, or
   (b) where a person is convicted of a relevant offence, in addition to any other penalty which the court may impose.

(3) On an application under subsection (2)(a), the court shall make an order for the forfeiture of any goods, material or articles only if it is satisfied that a relevant offence has been committed in relation to the goods, material or articles.

(4) The court may infer for the purposes of this section that such an offence has been committed in relation to any goods, material or articles if it is satisfied that such an offence has been committed in relation to goods, material or articles which are representative of them (whether by reason of being of the same design or part of the same consignment or batch or otherwise).

(5) The procurator-fiscal making the application under subsection (2)(a) shall serve on any person appearing to him to be the owner of, or otherwise to have an interest in, the goods, material or articles to which the application relates a copy of the application, together with a notice giving him the opportunity to appear at the hearing of the application to show cause why the goods, material or articles should not be forfeited.

(6) Service under subsection (5) shall be carried out, and such service may be proved, in the manner specified for citation of an accused in summary proceedings under the Criminal Procedure (Scotland) Act 1975.

(7) Any person upon whom notice is served under subsection (5)

and any other person claiming to be the owner of, or otherwise
to have an interest in, goods, material or articles to which an
application under this section relates shall be entitled to appear
at the hearing of the application to show cause why the goods,
material or articles should not be forfeited.

(8) The court shall not make an order following an application
under subsection (2)(a) –

   (a) if any person on whom notice is served under subsection
(5) does not appear, unless service of the notice on that
person is proved; or

   (b) if no notice under subsection (5) has been served, unless the
court is satisfied that in the circumstances it was reasonable
not to serve such notice.

(9) Where an order for the forfeiture of any goods, material or
articles is made following an application under subsection
(2)(a), any person who appeared, or was entitled to appear, to
show cause why goods, material or articles should not be
forfeited may, within 21 days of the making of the order, appeal
to the High Court by Bill of Suspension; and section 452(4)(a)
to (e) of the Criminal Procedure (Scotland) Act 1975 shall apply
to an appeal under this subsection as it applies to a stated case
under Part II of that Act.

(10) An order following an application under subsection (2)(a) shall
not take effect –

   (a) until the end of the period of 21 days beginning with the
day after the day on which the order is made; or

   (b) if an appeal is made under subsection (9) above within that
period, until the appeal is determined or abandoned.

(11) An order under subsection (2)(b) shall not take effect –

   (a) until the end of the period within which an appeal against
the order could be brought under the Criminal Procedure
(Scotland) Act 1975; or

   (b) if an appeal is made within that period, until the appeal is
determined or abandoned.

(12) Subject to subsection (13), goods, material or articles forfeited
under this section shall be destroyed in accordance with such
directions as the court may give.

(13) On making an order under this section the court may if it
considers it appropriate to do so, direct that the goods, material
or articles to which the order relates shall (instead of being

destroyed) be released, to such person as the court may specify, on condition that that person causes the offending sign to be erased, removed or obliterated.

(14) For the purposes of this section –

'relevant offence' means an offence under section 92 (unauthorised use of trade mark, &c in relation to goods) or under the Trade Descriptions Act 1968 or any offence involving dishonesty or deception,

'the court' means –

(a) in relation to an order made on an application under subsection (2)(a), the sheriff, and

(b) in relation to an order made under subsection (2)(b), the court which imposed the penalty.

Annotations

Date in force: 31 October 1994.

Commencement order: SI 1994 No 2550.

Part IV
Miscellaneous and General Provisions

Miscellaneous

99 Unauthorised use of Royal arms, &c

(1) A person shall not without the authority of Her Majesty use in connection with any business the Royal arms (or arms so closely resembling the Royal arms as to be calculated to deceive) in such manner as to be calculated to lead to the belief that he is duly authorised to use the Royal arms.

(2) A person shall not without the authority of Her Majesty or of a member of the Royal family use in connection with any business any device, emblem or title in such a manner as to be calculated to lead to the belief that he is employed by, or supplies goods or services to, Her Majesty or that member of the Royal family.

(3) A person who contravenes subsection (1) commits an offence and is liable on summary conviction to a fine not exceeding level 2 on the standard scale.

(4) Contravention of subsection (1) or (2) may be restrained by

injunction in proceedings brought by –

(a) any person who is authorised to use the arms, device, emblem or title in question, or

(b) any person authorised by the Lord Chamberlain to take such proceedings.

(5) Nothing in this section affects any right of the proprietor of a trade mark containing any such arms, device, emblem or title to use that trade mark.

Annotations
Date in force: 31 October 1994.
Commencement order: SI 1994 No 2550.

100 Burden of proving use of trade mark

If in any civil proceedings under this Act a question arises as to the use to which a registered trade mark has been put, it is for the proprietor to show what use has been made of it.

Annotations
Date in force: 31 October 1994.
Commencement order: SI 1994 No 2550.

101 Offences committed by partnerships and bodies corporate

(1) Proceedings for an offence under this Act alleged to have been committed by a partnership shall be brought against the partnership in the name of the firm and not in that of the partners; but without prejudice to any liability of the partners under subsection (4) below.

(2) The following provisions apply for the purposes of such proceedings as in relation to a body corporate –

(a) any rules of court relating to the service of documents;

(b) in England and Wales or Northern Ireland, Schedule 3 to the Magistrates' Courts Act 1980 or Schedule 4 to the Magistrates' Courts (Northern Ireland) Order 1981 (procedure on charge of offence).

(3) A fine imposed on a partnership on its conviction in such proceedings shall be paid out of the partnership assets.

(4) Where a partnership is guilty of an offence under this Act, every partner, other than a partner who is proved to have been

ignorant of or to have attempted to prevent the commission of the offence, is also guilty of the offence and liable to be proceeded against and punished accordingly.

(5) Where an offence under this Act committed by a body corporate is proved to have been committed with the consent or connivance of a director, manager, secretary or other similar officer of the body, or a person purporting to act in any such capacity, he as well as the body corporate is guilty of the offence and liable to be proceeded against and punished accordingly.

Annotations
Date in force: 31 October 1994.
Commencement order: SI 1994 No 2550.

Interpretation

102   **Adaptation of expressions for Scotland**

In the application of this Act to Scotland –
'account of profits' means accounting and payment of profits;
'accounts' means count, reckoning and payment;
'assignment' means assignation;
'costs' means expenses;
'declaration' means declarator;
'defendant' means defender;
'delivery up' means delivery;
'injunction' means interdict;
'interlocutory relief' means interim remedy; and
'plaintiff' means pursuer.

Annotations
Date in force: 31 October 1994.
Commencement order: SI 1994 No 2550.

103   **Minor definitions**

(1) In this Act –
'business' includes a trade or profession;
'director', in relation to a body corporate whose affairs are managed by its members, means any member of the body;
'infringement proceedings', in relation to a registered trade mark, includes proceedings under section 16 (order for

delivery up of infringing goods, &c);
'publish' means make available to the public, and references to
    publication –
    (a) in relation to an application for registration, are to
        publication under section 38(1), and
    (b) in relation to registration, are to publication under
        section 40(4);
'statutory provisions' includes provisions of subordinate
    legislation within the meaning of the Interpretation Act
    1978;
'trade' includes any business or profession.
(2) References in this Act to use (or any particular description of
    use) of a trade mark, or of a sign identical with, similar to, or
    likely to be mistaken for a trade mark, include use (or that
    description of use) otherwise than by means of a graphic
    representation.
(3) References in this Act to a Community instrument include
    references to any instrument amending or replacing that
    instrument.

Annotations
Date in force: 31 October 1994.
Commencement order: SI 1994 No 2550.

104   Index of defined expressions

In this Act the expressions listed below are defined by or otherwise
fall to be construed in accordance with the provisions indicated –

299

date of filing	section 33(1)
date of registration	section 40(3)
defendant (in Scotland)	section 102
delivery up (in Scotland)	section 102
director	section 103(1)
earlier right	section 5(4)
earlier trade mark	section 6
exclusive licence and licensee	section 29(1)
infringement (of registered trade mark)	sections 9(1) and (2) and 10
infringement proceedings	section 103(1)
infringing articles	section 17
infringing goods	section 17
infringing material	section 17
injunction (in Scotland)	section 102
interlocutory relief (in Scotland)	section 102
the International Bureau	section 53
international trade mark (UK)	section 53
Madrid Protocol	section 53
Paris Convention	section 55(1)(a)
plaintiff (in Scotland)	section 102
prescribed	section 78(1)(b)
protected under the Paris Convention	
– well-known trade marks	section 56(1)
– state emblems and official signs or hallmarks	section 57(1)
– emblems, &c of international organisations	section 58(2)
publish and references to publication	section 103(1)
register, registered (and related expressions)	section 63(1)
registered trade mark agent	section 83(1)
registrable transaction	section 25(2)
the registrar	section 62
rules	section 78
statutory provisions	section 103(1)
trade	section 103(1)
trade mark	
– generally	section 1(1)
– includes collective mark or certification mark	section 1(2)

United Kingdom (references include Isle of Man)	section 108(2)
use (of trade mark or sign)	section 103(2)
well-known trade mark (under Paris Convention)	section 56(1)

Annotations
Date in force: 31 October 1994.
Commencement order: SI 1994 No 2550.

Other general provisions

105 Transitional provisions

The provisions of Schedule 3 have effect with respect to transitional matters, including the treatment of marks registered under the Trade Marks Act 1938, and applications for registration and other proceedings pending under that Act, on the commencement of this Act.

Annotations
Date in force: 31 October 1994 (certain purposes); 29 September 1994 (remaining purposes).
Commencement order: SI 1994 No 2550.

106 Consequential amendments and repeals

(1) The enactments specified in Schedule 4 are amended in accordance with that Schedule, the amendments being consequential on the provisions of this Act.

(2) The enactments specified in Schedule 5 are repealed to the extent specified.

Annotations
Date in force: 31 October 1994.
Commencement order: SI 1994 No 2550.

107 Territorial waters and the continental shelf

(1) For the purposes of this Act the territorial waters of the United Kingdom shall be treated as part of the United Kingdom.

(2) This Act applies to things done in the United Kingdom sector of the continental shelf on a structure or vessel which is present

there for purposes directly connected with the exploration of the sea bed or subsoil or the exploitation of their natural resources as it applies to things done in the United Kingdom.

(3) The United Kingdom sector of the continental shelf means the areas designated by order under section 1(7) of the Continental Shelf Act 1964.

Annotations

Date in force: 31 October 1994.

Commencement order: SI 1994 No 2550.

108 Extent

(1) This Act extends to England and Wales, Scotland and Northern Ireland.

(2) This Act also extends to the Isle of Man, subject to such exceptions and modifications as Her Majesty may specify by Order in Council; and subject to any such Order references in this Act to the United Kingdom shall be construed as including the Isle of Man.

Annotations

Date in force: 31 October 1994.

Commencement order: SI 1994 No 2550.

109 Commencement

(1) The provisions of this Act come into force on such day as the Secretary of State may appoint by order made by statutory instrument.

Different days may be appointed for different provisions and different purposes.

(2) The references to the commencement of this Act in Schedules 3 and 4 (transitional provisions and consequential amendments) are to the commencement of the main substantive provisions of Parts I and III of this Act and the consequential repeal of the Trade Marks Act 1938.

Provision may be made by order under this section identifying the date of that commencement.

Annotations

Date in force: 31 October 1994.

Commencement order: SI 1994 No 2550.

110 Short title

This Act may be cited as the Trade Marks Act 1994.

Annotations

Date in force: 31 October 1994 (certain purposes); 29 September 1994 (remaining purposes).

Commencement order: SI 1994 No 2550.

SCHEDULE 1
Collective Marks

Section 49

General

1

The provisions of this Act apply to collective marks subject to the following provisions.

Signs of which a collective mark may consist

2

In relation to a collective mark the reference in section 1(1) (signs of which a trade mark may consist) to distinguishing goods or services of one undertaking from those of other undertakings shall be construed as a reference to distinguishing goods or services of members of the association which is the proprietor of the mark from those of other undertakings.

Indication of geographical origin

3

(1) Notwithstanding section 3(1)(c), a collective mark may be registered which consists of signs or indications which may serve, in trade, to designate the geographical origin of the goods or services.

(2) However, the proprietor of such a mark is not entitled to prohibit the use of the signs or indications in accordance with

honest practices in industrial or commercial matters (in particular, by a person who is entitled to use a geographical name).

Mark not to be misleading as to character or significance

4

(1) A collective mark shall not be registered if the public is liable to be misled as regards the character or significance of the mark, in particular if it is likely to be taken to be something other than a collective mark.

(2) The registrar may accordingly require that a mark in respect of which application is made for registration include some indication that it is a collective mark.

Notwithstanding section 39(2), an application may be amended so as to comply with any such requirement.

Regulations governing use of collective mark

5

(1) An applicant for registration of a collective mark must file with the registrar regulations governing the use of the mark.

(2) The regulations must specify the persons authorised to use the mark, the conditions of membership of the association and, where they exist, the conditions of use of the mark, including any sanctions against misuse.

Further requirements with which the regulations have to comply may be imposed by rules.

Approval of regulations by registrar

6

(1) A collective mark shall not be registered unless the regulations governing the use of the mark –
  (a) comply with paragraph 5(2) and any further requirements imposed by rules, and

(b) are not contrary to public policy or to accepted principles of morality.

(2) Before the end of the prescribed period after the date of the application for registration of a collective mark, the applicant must file the regulations with the registrar and pay the prescribed fee.

If he does not do so, the application shall be deemed to be withdrawn.

7

(1) The registrar shall consider whether the requirements mentioned in paragraph 6(1) are met.

(2) If it appears to the registrar that those requirements are not met, he shall inform the applicant and give him an opportunity, within such period as the registrar may specify, to make representations or to file amended regulations.

(3) If the applicant fails to satisfy the registrar that those requirements are met, or to file regulations amended so as to meet them, or fails to respond before the end of the specified period, the registrar shall refuse the application.

(4) If it appears to the registrar that those requirements, and the other requirements for registration, are met, he shall accept the application and shall proceed in accordance with section 38 (publication, opposition proceedings and observations).

8

The regulations shall be published and notice of opposition may be given, and observations may be made, relating to the matters mentioned in paragraph 6(1).

This is in addition to any other grounds on which the application may be opposed or observations made.

Regulations to be open to inspection

9

The regulations governing the use of a registered collective mark shall be open to public inspection in the same way as the register.

Appendix

Amendment of regulations

10

(1) An amendment of the regulations governing the use of a registered collective mark is not effective unless and until the amended regulations are filed with the registrar and accepted by him.

(2) Before accepting any amended regulations the registrar may in any case where it appears to him expedient to do so cause them to be published.

(3) If he does so, notice of opposition may be given, and observations may be made, relating to the matters mentioned in paragraph 6(1).

Infringement: rights of authorised users

11

The following provisions apply in relation to an authorised user of a registered collective mark as in relation to a licensee of a trade mark –

(a) section 10(5) (definition of infringement: unauthorised application of mark to certain material);

(b) section 19(2) (order as to disposal of infringing goods, material or articles: adequacy of other remedies);

(c) section 89 (prohibition of importation of infringing goods, material or articles: request to Commissioners of Customs and Excise).

12

(1) The following provisions (which correspond to the provisions of section 30 (general provisions as to rights of licensees in case of infringement)) have effect as regards the rights of an authorised user in relation to infringement of a registered collective mark.

(2) An authorised user is entitled, subject to any agreement to the contrary between him and the proprietor, to call on the proprietor to take infringement proceedings in respect of any matter which affects his interests.

(3) If the proprietor –
   (a) refuses to do so, or
   (b) fails to do so within two months after being called upon,
   the authorised user may bring the proceedings in his own name
   as if he were the proprietor.
(4) Where infringement proceedings are brought by virtue of this
   paragraph, the authorised user may not, without the leave of the
   court, proceed with the action unless the proprietor is either
   joined as a plaintiff or added as a defendant.
   This does not affect the granting of interlocutory relief on an
   application by an authorised user alone.
(5) A proprietor who is added as a defendant as mentioned in sub-
   paragraph (4) shall not be made liable for any costs in the action
   unless he takes part in the proceedings.
(6) In infringement proceedings brought by the proprietor of a
   registered collective mark any loss suffered or likely to be
   suffered by authorised users shall be taken into account; and the
   court may give such directions as it thinks fit as to the extent to
   which the plaintiff is to hold the proceeds of any pecuniary
   remedy on behalf of such users.

Grounds for revocation of registration

13

Apart from the grounds of revocation provided for in section 46,
the registration of a collective mark may be revoked on the
ground –
(a) that the manner in which the mark has been used by the
   proprietor has caused it to become liable to mislead the public
   in the manner referred to in paragraph 4(1), or
(b) that the proprietor has failed to observe, or to secure the
   observance of, the regulations governing the use of the mark,
   or
(c) that an amendment of the regulations has been made so that the
   regulations –
   (i) no longer comply with paragraph 5(2) and any further
      conditions imposed by rules, or
   (ii) are contrary to public policy or to accepted principles
      of morality.

Grounds for invalidity of registration

14

Apart from the grounds of invalidity provided for in section 47, the registration of a collective mark may be declared invalid on the ground that the mark was registered in breach of the provisions of paragraph 4(1) or 6(1).

Annotations

Date in force: 31 October 1994 (paras 1–5, 7–14, para 6 in part); 29 September 1994 (remainder).

Commencement order: SI 1994 No 2550.

SCHEDULE 2
Certification Marks

Section 50

General

1

The provisions of this Act apply to certification marks subject to the following provisions.

Signs of which a certification mark may consist

2

In relation to a certification mark the reference in section 1(1) (signs of which a trade mark may consist) to distinguishing goods or services of one undertaking from those of other undertakings shall be construed as a reference to distinguishing goods or services which are certified from those which are not.

Indication of geographical origin

3

(1) Notwithstanding section 3(1)(c), a certification mark may be registered which consists of signs or indications which may

serve, in trade, to designate the geographical origin of the goods or services.

(2) However, the proprietor of such a mark is not entitled to prohibit the use of the signs or indications in accordance with honest practices in industrial or commercial matters (in particular, by a person who is entitled to use a geographical name).

Nature of proprietor's business

4

A certification mark shall not be registered if the proprietor carries on a business involving the supply of goods or services of the kind certified.

Mark not to be misleading as to character or significance

5

(1) A certification mark shall not be registered if the public is liable to be misled as regards the character or significance of the mark, in particular if it is likely to be taken to be something other than a certification mark.

(2) The registrar may accordingly require that a mark in respect of which application is made for registration include some indication that it is a certification mark.

Notwithstanding section 39(2), an application may be amended so as to comply with any such requirement.

Regulations governing use of certification mark

6

(1) An applicant for registration of a certification mark must file with the registrar regulations governing the use of the mark.

(2) The regulations must indicate who is authorised to use the mark, the characteristics to be certified by the mark, how the

certifying body is to test those characteristics and to supervise the use of the mark, the fees (if any) to be paid in connection with the operation of the mark and the procedures for resolving disputes.

Further requirements with which the regulations have to comply may be imposed by rules.

· *Approval of regulations, &c*

7

(1) A certification mark shall not be registered unless –
  (a) the regulations governing the use of the mark –
    (i) comply with paragraph 6(2) and any further requirements imposed by rules, and
    (ii) are not contrary to public policy or to accepted principles of morality, and
  (b) the applicant is competent to certify the goods or services for which the mark is to be registered.

(2) Before the end of the prescribed period after the date of the application for registration of a certification mark, the applicant must file the regulations with the registrar and pay the prescribed fee.

   If he does not do so, the application shall be deemed to be withdrawn.

8

(1) The registrar shall consider whether the requirements mentioned in paragraph 7(1) are met.

(2) If it appears to the registrar that those requirements are not met, he shall inform the applicant and give him an opportunity, within such period as the registrar may specify, to make representations or to file amended regulations.

(3) If the applicant fails to satisfy the registrar that those requirements are met, or to file regulations amended so as to meet them, or fails to respond before the end of the specified period, the registrar shall refuse the application.

(4) If it appears to the registrar that those requirements, and the other requirements for registration, are met, he shall accept the

application and shall proceed in accordance with section 38 (publication, opposition proceedings and observations).

9

The regulations shall be published and notice of opposition may be given, and observations may be made, relating to the matters mentioned in paragraph 7(1).

This is in addition to any other grounds on which the application may be opposed or observations made.

Regulations to be open to inspection

10

The regulations governing the use of a registered certification mark shall be open to public inspection in the same way as the register.

Amendment of regulations

11

(1) An amendment of the regulations governing the use of a registered certification mark is not effective unless and until the amended regulations are filed with the registrar and accepted by him.

(2) Before accepting any amended regulations the registrar may in any case where it appears to him expedient to do so cause them to be published.

(3) If he does so, notice of opposition may be given, and observations may be made, relating to the matters mentioned in paragraph 7(1).

Consent to assignment of registered certification mark

12

The assignment or other transmission of a registered certification mark is not effective without the consent of the registrar.

Appendix

Infringement: rights of authorised users

13

The following provisions apply in relation to an authorised user of a registered certification mark as in relation to a licensee of a trade mark –
(a) section 10(5) (definition of infringement: unauthorised application of mark to certain material);
(b) section 19(2) (order as to disposal of infringing goods, material or articles: adequacy of other remedies);
(c) section 89 (prohibition of importation of infringing goods, material or articles: request to Commissioners of Customs and Excise).

14

In infringement proceedings brought by the proprietor of a registered certification mark any loss suffered or likely to be suffered by authorised users shall be taken into account; and the court may give such directions as it thinks fit as to the extent to which the plaintiff is to hold the proceeds of any pecuniary remedy on behalf of such users.

Grounds for revocation of registration

15

Apart from the grounds of revocation provided for in section 46, the registration of a certification mark may be revoked on the ground –
(a) that the proprietor has begun to carry on such a business as is mentioned in paragraph 4,
(b) that the manner in which the mark has been used by the proprietor has caused it to become liable to mislead the public in the manner referred to in paragraph 5(1),
(c) that the proprietor has failed to observe, or to secure the observance of, the regulations governing the use of the mark,
(d) that an amendment of the regulations has been made so that the regulations –
  (i) no longer comply with paragraph 6(2) and any further conditions imposed by rules, or
  (ii) are contrary to public policy or to accepted principles of morality, or

312

(e) that the proprietor is no longer competent to certify the goods or services for which the mark is registered.

Grounds for invalidity of registration

16

Apart from the grounds of invalidity provided for in section 47, the registration of a certification mark may be declared invalid on the ground that the mark was registered in breach of the provisions of paragraph 4, 5(1) or 7(1).

Annotations

Date in force: 31 October 1994 (paras 1–6, 8–16, para 7 in part); 29 September 1994 (remainder).

Commencement order: SI 1994 No 2550.

SCHEDULE 3
Transitional Provisions

Section 105

Introductory

1

(1) In this Schedule –

'existing registered mark' means a trade mark, certification trade mark or service mark registered under the 1938 Act immediately before the commencement of this Act;

'the 1938 Act' means the Trade Marks Act 1938; and

'the old law' means that Act and any other enactment or rule of law applying to existing registered marks immediately before the commencement of this Act.

(2) For the purposes of this Schedule –

(a) an application shall be treated as pending on the commencement of this Act if it was made but not finally determined before commencement, and

(b) the date on which it was made shall be taken to be the date of filing under the 1938 Act.

Existing registered marks

2

(1) Existing registered marks (whether registered in Part A or B of the register kept under the 1938 Act) shall be transferred on the commencement of this Act to the register kept under this Act and have effect, subject to the provisions of this Schedule, as if registered under this Act.

(2) Existing registered marks registered as a series under section 21(2) of the 1938 Act shall be similarly registered in the new register.

Provision may be made by rules for putting such entries in the same form as is required for entries under this Act.

(3) In any other case notes indicating that existing registered marks are associated with other marks shall cease to have effect on the commencement of this Act.

3

(1) A condition entered on the former register in relation to an existing registered mark immediately before the commencement of this Act shall cease to have effect on commencement.

Proceedings under section 33 of the 1938 Act (application to expunge or vary registration for breach of condition) which are pending on the commencement of this Act shall be dealt with under the old law and any necessary alteration made to the new register.

(2) A disclaimer or limitation entered on the former register in relation to an existing registered mark immediately before the commencement of this Act shall be transferred to the new register and have effect as if entered on the register in pursuance of section 13 of this Act.

Effects of registration: infringement

4

(1) Sections 9 to 12 of this Act (effects of registration) apply in relation to an existing registered mark as from the commencement of this Act and section 14 of this Act (action for infringement) applies in relation to infringement of an existing registered mark committed after the commencement of this

Act, subject to sub-paragraph (2) below.

The old law continues to apply in relation to infringements committed before commencement.

(2) It is not an infringement of –

(a) an existing registered mark, or

(b) a registered trade mark of which the distinctive elements are the same or substantially the same as those of an existing registered mark and which is registered for the same goods or services,

to continue after commencement any use which did not amount to infringement of the existing registered mark under the old law.

Infringing goods, material or articles

5

Section 16 of this Act (order for delivery up of infringing goods, material or articles) applies to infringing goods, material or articles whether made before or after the commencement of this Act.

Rights and remedies of licensee or authorised user

6

(1) Section 30 (general provisions as to rights of licensees in case of infringement) of this Act applies to licences granted before the commencement of this Act, but only in relation to infringements committed after commencement.

(2) Paragraph 14 of Schedule 2 of this Act (court to take into account loss suffered by authorised users, &c) applies only in relation to infringements committed after commencement.

Co-ownership of registered mark

7

The provisions of section 23 of this Act (co-ownership of registered mark) apply as from the commencement of this Act to an existing registered mark of which two or more persons were immediately before commencement registered as joint proprietors.

But so long as the relations between the joint proprietors remain such as are described in section 63 of the 1938 Act (joint ownership) there shall be taken to be an agreement to exclude the operation of subsections (1) and (3) of section 23 of this Act (ownership in undivided shares and right of co-proprietor to make separate use of the mark).

Assignment, &c of registered mark

8

(1) Section 24 of this Act (assignment or other transmission of registered mark) applies to transactions and events occurring after the commencement of this Act in relation to an existing registered mark; and the old law continues to apply in relation to transactions and events occurring before commencement.

(2) Existing entries under section 25 of the 1938 Act (registration of assignments and transmissions) shall be transferred on the commencement of this Act to the register kept under this Act and have effect as if made under section 25 of this Act.

Provision may be made by rules for putting such entries in the same form as is required for entries made under this Act.

(3) An application for registration under section 25 of the 1938 Act which is pending before the registrar on the commencement of this Act shall be treated as an application for registration under section 25 of this Act and shall proceed accordingly.

The registrar may require the applicant to amend his application so as to conform with the requirements of this Act.

(4) An application for registration under section 25 of the 1938 Act which has been determined by the registrar but not finally determined before the commencement of this Act shall be dealt with under the old law; and sub-paragraph (2) above shall apply in relation to any resulting entry in the register.

(5) Where before the commencement of this Act a person has become entitled by assignment or transmission to an existing registered mark but has not registered his title, any application for registration after commencement shall be made under

section 25 of this Act.

(6) In cases to which sub-paragraph (3) or (5) applies section 25(3) of the 1938 Act continues to apply (and section 25(3) and (4) of this Act do not apply) as regards the consequences of failing to register.

Licensing of registered mark

9

(1) Sections 28 and 29(2) of this Act (licensing of registered trade mark; rights of exclusive licensee against grantor's successor in title) apply only in relation to licences granted after the commencement of this Act; and the old law continues to apply in relation to licences granted before commencement.

(2) Existing entries under section 28 of the 1938 Act (registered users) shall be transferred on the commencement of this Act to the register kept under this Act and have effect as if made under section 25 of this Act.

Provision may be made by rules for putting such entries in the same form as is required for entries made under this Act.

(3) An application for registration as a registered user which is pending before the registrar on the commencement of this Act shall be treated as an application for registration of a licence under section 25(1) of this Act and shall proceed accordingly.

The registrar may require the applicant to amend his application so as to conform with the requirements of this Act.

(4) An application for registration as a registered user which has been determined by the registrar but not finally determined before the commencement of this Act shall be dealt with under the old law; and sub-paragraph (2) above shall apply in relation to any resulting entry in the register.

(5) Any proceedings pending on the commencement of this Act under section 28(8) or (10) of the 1938 Act (variation or cancellation of registration of registered user) shall be dealt with under the old law and any necessary alteration made to the new register.

Pending applications for registration

10

(1) An application for registration of a mark under the 1938 Act which is pending on the commencement of this Act shall be dealt with under the old law, subject as mentioned below, and if registered the mark shall be treated for the purposes of this Schedule as an existing registered mark.

(2) The power of the Secretary of State under section 78 of this Act to make rules regulating practice and procedure, and as to the matters mentioned in subsection (2) of that section, is exercisable in relation to such an application; and different provision may be made for such applications from that made for other applications.

(3) Section 23 of the 1938 Act (provisions as to associated trade marks) shall be disregarded in dealing after the commencement of this Act with an application for registration.

Conversion of pending application

11

(1) In the case of a pending application for registration which has not been advertised under section 18 of the 1938 Act before the commencement of this Act, the applicant may give notice to the registrar claiming to have the registrability of the mark determined in accordance with the provisions of this Act.

(2) The notice must be in the prescribed form, be accompanied by the appropriate fee and be given no later than six months after the commencement of this Act.

(3) Notice duly given is irrevocable and has the effect that the application shall be treated as if made immediately after the commencement of this Act.

Trade marks registered according to old classification

12

The registrar may exercise the powers conferred by rules under section 65 of this Act (adaptation of entries to new classification) to

secure that any existing registered marks which do not conform to
the system of classification prescribed under section 34 of this Act
are brought to conformity with that system.

This applies, in particular, to existing registered marks classified
according to the pre-1938 classification set out in Schedule 3 to the
Trade Marks Rules 1986.

Claim to priority from overseas application

13

Section 35 of this Act (claim to priority of Convention application)
applies to an application for registration under this Act made after
the commencement of this Act notwithstanding that the Convention
application was made before commencement.

14

(1) Where before the commencement of this Act a person has duly
filed an application for protection of a trade mark in a relevant
country within the meaning of section 39A of the 1938 Act which
is not a Convention country (a 'relevant overseas application'),
he, or his successor in title, has a right to priority, for the purposes
of registering the same trade mark under this Act for some or all
of the same goods or services, for a period of six months from the
date of filing of the relevant overseas application.

(2) If the application for registration under this Act is made within
that six-month period –
   (a) the relevant date for the purposes of establishing which
   rights take precedence shall be the date of filing of the
   relevant overseas application, and
   (b) the registrability of the trade mark shall not be affected by
   any use of the mark in the United Kingdom in the period
   between that date and the date of the application under
   this Act.

(3) Any filing which in a relevant country is equivalent to a regular
national filing, under its domestic legislation or an international
agreement, shall be treated as giving rise to the right of priority.

A 'regular national filing' means a filing which is adequate to
establish the date on which the application was filed in that

country, whatever may be the subsequent fate of the application.

(4) A subsequent application concerning the same subject as the relevant overseas application, filed in the same country, shall be considered the relevant overseas application (of which the filing date is the starting date of the period of priority), if at the time of the subsequent application –

(a) the previous application has been withdrawn, abandoned or refused, without having been laid open to public inspection and without leaving any rights outstanding, and

(b) it has not yet served as a basis for claiming a right of priority.

The previous application may not thereafter serve as a basis for claiming a right of priority.

(5) Provision may be made by rules as to the manner of claiming a right to priority on the basis of a relevant overseas application.

(6) A right to priority arising as a result of a relevant overseas application may be assigned or otherwise transmitted, either with the application or independently.

The reference in sub-paragraph (1) to the applicant's 'successor in title' shall be construed accordingly.

(7) Nothing in this paragraph affects proceedings on an application for registration under the 1938 Act made before the commencement of this Act (see paragraph 10 above).

Duration and renewal of registration

15

(1) Section 42(1) of this Act (duration of original period of registration) applies in relation to the registration of a mark in pursuance of an application made after the commencement of this Act; and the old law applies in any other case.

(2) Sections 42(2) and 43 of this Act (renewal) apply where the renewal falls due on or after the commencement of this Act; and the old law continues to apply in any other case.

(3) In either case it is immaterial when the fee is paid.

Pending application for alteration of registered mark

16

An application under section 35 of the 1938 Act (alteration of registered trade mark) which is pending on the commencement of this Act shall be dealt with under the old law and any necessary alteration made to the new register.

Revocation for non-use

17

(1) An application under section 26 of the 1938 Act (removal from register or imposition of limitation on ground of non-use) which is pending on the commencement of this Act shall be dealt with under the old law and any necessary alteration made to the new register.

(2) An application under section 46(1)(a) or (b) of this Act (revocation for non-use) may be made in relation to an existing registered mark at any time after the commencement of this Act.

Provided that no such application for the revocation of the registration of an existing registered mark registered by virtue of section 27 of the 1938 Act (defensive registration of well-known trade marks) may be made until more than five years after the commencement of this Act.

Application for rectification, &c

18

(1) An application under section 32 or 34 of the 1938 Act (rectification or correction of the register) which is pending on the commencement of this Act shall be dealt with under the old law and any necessary alteration made to the new register.

(2) For the purposes of proceedings under section 47 of this Act (grounds for invalidity of registration) as it applies in relation to

an existing registered mark, the provisions of this Act shall be deemed to have been in force at all material times.

Provided that no objection to the validity of the registration of an existing registered mark may be taken on the ground specified in subsection (3) of section 5 of this Act (relative grounds for refusal of registration: conflict with earlier mark registered for different goods or services).

Regulations as to use of certification mark

19

(1) Regulations governing the use of an existing registered certification mark deposited at the Patent Office in pursuance of section 37 of the 1938 Act shall be treated after the commencement of this Act as if filed under paragraph 6 of Schedule 2 to this Act.

(2) Any request for amendment of the regulations which was pending on the commencement of this Act shall be dealt with under the old law.

Sheffield marks

20

(1) For the purposes of this Schedule the Sheffield register kept under Schedule 2 to the 1938 Act shall be treated as part of the register of trade marks kept under that Act.

(2) Applications made to the Cutlers' Company in accordance with that Schedule which are pending on the commencement of this Act shall proceed after commencement as if they had been made to the registrar.

Certificate of validity of contested registration

21

A certificate given before the commencement of this Act under section 47 of the 1938 Act (certificate of validity of contested registration) shall have effect as if given under section 73(1) of this Act.

Trade mark agents

22

(1) Rules in force immediately before the commencement of this Act under section 282 or 283 of the Copyright, Designs and Patents Act 1988 (register of trade mark agents; persons entitled to described themselves as registered) shall continue in force and have effect as if made under section 83 or 85 of this Act.

(2) Rules in force immediately before the commencement of this Act under section 40 of the 1938 Act as to the persons whom the registrar may refuse to recognise as agents for the purposes of business under that Act shall continue in force and have effect as if made under section 88 of this Act.

(3) Rules continued in force under this paragraph may be varied or revoked by further rules made under the relevant provisions of this Act.

Annotations

Date in force: 31 October 1994 (paras 1–9, 13, 15–22, paras 10–12, 14 in part); 29 September 1994 (remainder).

Commencement order: SI 1994 No 2550.

SCHEDULE 4
Consequential Amendments

Section 106(1)

General adaptation of existing references

1

(1) References in statutory provisions passed or made before the commencement of this Act to trade marks or registered trade marks within the meaning of the Trade Marks Act 1938 shall, unless the context otherwise requires, be construed after the commencement of this Act as references to trade marks or registered trade marks within the meaning of this Act.

(2) Sub-paragraph (1) applies, in particular, to the references in the following provisions –

Industrial Organisation and Development Act 1947	Schedule 1, paragraph 7.
Crown Proceedings Act 1947	section 3(1)(b).
Horticulture Act 1960	section 15(1)(b).
Printer's Imprint Act 1961	section 1(1)(b).
Plant Varieties and Seeds Act 1964	section 5A(4).
Northern Ireland Constitution Act 1973	Schedule 3, paragraph 17.
Patents Act 1977	section 19(2); section 27(4); section 123(7).
Unfair Contract Terms Act 1977	Schedule 1, paragraph 1(c).
Judicature (Northern Ireland) Act 1978	section 94A(5).
State Immunity Act 1978	section 7(a) and (b).
Supreme Court Act 1981	section 72(5); Schedule 1, paragraph 1(i).
Civil Jurisdiction and Judgments Act 1982	Schedule 5, paragraph 2; Schedule 8, paragraph 2(14) and 4(2).
Value Added Tax Act 1983	Schedule 3, paragraph 1
Companies Act 1985	section 396(3A)(a) or (as substituted by the Companies Act 1989) section 396(2)(d)(i); section 410(4)(c)(v); Schedule 4, Part I, Balance Sheet Formats 1 and 2 and Note (2); Schedule 9, Part I, paragraphs 5(2)(d) and 10(2).
Law Reform (Miscellaneous Provisions) (Scotland) Act 1985	section 15(5).
Atomic Energy Authority Act 1986	section 8(2).
Companies (Northern Ireland) Order 1986	article 403(3A)(a) or (as substituted by the

Companies (Northern Ireland) Order 1986 - *contd*	Companies (No 2) (Northern Ireland) Order 1990) article 403(2)(d)(i); Schedule 4, Part I, Balance Sheet Formats 1 and 2 and Note (2); Schedule 9, Part I, paragraphs 5(2)(d) and 10(2).
Consumer Protection Act 1987	section 2(2)(b).
Consumer Protection (Northern Ireland) Order 1987	article 5(2)(b).
Income and Corporation Taxes Act 1988	section 83(a).
Taxation of Chargeable Gains Act 1992	section 275(h).
Tribunals and Inquiries Act 1992	Schedule 1, paragraph 34.

Patents and Designs Act 1907 (c 29)

2

(1)–(3) (. . .)

(4) The repeal by the Patents Act 1949 and the Registered Designs Act 1949 of the whole of the 1907 Act, except certain provisions, shall be deemed not to have extended to the long title, date of enactment or enacting words or to so much of section 99 as provides the Act with its short title.

3–9

(. . .)

Annotations

Date in force: 31 October 1994.

Commencement order: SI 1994 No 2550.

Para 2: sub-paras (1)–(3) amend the Patents and Designs Act 1907, ss62, 63.

Paras 3–9: amend the Patents, Designs, Copyright and Trade Marks (Emergency) Act 1939, ss4(1)(c), 6(1), 7(1)(a), 10(1), the Trade Descriptions Act 1968, s34, the Solicitors Act 1974, s22(2), (3A), the House of Commons Disqualification Act 1975, Sch 1, Part III, the Copyright, Designs and Patents Act 1988, ss114(6), 204(6), 231(6), 280(1) and the Tribunals and Inquiries Act 1992, Sch 1, Part I, and substitute the Patents, Designs, Copyright and Trade Marks (Emergency) Act 1939, s3 and the Restrictive Trade Practices Act 1976, Sch 3, para 4.

SCHEDULE 5
Repeals and Revocations

Section 106(2)

Chapter or number	Short title	Extent of repeal or revocation
1891 c 50.	Commissioners for Oaths Act 1891.	In section 1, the words 'or the Patents, Designs and Trade Marks Acts, 1883 to 1888,'.
1907 c 29.	Patents and Designs Act 1907.	In section 63(2), the words from 'and those salaries' to the end.
1938 c 22.	Trade Marks Act 1938.	The whole Act.
1947 c 44.	Crown Proceedings Act 1947.	In section 3(1)(b), the words 'or registered service mark'.
1949 c 87.	Patents Act 1949.	Section 92(2).
1964 c 14.	Plant Varieties and Seeds Act 1964.	In section 5A(4), the words 'under the Trade Marks Act 1938'.
1967 c 80.	Criminal Justice Act 1967.	In Schedule 3, in Parts I and IV, the entries relating to the Trade Marks Act 1938.
1978 c 23.	Judicature (Northern Ireland) Act 1978.	In Schedule 5, in Part II, the paragraphs amending the Trade Marks Act 1938.
1984 c 19.	Trade Marks (Amendment) Act 1984.	The whole Act.
1985 c 6.	Companies Act 1985.	In section 396 – (a) in subsection (3A)(a), and (b) in subsection (2)(d)(i) as inserted by the Companies Act 1989, the words 'service mark,'.
1986 c 12.	Statute Law (Repeals) Act 1986.	In Schedule 2, paragraph 2.

Chapter or number	Short title	Extent of repeal or revocation
1986 c 39.	Patents, Designs and Marks Act 1986.	Section 2; Section 4(4); In Schedule 1, paragraphs 1 and 2; Schedule 2.
SI 1986/1032 (NI 6).	Companies (Northern Ireland) Order 1986.	In article 403 – (a) in paragraph (3A)(a), and (b) in paragraph (2)(d)(i) as inserted by the Companies (No 2) (Northern Ireland) Order 1990, the words 'service mark,'.
1987 c 43.	Consumer Protection Act 1987.	In section 45 – (a) in subsection (1), the definition of 'mark' and 'trade mark'; (b) subsection (4).
SI 1987/2049.	Consumer Protection (Northern Ireland) Order 1987.	In article 2 – (a) in paragraph (2), the definitions of 'mark' and 'trade mark'; (b) paragraph (3).
1988 c 1.	Income and Corporation Taxes Act 1988.	In section 83, the words from 'References in this section' to the end.
1988 c 48.	Copyright, Designs and Patents Act 1988.	Sections 282 to 284; In section 286, the definition of 'registered trade mark agent'; Section 300.
1992 c 12.	Taxation of Chargeable Gains Act 1992.	In section 275(h), the words 'service marks' and 'service mark'.

Annotations

Date in force: 31 October 1994.

Commencement order: SI 1994 No 2550.

The Trade Marks Rules 1994

Made - - - 5 October 1994.

The Secretary of State, in exercise of the powers conferred upon him by sections 4(4), 13(2), 25(1), (5) and (6), 34(1), 35(5), 38(1) and (2), 39(3), 40(4), 41(1) and (3), 43(2), (3), (5) and (6), 44(3), 45(2), 63(2) and (3), 64(4), 65, 66(2), 67(1) and (2), 68(1) and (3), 69, 76(1), 78, 80(3), 81, 82 and 88 of, paragraph 6(2) of Schedule 1 to, paragraph 7(2) of Schedule 2 to, and paragraphs 10(2), 11(2), 12 and 14(5) of Schedule 3 to, the Trade Marks Act 1994, after consultation with the Council on Tribunals pursuant to section 8(1) of the Tribunals and Inquiries Act 1992, hereby makes the following Rules: –

Preliminary

1 Citation and commencement

These Rules may be cited as the Trade Marks Rules 1994 and shall come into force on 31 October 1994.

Annotations

Date in force: 31 October 1994.

2 Interpretation

(1) In these Rules, unless the context otherwise requires –
'the Act' means the Trade Marks Act 1994;
'the Journal' means the Trade Marks Journal published in accordance with rule 65 below;
'the Office' means the Patent Office;
'old law' means the Trade Marks Act 1938 (as amended) and any rules made thereunder existing immediately before the commencement of the Act;
'proprietor' means the person registered as the proprietor of the trade mark;
'publish' means publish in the Journal;
'send' includes give;

'specification' means the statement of goods or services in respect of which a trade mark is registered or proposed to be registered;

'United Kingdom' includes the Isle of Man.

(2) In these Rules, except where otherwise indicated, a reference to a section is a reference to that section in the Act, a reference to a rule is a reference to that rule in these Rules, a reference to a Schedule is a reference to that Schedule to these Rules and a reference to a form is a reference to that form as published by the registrar under rule 3 below.

(3) In these Rules references to the filing of any application, notice or other document are to be construed as references to its being sent or delivered to the registrar at the Office.

Annotations

Date in force: 31 October 1994.

3 Forms and directions of the registrar under s66

(1) Any forms required by the registrar to be used for the purpose of registration of a trade mark or any other proceedings before him under the Act pursuant to section 66 and any directions with respect to their use shall be published and any amendment or modification of a form or of the directions with respect to its use shall be published.

(2) A requirement under this rule to use a form as published is satisfied by the use either of a replica of that form or of a form which is acceptable to the registrar and contains the information required by the form as published and complies with any directions as to the use of such a form.

Annotations

Date in force: 31 October 1994.

The Act: Trade Marks Act 1994.

4 Requirement as to fees

(1) The fees to be paid in respect of any application, registration or any other matter under the Act and these Rules shall be those (if any) prescribed in relation to such matter by rules under section 79 (fees).

(2) Any form required to be filed with the registrar in respect of any specified matter shall be subject to the payment of the fee (if any) prescribed in respect of that matter by those rules.

Annotations

Date in force: 31 October 1994.

The Act: Trade Marks Act 1994.

Application for registration

5   **Applications for registration; s32 (Form TM3)**

An application for the registration of a trade mark shall be filed on Form TM3 and shall be subject to the payment of the application fee and such class fees as may be appropriate.

Annotations

Date in force: 31 October 1994.

Section 32: Trade Marks Act 1994, s32.

6   **Claim to priority; ss35 & 36**

(1) Where a right to priority is claimed by reason of an application for protection of a trade mark duly filed in a Convention country under section 35 or in another country or territory in respect of which provision corresponding to that made by section 35 is made under section 36, particulars of that claim shall be included in the application for registration under rule 5 above and, where no certificate as is referred to in paragraph (2) below is filed with the application, such particulars shall include the country or countries and the date or dates of filing.

(2) Unless it has been filed at the time of the filing of the application for registration, there shall be filed, within three months of the filing of the application under rule 5, a certificate by the registering or other competent authority of that country certifying, or verifying to the satisfaction of the registrar, the date of the filing of the application, the country or registering or competent authority, the

representation of the mark, and the goods or services covered by the application.

Annotations
Date in force: 31 October 1994.
Sections 35, 36: Trade Marks Act 1994, ss35, 36.

7 Classification of goods and services; s34

(1) For the purposes of trade mark registrations in respect of goods dated before 27 July 1938, goods are classified in accordance with Schedule 3 to these Rules, except where a specification has been converted, whether under the old law or under rule 40 below, to Schedule 4.

(2) For the purposes of trade mark registrations in respect of goods dated on or after 27 July 1938 and for the purposes of any registrations dated before that date in respect of which the specifications were converted under the old law, and for the purposes of trade mark registrations in respect of services, goods and services are classified in accordance with Schedule 4, which sets out the current version of the classes of the International Classification of Goods and Services.

Annotations
Date in force: 31 October 1994.
Section 34: Trade Marks Act 1994, s34.

8 Application may relate to more than one class and shall specify the class (Form TM3A)

(1) An application may be made for registration in more than one class of Schedule 4.

(2) Every application shall specify the class in Schedule 4 to which it relates; and if the application relates to more than one class in that Schedule the specification contained in it shall set out the classes in consecutive numerical order and list under each class the goods or services appropriate to that class.

(3) If the specification contained in the application lists items by reference to a class in Schedule 4 in which they do not fall, the applicant may request, by filing Form TM3A, that his application be amended to include the appropriate class for those items, and upon the payment of such class

fee as may be appropriate the registrar shall amend his application accordingly.

Annotations

Date in force: 31 October 1994.

9 Prohibition on registration of mark consisting of arms; s4

Where a representation of any arms or insignia as is referred to in section 4(4) appears on a mark, the registrar shall refuse to accept an application for the registration of the mark unless satisfied that the consent of the person entitled to the arms has been obtained.

Annotations

Date in force: 31 October 1994.

Section 4: Trade Marks Act 1994, s4.

10 Address for service (Form TM33)

(1) For the purposes of any proceedings before the registrar under these Rules or any appeal from a decision of the registrar under the Act or these Rules, an address for service in the United Kingdom shall be filed by –

(a) every applicant for the registration of a trade mark;

(b) every person opposing an application for registration of a trade mark;

(c) every applicant applying to the registrar under section 46 for the revocation of the registration of a trade mark, under section 47 for the invalidation of the registration of a trade mark, or under section 64 for the rectification of the register;

(d) every person granted leave to intervene under rule 31(5) (the intervener); and

(e) every proprietor of a registered trade mark which is the subject of an application to the registrar for the revocation, invalidation or rectification of the registration of the mark.

(2) The address for service of an applicant for registration of a trade mark shall upon registration of the mark be deemed to be the address for service of the registered proprietor, subject to any filing to the contrary under paragraph (1) above or rule 38(2) below.

(3) In any case in which an address for service is filed at the same time as the filing of a form required by the registrar under rule 3 which requires the furnishing of an address for service, the address shall be filed on that form and in any other case it shall be filed on Form TM33.

(4) Anything sent to any applicant, opponent, intervener or registered proprietor at his address for service shall be deemed to be properly sent; and the registrar may, where no address for service is filed, treat as the address for service of the person concerned his trade or business address in the United Kingdom, if any.

(5) An address for service in the United Kingdom may be filed at any time by the proprietor of a registered trade mark and by any person having an interest in or charge on a registered trade mark which has been registered under rule 34.

(6) Where an address for service is not filed as required by paragraph (1) above, the registrar shall send the person concerned notice to file an address for service within two months of the date of the notice and if that person fails to do so –

  (a) in the case of an applicant as is referred to in sub-paragraph (a) or (c), the application shall be treated as abandoned;

  (b) in the case of a person as is referred to in sub-paragraph (b) or (d), he shall be deemed to have withdrawn from the proceedings; and

  (c) in the case of the proprietor referred to in sub-paragraph (e), he shall not be permitted to take part in any proceedings.

Annotations
Date in force: 31 October 1994.
The Act: Trade Marks Act 1994.

11 Deficiencies in application; s32

Where an application for registration of a trade mark does not satisfy the requirements of section 32(2), (3) or (4) or rule 5 or 8(2), the registrar shall send notice thereof to the applicant to remedy the deficiencies or, in the case of section 32(4), the default of payment and if within two months of the date of the notice the applicant –
(a) fails to remedy any deficiency notified to him in respect of

section 32(2), the application shall be deemed never to have been made; or

(b) fails to remedy any deficiency notified to him in respect of section 32(3) or rule 5 or 8(2) or fails to make payment as required by section 32(4), the application shall be treated as abandoned.

Annotations
Date in force: 31 October 1994.
Section 32: Trade Marks Act 1994, s32.

Publication, observations, oppositions and registration

12   Publication of application for registration; s38(1)

An application which has been accepted for registration shall be published.

Annotations
Date in force: 31 October 1994.
Section 38(1): Trade Marks Act 1994, s38(1).

13   Opposition proceedings; s38(2) (Forms TM7 & TM8)

(1) Notice of opposition to the registration of a trade mark shall be sent to the registrar on Form TM7 within three months of the date on which the application was published under rule 12, and shall include a statement of the grounds of opposition; the registrar shall send a copy of the notice and the statement to the applicant.

(2) Within three months of the date on which a copy of the statement is sent by the registrar to the applicant the applicant may file, in conjunction with notice of the same on Form TM8, a counter-statement; the registrar shall send a copy of the Form TM8 and the counter-statement to the person opposing the application.

(3) Within three months of the date on which a copy of the counter-statement is sent by the registrar to the person opposing the registration, that person shall file such evidence by way of statutory declaration or affidavit as he may consider necessary to adduce in support of his opposition and shall send a copy thereof to the applicant.

(4) If the person opposing the registration files no evidence under paragraph (3) above, he shall, unless the registrar otherwise directs, be deemed to have abandoned his opposition.

(5) If the person opposing the registration files evidence under paragraph (3) above or the registrar otherwise directs under paragraph (4) above, the applicant shall, within three months of the date on which either a copy of the evidence or a copy of the direction is sent to the applicant, file such evidence by way of statutory declaration or affidavit as he may consider necessary to adduce in support of his application, and shall send a copy thereof to the person opposing the application.

(6) Within three months of the date on which a copy of the applicant's evidence is sent to him, the person opposing the application may file evidence in reply by statutory declaration or affidavit which shall be confined to matters strictly in reply to the applicant's evidence, and shall send a copy thereof to the applicant.

(7) No further evidence may be filed, except that, in relation to any proceedings before him, the registrar may at any time if he thinks fit give leave to either party to file evidence upon such terms as he may think fit.

(8) Upon completion of the evidence the registrar shall, if a hearing is requested by any party to the proceedings, send to the parties notice of a date for the hearing.

Annotations

Date in force: 31 October 1994.

Section 38(2): Trade Marks Act 1994, s38(2).

14   Decision of registrar in opposition proceedings

(1) When the registrar has made a decision on the acceptability of an application for registration following the procedure under rule 13, he shall send the applicant and the person opposing the application written notice of it, stating the reasons for his decision.

(2) For the purpose of any appeal against the registrar's decision the date of the decision shall be the date when notice of the decision is sent under paragraph (1) above.

Annotations

Date in force: 31 October 1994.

15 Observations on application to be sent to applicant; s38(3)

The registrar shall send to the applicant a copy of any documents containing observations made under section 38(3).

Annotations
Date in force: 31 October 1994.
Section 38(3): Trade Marks Act 1994, s38(3).

16 Publication of registration; s40

On the registration of the trade mark the registrar shall publish the registration, specifying the date upon which the trade mark was entered in the register.

Annotations
Date in force: 31 October 1994.
Section 40: Trade Marks Act 1994, s40.

Amendment of application.

17 Amendment of application; s39 (Form TM21)

A request for an amendment of an application to correct an error or to change the name or address of the applicant or in respect of any amendment requested after publication of the application shall be made on Form TM21.

Annotations
Date in force: 31 October 1994.
Section 39: Trade Marks Act 1994, s39.

18 Amendment of application after publication; s39

(1) Where, pursuant to section 39, a request is made for amendment of an application which has been published and the amendment affects the representation of the trade mark or the goods or services covered by the application, the amendment or a statement of the effect of the amendment shall also be published.

(2) Notice of opposition to the amendment shall be sent to the

registrar on Form TM7 within one month of the date on which the application as amended was published under paragraph (1) above, and shall include a statement of the grounds of objection and, in particular, how the amendments would be contrary to section 39(2).

(3) The provisions of rule 13 shall apply to proceedings relating to the opposition to the amendment of the application as they apply to proceedings relating to opposition to the registration of a trade mark.

Annotations

Date in force: 31 October 1994.

Section 39: Trade Marks Act 1994, s39.

Division, merger and series of marks

19   Division of application; s41 (Form TM12)

(1) At any time before registration an applicant may send to the registrar a request on Form TM12 for a division of his application for registration (the original application) into two or more separate applications (divisional applications), indicating for each division the specification of goods or services; each divisional application shall be treated as a separate application for registration with the same filing date as the original application.

(2) Where the request to divide an application is sent after publication of the application, any objections in respect of, or opposition to, the original application shall be taken to apply to each divisional application and shall be proceeded with accordingly.

(3) Upon division of an original application in respect of which notice has been given to the registrar of particulars relating to the grant of a licence, or a security interest or any right in or under it, the notice and the particulars shall be deemed to apply in relation to each of the applications into which the original application has been divided.

Annotations

Date in force: 31 October 1994.

Section 41: Trade Marks Act 1994, s41.

20 Merger of separate applications or registrations; s41 (Form TM17)

(1) An applicant who has made separate applications for registration of a mark may, at any time before preparations for the publication of any of the applications have been completed by the Office, request the registrar on Form TM17 to merge the separate applications into a single application.

(2) The registrar shall, if satisfied that all the applications which are the subject of the request for merger –

  (a) are in respect of the same trade mark,

  (b) bear the same date of application, and

  (c) are, at the time of the request, in the name of the same person, merge them into a single application.

(3) The proprietor of two or more registrations of a trade mark may request the registrar on Form TM17 to merge them into a single registration; and the registrar shall, if satisfied that the registrations are in respect of the same trade mark, merge them into a single registration.

(4) Where any registration of a trade mark to be merged under paragraph (3) above is subject to a disclaimer or limitation, the merged registration shall also be restricted accordingly.

(5) Where any registration of a trade mark to be merged under paragraph (3) above has had registered in relation to it particulars relating to the grant of a licence or a security interest or any right in or under it, or of any memorandum or statement of the effect of a memorandum, the registrar shall enter in the register the same particulars in relation to the merged registration.

(6) The date of registration of the merged registration shall, where the separate registrations bear different dates, be the latest of those dates.

Annotations
Date in force: 31 October 1994.
Section 41: Trade Marks Act 1994, s41.

21 Registration of a series of trade marks; s41 (Form TM12)

(1) The proprietor of a series of trade marks may apply to the registrar on Form TM3 for their registration as a series in a

single registration and there shall be included in such application a representation of each mark claimed to be in the series; and the registrar shall, if satisfied that the marks constitute a series, accept the application.

(2) At any time before preparations of publication of the application have been completed by the Office, the applicant under paragraph (1) above may request on Form TM12 the division of the application into separate applications in respect of one or more marks in that series and the registrar shall, if he is satisfied that the division requested conforms with section 41(2), divide the application accordingly.

(3) At any time the applicant for registration of a series of trade marks or the proprietor of a registered series of trade marks may request the deletion of a mark in that series, and the registrar shall delete the mark accordingly.

(4) The division of an application into one or more applications under paragraph (2) above shall be subject to the payment of a divisional fee and such application and class fees as are appropriate.

Annotations

Date in force: 31 October 1994.

Section 41: Trade Marks Act 1994, s41.

Collective and certification marks

22 Filing of regulations for collective and certification marks; Schs 1 & 2 (Form TM35)

Within nine months of the date of the application for the registration of a collective or certification mark, the applicant shall file Form TM35 accompanied by a copy of the regulations governing the use of the mark.

Annotations

Date in force: 31 October 1994.

23 Amendment of regulations of collective and certification marks; Sch 1 para 10 and Sch 2 para 11 (Forms TM36 & TM7)

(1) An application for the amendment of the regulations governing the use of a registered collective or certification

mark shall be filed on Form TM36.

(2) Where it appears expedient to the registrar that the amended regulations should be made available to the public he shall publish a notice indicating where copies of the amended regulations may be inspected.

(3) Any person may, within three months of the date of publication of the notice under paragraph (2) above, make observations to the registrar on the amendments relating to the matters referred to in paragraph 6(1) of Schedule 1 in relation to a collective mark, or, paragraph 7(1) of Schedule 2 in relation to a certification mark; the registrar shall send a copy thereof to the proprietor.

(4) Any person may, within three months of the date of publication of the notice, file notice on Form TM7 to the registrar of opposition to the amendment, accompanied by a statement of the grounds of opposition, indicating why the amended regulations do not comply with the requirements of paragraph 6(1) of Schedule 1 or, as the case may be, paragraph 7(1) of Schedule 2.

(5) The registrar shall send a copy of the notice and the statement to the proprietor and thereafter the procedure in rule 13(2)–(8) shall apply to the proceedings as they apply to proceedings relating to opposition to an application for registration.

Annotations
Date in force: 31 October 1994.

Disclaimers, limitations and alteration or surrender of registered trade mark

24   Registration subject to disclaimer or limitation; s13

Where the applicant for registration of a trade mark or the proprietor by notice in writing sent to the registrar –

(a) disclaims any right to the exclusive use of any specified element of the trade mark, or

(b) agrees that the rights conferred by the registration shall be subject to a specified territorial or other limitation, the registrar shall make the appropriate entry in the register and publish such disclaimer or limitation.

Annotations
Date in force: 31 October 1994.
Section 13: Trade Marks Act 1994, s13.

25 Alteration of registered trade marks; s44 (Forms TM25 & TM7)

(1) The proprietor may request the registrar on Form TM25 for such alteration of his registered mark as is permitted under section 44; and the registrar may require such evidence by statutory declaration or otherwise as to the circumstances in which the application is made.

(2) Where, upon the request of the proprietor, the registrar proposes to allow such alteration, he shall publish the mark as altered.

(3) Any person claiming to be affected by the alteration may within three months of the date of publication of the alteration under paragraph (2) send a notice on Form TM7 to the registrar of opposition to the alteration and shall include a statement of the grounds of opposition; the registrar shall send a copy of the notice and the statement to the proprietor and thereafter the procedure in rule 13(2)–(8) shall apply to the proceedings as they apply to proceedings relating to opposition to an application for registration.

Annotations
Date in force: 31 October 1994.
Section 44: Trade Marks Act 1994, s44.

26 Surrender of registered trade mark; s45 (Forms TM22 & TM23)

(1) Subject to paragraph (2) below, the proprietor may surrender a registered trade mark, by sending notice to the registrar –
   (a) on Form TM22 in respect of all the goods or services for which it is registered; or
   (b) on Form TM23, in respect only of those goods or services specified by him in the notice.

(2) A notice under paragraph (1) above shall be of no effect unless the proprietor in that notice –
   (a) gives the name and address of any person having a

registered interest in the mark, and
- (b) certifies that any such person –
  - (i) has been sent not less than three months' notice of the proprietor's intention to surrender the mark, or
  - (ii) is not affected or if affected consents thereto.
(3) The registrar shall, upon the surrender taking effect, make the appropriate entry in the register and publish the same.

Annotations
Date in force: 31 October 1994.
Section 45: Trade Marks Act 1994, s45.

Renewal and restoration

27   **Reminder of renewal of registration; s43**

At any time not earlier than six months nor later than one month before the expiration of the last registration of a trade mark, the registrar shall (except where renewal has already been effected under rule 28 below) send to the registered proprietor notice of the approaching expiration and inform him at the same time that the registration may be renewed in the manner described in rule 28 below.

Annotations
Date in force: 31 October 1994.
Section 43: Trade Marks Act 1994, s43.

28   **Renewal of registration; s43 (Form TM11)**

Renewal of registration shall be effected by filing a request for renewal on Form TM11 at any time within the period of six months ending on the date of the expiration of the registration.

Annotations
Date in force: 31 October 1994.
Section 43: Trade Marks Act 1994, s43.

29   **Delayed renewal and removal of registration; s43 (Form TM11)**

(1) If on the expiration of the last registration of a trade mark, the renewal fee has not been paid, the registrar shall publish that fact; and if, within six months from the date of the expiration of

the last registration, the request for renewal is filed on Form TM11 accompanied by the appropriate renewal fee and additional renewal fee, the registrar shall renew the registration without removing the mark from the register.

(2) Where no request for renewal is filed as aforesaid, the registrar shall, subject to rule 30 below, remove the mark from the register.

(3) Where, in the case of a mark the registration of which (by reference to the date of application for registration) becomes due for renewal, the mark is registered at any time within six months before the date on which renewal is due, the registration may be renewed by the payment of –

(a) the renewal fee within six months after the actual date of registration; or

(b) the renewal fee and additional renewal fee within the period commencing on the date six months after the actual date of registration (that is to say, at the end of the period referred to in paragraph (a)) and ending on the date six months after the due date of renewal;

and, where the fees referred to in paragraph (b) are not paid within the period specified in that paragraph the registrar shall, subject to rule 30 below, remove the mark from the register.

(4) Where, in the case of a mark the registration of which (by reference to the date of application for registration) becomes due for renewal, the mark is registered after the date of renewal, the registration may be renewed by the payment of the renewal fee within six months of the actual date of registration; and where the renewal fee is not paid within that period the registrar shall, subject to rule 30 below, remove the mark from the register.

(5) The removal of the registration of a trade mark shall be published.

Annotations
Date in force: 31 October 1994.
Section 43: Trade Marks Act 1994, s43.

30 Restoration of registration; s43 (Form TM13)

(1) Where the registrar has removed the mark from the register for failure to renew its registration in accordance with rule 29

above, he may, upon a request filed on Form TM13 within six months of the date of the removal of the mark accompanied by the appropriate renewal fee and appropriate restoration fee, restore the mark to the register and renew its registration if, having regard to the circumstances of the failure to renew, he is satisfied that it is just to do so.

(2) The restoration of the registration shall be published, with the date of restoration shown.

Annotations

Date in force: 31 October 1994.

Section 43: Trade Marks Act 1994, s43.

Revocation, invalidation and rectification

31 Procedure on application for revocation, declaration of invalidity and rectification of the register; ss46, 47 & 64 (Forms TM26 & TM27)

(1) An application to the registrar for revocation under section 46 or declaration of invalidity under section 47 of the registration of a trade mark or for the rectification of an error or omission in the register under section 64 shall be made on Form TM26 together with a statement of the grounds on which the application is made.

(2) Where any application is made under paragraph (1) by a person other than the proprietor of the registered trade mark, the registrar shall send a copy of the application and the statement to the proprietor.

(3) Within three months of the date on which the registrar sends a copy of the application and the statement to the proprietor, the proprietor may file a counter-statement together with Form TM8 and the registrar shall send a copy thereof to the applicant:

Provided that where an application for revocation is based on the ground of non-use under section 46(1)(a) or (b), the proprietor shall file (within the period allowed for the filing of any counter-statement) evidence of the use by him of the mark; and if he fails so to file evidence the registrar may treat his opposition to the application as having been withdrawn.

(4) Subject to paragraph (2) above and paragraphs (6) and (7) below, the provisions of rule 13 shall apply to proceedings relating to the application as they apply to opposition proceedings for the registration of a trade mark, save that, in the case of an application for revocation on the grounds of non-use under section 46(1)(a) or (b), the application shall be granted where no counter-statement is filed.

(5) Any person, other than the registered proprietor, claiming to have an interest in proceedings on an application under this rule may file an application to the registrar on From TM27 for leave to intervene, stating the nature of his interest and the registrar may, after hearing the parties concerned if so required, refuse such leave or grant leave upon such terms or conditions (including any undertaking as to costs) as he thinks fit.

(6) Any person granted leave to intervene (the intervener) shall, subject to the terms and conditions imposed in respect of the intervention, be treated as a party for the purposes of the application of the provisions of rule 13 to the proceedings on an application under this rule.

(7) When the registrar has made a decision on the application following any opposition, intervention or proceedings held in accordance with this rule, he shall send the applicant, the person opposing the application and the intervener (if any) written notice of it, stating the reasons for his decision; and for the purposes of any appeal against the registrar's decision the date when the notice of the decision is sent shall be taken to be the date of the decision.

Annotations

Date in force: 31 October 1994.

Sections 46, 47, 64: Trade Marks Act 1994, ss46, 47, 64.

The register

32 Form of register; s63(1)

The register required to be maintained by the registrar under section 63(1) need not be kept in documentary form.

Annotations

Date in force: 31 October 1994.

Section 63(1): Trade Marks Act 1994, s63(1).

33 Entry in register of particulars of registered trade marks; s63(2) (Form TM24)

In addition to the entries in the register of registered trade marks required to be made by section 63(2)(a), there shall be entered in the register in respect of each trade mark registered therein the following particulars –

(a) the date of registration as determined in accordance with section 40(3) (that is to say, the date of the filing of the application for registration);

(b) the actual date of registration (that is to say, the date of the entry in the register);

(c) the priority date (if any) to be accorded pursuant to a claim to a right to priority made under section 35 or 36;

(d) the name and address of the proprietor;

(e) the address for service (if any) as furnished pursuant to rule 10 above;

(f) any disclaimer or limitation of rights under section 13(1)(a) or (b);

(g) any memorandum or statement of the effect of any memorandum relating to a trade mark of which the registrar has been notified on Form TM24;

(h) the goods or services in respect of which the mark is registered;

(i) where the mark is a collective or certification mark, that fact; and

(j) where the mark is registered pursuant to section 5(5) with the consent of the proprietor of an earlier trade mark or other earlier right, that fact.

Annotations

Date in force: 31 October 1994.

Sections 5(5), 13(1), 35, 36, 40(3), 63(2): Trade Marks Act 1994, ss5(5), 13(1), 35, 36, 40(3), 63(2).

34 Entry in register of particulars of registrable transactions; s25

Upon application made to the registrar by such person as is mentioned in section 25(1)(a) or (b) there shall be entered in the register the following particulars of registrable transactions, that is to say –

(a) in the case of an assignment of a registered trade mark or any right in it –

(i) the name and address of the assignee,

      (ii) the date of the assignment, and

      (iii) where the assignment is in respect of any right in the mark, a description of the right assigned;

(b) in the case of the grant of a licence under a registered trade mark –

      (i) the name and address of the licensee,

      (ii) where the licence is an exclusive licence, that fact,

      (iii) where the licence is limited, a description of the limitation, and

      (iv) the duration of the licence if the same is or is ascertainable as a definite period;

(c) in the case of the grant of any security interest over a registered trade mark or any right in or under it –

      (i) the name and address of the grantee,

      (ii) the nature of the interest (whether fixed or floating), and

      (iii) the extent of the security and the right in or under the mark secured;

(d) in the case of the making by personal representatives of an assent in relation to a registered trade mark or any right in or under it –

      (i) the name and address of the person in whom the mark or any right in or under it vests by virtue of the assent, and

      (ii) the date of the assent; and

(e) in the case of a court or other competent authority transferring a registered trade mark or any right in or under it –

      (i) the name and address of the transferee,

      (ii) the date of the order, and

      (iii) where the transfer is in respect of a right in the mark, a description of the right transferred;

and, in each case, there shall be entered the date on which the entry is made.

Annotations

Date in force: 31 October 1994.

Section 25: Trade Marks Act 1994, s25.

35 Application to register or give notice of transaction; ss25 & 27(3) (Forms TM16, TM24, TM50 & TM51)

(1) An application to register particulars of a transaction to which section 25 applies or to give notice to the registrar of particulars of a transaction to which section 27(3) applies shall be made, subject to paragraph (2) below,

    (a) relating to an assignment or transaction other than a

transaction referred to in sub-paragraphs (b) to (d) below, on form TM16;

(b) relating to a grant of a licence, on form TM50;

(c) relating to an amendment to, or termination of a licence, on form TM51;

(d) relating to the grant, amendment or termination of any security interest, on form TM24; and

(e) relating to the making by personal representatives of an assent or to an order of a court or other competent authority, on form TM24.

(2) An application under paragraph (1) above shall –

(a) where the transaction is an assignment, be signed by or on behalf of the parties to the assignment;

(b) where the transaction falls within sub-paragraphs (b), (c) or (d) of paragraph (1) above, be signed by or on behalf of the grantor of the licence or security interest;

or be accompanied by such documentary evidence as suffices to establish the transaction.

(3) Where the transaction is effected by an instrument chargeable with duty, the application shall be subject to the registrar being satisfied that the instrument has been duly stamped.

(4) Where an application to give notice to the registrar has been made of particulars relating to an application for registration of a trade mark, upon registration of the trade mark, the registrar shall enter those particulars in the register.

Annotations

Date in force: 31 October 1994.

Sections 25, 27(3): Trade Marks Act 1994, ss25, 27(3).

36 Public inspection of register; s63(3)

(1) The register shall be open for public inspection at the Office during the hours of business of the Office as published in accordance with rule 64 below.

(2) Where any portion of the register is kept otherwise than in documentary form, the right of inspection is a right to inspect the material on the register.

Annotations

Date in force: 31 October 1994.

Section 63(3): Trade Marks Act 1994, s63(3).

37 Supply of certified copies etc; s63(3) (Form TM31R)

The registrar shall supply a certified copy or extract or uncertified copy or extract, as requested on Form TM31R, of any entry in the register.

Annotations
Date in force: 31 October 1994.
Section 63(3): Trade Marks Act 1994, s63(3).

38 Request for change of name or address in register; s64(4) (Forms TM21 & TM33)

(1) The registrar shall, on a request made on Form TM21 by the proprietor of a registered trade mark or a licensee or any person having an interest in or charge on a registered trade mark which has been registered under rule 34, enter any change in his name or address as recorded in the register.

(2) The registrar may at any time, on a request made on Form TM33 by any person who has furnished an address for service under rule 10 above, if the address is recorded in the register, change it.

Annotations
Date in force: 31 October 1994.
Section 64(4): Trade Marks Act 1994, s64(4).

39 Removal of matter from register; s64(5) (Form TM7)

(1) Where it appears to the registrar that any matter in the register has ceased to have effect, before removing it from the register –
   (a) he may, where he considers it appropriate, publish his intention to remove that matter, and
   (b) where any person appears to him to be affected by the removal, he shall send notice of his intention to that person.

(2) Within three months of the date on which his intention to remove the matter is published, or notice of his intention is sent, as the case may be –
   (a) any person may file notice of opposition to the removal on form TM7; and

(b) the person to whom a notice is sent under paragraph (1)(b) above may file, in writing –

    (i) his objections, if any, to the removal, or

    (ii) a request to have his objections heard orally;

and where such opposition or objections are made, rule 47 shall apply.

(3) If the registrar is satisfied after considering any objections or opposition to the removal that the matter has not ceased to have effect, he shall not remove it.

(4) Where there has been no response to the registrar's notice he may remove the matter; where representations objecting to the removal of the entry have been made (whether in writing or orally) the registrar may, if he is of the view after considering the objections that the entry or any part thereof has ceased to have effect, remove it or, as appropriate, the part thereof.

Annotations

Date in force: 31 October 1994.

Section 64(5): Trade Marks Act 1994, s64(5).

Change of classification

40   Change of classification; ss65(2) & 76(1)

(1) Subject to section 65(3), the registrar may –

(a) in order to reclassify the specification of a registered trade mark founded on Schedule 3 to one founded on Schedule 4, or

(b) consequent upon an amendment of the International Classification of Goods and Services referred to in rule 7(2) above,

make such amendments to entries on the register as he considers necessary for the purposes of reclassifying the specification of the registered trade mark.

(2) Before making any amendment to the register under paragraph (1) above the registrar shall give the proprietor of the mark written notice of his proposals for amendment and shall at the same time advise him that –

(a) he may make written objections to the proposals, within three months of the date of the notice, stating the

> grounds of his objections, and

(b) if no written objections are received within the period specified the registrar will publish the proposals and he will not be entitled to make any objections thereto upon such publication.

(3) If the proprietor makes no written objections within the period specified in paragraph (2)(a) above or at any time before the expiration of that period gives the registrar written notice of his intention not to make any objections, the registrar shall as soon as practicable after the expiration of that period or upon receipt of the notice publish the proposals.

(4) Where the proprietor makes written objections within the period specified in paragraph (2)(a) above, the registrar shall, as soon as practicable after he has considered the objections, publish the proposals or, where he has amended the proposals, publish the proposals as amended; and his decision shall be final and not subject to appeal.

Annotations

Date in force: 31 October 1994.

Sections 65, 76(1): Trade Marks Act 1994, ss65, 76(1).

41 Opposition to proposals; ss65(3) & 76(1)

(1) Notice of any opposition shall be filed on Form TM7 within three months of the date of publication of the proposals under rule 40 above and there shall be stated in the notice the grounds of opposition and, in particular, how the proposed amendments would be contrary to section 65(3).

(2) The registrar may require or admit evidence directed to the questions in issue and if so requested by any person opposing the proposal give that person the opportunity to be heard thereon before deciding the matter.

(3) If no notice of opposition under paragraph (1) above is filed within the time specified, or where any opposition has been determined, the registrar shall make the amendments as proposed and shall enter in the register the date when they were made; and his decision shall be final and not subject to appeal.

Annotations

Date in force: 31 October 1994.

Sections 65(3), 76(1): Trade Marks Act 1994, ss65(3), 76(1).

Request for information, inspection of documents and confidentiality

42 Request for information; s67(1) (Form TM31C)

A request for information relating to an application for registration or to a registered trade mark shall be made on Form TM31C.

Annotations

Date in force: 31 October 1994.

Section 67(1): Trade Marks Act 1994, s67(1).

43 Information available before publication; s67(2)

Before publication of an application for registration the registrar shall make available for inspection by the public the application and any amendments made to it and any particulars contained in a notice given to the registrar under rule 35.

Annotations

Date in force: 31 October 1994.

Section 67(2): Trade Marks Act 1994, s67(2).

44 Inspection of documents; ss67 & 76(1)

(1) Subject to paragraphs (2) and (3) below, the registrar shall permit all documents filed or kept at the Office in relation to a registered mark or, where an application for the registration of a trade mark has been published, in relation to that application, to be inspected.

(2) The registrar shall not be obliged to permit the inspection of any such document as is mentioned in paragraph (1) above until he has completed any procedure, or the stage in the procedure which is relevant to the document in question, which he is required or permitted to carry out under the Act or these Rules.

(3) The right of inspection under paragraph (1) above does not apply to –

    (a) any document until fourteen days after it has been filed at the Office;

    (b) any document prepared in the Office solely for use therein;

    (c) any document sent to the Office, whether at its request or otherwise, for inspection and subsequent return to the sender;

(d) any request for information under rule 42 above;

(e) any document issued by the Office which the registrar considers should be treated as confidential;

(f.) any document in respect of which the registrar issues directions under rule 45 below that it be treated as confidential.

(4) Nothing in paragraph (1) shall be construed as imposing on the registrar any duty of making available for public inspection –

(a) any document or part of a document which in his opinion disparages any person in a way likely to damage him; or

(b) any document filed with or sent to the Office before 31 October 1994.

(5) No appeal shall lie from a decision of the registrar under paragraph (4) above not to make any document or part of a document available for public inspection.

Annotations

Date in force: 31 October 1994.

Sections 67, 76(1): Trade Marks Act 1994, ss67, 76(1).

45 Confidential documents

(1) Where a document other than a form required by the registrar and published in accordance with rule 3 above is filed at the Office and the person filing it requests, at the time of filing or within fourteen days of the filing, that it or a specified part of it be treated as confidential, giving his reasons, the registrar may direct that it or part of it, as the case may be, be treated as confidential, and the document shall not be open to public inspection while the matter is being determined by the registrar.

(2) Where such direction has been given and not withdrawn, nothing in this rule shall be taken to authorise or require any person to be allowed to inspect the document or part of it to which the direction relates except by leave of the registrar.

(3) The registrar shall not withdraw any direction given under this rule without prior consultation with the person at whose request the direction was given, unless the registrar is satisfied that such prior consultation is not reasonably practical.

(4) The registrar may where he considers that any document issued by the Office should be treated as confidential so direct, and upon such direction that document shall not be open to public inspection except by leave of the registrar.

(5) Where a direction is given under this rule for a document to be treated as confidential a record of the fact shall be filed with the document.

Annotations

Date in force: 31 October 1994.

Agents

46 Proof of authorisation of agent may be required; s82 (Form TM33)

(1) Where an agent has been authorised under section 82, the registrar may in any particular case require the personal signature or presence of the agent or the person authorising him to act as agent.

(2) Where after a person has become a party to proceedings before the registrar, he appoints an agent for the first time or appoints one agent in substitution for another, the newly appointed agent shall file Form TM33, and any act required or authorised by the Act in connection with the registration of a trade mark or any procedure relating to a trade mark may not be done by or to the newly appointed agent until on or after the date on which he files that form.

(3) The registrar may by notice in writing sent to an agent require him to produce evidence of his authority.

Annotations

Date in force: 31 October 1994.
The Act: Trade Marks Act 1994.

47 Registrar may refuse to deal with certain agents; s88

The registrar may refuse to recognise as agent in respect of any business under the Act –

(a) a person who has been convicted of an offence under section 84;

(b) an individual whose name has been erased from and not restored to, or who is suspended from, the register of trade mark agents on the ground of misconduct;

(c) a person who is found by the Secretary of State to have been guilty of such conduct as would, in the case of an individual registered in that register, render him liable to have his name erased from it on the ground of misconduct;

(d) a partnership or body corporate of which one of the partners or directors is a person whom the registrar could refuse to recognise under paragraph (a), (b) or (c) above.

Annotations

Date in force: 31 October 1994.

The Act: Trade Marks Act 1994.

Decision of registrar, evidence and costs

48 Decisions of registrar to be taken after hearing

(1) Without prejudice to any provisions of the Act or these Rules requiring the registrar to hear any party to proceedings under the Act or these Rules, or to give such party an opportunity to be heard, the registrar shall, before taking any decision on any matter under the Act or these Rules which is or may be adverse to any party to any proceedings before him, give that party an opportunity to be heard.

(2) The registrar shall give that party at least fourteen days' notice of the time when he may be heard unless that party consents to shorter notice.

Annotations

Date in force: 31 October 1994.

The Act: Trade Marks Act 1994.

49 Evidence in proceedings before registrar; s69

(1) Where under these Rules evidence may be admitted by the registrar in any proceedings before him, it shall be by the filing of a statutory declaration or affidavit.

(2) The registrar may in any particular case take oral evidence in lieu of or in addition to such evidence and shall, unless he

otherwise directs, allow any witness to be cross-examined on his statutory declaration, affidavit or oral evidence.

Annotations
Date in force: 31 October 1994.
Section 69: Trade Marks Act 1994, s69.

50 Making and subscription of statutory declaration or affidavit

(1) Any statutory declaration or affidavit filed under the Act or these Rules shall be made and subscribed as follows –
  (a) in the United Kingdom, before any justice of the peace or any commissioner or other officer authorised by law in any part of the United Kingdom to administer an oath for the purpose of any legal proceedings;
  (b) in any other part of Her Majesty's dominions or in the Republic of Ireland, before any court, judge, justice of the peace or any officer authorised by law to administer an oath there for the purpose of any legal proceedings; and
  (c) elsewhere, before a commissioner for oaths, notary public, judge or magistrate.
(2) Any document purporting to have affixed, impressed or subscribed thereto or thereon the seal or signature of any person authorised by paragraph (1) above to take a declaration may be admitted by the registrar without proof of the genuineness of the seal or signature, or of the official character of the person or his authority to take the declaration.

Annotations
Date in force: 31 October 1994.
The Act: Trade Marks Act 1994.

51 Registrar's power to require documents, information or evidence

At any stage of any proceedings before the registrar, he may direct that such documents, information or evidence as he may reasonably require shall be filed within such period as he may specify.

Annotations
Date in force: 31 October 1994.

Appendix

52 Registrar to have power of an official referee; s69

(1) The registrar shall in relation to the examination of witnesses on oath and the discovery and production of documents have all the powers of an official referee of the Supreme Court.

(2) The rules applicable to the attendance of witnesses before such a referee shall apply in relation to the attendance of witnesses in proceedings before the registrar.

Annotations
Date in force: 31 October 1994.
Section 69: Trade Marks Act 1994, s69.

53 Hearings before registrar to be in public

(1) The hearing before the registrar of any dispute between two or more parties relating to any matter in connection with an application for the registration of a mark or a registered mark shall be in public unless the registrar, after consultation with those parties who appear in person or are represented at the hearing, otherwise directs.

(2) Nothing in this rule shall prevent a member of the Council on Tribunals or of its Scottish Committee from attending a hearing in his capacity as such.

Annotations
Date in force: 31 October 1994.

54 Costs of proceedings; s68

The registrar may, in any proceedings before him under the Act or these Rules, by order award to any party such costs as he may consider reasonable, and direct how and by what parties they are to be paid.

Annotations
Date in force: 31 October 1994.
The Act: Trade Marks Act 1994.

55 Security for costs; s68

(1) The registrar may require any person who is a party in any proceedings before him under the Act or these Rules to give security for costs in relation to those proceedings; and he may require security for the costs of any appeal from his decision.

(2) In default of such security being given, the registrar, in the case of the proceedings before him, or, in the case of an appeal, the person appointed under section 76 may treat the party in default as having withdrawn his application, opposition, objection or intervention, as the case may be.

Annotations
Date in force: 31 October 1994.
The Act: Trade Marks Act 1994.

56 Decision of registrar (Form TM5)

(1) When, in any proceedings before him, the registrar has made a decision following a hearing or, if a hearing has not been requested, after considering any submission in writing, he shall send notice of his decision in writing to each party to the proceedings, and for the purpose of any appeal against the registrar's decision, subject to paragraph (2) below, the date of the decision shall be the date when the notice is sent.

(2) Where a statement of the reasons for the decision is not included in the notice sent under paragraph (1) above, any party may, within one month of the date on which the notice was sent to him, request the registrar on form TM5 to send him a statement of the reasons for the decision and upon such request the registrar shall send such a statement; and the date on which that statement is sent shall be deemed to be the date of the registrar's decision for the purpose of any appeal against it.

Annotations
Date in force: 31 October 1994.

Appeals

57 Appeal to person appointed; s76

(1) Notice of appeal to the person appointed under section 76 shall be sent to the registrar within one month of the date of the registrar's decision which is the subject of the appeal accompanied by a statement in writing of the appellant's grounds of appeal and of his case in support of the appeal.

(2) The registrar shall send the notice and the statement to the person appointed.

(3) Where any person other than the appellant was a party to the proceedings before the registrar in which the decision appealed against was made, the registrar shall send to that person a copy of the notice and the statement.

58 Determination whether appeal should be referred to court; s76(3)

(1) Within one month of the date on which the notice of appeal is sent by the registrar under rule 57(3) above;
 (a) the registrar, or
 (b) any person who was a party to the proceedings in which the decision appealed against was made,
 may request that the person appointed refer the appeal to the court.
(2) Where the registrar requests that the appeal be referred to the court, he shall send a copy of the request to each party to the proceedings.
(3) A request under paragraph (1)(b) above shall be sent to the registrar; the registrar shall send it to the person appointed and shall send a copy of the request to any other party to the proceedings.
(4) Within one month of the date on which a copy of a request is sent by the registrar under paragraph (2) or (3) above, the person to whom it is sent may make representations as to whether the appeal should be referred to the court.
(5) In any case where it appears to the person appointed that a point of general legal importance is involved in the appeal, he shall send to the registrar and to every party to the proceedings in which the decision appealed against was made, notice thereof.
(6) Within one month of the date on which a notice is sent under paragraph (5) above, the person to whom it was sent may make representations as to whether the appeal should be referred to the court.

59 Hearing of appeal; s76(4)

(1) Where the person appointed does not refer the appeal to the court, he shall send notice of the time and place appointed for the hearing of the appeal –
   (a) where no person other than the appellant was a party to the proceedings in which the decision appealed against was made, to the registrar and to the appellant, and
   (b) in any other case, to the registrar and to each person who was a party to those proceedings.
(2) The provisions of rule 48(2) and rules 49 to 55 shall apply to the person appointed and to proceedings before the person appointed as they apply to the registrar and to proceedings before the registrar.
(3) The person appointed shall send a copy of his decision, with a statement of his reasons therefor, to the registrar and to each person who was a party to the proceedings before him.

Annotations
Date in force: 31 October 1994.
Section 76(4): Trade Marks Act 1994, s76(4).

Correction of irregularities, calculation and extension of time

60 Correction of irregularities of procedure

(1) Any irregularity in procedure in or before the Office or the registrar may be rectified, subject to paragraph (2) below, on such terms as he may direct.
(2) In the case of an irregularity or prospective irregularity –
   (a) which consists of a failure to comply with any limitation as to times or periods specified in the Act, these Rules or the old law as that law continues to apply and which has occurred or appears to the registrar as likely to occur in the absence of a direction under this rule, and
   (b) which is attributable wholly or in part to an error, default or omission on the part of the Office or the registrar and which it appears to him should be rectified,
   he may direct that the time or period in question shall be

altered in such manner as he may specify.

(3) Paragraph (2) above is without prejudice to the registrar's power to extend any time or periods under rule 62 below.

Annotations

Date in force: 31 October 1994.

The Act: Trade Marks Act 1994.

61 Calculation of times and periods

(1) Where, on any day, there is –
   (a) a general interruption or subsequent dislocation in the postal services of the United Kingdom, or
   (b) an event or circumstances causing an interruption in the normal operation of the Office,

   the registrar may certify the day as being one on which there is an 'interruption' and, where any period of time specified in the Act or these Rules for the giving, making or filing of any notice, application or other document expires on a day so certified the period shall be extended to the first day next following (not being an excluded day) which is not so certified.

(2) Any certificate of the registrar given pursuant to this rule shall be posted in the Office.

(3) If in any particular case the registrar is satisfied that the failure to give, make or file any notice, application or other document within any period of time specified in the Act or these Rules for such giving, making or filing was wholly or mainly attributable to a failure or undue delay in the postal services in the United Kingdom, the registrar may, if he thinks fit, extend the period so that it ends on the day of the receipt by the addressee of the notice, application or other document (or, if the day of such receipt is an excluded day, on the first following day which is not an excluded day), upon such notice to other parties and upon such terms as he may direct.

(4) In this rule 'excluded day' means a day which is not a business day of the Office under the registrar's direction pursuant to section 80, as published in accordance with rule 64 below.

Annotations

Date in force: 31 October 1994.

The Act: Trade Marks Act 1994.

62   Alteration of time limits (Form TM9)

(1) The time or periods –
   (a) prescribed by these Rules, other than the times or periods prescribed by the rules mentioned in paragraph (3) below, or
   (b) specified by the registrar for doing any act or taking any proceedings,

   may, at the request of the person or party concerned, be extended by the registrar as he thinks fit, upon such notice to any other person or party affected and upon such terms as he may direct.

(2) A request for the extension of a period prescribed by these Rules which is filed after the application has been published under rule 12 above shall be on Form TM9 and shall in any other case be on that form if the registrar so directs.

(3) The rules excepted from paragraph (1) above are rule 10(6) (failure to file address for service), rule 11 (deficiencies in application), rule 13(1) (time for filing opposition), rule 13(2) (time for filing counter-statement), rule 29 (delayed renewal) and rule 30 (restoration of registration).

(4) Subject to paragraph (5) below, a request for extension under paragraph (1) above shall be made before the time or period in question has expired.

(5) Where the request for extension is made after the time or period has expired, the registrar may, at his discretion, extend the period or time if he is satisfied with the explanation for the delay in requesting the extension and it appears to him that any extension would not disadvantage any other person or party affected by it.

(6) Where the period within which any party to any proceedings before the registrar may file evidence under these Rules is to begin upon the expiry of any period in which any other party may file evidence and that other party notifies the registrar that he does not wish to file any, or any further, evidence the registrar may direct that the period within which the first mentioned party may file evidence shall begin on such date as may be specified in the direction and shall notify all parties to the dispute of that date.

Annotations

Date in force: 31 October 1994.

Filing of documents, hours of business, Trade Marks Journal and translations

63 **Filing of documents by electronic means**

The registrar may, at his discretion, permit as an alternative to the sending by post or delivery of the application, notice or other document in legible form the filing of the application, notice or other document by electronic means subject to such terms or conditions as he may specify either generally by published notice or in any particular case by written notice to the person desiring to file any such documents by such means.

Annotations

Date in force: 31 October 1994.

64 **Directions on hours of business; s80**

Any directions given by the registrar under section 80 specifying the hours of business of the Office and business days of the Office shall be published and posted in the Office.

Annotations

Date in force: 31 October 1994.

Section 80: Trade Marks Act 1994, s80.

65 **Trade Marks Journal; s81**

The registrar shall publish a journal, entitled 'The Trade Marks Journal', containing particulars of any application for the registration of a trade mark (including a representation of the mark), such information as is required to be published under these Rules and such other information as the registrar thinks fit.

Annotations

Date in force: 31 October 1994.

Section 81: Trade Marks Act 1994, s81.

66 **Translations**

(1) Where any document or part thereof which is in a language other than English is filed or sent to the registrar in pursuance of the Act or these Rules, the registrar may require that there be furnished a translation into English of the document or that

part, verified to the satisfaction of the registrar as corresponding to the original text.

(2) The registrar may refuse to accept any translation which is in his opinion inaccurate and thereupon another translation of the document in question verified as aforesaid shall be furnished.

Annotations
Date in force: 31 October 1994.
The Act: Trade Marks Act 1994.

Transitional provisions and revocations

67 Pending applications for registration; Sch 3, para 10(2)

Where an application for registration of a mark made under the old law is advertised on or after 31 October 1994, the period within which notice of opposition may be filed shall be three months from the date of advertisement, and such period shall not be extendible.

Annotations
Date in force: 31 October 1994.
Sch 3, para 10(2): Trade Marks Act 1994, Sch 3, para 10(2).

68 Form for conversions of pending application; Sch 3, para 11(2)

A notice to the registrar under paragraph 11(2) of Schedule 3 to the Act, claiming to have the registrability of the mark determined in accordance with the provisions of the Act, shall be in the form set out in Schedule 2 to these Rules.

Annotations
Date in force: 31 October 1994.
The Act: Trade Marks Act 1994.

69 Revocation of previous Rules

(1) The rules specified in Schedule 1 are hereby revoked.

(2) Except as provided by rule 67 above, where –
    (a) immediately before these Rules come into force, any time or period prescribed by the Rules hereby revoked has effect in relation to any act or proceeding and has not

Appendix

> expired, and
> (b) the corresponding time or period prescribed by these Rules would have expired or would expire earlier,
> the time or period prescribed by those Rules and not by these Rules shall apply to that act or proceeding.

Annotations
Date in force: 31 October 1994.

SCHEDULE 1
Revocations

Rule 69

Rules revoked	Reference
The Trade Marks and Service Marks Rules 1986	SI 1986/1319
The Trade Marks and Service Marks (Amendment) Rules 1988	SI 1988/1112
The Trade Marks and Service Marks (Amendment) Rules 1989	SI 1989/1117
The Trade Marks and Service Marks (Amendment) Rules 1990	SI 1990/1459
The Trade Marks and Service Marks (Amendment) (No 2) Rules 1990	SI 1990/1799
The Trade Marks and Service Marks (Amendment) Rules 1991	SI 1991/1431
The Trade Marks and Service Marks (Amendment) Rules 1994	SI 1994/2549

Annotations
Date in force: 31 October 1994.

SCHEDULE 2

Rule 68

Form TM15

Notice under Schedule 3, paragraph 11 of the Act: Claim to have registrability of a mark applied for before 31 October 1994 determined under the Act (Conversion of application)

1

Your reference

2

Give details of the application you made under the Trade Marks Act 1938

Number   Class

3

Full name, address and postcode of the applicant

Trade Marks ADP number (if you know it)

4

Name of agent (if appropriate) address for service in the United Kingdom which all correspondence should be sent to (including postcode)

Trade Marks ADP number (if you know it)

I claim to have the registrability of the mark determined in accordance with the provisions of the Trade Marks Act 1994. I acknowledge that this notice is irrevocable.

Signature

Name (block capitals)

Date

Name and daytime telephone number of person we should contact

State the number of any sheets attached to this form

Reminder

You cannot amend a mark under the 1994 Act. If you want to amend the mark you must file form TM21 before or with this form.

The new filing date of your converted application will be the 31st October 1994, which is the commencement date of the 1994 Act.

Form TM15

Annotations
Date in force: 31 October 1994.
The Act: Trade Marks Act 1994.

Appendix

SCHEDULE 3
Classification of Goods (Pre-1938)

Rule 7(1)

Class 1 Chemical substances used in manufactures, photography, or philosophical research, and anti-corrosives.

Class 2 Chemical substances used for agricultural, horticultural, veterinary and sanitary purposes.

Class 3 Chemical substances prepared for use in medicine and pharmacy.

Class 4 Raw, or partly prepared, vegetable, animal, and mineral substances used in manufactures, not included in other Classes.

Class 5 Unwrought and partly wrought metals used in manufacture.

Class 6 Machinery of all kinds, and parts of machinery, except agricultural and horticultural machines and their parts included in Class 7.

Class 7 Agricultural and horticultural machinery, and parts of such machinery.

Class 8 Philosophical instruments, scientific instruments, and apparatus for useful purposes; instruments and apparatus for teaching.

Class 9 Musical instruments.

Class 10 Horological instruments.

Class 11 Instruments, apparatus, and contrivances, not medicated, for surgical or curative purposes, or in relation to the health of men or animals.

Class 12 Cutlery and edge tools.

Class 13 Metal goods, not included in other Classes.

Class 14 Goods of precious metals and jewellery, and imitations of such goods and jewellery.

Class 15 Glass.

Class 16 Porcelain and earthenware.

Class 17 Manufactures from mineral and other substances for building or decoration.

Class 18 Engineering, architectural, and building contrivances.

Class 19 Arms, ammunition, and stores, not included in Class 20.

Class 20 Explosive substances.

Class 21 Naval architectural contrivances and naval equipments

not included in other Classes.
Class 22 Carriages.
Class 23 (a) Cotton yarn;
(b) Sewing cotton.
Class 24 Cotton piece goods.
Class 25 Cotton goods not included in other Classes.
Class 26 Linen and hemp yarn and thread.
Class 27 Linen and hemp piece goods.
Class 28 Linen and hemp goods not included in other Classes.
Class 29 Jute yarns and tissues, and other articles made of jute, not included in other Classes.
Class 30 Silk, spun, thrown, or sewing.
Class 31 Silk piece goods.
Class 32 Silk goods not included in other Classes.
Class 33 Yarns of wool, worsted, or hair.
Class 34 Cloths and stuffs of wool, worsted, or hair.
Class 35 Woollen and worsted and hair goods, not included in other Classes.
Class 36 Carpets, floor-cloth, and oil-cloth.
Class 37 Leather, skins unwrought and wrought, and articles made of leather not included in other Classes.
Class 38 Articles of clothing.
Class 39 Paper (except paper hangings), stationery, and book-binding.
Class 40 Goods manufactured from india-rubber and gutta-percha not included in other Classes.
Class 41 Furniture and upholstery.
Class 42 Substances used as food or as ingredients in food.
Class 43 Fermented liquors and spirits.
Class 44 Mineral and aerated waters, natural and artificial, including ginger beer.
Class 45 Tobacco, whether manufactured or unmanufactured.
Class 46 Seeds for agricultural and horticultural purposes.
Class 47 Candles, common soap, detergents; illuminating, heating, or lubricating oils; matches; and starch, blue, and other preparations for laundry purposes.
Class 48 Perfumery (including toilet articles, preparations for the teeth and hair, and perfumed soap).
Class 49 Games of all kinds and sporting articles not included in other Classes.

Class 50   Miscellaneous: –
(1) Goods manufactured from ivory, bone or wood, not included in other Classes.
(2) Goods manufactured from straw or grass, not included in other Classes.
(3) Goods manufactured from animal and vegetable substances, not included in other Classes.
(4) Tobacco pipes.
(5) Umbrellas, walking sticks, brushes and combs for the hair.
(6) Furniture cream, plate powder.
(7) Tarpaulins, tents, rick-cloths, rope (jute or hemp), twine.
(8) Buttons of all kinds other than of precious metal or imitations thereof.
(9) Packing and hose.
(10) Other goods not included in the foregoing Classes.

Annotations

Date in force: 31 October 1994.

SCHEDULE 4
Classification of Goods and Services

Rule 7(2)

Goods

Class 1   Chemicals used in industry, science and photography, as well as in agriculture, horticulture and forestry; unprocessed artificial resins, unprocessed plastics; manures; fire extinguishing compositions; tempering and soldering preparations; chemical substances for preserving foodstuffs; tanning substances; adhesives used in industry.

Class 2   Paints, varnishes, lacquers; preservatives against rust and against deterioration of wood; colorants; mordants; raw natural resins; metals in foil and powder form for painters, decorators, printers and artists.

Class 3   Bleaching preparations and other substances for laundry use; cleaning, polishing, scouring and abrasive preparations; soaps; perfumery, essential oils, cosmetics, hair lotions; dentifrices.

Class 4   Industrial oils and greases; lubricants; dust absorbing, wetting and binding compositions; fuels (including motor spirit) and illuminants; candles, wicks.

Class 5   Pharmaceutical, veterinary and sanitary preparations; dietetic substances adapted for medical use, food for babies; plasters, materials for dressings; material for stopping teeth, dental wax; disinfectants; preparations for destroying vermin; fungicides, herbicides.

Class 6   Common metals and their alloys; metal building materials; transportable buildings of metal; materials of metal for railway tracks; non-electric cables and wires of common metal; ironmongery, small items of metal hardware; pipes and tubes of metal; safes; goods of common metal not included in other classes; ores.

Class 7   Machines and machine tools; motors and engines (except for land vehicles); machine coupling and transmission components (except for land vehicles); agricultural implements; incubators for eggs.

Class 8   Hand tools and implements (hand operated); cutlery; side arms; razors.

Class 9   Scientific, nautical, surveying, electric, photographic, cinematographic, optical, weighing, measuring, signalling, checking (supervision), life-saving and teaching apparatus and instruments; apparatus for recording, transmission or reproduction of sound or images; magnetic data carriers, recording discs; automatic vending machines and mechanisms for coin-operated apparatus; cash registers, calculating machines, data processing equipment and computers; fire-extinguishing apparatus.

Class 10   Surgical, medical, dental and veterinary apparatus and instruments, artificial limbs, eyes and teeth; orthopaedic articles; suture materials.

Class 11   Apparatus for lighting, heating, steam generating, cooking, refrigerating, drying, ventilating, water supply and sanitary purposes.

Class 12   Vehicles; apparatus for locomotion by land, air or water.

Appendix

Class 13   Firearms; ammunition and projectiles; explosives; fireworks.

Class 14   Precious metals and their alloys and goods in precious metals or coated therewith, not included in other classes; jewellery, precious stones; horological and chronometric instruments.

Class 15   Musical instruments.

Class 16   Paper, cardboard and goods made from these materials, not included in other classes; printed matter; bookbinding material; photographs; stationery; adhesives for stationery or household purposes; artists' materials; paint brushes; typewriters and office requisites (except furniture); instructional and teaching material (except apparatus); plastic materials for packaging (not included in other classes); playing cards; printers' type; printing blocks.

Class 17   Rubber, gutta-percha, gum, asbestos, mica and goods made from these materials and not included in other classes; plastics in extruded form for use in manufacture; packing, stopping and insulating materials; flexible pipes, not of metal.

Class 18   Leather and imitations of leather, and goods made of these materials and not included in other classes; animal skins, hides; trunks and travelling bags; umbrellas, parasols and walking sticks; whips, harness and saddlery.

Class 19   Building materials (non-metallic); non-metallic rigid pipes for building; asphalt, pitch and bitumen; non-metallic transportable buildings; monuments, not of metal.

Class 20   Furniture, mirrors, picture frames; goods (not included in other classes) of wood, cork, reed, cane, wicker, horn, bone, ivory, whalebone, shell, amber, mother-of-pearl, meerschaum and substitutes for all these materials, or of plastics.

Class 21   Household or kitchen utensils and containers (not of precious metal or coated therewith); combs and sponges; brushes (except paint brushes); brush-making materials; articles for cleaning purposes; steelwool; unworked or semi-worked glass (except glass used in building); glassware, porcelain and earthenware not included in other classes.

Class 22   Ropes, string, nets, tents, awnings, tarpaulins, sails, sacks and bags (not included in other classes); padding and stuffing materials (except of rubber or plastics); raw fibrous textile materials.

Class 23 Yarns and threads, for textile use.

Class 24 Textiles and textile goods, not included in other classes; bed and table covers.

Class 25 Clothing, footwear, headgear.

Class 26 Lace and embroidery, ribbons and braid; buttons, hooks and eyes, pins and needles; artificial flowers.

Class 27 Carpets, rugs, mats and matting, linoleum and other materials for covering existing floors; wall hangings (non-textile).

Class 28 Games and playthings; gymnastic and sporting articles not included in other classes; decorations for Christmas trees.

Class 29 Meat, fish, poultry and game; meat extracts; preserved, dried and cooked fruits and vegetables; jellies, jams, fruit sauces; eggs, milk and milk products; edible oils and fats.

Class 30 Coffee, tea, cocoa, sugar, rice, tapioca, sago, artificial coffee; flour and preparations made from cereals, bread, pastry and confectionery, ices; honey, treacle; yeast, baking-powder; salt, mustard; vinegar, sauces (condiments); spices; ice.

Class 31 Agricultural, horticultural and forestry products and grains not included in other classes; live animals; fresh fruits and vegetables; seeds, natural plants and flowers; foodstuffs for animals, malt.

Class 32 Beers; mineral and aerated waters and other non-alcoholic drinks; fruit drinks and fruit juices; syrups and other preparations for making beverages.

Class 33 Alcoholic beverages (except beers).

Class 34 Tobacco; smokers' articles; matches.

Services

Class 35 Advertising; business management; business administration; office functions.

Class 36 Insurance; financial affairs; monetary affairs; real estate affairs.

Class 37 Building construction; repair; installation services.

Class 38 Telecommunications.

Class 39 Transport; packaging and storage of goods; travel arrangement.

Class 40 Treatment of materials.

Class 41 Education; providing of training; entertainment; sporting and cultural activities.

Class 42 Providing of food and drink; temporary accommodation; medical, hygienic and beauty care; veterinary and agricultural services; legal services; scientific and industrial research; computer programming; services that cannot be placed in other classes.

Annotations

Date in force: 31 October 1994.

Comparison between the 1938 Act and the 1994 Act

Summarised below are the key differences between the 1938 Act and the 1994 Act.

Subject	1938 Act	1994 Act
The Register	Divided into Parts A and B	Unified register
Trade Marks Definition 1	Marks used for the purpose of indicating a connection in the course of trade	Signs capable of distinguishing the applicant's goods or services
Trade Marks Definition 2	Something applied to or attached to the goods	A sign may consist of the goods themselves
Registrability Definition 1	Onus on proprietor to establish registrability	Onus on registrar to establish grounds for refusal of registration
Registrability Definition 2	Test of inherently capable of distinguishing in fact and in law	Distinctiveness in fact only required
Registrar's discretion	Overriding discretion to refuse registration	No discretion to refuse registration
Multi-class applications/ registrations	Not available	Available

Subject	1938 Act	1994 Act
Assignment of applications	Not permitted	Permitted
Amendment of an application	More liberal s17(7)	More limited s39(2)
Divisional applications	Not available	Available
Merger of applications and registrations	Not available	Available
Advertisement prior to acceptance	Available pursuant to s18(1)	Not available
Observations after acceptance	Not available	Available under section 38(3)
Extensions of time: opposition	Allowed	Not allowed: three months maximum
Registrability: effect of consent	Registrar retained overriding discretion to refuse	Overcomes relative grounds for refusal: s5(5)
Compulsory disclaimers	May have been imposed by the registrar	Not applicable. Voluntary disclaimers and limitations only
Conditions of registration	May have been imposed by the registrar	Not applicable. Existing conditions will be removed
Association of trade marks	Available under section 23	Not available
Alteration of a registered trade mark	More liberal, section 35	More limited, section 44

Subject	1938 Act	1994 Act
Restoration of a removed registration	No time limit	Six month time limit
Conflicts with earlier trade marks	Prior registered marks in the United Kingdom only relevant	United Kingdom, Community and international registrations as well as well-known marks are now all relevant
Infringement	Limited to use on goods or services within the specification	Similar goods or services also protected as well as goods and services which are not similar under s10(3)
Comparative advertising	Often led to infringement: s4(1)(b)	No infringement if in accordance with honest practices in industrial or commercial matters: s10(6)
Use of a trade mark Definition 1	Printed or other visual representation, s68(2)	Not restricted to graphic representation, s103(2)
Use of a trade mark Definition 2	Use on goods or services of the same description was sufficient to avoid non-use, section 26	Use must be on the actual goods or services for which the mark is registered, section 49
Use of a trade mark Definition 3	Use by registered users deemed to be use by proprietor	Use by any third party with proprietor's consent sufficient to overcome non-use action, s46(1)

Subject	1938 Act	1994 Act
Non-use	Onus on applicant for expungement to establish non-use	Onus on proprietor to show use
Registered users/licensees	Licensees registered as registered users on substantive examination	Prescribed particulars of licences only recorded. No examination: s25
Trafficking	Recording as registered users prohibited: s28(6)	No express prohibition
Well known trade marks	Defensive registration for invented words only	Wide protection and remedies even if unregistered
Defensive registrations	Available	Not available: see well known trade marks
Collective marks	Not recognised	Available for registration: s49 and schedule 1
Invalidity: distinctiveness acquired since registration	Not relevant	Good defence to application for declaration of invalidity: s47(1) proviso
Deemed validity	Section 13: After 7 years for Part A marks	Prima facie evidence of validity, section 72; no deemed validity
Duration of registration	7+14 (etc) years	10+10 (etc) years

Schedule 1: Paris Convention for the Protection of Industrial Property

Status on 1 January 1994

State	Date on which State became party to the Convention
Algeria	March 1, 1966
Argentina	February 10, 1967
Australia	October 10, 1925
Austria	January 1, 1909
Bahamas	July 10, 1973
Bangladesh	March 3, 1991
Barbados	March 12, 1985
Belarus	December 25, 1991
Belgium	July 7, 1884
Benin	January 10, 1967
Bolivia	November 4, 1993
Bosnia and Herzegovina	March 6, 1992
Brazil	July 7, 1884
Bulgaria	June 13, 1921
Burkina Faso	November 19, 1963
Burundi	November 19, 1963
Cameroon	May 10, 1964
Canada	June 12, 1925
Central African Republic	November 19, 1963
Chad	November 19, 1963
Chile	June 14, 1991
China	March 19, 1985
Congo	September 2, 1963
Côte d'Ivoire	October 23, 1963
Croatia	October 8, 1991
Cuba	November 17, 1904
Cyprus	January 17, 1966
Czech Republic	January 1, 1993
Denmark[1]	October 1, 1894
Dominican Republic	July 11, 1890

Appendix

State	Date on which State became party to the Convention
Egypt	July 1, 1951
El Salvador	February 19, 1994
Finland	September 20, 1921
France[2]	July 7, 1884
Gabon	February 29, 1964
Gambia	January 21, 1992
Germany	May 1, 1903
Ghana	September 28, 1976
Greece	October 2, 1924
Guinea	February 5, 1982
Guinea-Bissau	June 28, 1988
Haiti	July 1, 1958
Holy See	September 29, 1960
Honduras	February 4, 1994
Hungary	January 1, 1909
Iceland	May 5, 1962
Indonesia	December 24, 1950
Iran, Islamic Republic of	December 16, 1959
Iraq	January 24, 1976
Ireland	December 4, 1925
Israel	March 24, 1950
Italy	July 7, 1884
Japan	July 15, 1899
Jordan	July 17, 1972
Kazakhstan	December 25, 1991
Kenya	June 14, 1965
Korea, Democratic People's Republic of	June 10, 1980
Korea, Republic of	May 4, 1980
Latvia[3]	September 7, 1993
Lebanon	September 1, 1924
Lesotho	September 28, 1989
Libya	September 28, 1976

380

State	Date on which State became party to the Convention
Liechtenstein	July 14, 1933
Luxembourg	June 30, 1922
Macedonia, Republic of (formerly a province of Yugoslavia)	September 8, 1991
Madagascar	December 21, 1963
Malawi	July 6, 1964
Malaysia	January 1, 1989
Mali	March 1, 1983
Malta	October 20, 1967
Mauritania	April 11, 1965
Mauritius	September 24, 1976
Mexico	September 7, 1903
Moldova, Republic of	December 25, 1991
Monaco	April 29, 1956
Mongolia	April 21, 1985
Morocco	July 30, 1917
Netherlands[4]	July 7, 1884
New Zealand[5]	July 29, 1931
Niger	July 5, 1964
Nigeria	September 2, 1963
Norway	July 1, 1885
Philippines	September 27, 1965
Poland	November 10, 1919
Portugal	July 7, 1884
Romania	October 6, 1920
Russian Federation	December 25, 1991
Rwanda	March 1, 1984
San Marino	March 4, 1960
Senegal	December 21, 1963
Slovakia	January 1, 1993
Slovenia	June 25, 1991
South Africa	December 1, 1947
Spain	July 7, 1884
Sri Lanka	December 29, 1952
Sudan	April 16, 1984

Appendix

State	Date on which State became party to the Convention
Surinam	November 25, 1975
Swaziland	May 12, 1991
Sweden	July 1, 1885
Switzerland	July 7, 1884
Syria	September 1, 1924
Tanzania, United Republic of	June 16, 1963
Togo	September 10, 1967
Trinidad and Tobago	August 1, 1964
Tunisia	July 7, 1884
Turkey	October 10, 1925
Uganda	June 14, 1965
Ukraine	December 25, 1991
United Kingdom[6]	July 7, 1884
United States of America[7]	May 30, 1887
Uruguay	March 18, 1967
Uzbekistan	December 25, 1991
Vietnam	March 8, 1949
Yugoslavia	February 26, 1921
Zaire	January 31, 1975
Zambia	April 6, 1965
Zimbabwe	April 18, 1980

(Total: 117 States)

1 Denmark extended the application of the Stockholm Act to the Faröe Islands with effect from August 6, 1971.
2 Including all Overseas Departments and Territories.
3 Latvia acceded to the Paris Convention (Washington Act, 1911) with effect from August 20, 1925. It lost its independence on July 21, 1940, and regained it on August 21, 1991.
4 Ratification for the Kingdom in Europe, the Netherlands Antilles and Aruba.
5 The accession of New Zealand to the Stockholm Act, with the exception of Articles 1 to 12, extends to the Cook Islands, Niue and Tokelau.
6 The United Kingdom extended the application of the Stockholm Act to the territory of Hong Kong with effect from November 16, 1977, and to the Isle of Man with effect from October 29, 1983.
7 The United States of America extended the application of the Stockholm Act to all territories and possessions of the United States of America, including the Commonwealth of Puerto Rico, as from August 25, 1973.

Schedule 2: Madrid Agreement Concerning the International Registration of Marks

Status on 1 January 1994

State[1]	Date on which State became party to the Convention
Algeria	July 5, 1972
Austria	January 1, 1909
Belarus	December 25, 1991
Belgium[2]	July 15, 1892
Bosnia and Herzegovina	March 6, 1992
Bulgaria	August 1, 1985
China[3]	October 4, 1989
Croatia	October 8, 1991
Cuba[3]	December 6, 1989
Czech Republic	January 1, 1993
Egypt	July 1, 1952
France[4]	July 15, 1892
Germany	December 1, 1909
Hungary	January 1, 1909
Italy	October 15, 1894
Kazakhstan	December 25, 1991
Korea, Democratic People's Republic of	June 10, 1980
Liechtenstein	July 14, 1933
Luxembourg[2]	September 1, 1924
Macedonia, Republic of (formerly a province of Yugoslavia)	September 8, 1991
Monaco	April 29, 1956
Mongolia[3]	April 21, 1985
Morocco	July 30, 1917

Appendix

State[1]	Date on which State became party to the Convention
Netherlands[2,5]	March 1, 1893
Poland[3]	March 18, 1991
Portugal	October 31, 1893
Romania	October 6, 1920
Russian Federation	December 25, 1991
San Marino	September 25, 1960
Slovakia	January 1, 1993
Slovenia	June 25, 1991
Spain[6]	July 15, 1892
Sudan	May 16, 1984
Switzerland	July 15, 1892
Ukraine	December 25, 1991
Uzbekistan	December 25, 1991
Vietnam	March 8, 1949
Yugoslavia	February 26, 1921

(Total: 38 States)

1 All the States have declared, under Article 3*bis* of the Nice or Stockholm Act, that the protection arising from international registration shall not extend to them unless the proprietor of the mark so requests.
2 As from January 1, 1971, the territories in Europe of Belgium, Luxembourg and the Netherlands are, for the application of the Madrid Agreement (Marks), to be deemed a single country.
3 In accordance with Article 14(2)(d) and (f), this State declared that the application of the Stockholm Act was limited to marks registered from the date on which accession entered into force: China: October 4, 1989; Cuba: December 6, 1989; Mongolia: April 21, 1985; Poland: March 18, 1991.
4 Including all Overseas Departments and Territories.
5 The instrument of ratification of the Stockholm Act was deposited from the Kingdom in Europe. The Netherlands, which had extended the application of the Stockholm Act to Aruba with effect from November 8, 1986, suspended that application as from that date for an indefinite period.
6 Spain declared that it no longer wished to be bound by instruments earlier than the Nice Act. This declaration became effective on December 15, 1966. The Madrid Agreement (Marks) was thus not applicable between Spain and the following States between December 15, 1966, and the date indicated for each State: Austria (February 8, 1970), Hungary (March 23, 1967), Liechtenstein (May 29, 1967), Morocco (December 18, 1970), Vietnam (May 15, 1973).

Schedule 3: Protocol Relating to the Madrid Agreement Concerning the International Registration of Marks (1989)*

Status on 1 January 1994

Signatory states	Ratification
Austria	Spain
Belgium	
Denmark	
Egypt	
Finland	
France	
Germany	
Greece	
Hungary	
Ireland	
Italy	
Korea, Democratic People's Republic of	
Liechtenstein	
Luxembourg	
Monaco	
Mongolia	
Morocco	
Netherlands	
Portugal	
Romania	
Russian Federation	
Senegal	
Spain	
Sweden	
Switzerland	
United Kingdom	
Yugoslavia	
(Total: 27 States)	(Total: 1 State)

*This instrument is not yet in force.

Schedule 4: Trade Marks Registry Forms

Form Number	Title
TM3	Application to register a trade mark, (including certification marks and collective marks).
TM3A	Application for additional classes.
TM5	Request to the Registrar for a statement of grounds of decision.
TM7	Notice of opposition.
TM8	Form for counterstatement.
TM9	Request for an extension of time on an application.
TM11	Renewal of registration.
TM12	Request to divide an application.
TM13	Request for the restoration and renewal of a registration removed from the Register because of non-payment of the renewal fee.
TM15	Notice under Schedule 3, paragraph 11 of the 1994 Act: claim to have registrability of a mark applied for before 31 October 1994 determined under the 1994 Act. (Conversion of application).
TM16	Application to register a change of proprietor.
TM17	Request to merge either applications or registrations.
TM21	Request to change the details of an application or a registration.

Form Number	Title
TM22	Notice to surrender a registration.
TM23	Notice of a partial surrender of the specification of goods or services for which the mark is registered.
TM24	Application to record/cancel a registrable transaction or memoranda relating to a trade mark but not an assignment or licence.
TM25	Request for alteration of a registered mark.
TM26	Application for the revocation or rectification of a registration or for it to be declared invalid.
TM27	Application to intervene in proceedings for revocation or rectification of a registration.
TM31C	Request for information about applications and registered marks.
TM31R	Request for Registrar's general certificate.
TM33	Request to appoint an agent or to enter or change an address for service.
TM35	Filing of regulations governing the use of a certification or collective mark.
TM36	Application to amend the regulations governing the use of a certification or collective mark.
TM50	Application for the registration of a licensee for a registered trade mark.
TM51	Application to remove or amend a licence.

Index